Rural Development and Planning in India

About the Author

Dr. Vishwambhar Nath was one of the leading development economists of India. After getting a Master's degree in Geography from Government College Lahore in 1946, he received his PhD. in Geography from the University of Maryland in 1949.

Returning to India, he joined the Planning Commission in 1950 and was tasked to lead the Programme Evaluation Organization (PEO). In 1957, Dr. Nath joined the Indian Administrative Service (IAS) and served as a District Collector in the Sawai Madhopur and Pali districts of Rajasthan. In Sawai Madhopur, he helped with the creation of country's best known tiger reserve—the Ranthambor Sanctuary. In 1963, he rejoined the Planning Commission as the head of the Natural Resources and Urban Planning Divisions. He was deeply involved with many projects including the Plan for the Calcutta Metropolitan Region.

In 1966, Dr Nath was deputized to the United Nations Development Programme and began his UN service as a Professor, at a newly formed Economic and Social Development Training Institute for Middle East, in Kuwait. Later assignments included Development Planning positions in Sierra Leone and The Gambia and several consultancy appointments in West Africa.

Dr. Nath spent a year as a Visiting Professor of Geography at the University of Kentucky and after retiring from the UNDP, he spent two years as Visiting Scholar at Boston University.

Returning to India in 1986, Dr Nath was attached to the Center for Policy Research in Delhi and continued his writing and scholarly work until his sudden death on September 10, 2002.

Rural Development and Planning in India

Dr. V. Nath

CONCEPT PUBLISHING COMPANY PVT. LTD., NEW DELHI-110059

ISBN-13: 978-81-8069-697-8

First Published 2010

Published and Printed by

Concept Publishing Company Pvt. Ltd.
Regd. Office:
A/15-16, Commercial Block, Mohan Garden
New Delhi-110059 (India)
Phones: 25351460, 25351794, *Fax*: 091-11-25357109
Email: publishing@conceptpub.com,
Website: www.conceptpub.com

Editorial Office:
H-13, Bali Nagar, New Delhi-110 015, India.

Cataloging in Publication Data-- *Courtesy:* D.K. Agencies (P) Ltd. <docinfo@dkagencies.com>

Nath, Viswambhar, 1923-
Rural development and planning in India / V. Nath.
p. cm.
With special reference to Sawai Madhopur District of Rajasthan, India.
Includes bibliographical references and index.
ISBN 9788180696978

1. Rural development--India. 2. Rural development--India--Sawai Madhopur (District). 3. Rural development projects--India. 4. Rural development projects--India--Sawai Madhopur (District). 5. Sawai Madhopur (India : District)--Economic conditions. 6. Sawai Madhopur (India : District)--Rural conditions. I. Title.

DDC 307.14120954 22

Acknowledgements

As mentioned in Volume I, we are making an effort to publish Dr. Nath's writings on Economic Development in FIVE volumes. Each volume focusses on specific area of development and planning in India. The volumes are not being published sequentially but by subject matter, with the generous assistance of experts on the subjects.

During his lifetime, Dr. Vishwambhar Nath had the privilege of working in many important areas of economic development. He worked for the Population Census Commission in the early 1950s, for demarcation of agro-climatic regions in India; he headed the Programme Evaluation Organization of the Planning Commission from its inception in 1952 to 1958 and later was Chief of the Natural Resources and Urban Planning Divisions of the Planning Commission and was associated with preparation of the Plans for Calcutta Metropolitan region. Later, on behalf of UNDP he was involved with economic and social development planning in developing countries of the Middle East and West Africa. These assignments gave him an opportunity for deep understanding of the economic planning processes under different natural, social and cultural conditions. His experience as Collector and district development officer gave an opportunity for deep understanding of processes of implementation of development programmes and their impact on economic and social change in rural areas.

Over a period of 49 years of our companionship, I had the privilege to see how Dr. Nath's interest in the above mentioned and several other areas of development evolved, and how passionately he could connect different issues of development. It is my privilege to bring together as much of his published and unpublished writings as possible in Volumes so that all his thoughts are available to researchers and planners. The author, who suddenly passed away in September 2002, was involved in academic writing until the last day of his life.

The essays included in the volumes reflect not only Nath's own thinking but also the fine people with whom he worked and who worked for him in the several institutions with which he was associated.

I am thankful to many people who have encouraged me to continue with the task of getting these volumes published. My special thanks, however, are for Dr. Surender Aggarwal of Department of Geography, Delhi University who edited the first two volumes and Mrs. Suhasini Ramaswamy, who edited the third volume and the publisher, Mr. Ashok Kumar Mittal (Concept Publishing Company PVT. LTD.), who has undertaken to publish all the volumes. I am also thankful to my three children—Virendra, Arvind and Jyotsna—for allowing me the time and giving encouragement to complete this mission.

March 2010 **Kamla Nath**

Contents

Section III
Socio-Economic Structure of Villages in India

Section IV
The Village Studies : Socio-Economic Change in Village India

Introduction

In 2001, more than half a century after Independence, nearly 72 per cent of India's population lived in villages. Development with welfare would have no meaning if the level of income and welfare of the rural people did not increase. These are dependent on increase in agricultural production and balanced industrial development as well as adequate supplies and access to basic services—approach roads, clean and adequate water supplies, education, health as well as electricity for irrigation and for increase in comfort of living. Furthermore, expansion of communication facilities, in addition to motorable roads and availability of industrial goods are essential for enhancement of rural standard of living (Chapter 1).

The Government of India in initial stages of planning for development introduced the Community Development Programmes to meet the above needs of the rural and agricultural development (Chapter 2). Further attempts at technological change and introduction of high yielding varieties of seeds have led to great increase in agricultural incomes and well-being (Chapter 12). Secondary sources of rural incomes—small scale and cottage industries—though important in a scenario of rapid population growth and decrease in per capita availability of land, have not made major dents in rural incomes (Chapter 6) but poultry and dairying has developed as a source of income in some villages in several States.

Evaluation of the impact of major rural development programmes launched under the community development programme and other rural development schemes, *e.g.* increasing productivity of land, rural employment and local self-government etc. is a continuous process (Chapter 4). Lot of emphasis was and is being given to local self government as a tool for need-based and bottom up development planning by elected bodies *i.e. Panchayati Raj* institutions (Chapters 9, 10 and 11). These continue to interest scholars on rural development.

However, due to large variations in natural endowment of land, water and climate and dynamism of people in different States, regional imbalance in agricultural growth is a dominant feature, which had begun to attract attention in the early 1960s and the 70s (Chapter 5). It is becoming increasingly clear that while in some areas agriculture has started to display considerable dynamism, its progress in other areas is still very slow. Identification of the physical, economic and social factors, which are responsible for these differences, is vital for understanding the dynamics of agricultural change. A fruitful method of identifying these factors is through case studies of villages of specially rapid or slow progress.

It is with this objective in view that Dr Nath undertook studies of villages in Rajasthan and Central Punjab in the early 1960s and later reviewed the progress in both areas in early 2001 and mid-70s respectively. The Rajasthan villages in 1961 were still untouched by strides being made in Punjab around the same time under technological change in farming practices and use of improved seeds and irrigation (Green Revolution). The studies also bring out the impact of various agricultural practices and social reforms on social attitudes and occupational pattern as well as in emergence of new leadership. The many changes in agriculture in the villages in central Punjab and Rajasthan after the adoption of improved practices and the problems which agricultural progress and prosperity have themselves created in the villages have been analyzed. The Punjab study focussed on technological change in agriculture, progress in levels of living, health, education, transport and communication and in several other directions. In Rajasthan it was found that caste played an important part in involvement of people in agriculture and in non-agricultural skilled and unskilled jobs and directed the change in occupational mobility of people of different castes (Chapter 13). This in turn affected their attitudes towards education—of boys and girls, and towards treatment of diseases. Furthermore, it was found that work patterns of women of different castes outside the home were also determined by their caste, which in turn patterned the practices relating to marriage, divorce, widow remarriage and dowry and bride price. The work pattern of women and the availability of cash in the households, which came as a result of non-agricultural work, determined consumption patterns and child care practices. These were recorded by author's wife in a Punjab village adjacent to the one selected by the author and three villages in Rajasthan—two of which were also included in the author's study and are given in Appendices to the Chapters relating to the studies (Chapters 16 and 17).

Findings of the Punjab study in 1963 and the revisit in 1975 were published under the title "The New Village" (Chapter 17) and "The New Village Twelve Years After" (Chapter 18). The detailed findings of the Rajasthan study remained unpublished. However, several articles based on the findings of the study were published *e.g.* 'Village Caste and Community' (Chapter 12), 'Caste and Occupational Mobility' (Chapter 13); others on 'The Changing Role of Caste' and 'Emerging Leadership in Village India' as well as 'Self Sustainable Development: A Study of Four Decades of Rural Development in Three Villages of Eastern Rajasthan' (Chapters 14, 15 and 16) are included in this volume.

March 2010 **Kamla Nath**

because change had taken place in other parts of this district, in other districts of Rajasthan, and in other States of Northern India in which such lands were not available and no migration took place. But it had enabled the community to absorb the tensions created by the change. A majority of the *Chamaars* has become cultivating owners and is better off than before. The *Meenas* and other traditional cultivators have also more land given to them, and are happy with this result of the change, however, keenly they might resent the other effects. On the other hand, in other parts of the district (*e.g.* the Hinton *tehsil*, 60 miles to the north of Sawai Madhopur) where the pressure of the population on land is high and *Chamaars* have not been able to get much new land for cultivation there is keen competition between them and the other cultivators for the very small area of cultivable wastelands that are available for the allotment, and there is also greater tension.

Abolition of *jagirdari* itself assisted the change in several ways. First, it removed a powerful local influence, which was for preservation of tradition and against change; the *jagirdars* were active in support of *jajmani* system. Secondly, they did not allow any caste to become too assertive or powerful or social tensions to develop within their villages. The attitude of curbing "apishness" which was perhaps necessary for preserving their own position at the apex of the local power structure often worked against the *Meenas*, who were naturally the most powerful caste in the villages. But it also meant discouraging the aspirations of other castes which might disturb the traditional structure of social position and power. The influence of the *jagirdars* in curbing local tensions has been seen very clearly.

During the 1950s the political and administrative changes and special measures for uplift of scheduled castes proved to be noteworthy influences. These did not initiate the change in occupation of the *Chamaars* or their migration, which were already under way. But they were major factors in acceptance by the rest of the community of the *Chamaars* right to give up their traditional occupation to seek a higher social status, and need for improvement in their economic and social condition.

The Political System based on the Adult Suffrage

Every politician understands the importance of the large scheduled caste votes in such a system and is anxious to win it. Among the *Chamaars* themselves, realization of the power of their number grows with every successive election. Moreover, reservation of seats for the scheduled castes in legislatures, *Panchayat* and other bodies have produced a crop of young

SECTION I
RURAL DEVELOPMENT

1

Rural Development

Introduction

The developing countries of Asia, Africa and Latin America are undergoing social, economic and political changes at breakneck speed. The primary object of the changes is to minimize and eradicate, in time, poverty, illiteracy and disease among the deprived sections of the population and ensure that all the people of these countries have enough nutritious food, their children have access to facilities for primary education and a proportion of them have access to higher/or technical education so that they are equipped for white collar jobs or those of skilled workers. Furthermore, they have access to prevention and curative health care so that epidemic diseases are eradicated and no child or adult dies or is disabled for lack of medical care.

India after China, is the most populous country in the world, it exceeded one billion by the Census of 2001. The proportion of people below the poverty line i.e. those who do not get enough food calories derived from cereals and pulses to maintain themselves in health was estimated at least 25 per cent in 1996-97. Some estimates had put this proportion as high as one-third or even higher. Thus, the number of the poor was between 210 and 300 million in that year. The illiteracy rate was estimated at 48 per cent by the Census Commissioner in 1991. Infant mortality rate in 1998 was as high as 70 per 1000 live births and life expectancy of 63 years against the figure of 77 for U.K., which is a good representation of the rates in the western European developed countries. The rates represent, however, significant improvements since 1971—the illiteracy rate was 65.5 per cent in 1971 and life expectancy at birth in that year was 45.6 per cent. The death rate was 9.8 per 1000 in 1991 and has gone down to 8.5 by 2001[1]. The country has experienced social, economic and political changes during more than half a century since it became independent which can be described as truly revolutionary.

India has chosen a democratic form of government, although in most of its long history of more than three million, it has been an authoritarian and feudal society, marked by great inequalities in social status and political and economic power of different sections of its society.

The centre piece of this unequal social structure is the caste system, which dictates the social status of each caste group—its occupation, political and economic power. At the top of the social structure are the high castes—Brahmins, Rajputs and Mahajans (or traders). They own most of the wealth and land in rural areas and property in urban areas. At the bottom of the structure are the scheduled castes and the scheduled tribes. They are the poorer quarter of the population and have besides very low social status. The traditional occupation of the scheduled castes was labour on lands owned by the high castes. Furthermore, they performed tasks, such as flaying of hides and skins of dead animals, dressing them to make leather goods for shoes and for some operations on farms and scavenging which are considered 'dirty' by the high caste Hindus. To add insult to injury, they were considered untouchables, *i.e.* their touch was considered polluting by the high castes. In the villages, they could not draw water from the wells used by the high castes nor worship in the temples of the high castes.

They had their own drinking water wells and temples. In most parts of the country, they lived in hamlets spread around a central inhabited area, in which the people of the high castes lived and which the habitat gave its name. In States such as Punjab, Haryana and Rajasthan, Gujarat and western U.P. in which the relatively large, tightly nucleated village is the norm, they lived in a separate quarter of the village so that their physical contact with residents of these high castes was minimal.

All this has changed during the last half a century. Untouchability has been abolished by a directive principal of the Constitution—its practice is a cognizable offence—and is slowly disappearing in practice in both the rural and the urban areas. The owner of a teashop located in a small town a few miles from the village, does not ask the caste of his or her customers and people of the high castes do not have any hesitation in taking tea from the same shop. Similarly, the priests of the biggest temples in metropolitan cities do not ask the castes of the devotees; they accept gratefully offerings of all the devotees, regardless of their caste.

More important, as a result of the land reforms introduced in most of the States during the early 1950s, large areas of cultivable lands which were lying fallow have been allotted to the landless agricultural labourers most of whom belong to the scheduled castes in order to raise their social and economic status. Large areas of cultivable lands became available also as a result of abolition of exploitative intermediary tenures such as *zamindari* and *jagirdari*. Most of the cropland held by the *zamindars* in the former British province and their counterparts, the *jagirdars* in princely States were taken away from them and allotted to their tenants who used to cultivate the land and who belong to the scheduled castes or other backward castes. The former *zamindars* and *jagirdars* have accepted the change as inevitable as a result of the political change to a democratic society. It is only in parts of Bihar and of the Telugu speaking part of the former dominion of the Nizam of Hyderabad that there are cases of burning of villagers of the scheduled castes by their former high caste landowners or of killing of individual landowners by their former tenants.

The revolutionary social changes have produced great social tensions, one symptom of which is widespread monetary corruption among the political elite, a significant proportion of which have been elected to their high office by the use of money and muscle power. Monetary corruption has percolated also to the middle and lower rungs of the bureaucracy so that the citizen has to pay a bribe to the official who is to give him a piece of land for housing, connections for water or electricity in the urban area or the right to cultivable land in the rural areas conferred on him by the land reforms.

Political change has been so great that the Chief Ministers in most of the States belong to the dominant cultivating castes or other backward castes. The Constitution provides for reservation of one-fourth of the seats in Parliament and legislative bodies in the States for members of the scheduled castes and the scheduled tribes. Similar proportions of the ministers in the cabinets of most of the States belong to these formerly depressed castes.

Fifty years ago the position was radically different. The Prime Minister of India and Chief Ministers of most of the States belonged to the high castes. The proportion of ministers of the scheduled castes and the scheduled tribes was similar or lower than their proportion in the population. Furthermore, most of the ministers responsible for taking the major decisions on governance of the States belonged to the high castes. The ministers belonging to the scheduled castes and the scheduled tribes were responsible for decisions, which affected only the welfare of members of their own castes.

Economic Change

Indian society has been witness also to major economic changes during this period, initiated by the Government of India or of the States or by private entrepreneurs. As late as the mid-1950s, a decade after independence, India was a predominantly agricultural society in which more than half (56 %) of the gross domestic product was contributed by agriculture and less than half was produced by industries and services. Furthermore, the level of agricultural output was a gamble with the rains—agricultural output fell drastically in years of an unfavourable monsoon. Towards the end of the 1990s, however, output of foodgrains has reached almost 200 million tonnes or higher in years of favourable monsoon. It is three and a half times the output of less than 60 million in the mid-1950s. Furthermore, there have been eleven successive years of favourable monsoons. In fact, such a large proportion of the principal foodgrains—wheat and rice—is produced in the areas of assured and controlled water supply provided by canals, deep tubewells or wells powered by pumps using electric or diesel motors that output in these cereals is not affected greatly by the quantum or distribution of rainfall in the rainy season.

The cultivated areas irrigated by various sources mentioned above and tanks in villages have increased steadily from just over 20 per cent to about 30 per cent by the late 1990s. Output in the irrigated areas is due partly to improved methods of cultivation and farm management but mainly to use of dwarf, very high yielding varieties of rice and wheat, which give two to three times the yields of the older varieties.

There has been rapid increase also in output of other food crops—sugar and cooking oil, of fibres—cotton and jute, of beverages—tea and coffee, and tobacco. Part of the output is exported but most of it is for domestic consumption. The only food for which there is a deficit met by imports is of cooking oil.

The economy has been transformed in this period from one in which industries and services produced three-fourth of the GDP, whereas agriculture produced only 25 per cent or less.

The change was initiated in the late 1950s when the Government of India made large investments in establishing four large integrated steel mills; a plant for making heavy machine tools and those for making light machine tools; machines for generation, transmission and distribution of electricity and for making equipment for railways (rails, wagons and locomotives); exploration and development of oil fields, petroleum refining and construction of pipelines for transport of motor spirit, diesel and liquefied natural gas from the refineries to various parts of the country and opening a network of distribution of petroleum products throughout the country. Investments were made also in production of chemicals such as penicillin and even of photographic films.

Private industrialists with some exceptions concentrated their attention on expanding output of consumer goods (processed food, cloth, garments, shoes and other leather goods) and consumer durables such as motor vehicles (passenger cars, scooters, motor cycles, chassis for buses and trucks), T.V. receivers, refrigerators and air conditioners, furniture for offices and hospitals and furnishings for homes and offices.

By the 1990s, however, most of the investment including that in petroleum refining and manufacture of petrochemicals was being made by private industrialists. The efforts of the Government were diverted towards reducing losses of industrial enterprises established in the 1960s and 1970s through removing deficiencies in management and infrastructure. The 1970s also witnessed growth of information technology industries, computer software for export, which witnessed exponential growth in the subsequent two decades. By the end of the decade export of IT industries contributed a significant part of the export earnings of the country and were increasing very rapidly and are expected to increase equally rapidly for another two decades.

The policy of the Government of India, stated repeatedly in various statements made by the present government and its predecessors since the 1990s is to withdraw progressively from industries and economic services by closing down its loss making industrial enterprises; and to make no new investment in them. It plans also to induce private entrepreneurs to enter activities such as generation, transmission and distribution of electricity and construction and maintenance of highly used parts of national highways.

However, due to strong opposition in Parliament and by unions of workers, no loss making enterprise has been closed although the number of workers in many is being reduced steadily by various voluntary retirement schemes. Private investors have with some notable exceptions also shown a strong reluctance to invest in basic industries and the infrastructure mentioned above.

Rural Development

In 1991, more than 40 years after independence just over 70 per cent of the population lived in villages; in 1950/51 the proportion was more than

80 per cent. (Both estimates are according to the Censuses of Population conducted during the two years.) Development with welfare would have no meaning if the level of income and welfare of the rural people did not increase. Since most of the rural people are farmers or agricultural labourers their level of income depends principally on increase in agricultural output. Their welfare depends also on their having access to basic service facilities—approach roads to break their isolation from the cities; clean and adequate water supplies provided through improvement of existing sources—shallow surface wells and tanks in most parts of the country and artesian springs in the mountainous areas and creating new sources; providing facilities for primary education for all children of the primary school-going age and facilities for secondary or technical education for a proportion of them and finally providing easy access to facilities for preventive and curative medical care so that epidemic diseases are eradicated and the sick can get medical assistance within a short distance from their villages.

After these elementary facilities are created and agricultural output begins to increase an attempt should be made to bring all villages within a short distance of a motorable road on which buses and other motor vehicles ply so that dependence for transport on the bullock cart is minimized. Furthermore, as supplies of electricity increase, all villages must be electrified so that their dependence on oil for lighting and cow dung for cooking fuel is reduced. The oil can be used as food and the cow dung can be used for manure.

A sustained programme of basic adult literacy must be undertaken so that all adults have the basic skills of the three R's. This would assist them in their transactions with the traders when they go to sell their produce and buy cloth or other household needs. Since in many parts of the country literacy among girls is considered useless, the head of households must be convinced that literate girls will make better mothers and that making them literate will not make them reluctant to do farm work. The examples of Kerala and Goa may be quoted to convince them of this truth.

Increase in rural incomes will in turn increase demand for industrial goods—cloth, corrugated iron sheets for building their huts, so that they are less likely to collapse during the rains and several electronic goods.

Community Development Programme

The above were precisely the objects of the community development programme, which was launched in October 1952; initially in about 2000 villages located in all the States and were extended in a diluted version all over the country during the next ten years. The principal objects of the programme were two :

(i) to make major investments in rural infrastructure *i.e.* to provide to the villages approach roads, safe clean and adequate water supplies (by improving existing wells and tanks and other sources of water) and assisting them to build new ones; open primary and secondary schools to provide children facilities for primary and secondary education and primary health centres to provide preventive and curative health care.

(ii) to assist the villagers to improve methods of farming to increase agricultural output. The diseases of livestock would be controlled by providing veterinary facilities within easy reach of the villagers and teaching them better methods of improved animal husbandry.

The villagers were expected to pay half the cost of expansion of some of the infrastructure facilities through their labour or materials. Thus for construction of roads, they would provide the land and do the earthwork while the State governments would provide funds for metalling them so that they are not washed away during the rains. Similarly, they would construct buildings for primary schools while the State government would provide the teacher(s) and equipment for running the schools.

To increase agricultural output, the State governments would provide extension workers to teach them improved methods of cultivation and farm management. Financial assistance was provided to improve tanks for irrigation and construct new wells. Later when electric supplies became available as a result of completion of the various irrigation and power projects, started in the First Five Year Plan (1951-56), the farmers were assisted to install pump sets on their wells. Increased supplies of irrigation water also increased greatly the areas with assured supplies of water for farming. As a result, while less than 20 per cent of the farm land had assured water supplies in 1950/51, by the 1990s, almost 30 per cent of the crop land had such assured water supply provided by canals improved tanks and irrigation wells, powered by electric or diesel pumps.

The extension workers provided by the community development programme, supplemented by specialists in use of chemical fertilizers and pesticides assisted the farmers to plant dwarf varieties of wheat and rice which began to be available from the late 1960s and the early 1970s.

These varieties gave two to three times the yields of the older varieties when grown under conditions of adequate and assured moisture provided by deep tubewells and wells powered by electric or diesel operated pumps or canals and use of chemical fertilizers or organic manure and pesticides to control diseases of the cereals. As a result, yields of the two cereals began to increase progressively. By the end of the 1990s the country was producing almost 200 million tonnes, three and a half times the foodgrains (mainly wheat and rice) that it was producing in the mid-1950s which provide the bulk of calories for India's population, .

Per capita consumption of cereals has increased by about 10 per cent during the period 1970-71 to 1996-97. At the same time, there is an imbalance between the income of farmers of the 70 per cent cropped area that is not irrigated and the 30 per cent which is irrigated because yields of the cereals 'sorghum' and 'millets' which is grown in the unirrigated areas has not recorded as much increase as those of the areas irrigated and growing wheat and rice.

Production of sugarcane has also increased so rapidly that per capita consumption of sugar is also much higher than in the 1950s and even as late as 1970s. However, the increase is concentrated in areas which get adequate and assured moisture. Similarly, per capita consumption of milk, vegetables, poultry products (eggs and chicken) and fish has also increased. Excepting fish, which is produced and consumed mainly in coastal areas, milk and chicken are produced also in areas which have facilities of assured water supply provided mainly by irrigation. Milk and milk products (butter and cheese) are produced partly by producers' cooperatives to supply liquid milk and the other products to the cities and partly by individual producers in areas, which have good breeds of livestock (mainly milch buffaloes).

Production of poultry products (eggs and chicken) is also concentrated in the irrigated areas because these areas have the surplus of grains which, supplemented by other nutrients, are the main feed stock of the birds. Furthermore, these areas can afford the facilities of veterinary care needed to control diseases of livestock and birds.

Production of vegetables is partly to meet demands of the cities and partly for local consumption. Here again, there is an imbalance between the areas that have assured water supply provided by rainfall and/or irrigation and those, which have not.

Thus, regional imbalance is a dominant characteristic of the agricultural revolution that India has witnessed since the late 1960s and there does not seem to be any prospect of its reduction in the next decade.

Panchayati Raj Institutions

Establishments of these institutions were first recommended in 1954 by a committee, appointed by the Ministry of Community Development to evaluate progress of community development and national extension service. The principal recommendation of the Committee was that the responsibility for implementation of community development and other related rural development programmes should be transferred from officials to chosen representatives of the people. Towards this end, it recommended establishment of three institutions: *Panchayats*, *Panchayat Samitis* and *Zilla Parishads* at the levels of the village, the community development block and the district. The recommendations of the Committee were accepted by the Ministry of Community Development and Cooperation and the Minister requested the State governments to implement the recommendations by establishing these institutions at the three levels at the earliest. Beginning with Rajasthan in October 1959, the governments of all the States established these institutions in the early or mid-1960s. Establishment of the institutions was hailed by the political leaders in the central and State governments as a major step forward in the direction of "direct democracy". It fulfilled also a Directive Principal of the Constitution of India.

The three institutions, their mode of establishment and their powers and functions are :

The Panchayats : A body constituted for every village with a population of 1,000-5,000 (up to 10,000 in Kerala) or a group of villages with similar population.

The Panchayat Samiti : A body constituted for every community development block, an area with rural population between 60,000 (less in mountainous areas) and 150,000 or more in some southern States. The country had been divided into about 5,000 blocks for implementation of the Community Development Programme. The *Panchayat Samiti* was a body consisting of *Sarpanchs* (chairmen) of all the Panchayats in its area. It was a rather large body consisting up to 50 *Sarpanch* members.

The Zilla Parishad : A body constituted at the district level, in order to oversee community development and other rural development programmes within its jurisdiction. It would distribute the grants given by the State government for implementation of the community development and other rural development programmes. Since the country had nearly 500 districts in 1951 and about 5,000 blocks, every *zilla parishad* had an average of 10 blocks within its jurisdiction. Every Member of Legislative Assembly (MLA) was an *exofficio* non-voting member of one or two *Panchayat Samitis* within his constituency. Similarly, every Member of Parliament (MP) was an *exofficio* non-voting member of all the *Panchayat Samitis* and *Zilla Parishads* within his constituency.

The *panchayat* was to be a directly elected body. All adults (men and women) in the village or villages within its jurisdiction were entitled to vote for election of its chairman (*Sarpanch*) and other members. The *Panchayat Samiti* and the *Zilla Parishad* were both constituted through indirect election. The *Samiti* consisted of the *Sarpanchs* of all *panchayats* within its jurisdiction as its members. The *Zilla Parishad* had as members all the chairmen (*Pradhans*) of all the *Samitis* within its jurisdiction.

In Maharashtra and some southern States, an older administrative unit *taluka* and the community development block were co-terminus.

There was at the level of the *Panchayat Samiti*, a team of one or more extension officers for raising agricultural output, a veterinarian who treated diseases of farm animals and advised villagers on improving livestock and a veterinary dispensary, a 6-bed hospital with a doctor, a dispenser and one or more nurses. It had also a lady health visitor who advised the rural women on basics of hygiene, nutrition and childcare. There were also one or more dispensaries in every community development block. This organization provided villagers with curative and preventive health care. There was also an inspector of education, who supervised working of all the primary and secondary schools within the *Panchayat Samiti* under his supervision. The area of every *Panchayat* had to have a primary school. A number of secondary schools were to be located in large villages or small towns to provide secondary school students within its jurisdiction. A *samiti* had also an inspector of cooperative societies and a secretary of a cooperative society in every large village. Their duty was to provide the villagers with loans for buying improved seed, fertilizers at low rates of interest and to ensure that the loans were repayed in time.

According to the Committee the Collector was supposed to be the friend, philosopher and guide of the *Panchayati Raj* institutions. He had a senior officer of the State administrative service to assist him in his duties relating to rural development programmes. This officer, designated as District Development officer was also the Secretary of the *Zilla Parishad*.

The Collector was supposed to attend all meetings of the *Zilla Parishad* which had its own chairman called *Pramukh*. He could attend the meeting of any *Panchayat Samiti* that he considered necessary. His duties were to keep the State government informed about the functioning of the *Panchayati Raj* institutions. Thus, he could report to the government any major deficiencies in functioning of any *Panchayat Samiti* or even the *Zilla Parishad*. On receiving his report, the State government would direct him to conduct an enquiry and submit his report for necessary action. He would enquire also about corruption or unacceptable behaviour of any *Sarpanch*.

The district and division level officers of the development departments were expected to attend all meetings of the *Zilla Parishad* and if requested by the Collector also attend meeting of any *Panchayat Samiti*. Their attendance would acquaint them with the views of these representatives of the people about the functioning of their departments. They were supposed to rectify immediately complaints about malfunctioning of their departments.

The governments of several States abolished the *Zilla Parishads* and *Panchayat Samitis* in the late 1960s or early 1970s — barely 10 years after their formation because their functioning was not considered satisfactory by the governments. They began to be revived with greatly increased powers and grants and loans given by the State governments in the 1980s and 1990s. Establishing them has been made mandatory on the State governments by the 73rd amendment to the Constitution, which was enacted in 1995. However, State governments of some States have still not revived them.

A number of committees headed by distinguished political leaders have been appointed by the Government of India from time to time to enquire into the deficiencies of these institutions. The State governments have taken these deficiencies into consideration while establishing the new institutions.

The committee, which had recommended establishment of these institutions in 1957, had expected that these institutions would be non-political. This was an unrealistic expectation in the social situation in the villages with great inequalities in income and social status of residents of influential members of the high castes and those of the scheduled castes. In reviving the institutions, the State governments have realized that the institutions cannot but be political so much so that loss of control of these institutions in a large number of districts or of municipal bodies of the most important cities is considered by the political party which is in power in the State government to be an indicator of decline in its popularity. Consequently, the party in power in the State government tries very hard to remain in power in these institutions.

Other Rural Development Programmes

Employment Generation by Building or Repair of Public Works in Selected Regions

These programmes have received varying emphasis during this 50-year period depending upon the commitment of the various governments to eradication of poverty among the rural poor—landless agricultural labourers belonging mainly to the scheduled castes, in villages in the plains; members of the scheduled tribes in the hilly, tribal areas of peninsular India; both farmers and landless labourers in the western and eastern Himalayan regions in which the fields are small and there is heavy soil erosion during the summer monsoons and many fields get washed away; the semi-desert and desert areas of western Rajasthan.

The areas with concentration of rural poverty are:

(i) hilly, tribal areas inhabited mainly by tribal people of Chhota Nagpur plateau region of Bihar, West Bengal, Madhya Pradesh, large parts of Andhra Pradesh, parts of Maharashtra and Gujarat and southern Rajasthan;
(ii) semi-desert and desert regions of western Rajasthan;
(iii) parts of U.P. and Bihar plains in which the farmers have very small holdings and there are large number of landless labourers. Furthermore, in both States, large areas of potentially fertile land are covered with coarse sand or small stones brought down by the monsoon floods;
(iv) the small valleys in the mountainous areas of the western Himalayan region, located in Himachal Pradesh, Jammu & Kashmir and western U.P.; and
(v) similar areas in Assam, a small part of West Bengal and the seven States of the north-east.

The programmes include:

(i) building or repair of roads—including both approach roads to villages and State and national highways. The villagers do the earth work and the State highway departments metal the State and national highways;
(ii) construction or repair of drinking water sources—tanks and wells in villages of the plains and small reservoirs below artesian springs in mountainous areas;

(iii) construction and repair of irrigation sources such as wells and tanks in the villages in the plains; and

(iv) soil conservation-*cum*-irrigation works—restoration of check dams and thus create small reservoirs used for irrigation during the peak monsoon season. Similar soil conservation works in the eastern and western Himalayan regions.

The work combined with forestation has two benefits:

(i) the small fields in the hills which were washed away by floods are restored and their chances of being washed away in the next season are reduced.

(ii) The areas covered by sand and coarse pebbles in sub-mountain region of U.P. and Bihar are cleared of these and rendered fit for crop production.

Construction and repair of roads, check dams and drinking water sources are the most widespread work undertaken in all the regions mentioned above.

In the semi-desert and desert areas of western Rajasthan, the programme consists of:

(i) construction of new wells and repair of old tanks, step wells and wells; and

(ii) clearing crop lands of silt and coarse sands deposited during the drought.

There are areas, which get affected by natural disasters such as cyclones, which visit coastal areas of the east and west coast and the northern planes in Assam which get flooded during the monsoon. In such areas, millions are rendered homeless because their huts have been washed away; thousands of cattle are also washed away and people can return to their homes only when the floods recede. In such areas, food, clothing and blankets are air dropped to sustain the people until the floods recede. Thereafter money is provided to clear the land of water and to buy livestock to replace those that had perished; money is also provided to help them rebuild their huts. Building materials such as cement and corrugated iron sheets are also distributed by the offices of the Collectors and Sub-Divisional offices. These officers are in-charge of overseeing the relief work.

The programmes can be called also 'food for work'. The men and women employed in them are provided a part of their wages in balanced food (cereals, sugar and cooking oil) and the rest as money to enable them to buy other needs of life including kerosene for cooking. An efficient public distribution system *i.e.* ration shops in which they can buy the basic foods at prices fixed by the government is an integral part of the programme. The programmes are most effective when distribution of balanced food is accompanied by education of pregnant and lactating mothers and those with small children, the basics of nutrition, personal hygiene and care of children.

Finance for these programmes is provided partly by the central government and partly by the governments of the States. Such programmes are financed also by the World Food Programme of the Food and Agricultural Organization of the United Nations, several western donors and by the World Bank and the Asian Development Bank as part of their efforts for alleviation of poverty. Finance for the disaster relief programme is provided mainly by the Central government. The International Red Cross distributes clothes and blankets to people marooned in floods and also sends doctors and Para-medical personnel to prevent spread of epidemic diseases in the extremely unsanitary conditions around the marooned people.

Campaigns for reducing literacy and securing admission of all children in schools; and campaigns for eradicating widespread diseases and improving health of mothers and children; family welfare (including family limitation) for all women in reproductive age groups.

These programmes have received increased emphasis during the last decade because of increasing realization that educated and healthy population is a *sine qua non* of sustained economic growth. The programmes have received emphasis also because of the findings of the Census of Population of 1991 and of various rounds of the National Sample Survey, which found that, India has the largest number of illiterates in the world. The illiteracy rates in several States are larger even than in some of the least developed countries of Africa.

Similarly, despite 50 years or more in providing health care to all, millions of people suffer from easily preventable diseases such as diseases of the digestive tract—diarrhoea, dysentery and cholera during the monsoon and post-monsoon months; diseases of the respiratory tract—bronchitis, pneumonia and even tuberculosis in the post-monsoon, cool season in northern and central India; malaria, which had been eradicated in the late 1950s has staged a slow come-back in some areas in which it was eradicated.

In some States, particularly Bihar, large parts of U.P., Madhya Pradesh and Rajasthan, illiteracy rates are very high and percentage of children going to schools is very low.[2] Furthermore, incidence of the above mentioned communicable diseases is also very high. Family welfare programmes beginning with provision of medical assistance in cases of sickness is not available, because the primary health centres built at Block headquarters are non-functional because of absence of doctors, dispensers and nurses and because some essential diagnostic equipment has not been installed. The doctors and para-medical personnel are reluctant to work in the Block headquarters, usually small towns because of lack of facilities for education of their children. Furthermore, in many cases, residences for doctors and para-medical personnel, has either not been built or have no electricity and water supplies.

Regional Imbalance in Rural Development[3]

During the last 50 years of rural development there has emerged a large and increasing imbalance between areas, which have assured and controlled irrigation and others in which crop production depends upon the rains. In the former, the farmers obtain high yields of the principal cereals—wheat and rice with use of very high yielding dwarf varieties along with use of chemical fertilizers and/or organic manure and pesticides. The large farmers use tractors and other machines such as mechanical hullers for wheat and maize. Some of these areas which produce sugarcane or cotton, yields per hectare are high because improved high yield varieties of the crops can be grown. Farmers get employment through most of the year because raising two crops from most of the fields is the norm. Agricultural labourers can also find employment through most of the year in agriculture, in handling produce in the markets, in the processing industries, mills for producing rice or wheat flour, cotton textile mills, sugar mills and those producing cooking oil or *vanaspati*. Production of perishable foods—milk, poultry products and vegetables is also concentrated in these areas. They have the milch buffaloes which give high yields of milk when fed with nutritious fodder (fodder crops and grains) can be provided. Most of the chicken and eggs are produced also in these areas because they have the surplus of grains, which together with other nutrients provide feed for the birds. Veterinary services to control diseases of the livestock and birds can also be effectively used.

Production of vegetables with some exception is also concentrated in these areas because they can provide assured water supplies for growing them. The level of living of the rural population is high because they have the income to buy mill made clothes, furnishings, soap and toiletries and cooking gas for their homes. Most of the homes are *pucca* and may have electricity. The villages are also located along motorable roads. The landless agricultural labourers can find adequate employment also in the numerous industries in these areas.

In the unirrigated areas on the other hand the principal cereals grown are coarse grains (sorghum and millets) in the monsoon season and gram in the post-monsoon season in areas, which have moisture in the post-monsoon season. Oilseeds (groundnut) and cotton are the principal cash crops. Yields are generally low. Furthermore, yields vary greatly depending upon whether rainfall has been adequate or timely. Farmers as well as agricultural labourers cannot get more than 100 days work and food for work programmes have to be undertaken for them.

This regional imbalance between farmers and agricultural labourers in the irrigated areas on the one hand and the unirrigated areas on the other is a prominent feature of the Indian rural scene of which there seems to be no prospect for reduction in the foreseeable future.

NOTES

1. Statistical Outline of India 2003-2004; Tat Services Ltd.
2. A nearly inseparable obstacle in reducing illiteracy is that in most of these States, the rural people feel that literacy, particularly of girls is useless. A sustained programme must be undertaken to convince the people that knowledge of the 3 R's will help them in their dealing with the traders when they sell their crops or buy cloth, sugar and building material such as corrugated iron sheets. It will help them also in calculation of their wages when they work in public works such as construction or repair of roads.

   Among the State governments, Madhya Pradesh has during the last decade organized a programme for increasing literacy with considerable success. No other State government has taken such an initiative so far.
3. For more detailed analyses of the subject see Nath, V. 2008: *Growth of Indian Agriculture : A Regional Analysis.*

REFERENCE

Nath, V. : *Regional Planning* and *Development in India* 2008, Concept Publisher, New Delhi.

2

Rural Development and Planning in India

Introduction

Rural development programming has laid the foundation for the progress in the rural areas of the country from a poor primarily, agricultural society to a diversified prosperous and progressive society in which manufacturing and services contribute more than 75 per cent of the GDP during the more than half a century of Independence. In 1951, almost 83 per cent of India's population lived in rural areas and their progress is essential for economic development of the country. It was the main endeavour of Planning in India to raise the income levels of the rural population. Agricultural development became a top priority for investment in the First Plan. Although the priorities changed in the subsequent Plans but welfare of the rural population through providing development inputs has remained one of the major concerns of the Government and planning bodies in the country through various schemes launched from time to time.

The thrust of attention is on all the rural people but particularly towards rural poor by providing incentives for development so as to link economic activities into a well-planned infrastructure. Thus rural development is a multi-dimensional process in which governments as well as several civil society groups have introduced development programmes.

The government strategies/approach and programmes have been in the area of (a) multi-purpose integrated development approach, (b) minimum package approach, (c) target group approach, and (d) area development approach/spatial development approach.

The Main Programmes under various Approaches include

The Community Development Programmes, Jawahar Rozgar Yojana, Employment Assurance Scheme, Million Wells Scheme, DWCRA,

TRYSEM, Indira Awas Yojana, DPAP, DDP, Waste Land Development Programme, Watershed Development Programme, National Social Assistance Programme and the recently launched and heavily funded National Rural Employment Guarantee Scheme (NREG). Besides introduction of high yielding varieties of seeds and provision of other technical inputs, which increased agricultural production and income substantially, so did the development of infrastructure *e.g.* provision of water and expansion of land under irrigation, roads and electricity etc.

Integrated Rural Development

The Community Development Programme started on 1st October 1952 at the instance of the then Prime Minister, Pandit Nehru, who inaugurated it by carrying some earth for digging a well in a Delhi village. Tremendous interest in it was aroused within India and throughout the world. Delegates came from least developed (LD) and developing countries round the world to observe its working, so that they could start similar programmes in their countries. Some economic and technical assistance for the programme was provided by the USA, UK, West Germany and smaller European countries, notably the Netherlands. However, it was a programme financed primarily by the Indian Government at the Centre and State governments and implemented by Indian officers. I got an opportunity to study the programme in the field as Deputy Director and Director of Programme Evaluation Organization (PEO) for 5 years (1953-1958) which had been constituted especially for concurrent evaluation of progress of the Programme, bring out the areas in which it had succeeded and others in which it was failing to achieve its objects due to various difficulties. Furthermore, it made recommendations for improving implementation of the Programme.

The Programme started in 1952 on 60 projects covering about 18,000 villages but was spread rapidly in a diluted version to cover the whole country by 1961. Funds and workers in the programme have been increasing progressively as programme's specific objectives such as for increasing agricultural production rapidly, to greatly reduce rural unemployment or under-employment, to provide housing to the rural poor have been undertaken from time to time, as these problems have become urgent.

Two main components of the programme were :

(i) Extending essential service facilities like approach roads to villages, improving and increasing sources of water supply for provision of adequate and clean drinking water from wells, tanks, primary and secondary schools, health care centres (mini-hospitals) and dispensaries.

(ii) Teaching farmers techniques for improvement of agricultural production and of prevention and control of disease among livestock in order to increase production of milk, meat and wool, and having healthier farm animals.

The Central Government created a separate organization, the Community Development Administration, to provide guidelines and a portion of the finance for implementation of the programme. The State governments deputed their most dynamic officers to implement the programme. The administrative structure for formulation and implementation of the programme extended from the Central Government and State governments to districts, community development blocks to the villages.

The Programme aroused great interest and expectations among the rural people. They began to feel that the government was making a determined and sincere effort for their welfare. Since making contributions in land, locally available materials and labour had to be made by the rural people themselves, the people made these contributions to create the essential service facilities for themselves. As a result living conditions for the villagers began to improve progressively.

Progress on the Programme for improvement of agricultural production and reducing diseases and improving productivity of animals was slower. One reason for this was that the community development organization did not suggest any methods better than those, which the best farmers were following already.

However, with extension of irrigation, through increase in number of irrigation wells, and of wells fitted with electric or diesel operated pumps, and deep tube-wells, improvement of tanks etc. and extension of canals from the large irrigation, power and flood control projects, the area with adequate and controlled supplies of irrigated water increased progressively and so did the production.

For successful implementation of the programme by Central and State government officers, it was considered essential that the officers were trained in implementation of the programme and that the programme was evaluated continuously. To achieve these objectives a Central Institute for Community Development (CICD) was started in the spring of 1959 while an organization for evaluation of the project called the Programme Evaluation Organization (PEO) was started in 1952, along with the CDP.[1]

High Yielding Varieties of Seeds

The real breakthrough in increasing agricultural production came however in the late 1960s and early 1970s, when new, very high yielding varieties of seeds of wheat and rice, first produced through research in Mexico (wheat) and in the Philippines (rice) respectively, were developed and adapted by Indian research scientists to suit conditions in the areas growing these crops and had the necessary climate and soil. These varieties gave very high (two to three times) yields in the cropped areas which had adequate and assured water supply provided by canals, wells or tube-wells and which could benefit with use of improved organic manure and chemical fertilizers and use of improved farm implements including tractors and pesticides as needed.

As a result agricultural output began to improve rapidly and the country which had to import as much as 9-10 million tonnes of wheat from the USA in the mid-1960s became self sufficient in cereals by 1970-71. Production of cereals has been increasing steadily since then, so that India, which produced about 60 million tonnes of cereals in the late 1950s, has been producing more than 190 million tonnes by the mid-1990s. Production of milk, fruit and vegetables has also increased progressively with consequent improvement in quality of food consumed by large sections of the rural and urban population. The production of cash crops—sugarcane, cotton, jute, tea, and coffee and wool—has also been increasing progressively. Production of milk, fruit and vegetables has increased manifolds. The only crops for which production has not kept pace with increasing consumption and the deficit has to be met by imports are oilseeds and to a smaller extent pulses.

There is in the most progressive areas, such as Punjab, Haryana, Western U.P., Coastal Andhra Pradesh and Tamil Nadu, and areas with assured water supplies provided either by adequate and assured rainfall or by irrigation in other States such as the sugar producing areas of Maharashtra, a rapidly growing class of middle income farmers with demand for processed consumer goods such as readymade garments, footwear and cooking gas and consumer durables such as fans, air coolers, refrigerators, bicycles, and scooters or mopeds, has emerged.

Extension of the Network of Motorable Roads

The proportion of villages within two km. of motorable roads has been increasing progressively with the result that motorized vehicles—buses, trucks, or tempos for public transport and motor cycles, scooters and mopeds—are the principal means of private transport in the rural areas over large parts of the country. Use of bullock carts as the principal means of rural transport has been reduced progressively.

Almost all the villages in most of the States have been provided with electricity. So that the area irrigated by wells fitted with electric pumps and deep tube wells has increased progressively. Since these areas provide adequate and controlled water supply, farmers with even small (three to five acres) holdings can use high yielding varieties of wheat and rice, sugarcane and cotton and obtain high yields from them. In those areas farmers have high enough income to afford electricity in their homes and can use fans, air coolers and refrigerators. They can produce their own vegetables and have milch animals to produce milk for consumption and sale. There is enough demand of labour for the landless labourers in the busy agricultural season, in handling the increased produce in the markets or in processing industries such as wheat and rice and sugar mills, cotton gins and textile mills. There is growing demand in these areas of soap, hair oil, cosmetics, pharmaceuticals drugs etc. The manufacturers of all such products look upon the rural areas as the principal growth areas for demand for their goods.

Rural Development Programmes

The CD Programme and its successors, programmes for rural employment, intensive agricultural development, elimination of poverty, adult literacy, basic health care and welfare of the poor especially the scheduled castes and the scheduled tribes has aroused great enthusiasm among the rural people about the efforts sponsored by the Government to improve their economic and social conditions. Tens of thousands of primary schools and village dispensaries have been started. The country is able to feed its population despite a nearly three-fold increase in it. Furthermore consumption of food (including protective foods) such as milk, vegetables, eggs, and fish, sugar and cooking oil has gone up. The rural level of living is better. The radio and television receivers are the proud possession of every slum dweller in the cities and millions of rural homes are lighted. The isolation of the village is broken. In most States nearly all the villages are within a two km. radius of a motorable road. Rural electrification is universal in most of the States and the States provide almost free electricity to all farmers in the interest of promoting agricultural output. Furthermore, minimum prices are guaranteed to farmers for their produce in order to provide an adequate income to all the farmers. Information on minimum prices is published and the government buys surplus produce of all so that exploitation by the merchants in the market is reduced. Most of the surplus is by large farmers, but most of the small farmers also do have the means to buy food when they need. The Public Distribution System (PDS) ensures/guarantees that. In 50 years of independence there has been no famine, although earlier famine was a daily occurrence.

Despite these improvements, there has been very slow increase in production in the large areas, which do not have irrigation or adequate rainfall. These areas comprise about 70 per cent of the cropped area; they await seed varieties, which give higher yields of its main food crops—sorghum and millets—and cash crops—cotton and oilseeds. There is need for agriculture research focussed on evolving seed varieties of these crops, which can increase crop yields in areas with variable water supplies. The increase in agricultural output as a result of use of these varieties will besides increasing production reduce under-employment and unemployment in rural areas and consequent emigration to the cities.

Until recently about one-third of the population was poor—*i.e.* it got less calories than needed for health but this proportion seems to be declining now. However, most of the poor are concentrated in hilly and forested areas of Madhya Pradesh, Bihar and Orissa and other States, which suffer from difficulties of communication or in States such as central and eastern U.P., Bihar and parts of West Bengal, where people are too poor to buy the food.

The principal problem, therefore, is under-employment or unemployment of large numbers of poor people in the villages. Programmes must be devised to provide employment to them in their home States.

The NREGS launched in 2005 has had its initial problems in implementation. Latest research indicates that while in some States the programme is making good progress, in some others, there are major seepages in the funds provided for the scheme and the proportion of rural poor benefiting form it is rather small.

The Unirrigated Areas

Despite the increase in irrigated area, during the last 50 years, almost 70 per cent of the cropland lacks irrigation. In several areas such as the Assam plains and hills, West Bengal and coastal Orissa, large parts of the west and east coasts rainfall is adequate and assured and rice, gram, wheat, sugarcane, pulses and other crops can be grown without irrigation and give high yields. The principal problems in some of these areas, such as the sub-mountain areas of West Bengal, Bihar and U.P., is that large areas are rendered unproductive because of being covered with coarse sands brought down by floods of the rivers during the summer monsoon. Large areas in central U.P. are rendered unproductive because of excess salinity or alkalinity of the soil.

The primary need in these areas is reclamation of the lands by controlling ravages of floods and reduction of salinity or alkalinity. Determined action by the present Government of West Bengal has reduced the area rendered unproductive by the floods of the Teesta River and other rivers in North Bengal. Furthermore, the areas with assured water supply have increased by increase in the number of wells fitted with electric pumps. The Government also implemented the land reforms for abolition of the old *zamindari* system and giving ownership of land to the actual cultivators thus providing the latter with a powerful incentive to invest labour and capital, use of improved varieties of seeds, organic manure and chemical fertilizers to increase output of the principal crop—rice and jute—so that total production of rice has recorded an impressive increase for nearly 30 years that the Government led by the Communist Party has been in power. Similar action by the Governments of U.P. and Bihar has been lacking, so that crop yields are low, and the farmers cannot produce enough crops of rice, wheat or other grains for the needs of their families and are besides underemployed for part of the year.

In the unirrigated areas of other States—Telengana in Andhra Pradesh, large parts of Tamil Nadu, Karnataka, Maharashtra, Gujarat, Madhya Pradesh, and Rajasthan—similarly farmers depend upon uncertain and frequently deficient rainfall. Yields of the food crops (sorghum and millets) or cash crops (cotton and oilseeds) are generally low and vary greatly with adequacy, and timeliness of the monsoon rains. Seed variety, which, would give dependable yields under conditions of variable moisture have not yet been evolved. The farmers can barely produce enough food crops for their own needs, with little surplus for sale. Yields of the cash crops—cotton and oilseeds—are also barely sufficient to give farmers enough cash to meet their needs for essential consumer goods, such as cloth, services such as education of their children and obtaining medical assistance in case of sickness.

In these areas agricultural output can be increased through :

(i) agricultural research concentrated on evolving seed varieties of the principal crops—sorghum, millets, greens, cotton and oilseeds so that they give higher yields under conditions of inadequate and uncertain rainfalls;

(ii) reducing intensity of floods in the monsoon season by plantation of trees or protective bushes which hold water in the Himalayan foothills;

(iii) reclamation of lands infested with salinity and alkalinity in U.P.;

(iv) increasing employment opportunities in those areas through the land reclamation measures mentioned above and improving communication through construction of approach roads and increasing irrigated area through construction of small check dams in the sub-Himalayan areas;

(v) the agro-processing industries based on the agricultural output will provide additional employment; and

(vi) improving education and preventive and curative health care programmes so that children can go to school and the needed medical care can be obtained by the people at low cost; remittances from migrants to cities will remain an important source of income of families in the region. However, with progressive reduction of emigration, there will be larger manpower to undertake the programmes mentioned above.

Currently the responsibility for implementation of rural development programmes has been entrusted to *Panchayati Raj* Institutions (PRI) in order to secure greater involvement in these programmes of the rural people through their representatives in the institutions. However, the *Panchayati Raj* institutions are political bodies. In large numbers of them inter-caste and inter-personal disputes occupy the time of institutions and development takes the backseat. There is, therefore, need for rethinking on the structure and functions of these institutions so that welfare-oriented development becomes the top priority task of these institutions.

The institutions should be restructured so that they pay greater attention to development porogrammes. For instance, greater representation of women in the institutions will mean greater attention to programmes of health care and education because these are of vital concern to the women.

Emphasis on education and health care programmes means that the people who migrate to the cities are healthier and have education and some skills to take up jobs such as messengers, and artisans and can have higher income and afford to live in *pucca* homes in 'unauthorized' colonies in which they have electricity and safe water supply. The infrastructures in them are better than in the slums. The migrants to Delhi from Punjab and Haryana—States with high agricultural productivity—are already artisans, messengers in offices, drivers and repair-men of motor vehicles and live in the 'unauthorized colonies'. These States in fact import labourers in the busy agricultural season from eastern U.P. and Bihar because there is shortage of local labour in them.

The migration of the rural people is both seasonal and permanent. The farmers migrate when there is no work to be done on the farms after sowing and harvesting their crops. The landless migrate on a permanent basis, however. Both groups do the lowest paid semi-skilled labour jobs and live in the slums of the large cities, in which rents are low but there is no provision for safe drinking water or drainage for disposal of silage water. As a result, there is much disease and high mortality, particularly among children and women in these areas.

The slum dwellers in Delhi, Mumbai and Calcutta are all from eastern U.P., Bihar and Orissa, parts of Rajasthan, which are areas of rural poverty.

Effects of Rural Development Programmes After 50 Years

The Community Development Programme, N.E.S. programme, and later additions—HYV seed and irrigation and Rural Employment Programme have led to major increases in agricultural output, particularly cereals but also of sugar, cotton, jute, tea and coffee to meet domestic demand and also increase in exports of the latter three—jute, tea and coffee. Major deficiency in production of oilseeds, however, had to be met by imports of cooking oil.

In spite of above advances in agriculture India has the largest number of people below poverty line, illiterate, and people without access to safe and adequate drinking water. There are large regional disparities in economic development.

Access to essential infrastructure facilities, universal rural electrification, adequate road network, higher proportion of literate population, low percentages of rural population below poverty line is concentrated in some advanced States while poverty and hunger is concentrated in other areas of the country (Table 2.1 and 2.2).

Distribution of Hunger and of Rural Poor

There are large regional differences in the incidence of hunger. It is least in the 30 per cent of the area in which there is security of production as a result of adequate and dependable rainfall or irrigation. There is little hunger in States such as Punjab, Haryana, a part of western U.P., coastal

Andhra Pradesh, most of Tamil Nadu, which have benefited from the Green Revolution which raised yield of the principal food crops—wheat and rice with use of high breed seeds, fertilizers and pesticides.

Similarly in areas such as coastal Gujarat and western Maharashtra which are industrialized and farmers have the means to buy food in case of need, hunger is confined to (i) hilly and forested areas of Peninsular India—parts of Andhra Pradesh and Karnataka, Marathwada and Vidarbha regions of Maharashtra, a large part of western Rajasthan, Sourashtra in Gujarat in which most of the cropland is unirrigated and production depends upon vagaries of the monsoon rainfall; and (ii) Inland Orissa, Chhota Nagpur region of Bihar, most of Madhya Pradesh and parts of Maharashtra, Gujarat and south-east Rajasthan which are forested and inhabited by tribal. Hunger in these parts is due partly to low production and partly to difficulties of commercialization.

Large parts of U.P. and Bihar which are densely populated and do not produce enough food despite having fertile plains; hunger is the legacy of the *zamindari* system and social backwardness of the people.

However, in other areas where agricultural development accompanied by increase in area under irrigation and improved varieties of seeds, fertilizers and technological advances, has led to improvement in levels of living and social change. Tens of thousands of new schools were opened. Every village above a certain population had a primary school, which served also for a group of villages. Tens of thousands of new drinking water wells were constructed. People of lower castes who were not allowed to draw water from the wells of high castes, were encouraged to construct their own wells. Tens of thousands of primary health care centres were opened. Thousands of mini-hospitals (with six beds), one or two doctors and para-medical personnel were opened. These provided curative and preventive health care.

Thousands of miles of new approach roads and motorable roads were constructed so that every village had a bus within a km. of walking distance. There were problems of unwillingness of urban based teachers and doctors and para-medical personnel to man the schools and health care centres located in rural areas. Yet at the end of five decades of community development effort, 91 per cent of the children are in the primary schools in 1999; several villages had coverage of 96 per cent of children. All the villages have electricity; the proportion is 100 per cent in several States.

Panchayati Raj institutions have been opened and they have been functioning with varying degrees of efficiency. Food production has increased by three and a half times since the mid-1950s somewhat in excess of the increase in population. There has been no famine in the last fifty years. Yet according to a report of the UNFPA, one-third of the population—an estimated 325 million go hungry *i.e.* they consume less than 80 per cent of the minimum energy requirements. The principal reason for it is different stages of production and storage and maldistribution.

Table 2.1: Per Capita Availability of Selected Articles of Consumption

Sl. No.	*1998-99 grams per day*	*1980-81 grams per day*	*Increase 1998-99 over 1980-81*
1. Foodgrains per day	450.71	410.4	Marginal Increase
2. Edible Oil (kg. pa.)	9.5	3.8	Nearly three times
3. Sugar (kg. pa.)	14.9	7.3	Nearly double
4. Tea (gm. pa.)	676	511	Some increase
5. Fabrics (m. pa.)	28.2	17.3	Nearly double
6. Electricity Consumption k.wh. pa.	*1997-98* 64.3	13.5	Five Times
7. People Below Poverty Line	29.2	54.9	.

Source: Tata Consultancy Services; *Statistical Outline of India, 2000-2001*, Mumbai, Table 248, p. 213.

Table 2.2: Total Area Cropped and Irrigated and Output of Foodgrains*

Agriculture	*Ml. Hectares 1996-97*	
Net Area Irrigated	55.1	
Total Area Cropped	189.5	
Irrigated area/ Cropped Area (%)	38.7	
Output of Foodgrains Items	1996-97	*(In Ml. Tonnes.)* 1980-81
1. Foodgrains	199.3	129.6
2. Rice	81.3	53.6
3. Wheat	69.3	36.3
4. Pulses	14.5	10.6
5. Oilseeds	25.0	9.4
6. Tea	0.57	0.6
7. Sugarcane + Jaggery	277.3	154.2
8. *Cotton	14.2	7.0

* The per capita income at constant 1983-84 prices has increased three times between 1951-51 and 1988-89.

Source: Tata Consultancy Services (TCS), *Statistical Outline of India,* 2000-2001, Table 53, p. 50 and Table 35, p. 39.

NOTES

1. A brief note on PEO and CICD form part of this collection in subsequent chapters. The author had the privilege of being the first Director of the PEO and the first Vice Principal of CICD.
2. Intensive Agricultural District Programme : One of the most important ingredients of the programme is the package of improved practices for the selected crops such as the use of improved seeds, fertilizers, plant protection measures, improved implements and proper soil and water management. The package has been refined to include such cultural practices as proper placing of fertilizers, introducing changes in the time of sowing and other tillage and inter-cultural practices. The scheme of intensive agriculture has lent greater precision to planning of agricultural production as it has sharply defined the role of the government, the research organizations, the extension agency and the farmer. On the basis of the package of practices, the Village Level Workers (VLWs) were asked to develop farm plans for individual farmers. The scheme of intensive agriculture is scientific. It is the nearest approach to factory method of production in agriculture. It has removed a major difficulty in our agricultural planning by channelling precious inputs like fertilizers and plant protection chemicals into most productive areas, which are comparatively secure from hazards of weather.

ANNEXURE 2.1

Achievements of the Rural Development Programmes

Increased production of cereals to raise per capita availability: Increased production of milk, eggs, chicken, fish (in the coastal areas), vegetables and fruit to meet demands of the approximate 213 million plus urban population and partly of the numerous rural population especially in the prosperous areas.

Most of the villages in many States have electricity so that dependence on cow-dung for cooking and oil for lighting has been reduced. Most of the villages in many States are within two km. of a motorable road so that buses, tempo and mopeds or motor bicycles have taken the place of bullock carts as the means of rural transport.

Most of the villages in several States have primary schools and secondary schools in large villages so that literacy rates have increased considerably. The national literacy rate was over 52.2 per cent in 1991 having gone up from 36.5 per cent in 1971. In States such as Kerala and Goa it is over 90 per cent.

However, as has been mentioned above, there are large regional imbalances in economic development, in distribution of hunger and rural poor between irrigated and unirrigated areas.

Production of cereals and protective food is all concentrated in the irrigated areas. Unirrigated areas can barely produce enough cereals (sorghums and millets) for self-consumption and cotton or oil seeds for sale for meeting their requirements of cash to buy the goods that they need. In bad monsoon periods they suffer from scarcity of food or fodder for the livestock. These areas comprise large parts of Madhya Pradesh, inland Orissa, Rajasthan, U.P., Bihar and West Bengal.

The imbalance would increase progressively unless steps are taken at the initiative of the State governments. Some of the successful initiatives from State governments which have made a difference in rural areas with no security of water supply have been in West Bengal in its measures for (i) land reforms, (ii) in provision of loans for pump sets for the poor, (iii) health care, and (iv) control of floods. In Punjab, Haryana, Madhya Pradesh and Rajasthan provision of educational facilities is an example. Besides, the government of Rajasthan has increased greatly tourism to the State through its Tourism Department. However, in Orissa the cyclone affected villages have not returned to normalcy despite all the assistance.

3

Progress of Rural Development Programmes

*Regional Differences**

The experience with agricultural and rural development programmes of more than a decade has shown that progress of these programmes is significantly better in some States than in others. Even within the State progress has been markedly uneven.

A study of these differences is important because in all these programmes success depends in large part upon the response of the local people—their understanding of the objects and methods of the programmes, their capacity to avail of the assistance offered, etc. Further, the success or failure of these programmes affects the economy and social life of large numbers of people.

This Chapter points to the emergence of regional differences in the progress of rural development programmes and emphasizes the need for detailed and systematic studies to identify these differences and to locate their causes. Such studies are essential for remedial action to remove these disparities and to enable areas of low progress to overcome their handicaps and achieve a more satisfactory rate of progress.

Some data on inter-State differences in progress have been given for two fields: cooperative credit and technological change in agriculture. The data are primarily illustrative; they are not intended for comparisons of progress among different States. In the case of technological change in agriculture, data have been given for only two indicators: use of chemical fertilizers and installation of mechanical pumps (electrically and oil operated engine) for irrigation. These data would need to be supplemented by other indicators of technological change (*e.g.* use of improved seed)

---

*Published in *The Economic Weekly*, Annual Number, February 1963, pp. 175-177.

as well as by statistics of increase of agricultural production for a comparative picture of agricultural progress in different States. However, the indicators selected are useful as pointers to progress in the particular fields and, therefore, adequate for the limited purpose of this Chapter.

The other limitation of the data is that they are for States as a whole. It is known that in case of many programmes, areas of good as well as poor progress—differences between which are as large, as or even larger than those between States—are found within the same State. Thus Maharashtra and Andhra Pradesh which make a good showing in cooperative credit included areas *e.g.* most districts of Marathwada in Maharashtra and Telengana, which formed part of the former Hyderabad State, in Andhra, in which the cooperative movement is much less developed than in States like Punjab which make only a medium showing. The progress indicated by data for the whole State is in these cases due primarily to spectacular progress in some districts, *e.g.* several of the districts of the former Bombay State, which now form part of Maharashtra. Thus the credit advanced by cooperatives in the Jalgaon district of the old Bombay State alone is of the order of Rs. 8 crore in 1960-61, which is equal to the total credit advanced in the four eastern States of Bihar, West Bengal, Orissa and Assam.

Such areas of spectacular progress as well as areas of particularly poor progress should be identified through detailed studies so that analysis of the factors responsible for these disparities can be understood. The value of such case studies hardly needs any emphasis.

Cooperative Credit

Data on agricultural credit advanced by primary (agricultural credit and multi-purpose) societies in the three years 1951-52, 1956-57 and 1959-60 are given in Table 3.1. The States have been arranged in four regional groups to bring out regional differences more clearly. The period covered is one of rapid expansion in cooperative credit, primarily due to the availability of large funds from the Reserve Bank of India from the early fifties. The increase for the country as a whole is seven times during this period. Several of the States show comparable or higher rates of increase; but in certain others, progress has been much below the national average. Andhra, Madras, Gujarat, Maharashtra and U.P. are the big five in cooperative credit; followed by Mysore, Punjab and Madhya Pradesh. The differences in the volume of cooperative credit are due in part to differences in the size and cropped area of the States; the high figure for

U.P. is due partly to its large size. The influence of this factor has been eliminated in column 8 of Table 3.1 in which cooperative credit per 1,000 acres of cropped area has been given.

The regional differences that have emerged are:

Southern Region : All the States in this region show rapid and constant progress. Andhra (in the former Madras area only) and Madras (Tamil Nadu) starting with well-developed cooperative movement, have maintained steady progress. In 1959-60, Madras achieved the figure of Rs. 10.31 of cooperative credit per acre of cropped area, which is the highest in the country. In Kerala, progress has been from small beginnings, but has been rapid, so that by 1959-60 the State had the third highest figure of cooperative credit per acre of cropped area. The percentage of overdues to outstanding loans is medium to low in all three States and the cooperative movement can be considered to be progressing satisfactorily. In Mysore, on the other hand, progress is slower and the percentage of overdues is also higher.

Western Region : Both Gujarat and Maharashtra show steady progress in cooperative credit. Together they account for about 30 per cent of the total cooperative credit in the country. The movement was already well developed in the former Bombay State areas of these States, but not so in other areas like Marathwada in Maharashtra, where it is even now less advanced than in the other areas.

Northern and Central Region : The four States grouped together in this region all show rapid advance during this period. In Punjab and parts of U.P. and M.P. the movement was already well developed; but in the other areas, advance has been from small beginnings. In Rajasthan, for instance, the movement was very small until the early 1950s, because a large number of the princely States, from which the new State was formed, did not have any cooperative movement worth the name. Only in a few of the larger princely States had a beginning been made with organization of cooperatives. But even in these, the movement was relatively less developed as it was started comparatively late, in the 1930s or the 1940s. In Madhya Pradesh, while in certain parts there were well-developed cooperatives, in others, like the areas of the former Vindhya Pradesh, conditions were similar to those in Rajasthan. The rapid progress recorded by both Rajasthan and Madhya Pradesh during this period has enabled them to overcome the disadvantage of a late start to a considerable extent. But this rate of progress will have to continue for some years more before these States can come up to the levels of Punjab and U.P.

Table 3.1 : Co-operative Credit Loans advanced by Primary Agricultural Credit and Multi-Purpose Societies

States	*Loans Advanced (Rs. Lakh)*			*Percentage Increase in 1959-60 over 1951-52*	*State Total as Per Cent of All-India Total*	*Gross Cropped Area in 1958-59*	*Co-operative Loans per Acre of Cropped Area*	*Overdues as Per Cent of Outstanding Loans in 1959-60*	*Number of Members in 1959-60*
	1951-52	1956-57	1959-60						
(1)	(2)	(3)	(4)	(5)	(6)	(7)	(8)	(9)	(10)
Southern									
Andhra	292	865	1750	499.3	10.39	29872	5.86	14	126
Madras	318	722	1737	446.2	10.31	17097	10.16	11	158
Mysore	NA	539	1203	NA	7.14	26031	4.62	33	105
Kerala	52	153	409	686.5	2.43	5537	7.39	20	750
Western									
Maharashtra	640	1207	2937	358.9	17.44	45836	6.41	27	1531
Gujarat	188	899	2126	1030.9	12.62	23570	9.02	25	750
Northern and Central									
Uttar Pradesh	257	656	2922	1037.0	17.35	53794	5.43	6	2883
Punjab	176	566	1129	541.5	6.70	24527	4.60	26	1126
Rajasthan	16	104	539	3268.8	3.20	33921	1.59	19	513
Madhya Pradesh	128	505	1301	916.4	7.73	43813	2.97	21	789

(Contd.)

Table 3.1 : (*Contd.*)

States	Loans Advanced (Rs. Lakhs)			Percentage increase in 1959-60 over 1951-52	State Total As Per Cent of All-India Total	Gross Cropped Area in 1958-59	Co-operative Loans per Acre of Cropped Area	Over dues as Per Cent of Outstanding Loans in 1959-60	Number of Members in 1959-60
	1951-52	1956-57	1959-60						
(1)	(2)	(3)	(4)	(5)	(6)	(7)	(8)	(9)	(10)
Eastern									
Assam	1.2	75.7	66.9	5475.0	0.40	6003	1.11	55	204
West Bengal	69	116	227	229.0	1.35	15055	1.51	43	571
Bihar	4	69	129	3125.0	0.77	27378	0.47	55	620
Orissa	41	170	235	473.2	1.40	14958	1.57	20	369
Total:									
All India	2421	6733	16840	695.6	100.00	367392	4.58	21	14468

Source : "Co-operative Movement in India: Trend of Progress in the States, 1950-51 to 1959-60", Government of India, Ministry of Community Development and Co-operation, 1961. Statements 1.6 and 1.7 to 16.6 and 16.7.

Table 3.2 : Technological Change in Agriculture—Use of Chemical Fertilizers and Number of Mechanical Pumps Used

States	Use of Chemical Fertilizers, 1959 NP$_2$O$_5$, K$_2$O		Figure for State as Per Cent of All India Total	No. of oil Engines and Electric Pumps Used for Irrigation						
	Total (tonnes)	Per Acre of Agricultural Land (lbs)		1951	1956	1961	Increase in 1961 over 1951	Figure for State as Per Cent of All India Total for 1961	Area Irrigated by Wells in 1958-59 ('000 acres)	No. of Pumps per 1000 Acres of Well Irrigated Area
(1)	(2)	(3)	(4)	(5)	(6)	(7)	(8)	(9)	(10)	(11)
Southern										
Andhra	36911	2.64	13.16	9526	19991	50964	435.0	13.66	728	70.0
Madras	40232	5.38	14.34	28684	53729	135313	371.7	36.28	1346	100.5
Mysore	11847	1.03	4.22	7461	11109	22520	201.8	6.04	304	74.1
Kerala	11322	4.65	4.04	2788	3227	5937	113.0	1.59	35	169.6
Western										
Maharashtra } Gujarat	42664	1.36	15.21	31588	48848	121484	284.6	32.57	2484	48.9
Northern and Central										
Uttar Pradesh	44170	1.87	15.75	3394	6319	11377	235.2	3.05	5754	2.0

(*Contd.*)

(Contd.)

States	Use of Chemical Fertilizers, 1959		Figure for State as Per Cent of All India Total	No. of oil Engines and Electric Pumps Used for Irrigation						
	NP_2O_5, K_2O									
	Total (tonnes)	Per Acre of Agricultural Land (lbs)		1951	1956	1961	Increase in 1961 over 1951	Figure for State as Per Cent of All India Total for 1961	Area Irrigated by Wells in 1958-59 ('000 acres)	No. of Pumps per 1000 Acres of Well Irrigated Area
(1)	(2)	(3)	(4)	(5)	(6)	(7)	(8)	(9)	(10)	(11)
Punjab	7124	0.67	2.54	1973	11896	NA	NA	NA	2322	NA
Rajasthan	3158	0.21	1.13	1644	1659	2941	78.9	0.79	1944	1.5
Madhya Pradesh	9913	0.51	3.53	2389	5730	11909	398.5	3.19	741	16.1
Eastern										
Assam	1644	0.62	0.59	74	376	127	71.6	0.03	—	—
West Bengal	12283	1.83	4.38	1173	1476	3893	231.9	1.04	39	99.8
Bihar	15129	1.35	5.39	886	3653	5117	477.5	1.37	681	7.5
Orissa	5172	0.77	1.84	129	936	1322	924.8	0.35	94	14.1
Total: All India	280467	—	—	91709	168949	373000	306.7	—	—	—

Sources: Fertilizer Statistics 1960, Fertilizer Association of India, New Delhi, 1961.
Indian Livestock Census 1956 and the Directorate of Economics and Statistics, Ministry of Food and Agriculture, New Delhi.

The Eastern Region : All the four Eastern States—Assam, West Bengal, Bihar and Orissa—show poor progress. The total cooperative credit advanced in these States in 1959-60 is only Rs. 6.6 crore or about 4 per cent of the total for the country. The number of cooperative societies and their membership is not too small (13 per cent of the total for the country), but the credit advanced by them is very small, mainly because a large proportion of the societies are not working satisfactorily. This is brought out by the high percentage of overdues in col. 9 of Table 3.1. Orissa is a little better off than the other three. In spite of a late start in a large part of the State, it can claim better progress and a better overdues position. But in the other three States the movement is clearly not making progress. These States have had experience of cooperation for as long as the rest of the country. So there is no question of their being handicapped by a late start or lack of administrative experience. In their case it is clearly a case of poor response, which needs to be investigated in detail.

Technological Change in Agriculture

In the use of fertilizer also the southern and western States are much ahead of the rest of the country. Together, they account for nearly 60 per cent of the total fertilizer used (*see* Table 3.2). In contrast, use of fertilizer is limited in most of the eastern and all the northern and western States except U.P.; the large figure for U.P. is due to its size. The influence of this factor is eliminated in col. 3 of Table 3.2 in which figures of use of fertilizer per acre of cropped area have been given. These figures range from 0.2 lbs per acre in Rajasthan to 4.65 lbs in Kerala and 5.38 lbs in Madras. Differences in use of fertilizers are due in part to differences in climate and cropping pattern. In the country, use of fertilizer has so far been successful only in areas of assured rainfall and/or irrigation facilities. The principal fertilizers used are nitrogenous and are used largely for irrigated paddy. In contrast, the millet growing areas of low and uncertain rainfall use very little fertilizer; the low figure for Rajasthan is due mainly to this.

But, this factor does not explain the marked differences between Madras and Andhra on the one hand and the eastern States of West Bengal and Assam on the other in the use of fertilizer; the per acre figure for Bengal is one-third and for Assam one-ninth of that for Madras. The differences would have been even greater if paddy lands alone were considered since the average for Madras is depressed by the inclusion of large areas under millets and other dry zone crops. The much higher use of fertilizers in Madras (and Andhra and Kerala) appears to be due mainly to better acceptance by the cultivators. The reason for this as also for the poor acceptance in Bengal and Assam where the climatic conditions are equally favourable and fertilizer equally needed would be a fruitful subject for study.

A similar picture emerges from figures of installation of pumping sets driven by oil engines or electric motors. Madras, Andhra, Maharashtra and Gujarat are prominent with more than 80 per cent of the total pump sets in the country. The six States of the southern and western regions together account for 90 per cent of the total. In contrast, the number of pump sets in the northern and eastern States is very small. Here again, we should draw attention to the figures given in column. 11 of Table 3.2, which show the number of pump sets per 1,000 acres of area irrigated by wells, because these eliminate the influence of the size of area under well irrigation in different States. These figures show striking contrasts between the southern States on the one hand and the northern States like U.P. and Rajasthan on the other. The latter have large numbers of wells but very few pumping sets.

These differences again are not due to any differences in natural conditions : mechanical pumping will benefit the farmer just as much in U.P. and Rajasthan as in Madras and Andhra. The differences are due partly to greater rural electrification in the southern States, which facilitates installation of electric motors and partly to better response to mechanical pumping by cultivators.

Intra-State Differences

The very limited data presented here points to striking differences in progress in different States. Similar analysis should be carried out for the entire range of rural development activities and for areas smaller than States (districts or groups of districts) so that differences in progress between different areas are more clearly and accurately identified. The value of such analysis need hardly be emphasized. Identification of regional differences and demarcation of areas of outstanding and poor progress is essential so that programmes and policies can be modified to suit particular regional conditions and the example of areas of outstanding progress can be followed by others and the causes which hamper progress in the latter can be removed.

4

Evaluation of Rural Development Programmes

*The Programme Evaluation Organization (PEO)**

All purposive, planned and organized action in any field—social, private or governmental—implies (a) a goal or an end to be achieved; (b) the organized deployment of resources—human, material and institutional—to achieve the end; and (c) an assessment of results. The assessment of results is of special significance in development planning where it is necessary to know how far the targets have been attained and what are the reasons for the shortfalls, if any, in terms of quality or quantity of the end-products.

A review of activities and appraisal of results are normally undertaken by the administrative agencies themselves through a system of regular checks, inspections, stock-taking, etc. Besides such administrative assessment, there is another type of assessment or evaluation which is concerned primarily with study of (i) effectiveness of methods of operation and of approach to the people, and (ii) progress in terms of impact of the activities on the social and economic life of the people. This latter type of assessment is particularly important in programmes like the Community Projects and National Extension Services which aim not merely at accomplishing stated administrative tasks, but primarily at inducing fundamental social and economic changes. The work of the Programme Evaluation Organization (PEO) is concerned with this latter type of study. Considering that the evaluating agency should be in close and constant touch with the people and as near as possible to the authorities responsible for planning of the programmes; the P.E.O. was from its very inception constituted as an independent organization but attached to the Planning Commission.

---

* Published in *Indian Journal of Public Administration*, October 2, 1967, pp. 339-348.

The need for evaluation of methods of approach and of results of extension was, for the first time, stressed by the Grow More Food Enquiry Committee in 1952 (Government of India, p. 57). The Committee recommended setting up of suitable organizations for the purpose in the Central and State governments. In the First Five Year Plan, the Planning Commission emphasized that "systematic evaluation should become a normal administrative practice in all branches of public activity.

The PEO was established in October 1952, with Professor D.G. Karve, an eminent Indian economist, as the founder Director of the Organization. A substantial grant towards the cost of operation of the Organization for the first three years was given by the Ford Foundation. It is noteworthy that the P.E.O. started functioning at the same time as the first Community Development Projects were started in the country. Its setting up with the beginning of the Community Development Programme (CDP) has been of considerable advantage to both sides. The results of observations of the evaluation officers have been available to the administrators almost from the beginning. The PEO, on its side, has had the advantage of observing the progress of the development programme at the various stages and to develop and adapt its methods of evaluation to meet the changes in the size and content of the Programme.

Objects

The objects of the work of the Organization were to keep all concerned apprised of the progress of the Programme objectives; point out various extension methods which are proving effective and those which are not; and furnish the insights into the impact of the CDP upon the rural economy and social life.

The importance of the evaluation carried out by the P.E.O. is better seen in the context of the character and objectives of the National Extension Service (NES) and CDP itself. The programme represents the biggest effort yet made to reach the rural people, to teach them improved methods of productive activity and of better living and to provide them with effective assistance towards the realization of these ends. It is a comprehensive programme touching all aspects of rural life and every section of the rural population, and can well be considered the beginning of an intensive and expanding effort to regenerate rural life in our times. To cope with the new responsibilities the entire rural administration is being progressively transformed. The existing development services are being greatly expanded and new services are being created. The NES represents the basic structure of rural development administration through which the increasing development activities of the Welfare State are to reach the rural people. But this is not merely a programme of providing State assistance. The ultimate object is to develop individuals and institutions so that they may themselves progressively take up the initiative for development; hence, the emphasis on the educational process and on the growth of popular institutions.

Structure of the Organization

The P.E.O. is an independent organization working under the general direction of the Planning Commission. The most important part of the Organization is its field agency, which consists of about 20 Project Evaluation Officers. These officers are located in carefully selected project areas in different parts of the country. All the States and the major geographical and agricultural regions of the country are represented in the project areas. To provide guidance to the field staff and to maintain more active contact with the State governments than what would be possible from the Central office, there were to start with three Regional Evaluation Officers. The central staff consisted of the Director and other officers who are responsible for providing overall direction and guidance and for the collation and interpretation of the results of field studies and surveys. The Project Evaluation Officer is the key functionary in the set up because he is the primary observer of the progress of the programme and is in addition responsible for the conduct of evaluation surveys in his area. He maintains continuous and active contact with the development staff up to the district level, and, through field visits and rural surveys, with the people of the area. Thus, the set-up of the Organization provides for effective contacts and observations at all levels from the field to the Central Government.

Programme of Work of the PEO

The work of the PEO falls into two main parts : (1) General Evaluation, and (2) Evaluation Surveys and Studies. Each of these is described in some detail below :

General Evaluation

In the first year of working of the PEO, general evaluation received somewhat greater emphasis than other phases of its work. At that time, the Community Projects had just started functioning and had many new features. However, as a result of experience in the field for about one year, major changes were introduced in the organizational structure and the content of the programme and the methods of approach to the people. The extent of these changes can only be appreciated by comparing a National Extension or Community Development Block of today with the Community Projects, which went into operation in October 1952. In the process of assessing the success of particular activities or approaches, and indicating the need for change, the reports of the P.E.O. have played a very useful role.

The most notable contribution of the P.E.O. in this field of general evaluation has been through its annual Evaluation Reports. Each Report contains a comprehensive review of progress of the Programme during the year, which is based on the experiences of the evaluation officers and on results of important studies conducted by the Organization.

Besides the Annual Reports, a large number of other reports relating to particular programme or particular situation in the field are made available from time to time to the Ministry of Community Development and the Planning Commission. The objective reporting by the Organization has been invaluable in providing insights on how the Programme was progressing, which activities were proving more successful than others, and what problems were being experienced.

Evaluation Surveys and Studies

During the initial few years of its establishment the P.E.O. conducted a number of surveys and studies. Most of these were designed specifically to serve as aids to evaluation. Some of the more important ones have been concerned with (i) investigation of the reasons why the rural people accept certain improved practices or participate in certain development programmes and not in others, (ii) quantitative assessment of such acceptance or participation, and (iii) measurement of the economic or social effects of the development programme upon the rural population. In the initial period the studies included were the Bench-Mark Survey, the Acceptance of Practices Survey, the Survey on Cotton Extension in PEPSU and Studies of Rural Social Organization.

The Bench-Mark Survey : Data collected and tabulated for bench-mark survey established a base-line from which changes in specified conditions can be measured over a period of time *e.g*, the effects of adoption of new practices upon production, income, employment and levels of living of the rural population by collecting data on such items as occupation and employment status, literacy, incidence of sickness, patterns of land holding, land utilization and crop production, investment in specified land improvements, extent of adoption of improved agricultural practices and participation in Community Programmes and developmental institutions.

Data is obtained, for selected families (from about 100 families in each block), on their assets and liabilities, capital formation, production and disposal of crops in case of cultivators, and employment and earnings in case of agricultural labourers. Changes in these conditions are measured by means of repeated surveys at stated intervals.

The bench-mark survey has made available detailed data on important aspects of the rural economy, which are of considerable interest for development workers, and the repeat surveys will make possible assessment of the extent and direction of change in these, under the impact of the development programme.

The Acceptance of Practices Enquiry makes deeper investigation of selected farms on the incentives provided and methods of persuasion used for encouraging the adoption of improved practices in agriculture, animal husbandry, health and sanitation, irrigation, and other fields; and the reasons for adoption, partial adoption or non-adoption of improved practices by the people; the advantages of new practices; the present attitudes of the people towards the new practices, the incentives or facilities which were considered necessary for their continued or increased adoption in future.

The Survey on Cotton Extension studied in PEPSU was undertaken to analyze the relative economy of growing the old and new varieties of cotton under different conditions of soil and irrigation, and of the economic feasibility of various cultivation practices, which were being advocated by the projects along with propagation of the new variety. Some 'sponsored' practices were found to be acceptable to cultivators, while others, which were being simultaneously advocated were not proving acceptable.

Studies of Rural Social Organization

As development programmes become more comprehensive in their scope and seek to have an increasing influence on the life of the rural people, the need for detailed basic data on social and economic aspects of rural life is increasingly felt. The gaps in our existing knowledge of rural life are particularly serious on the social side. In view of the importance of such data for its work, the P.E.O. has conducted two studies of rural social organization and leadership during the first-three years of its operation. The first study, which was undertaken in a north Indian village near Delhi, analyzed in detail the factors influencing group formation and patterns of leadership in the village. The second study brought out the main facts about leadership and groups in a village in Mysore, and showed how these had affected, and had in turn, been themselves influenced by development activities. Since then many studies of village institutions and leadership have been conducted which, analyze the factors in the economic and social structure of the villages, particularly caste, which have an influence on the success or failure of popular institutions like *Panchayats.*

Some other P.E.O. enquiries have been related to more intensive studies of subjects like agricultural extension, administrative coordination, training programmes for village leaders and village artisans. At any given time, one or more such studies would be in progress in the evaluation centres.

Evaluation by other Agencies

Although the P.E.O. has a distinct and important role in the evaluation of the CDP and NES, its work can obviously form only a small portion of the truly enormous task of assessment of progress and location of deficiencies connected with this Programme. The Organization has, therefore, all along impressed upon the Programme Administration that a large part of the assessment has necessarily to consist of self-evaluation. To the extent self-evaluation is continuous, objective and vigorous; the Programme will retain its resilience and capacity to grow. The monthly meetings of the Project or block staff at which progress of the work is reviewed and reasons for outstanding success or shortfall are examined is one instance of self-evaluation. More significant perhaps are the seminars—Inter-State, Intra-State and Intra-District—which have become a regular feature of the Programme. At these seminars, development workers from different States or areas, of varying status, and representing different fields of activity, are brought together. The seminars afford a valuable opportunity for exchange of ideas and experiences among the workers and constitute an important instrument of self-evaluation.

The P.E.O. is a unit of the Central Government. Its scope of operation and the range of its activities are limited by its size, which must necessarily remain comparatively small. As the size of the Programme increases, and increasingly large areas are covered by it, it becomes necessary that evaluation by the Central Organization is supplemented by similar work by the State governments. The Central Organization will tend to concentrate on study of broad trends in the Programme. More intensive examination of particular developments, which are of special interest to an individual State, or of assessment of progress within the area of a State, can best be accomplished by State evaluation units. The need for establishing such units is being gradually realized and some States have already initiated evaluation activity.

Reference has been made above to paucity of basic data on economic and social aspects of village life. In this field, the universities and research institutes are particularly well equipped to make a contribution. The wider scope for choice of techniques and detailed examination of basic issues, which are possible in studies by Universities, make them particularly suitable for this kind of work. An organization like the P.E.O. can indicate to them the problems which are arising in the operation of the Programme, and on which guidance, based on research, would be valuable. The P.E.O. has already acquired some experience of fruitful cooperation with Universities.

Conclusion

The brief evaluation of the working of P.E.O. in the early few years after its establishment, when the author was closely related to its working shows the usefulness of independent evaluation in the implementation of the CD and NES programmes. The findings of the P.E.O. have been useful not only in making an objective appraisal of progress achieved but also in planning of future activities in the light of the past experience and the attitudes and the reactions of the people. A stage has, in fact, been now reached when it is felt that such objective assessment by an independent agency not charged with any administrative responsibility should be extended to other fields of development activity also. In all fields of development effort, in which the objectives are not merely the accomplishment of stated administrative tasks but are related to consciously inducing social and economic changes, evaluation can be a valuable aid to administrative action. By furnishing an objective appraisal of progress, by indicating which methods are proving effective and which are not and by furnishing more detailed quantitative data through specially carried out surveys, it can provide valuable material for the guidance of the field workers. In this connection, the following observations of the Planning Commission in its report on the Second Five Year Plan are noteworthy:

> "The need for evaluation exists in all fields of development and more especially in those in which new or expanded activities are being undertaken. In all planned development many unknown factors have to be reckoned with. Understanding of the interaction of different elements that enter into programmes, which bear closely on the life of the people, can be of material help in enhancing their contribution to the welfare of the community. Evaluation has, therefore, to be increasingly oriented towards studies of a selective and intensive type, motivated by and leading to purposive action." (Government of India, Planning Commission, 1956, p. 251)

REFERENCES

Government of India, Ministry of Food and Agriculture, *Report of the Grow More Food Enquiry Committee*, 1952.

Planning Commission, Government of India, *Second Five-Year Plan,* 1956.

ANNEXURE 4.1

The National Institute of Rural Development

*The First Year (1959-60)**

National Institute of Rural Development, then called the Central Institute of Community Development was started by the Ministry of Community Development of the Government of India in the spring of 1959 and was located in Mussorie, a hill station in Uttar Pradesh in Radha Estate. The estate consisted of a number of buildings, one of which housed the lecture hall, seminar rooms and offices of the Principal and other staff of the institute. Other buildings included residences of the Principal, the Vice Principal, the Professors and other staffs of the Institutes, a dining hall and buildings for residence of about 30 trainees.

The building in which the institute's lecture hall was located had a magnificent view of the Doon Valley and the plains beyond. The Principal's house, which had been the palace of the Nawab, was a beautiful building with a good view of Mussoorie town on one side and of the National Academy of Public Administration on the other. The Vice Principal's residence located just below it had similar views. The Central Institute and National Academy were separated by a valley covered with pine trees. The Academy was located in a group of buildings, which had formed part until 1957 of a hotel, managed by an old Portuguese, adjoining snow clad peaks of the Himalayas.

The Institute had been started to fulfil the role of the apex institute for training and research in Community Development and *Panchayati Raj* Programme. The Community Development Programme, a programme of integrated rural development had been started on October 2nd, 1952 at the personal initiative of Prime Minister Pandit Nehru. The twin objective of the Programme were: (i) to provide essential service facilities to villagers, approach roads, primary and secondary schools for boys and girls, facilities for primary health care, provision of adequate and safe drinking water, improvement of minor irrigation facilities such as wells and tanks which were needed to improve their quality of life, and (ii) to provide to the farmers training in use of improved agricultural production

* Part of a series of Lectures delivered at the National Institute of Rural Development, Hyderabad in 1991 on Panchayati Raj.

and animal husbandry practices in order to increase production and income. Higher agricultural output would also provide larger opportunities for employment of landless labourers for work in agriculture and on public works located near their villages.

A separate organization, the Community Development Administration was created within the Government of India to oversee implementation of the Programme by the State governments; provide them grants and loans for construction of the infrastructure facilities and for creating the administrative machinery for implementation of the Programme. The Reserve Bank of India provided large funds for establishing a network of cooperative societies, which would provide to the farmers short-term credit for buying improved seed, chemical fertilizers, pesticides and improved implements for increasing agricultural output. The CDA was headed by Mr. S.K. Dey, a dedicated social worker who became later the Minister for Community Development.

The Programme was started initially in 60 project areas. The areas were carefully selected for their potential for increasing production and improving the living conditions of the villages rapidly. Each project area was divided into 3 blocks; each block consists of 100-150 villages with a population of 60,000-150,000. Some of the large States such as U.P., Bihar and the Madras and Bombay Presidency had two or three projects while the smaller State had only one project.

From these small beginnings, the Programme was quickly expanded to cover the entire country by Community Development and National Extension Service Blocks by 1961. The N.E.S. was a diluted version of the Community Development Programme; the personnel and funds provided for agricultural and animal husbandry extension and for expansion of infrastructure facilities in villages were smaller in the N.E.S. blocks than in community development blocks.

The Programme generated great enthusiasm both among the rural people in the community development project areas and the officials of the State governments. The rural people began to feel that the government was genuinely interested in their welfare and responded in implementation of the Programme with enthusiasm. The State governments deputed some of their most dynamic ICS and lower level officers to implement this Programme. I remember that in one community development project in Punjab farmers of a group of villages had cut down their standing crop of wheat over a 100-150 ft. wide and twenty miles long stretch to provide land for construction of an approach road to their village. They did get the road!

In large numbers of villages, the villagers made contribution in form of cash, labour and materials to construct buildings for primary or 8-grade schools for boys and girls, construct or improve drinking water or for irrigation and construction of offices of *Panchayats* or cooperative societies.

Setting of Three-tier *Panchayati Raj* Institutions in 1991

Although establishment of village level *Panchayats* is one of the directive principles of the State under the Constitution of India, the proposal to establish a 3-tier system of *Panchayati Raj* institutions was made in 1957 by a committee headed by a prominent member of the Lok Sabha and appointed by the Ministry of Community Development. The Committee recommended constitution of a *Panchayat* for every medium sized village or a group of small villages, a *Panchayat Samiti* at the level of the community development block and *Zilla Parishad* at the district level. The principal object of establishing the institutions was to increase participation by the rural people in implementation of the Community Development and the other rural development programmes. The institutions were to be constituted by direct election to the *Panchayats* and indirect election to the *Panchayat Samitis and Zilla Parishads*. The staff of the Community Development Programme was expected to work under the day-to-day direction of the Chairman and the other members of the *Panchayat Samiti* and the Presidents of the *Panchayats* while taking technical direction from officials in their respective departments. The district level officers of the development departments were to function as advisers to the *Zilla Parishads*. The Collector was expected to function as a 'friend, philosopher and guide of the institutions'; giving their executive timely advice for improving development work and assisting in resolving conflicts among their members.

Although the institutions were to be constituted by direct and indirect elections, they were expected to be non-political bodies constituted for the sole purpose of increasing participation of the rural people in rural development programme. This expectation of the committee was not fulfilled, however, and the working of the institutions established in most of the States during the 1960s was so dominated by inter-personal and inter-group conflicts that they began to be abolished by the late 1960s. They began to be revived with greater funds and powers for administration of rural development programmes during 1980s. Establishing them had been made mandatory on the State governments by the 73rd Amendment to the Constitution of India. But it is now recognized by all concerned that the institutions cannot but be political and that the ruling political party in every State would ensure that its leaders have control over working of these institutions in as many districts of the State as possible. Elections to these bodies in most of the States are contested as keenly as those to the State legislature or the parliament.

I had been associated with evaluation of the Programme from the beginning as Deputy Director (and later as Director) of the Programme Evaluation Organization. The P.E.O. had been established within the Planning Commission to undertake concurrent evaluation of the Community Development Programme through observation of working in different aspects of the Programme in selected project areas and conducting surveys aimed at measuring the impact of the Programme in economic and social conditions of the rural people. Funds for establishing the organization and running it for the first-three years were provided by the Ford Foundation, an American Foundation which provided large funds for assisting India's rural development programme and for establishing several training institutions including the Small Industries Training Institute located in Hyderabad and the Indian Institute of Management located in Ahmedabad. The Foundation had provided assistance also for establishing the Central Institute by financing appointment of two professors for three years each. The Annual Evaluation Reports prepared by the P.E.O. were read by the Development Commissioners of the States with great interest and an attempt was made to initiate action on their recommendations.

Notwithstanding the Minister's keen interest in establishing the Institute, it had uncertain beginnings. The first three courses were organized in the summer of 1959 with Development Commissioners of two States and Mr. B. Mukherjee I.C.S. and Joint Secretary in the Ministry of Community Development as Principal.

Mr. S. Chakravarti (I.C.S.), a senior officer of the Andhra Pradesh cadre was appointed the first Principal for three years and I was appointed the Vice Principal. Both of us assumed charge of our posts at about the same time in October 1959.

The institute conducted two 6-8 week courses during October-December 1959 before it closed for the winter to reopen in March 1960. Each course was attended by Collectors, Presidents of *Zilla Parishads,* Deputy Development Commissioners and division level officers of departments such as agriculture, animal husbandry, education, cooperation, primary health care, minor irrigation etc., which were closely associated with implementation of the Community Development

Programme. Each course consisted of (i) lectures by the staff of the Institute, senior officials of the Ministry of Community Development or distinguished visitors, Indian or foreign, to the Institute on various aspects of rural development; and (ii) preparation of reports on working of the rural development; and *Panchayati Raj* programmes in their States by groups of trainees. Discussions on the papers prepared by the different groups and after every lecture by a visitor were so animated that one visiting experts of the Ford Foundation was constrained to remark, "You Indians, love to debate!"

During the three-month closing period of the Institute Mr. Chakravarti and I travelled to several States to see the working of the training centres for Block Development Officers and other extension officers that had been opened in all States. The training centres in West Bengal was located in Sriniketan which was located next to Shanti Niketan and where poet Rabindra Nath Tagore had initiated a rural development programme among a group of villages way back in the 1930s. I did not know about the poet's interest in this field but apparently he had been a pioneer in this field.

During the course of this tour we visited also the Extension Training Centre located at Rajendra Nagar on the outskirt of Hyderabad. After seeing it Mr. Chakravarti decided to recommend to the Minister to shift the institute to Rajendra Nagar. The shift would avoid the need to close the institute in winter. Furthermore, Hyderabad was more central than Mussoorie reaching which involved travel over a long distance for trainees for the southern States. Thirdly, there would be room to expand the institute if a sufficiently large area of land was acquired for building its campus. The shifting of the institute to its present campus followed a few years later.

The Central Institute conducted four six-week courses during the six months March-October during which I was at the institute. One of the distinguished visitors to the institute during this period was the renowned socialist leader, Jai Prakash Narain. He was a frail looking man in his late 50s. He spoke to us for three hours in a faltering voice in which he explained his concept for rural development and *Sarvodaya* and the rural development work that he and his followers were doing in the centre that he had established near his home in Bihar.

The Institute's programme of financing research on working of Community Development and *Panchayati Raj* Programmes through universities was also initiated during the first year. The most interesting proposal on study of *Panchayati Raj* institutions in Rajasthan came from (late) Prof. Iqbal Narain, Professor of Public Administration in the University of Rajasthan. He and I had several discussions aimed at finalizing the design of his proposed study. I was happy to see several years later the results of his studies published in books which are still among the best studies on working of *Panchayati Raj* institutions.

I had the privilege of being invited to deliver a series of three lectures on *Panchayati Raj* by the Director General of the Institute in 1991. It was a pleasure to see the sprawling tree lined campus of the Institute, an oasis of green in a bleak landscape. Discussions with the faculty of the institute revealed that the conduct of the training programme had not changed materially during the intervening forty years. Discussion on seminar papers prepared by groups of trainees still continued to be animated. However, the institute had launched a successful programme of action research, which was obviously not possible at Mussoorie.

The Institute should initiate, if it has not done already, a programme of training women members of *Panchayati Raj* institutions. There are a growing number of women who have fulfilled successfully the roles of Chairman of *Panchayat Samitis* and *Zilla Parishads.* And with enactment of legislation of reserving one-third of seats in representative institutions from the *Panchayats* to the Parliament for women, the number of women executives of *Panchayati Raj* institutions has increased rapidly. These women leaders shall have a crucial role in giving greater emphasis to programmes such as eradication of female illiteracy, providing better health care to women and children and faster acceptance of family planning. One wing of the Institute should be devoted exclusively to training women leaders.

5

The Growth of Indian Agriculture

*A Regional Analysis**

Since agriculture is the largest single sector in the Indian economy, providing about 50 per cent of the gross national product and nearly 70 per cent of the employment, an adequate agricultural growth rate is essential for sustained economic progress. The growth rate of agricultural output has a considerable influence on the overall growth rate of the economy and on the productivity of a large part of the work force. Moreover, a rapid increase in agricultural output is essential to meet the increasing demand for food and other agricultural products, which results from the rapid population growth (currently estimated at 2.5% per year) and from the rise in per capita consumption. This is particularly important, since India had a food supply deficit, even at extremely low levels of per capita consumption, at the beginning of the economic development process.

The importance of adequate agricultural growth to the success of India's efforts at planned economic development was demonstrated dramatically, if painfully, during the years 1965-1967, when the country experienced widespread drought and a steep drop in agricultural output. Foodgrain production, for instance, declined from 89 million metric tonnes in 1964-1965 to 72 million tonnes in 1965-1966 and rose only slightly to 78 million tonnes in 1966-1967. The fall in production led to scarcity and local famines, and large imports of 9 to 10 million tonnes of foodgrains annually were necessary. But agricultural production in 1967-1968 and 1968-1969 has been high again, with foodgrain production in both years

* First published in the *Geographical Review,* Vol. LIX, No. 3, 1969, pp. 348-372, New York and reprinted in V. Nath: *Regional Development and Planning in India,* 2008, Concept Publishers, New Delhi.

estimated at around 95 million tonnes, mainly as a result of more favourable monsoons. But the drought experience has led to a reappraisal of development objectives and to the initiation in 1966 of an agricultural development programme that concentrates on new high-yielding seed varieties, chemical fertilizers, pesticides, and efficient water management in selected areas to increase output rapidly. (Saran and Chawla, 1967, pp. 461-483)

India's three Five-Year Plans included large outlays for increasing agricultural production: expenditures amounted to rupees 36,330 million, or 23.9 per cent of the total spent. But it is noteworthy that, whereas in the First Plan, which had been drawn up against the background of an acute food shortage, agricultural expenditure formed 36.9 per cent of the total, the proportion declined to 22.3 per cent in the Second Plan and to 21.8 per cent in the Third Plan. (Saran and Chawla, 1967, p. 480) The reduced emphasis on agriculture followed improvement in the food-supply position during the First Plan. The reappraisal of development objectives and priorities, which took place after the drought years, will probably result in agriculture receiving a greater proportion of the total investment in the Fourth Plan (which begins this year) than it received in the earlier plans.

The study presented in this chapter describes the principal features of agricultural growth in the period 1952-1953 to 1964-1965, which covers thirteen of the fifteen years of the first three Five Year Plans[1] (Ministry of Food and Agriculture, 1966, p. 3). It brings out regional differences in growth rates and examines their relationship with the availability of moisture, with such variables as population growth, with levels of productivity per hectare and per worker, and with some indicators of modern technology. The analysis is by States because data on agricultural growth rates and other economic variables are available only by States.[1] However, the State is rather a large unit for analyses of this type: several States include within their border areas with very different physical conditions, cropping patterns, and levels of economic development. It is recognized that contrasts within States can be as great as the inter-State differences. The district is, therefore, a more suitable unit for such analysis, and it is hoped that data on agricultural growth rates and the relevant physical and economic variables will become available by districts before long. Then a more precise delineation of patterns of agricultural growth and their correlation with the relevant variables will be possible.[3] (Directorate of Economics and Statistics, 1965).

Table 5.1 : Growth Rates in Agriculture and Related Data for India and Fourteen States

Linear Growth Rates 1952/53-1964/65 (% per year)	*India*	*Punjab*	*Gujarat*	*Madras*	*Mysore*	*Bihar*	*Maha-rashtra*	*Raja-sthan*	*Andhra Pradesh*	*Madhya Pradesh*	*Orissa*	*Kerala*	*West Bengal*	*Uttar Pradesh*	*Assam*
All crops															
1. Output	3.42	5.56	5.12	4.91	4.06	3.21	3.19	3.08	3.06	2.79	2.72	2.52	2.07	1.82	1.25
2. Area	1.28	2.06	0.46	1.13	0.83	0.71	0.44	3.23	0.27	1.35	0.84	1.38	0.60	0.74	1.32
3. Productivity	1.91	2.86	4.52	3.46	3.03	2.39	2.62	–0.08	2.72	1.30	1.78	1.00	1.41	1.01	–0.07
Foodgrains :															
4. Output	2.75	4.30	–2.09	4.89	3.71	3.28	2.29	2.68	3.65	2.58	2.60	4.37	1.16	0.91	0.80
5. Area	1.02	1.63	–2.19	0.75	0.91	0.64	0.33	3.03	0.84	1.28	0.79	0.51	0.26	0.40	1.36
6. Productivity	1.60	2.26	5.34	3.92	2.64	2.55	1.94	–0.23	2.63	1.16	1.75	3.74	0.90	0.49	–0.48
Non-food grain crops :															
7. Output	4.79	9.46	8.03	4.96	4.91	2.61	5.15	4.89	1.83	4.50	3.40	1.83	4.23	4.28	1.62
8. Area	2.56	4.90	5.93	2.45	0.59	1.84	0.83	5.13	–1.59	1.67	1.65	2.06	4.29	2.19	1.21
9. Productivity	1.79	3.08	1.64	2.05	4.03	0.78	3.65	–0.09	3.93	2.44	1.54	–0.20	–0.09	1.72	0.35
10. Growth rate of population, 1951-1961 (%)	21.50	25.84	26.88	11.85	21.57	19.78	23.60	26.20	15.65	24.17	19.82	24.76	32.79	16.60	34.45
11. Growth rate of male agricultural workers, 1951-1961 (%)	26.38	12.00	28.56	]41.34	42.11	19.89	28.56	29.04	31.90	20.68	31.86	–5.70	36.76	15.57	35.33
Relative Growth Rates (% per year) :															
12. Of agricultural production relative to population	1.05	2.36	1.92	3.33	1.57	1.03	0.67	0.36	1.29	0.30	0.61	0.03	–0.91	0.14	–1.63

(Contd.)

Table 5.1 : (*Contd.*)

Linear Growth Rates 1952/53-1964/65 (% per year) *All crops*	*India*	*Punjab*	*Gujarat*	*Madras*	*Mysore*	*Bihar*	*Maha-rashtra*	*Raja-sthan*	*Andhra Pradesh*	*Madhya Pradesh*	*Orissa*	*Kerala*	*West Bengal*	*Uttar Pradesh*	*Assam*
13. Of foodgrain production relative to population	0.49	1.36	–0.47	3.31	1.28	1.09	–0.06	0.05	1.80	0.13	0.52	1.52	–1.60	–0.64	–1.97
14. Of agricultural production relative to number of male agricultural workers	0.62	3.89	1.76	0.55	0.99	1.02	0.25	0.14	–0.10	0.60	–0.35	3.28	–1.18	0.23	–1.69
Linear Growth Rates 1952/53-1964/65 (% per year) :															
Foodgrain crops															
Rice															
15. Output	3.64	12.31	5.98	6.04	5.96	3.63	3.38	5.56	5.15	2.34	2.88	4.42	1.42	5.08	0.78
16. Area	1.57	9.21	1.13	3.19	1.97	0.23	1.75	6.48	3.19	1.28	1.14	0.53	0.13	1.97	1.32
17. Productivity	1.80	1.80	4.61	2.19	3.33	3.36	1.41	–0.50	1.56	0.93	1.60	3.70	1.29	2.61	–0.47
(Percent)	(100.0)	(1.5)		(11.0)	(4.1)	(12.8)	(3.8)		(11.5)	(8.5)	(11.5)	(3.1)	(14.4)	(9.0)	(4.9)
Wheat															
18. Output	3.80	6.79	3.59		4.88	2.35	4.17	2.24		3.61				1.65	
19. Area	2.57	3.92	0.15		0.98	0.98	2.10	3.36		4.50				0.78	
20. Productivity	1.00	2.09	3.22		3.46	1.18	1.85	–0.85		–0.53				0.80	
(Percent)	(100.0)	(27.2)	(3.3)		(0.9)	(4.1)	(3.7)	(9.3)		(18.5)				(30.2)	
Jowar															
21. Output	1.99	0.66	1.28	4.61	2.71		2.95	–0.59	1.62	2.81				–1.31	

(*Contd.*)

Table 5.1: (Contd.)

Linear Growth Rates 1952/53-1964/65 (% per year)	India	Punjab	Gujarat	Madras	Mysore	Bihar	Maha-rashtra	Raja-sthan	Andhra Pradesh	Madhya Pradesh	Orissa	Kerala	West Bengal	Uttar Pradesh	Assam
All crops															
22. Area	0.40	0.42	–1.59	0.10	1.78		0.87	0.59	0.18	–0.24				–0.78	
23. Productivity	1.57	0.15	3.21	4.46	0.91		1.91	–1.10	1.26	3.22				–0.58	
(Percent)	(100.0)	(0.5)	(4.5)	(6.2)	(14.6)		(34.4)	(3.8)	(13.9)	(16.0)				(5.9)	
Bajra															
24. Output	1.34	–2.32	–0.37	3.60			1.48	4.13	0.74					–1.12	
25. Area	–0.20	–2.59	–4.04	–2.24			–1.12	3.73	–0.89					–0.94	
26. Productivity	1.62	0.55	5.96	7.63			3.10	0.51	1.88					–0.27	
(Percent)	(100.0)	(8.0)	(16.1)	(7.7)			(12.3)	(25.2)	(8.0)					(15.2)	
Gram															
27. Output	0.85	1.35				–0.29		5.19		1.91				–0.04	
28. Area	1.16	2.01				–0.80		6.12		0.91				–0.08	
29. Productivity	–0.24	–0.66				0.57		–0.50		0.95				0.05	
(Percent)	(100.0)	(27.4)				(4.8)		(12.9)		(16.4)				(31.2)	
Non-foodgrain crops															
Cotton															
30. Output	3.81	9.35	6.48	5.56	2.06		2.45	5.85	0.74	–0.98					
31. Area	1.27	5.78	2.65	1.11	0.66		0.63	2.70	–0.48	–0.87					
32. Productivity	2.25	2.89	3.08	3.87	1.23		1.70	2.74	1.29	–0.17					
(Percent)	(100.0)	(19.7)	(26.6)	(7.6)	(7.2)		(24.3)	(3.2)	(2.9)	(7.0)					
Groundnuts															
33. Output	5.64		11.04	5.49	0.72		6.06		–2.00	11.12					
34. Area	4.40		15.04	3.69	0.87		1.28		–3.16	8.15					

(Contd.)

Table 5.1 : (Contd.)

Linear Growth Rates 1952/53-1964/65 (% per year)	India	Punjab	Gujarat	Madras	Mysore	Bihar	Maha-rashtra	Raja-sthan	Andhra Pradesh	Madhya Pradesh	Orissa	Kerala	West Bengal	Uttar Pradesh	Assam
All crops															
35. Productivity	0.84		–1.11	1.24	–0.10		4.18		1.58	1.84					
(Percent)	(100.0)		(24.0)	(20.0)	(10.9)		(14.1)		(14.3)	(5.4)					
Sugarcane															
36. Output	7.83	9.28	17.86	10.50	14.58	0.65	9.83	6.34	13.21	7.96			6.73	4.13	3.18
37. Area	4.93	5.71	16.83	10.56	7.60	2.20	7.97	7.76	8.56	9.91			7.32	3.72	1.23
38. Productivity	1.93	2.26	0.53	0.04	4.02	–1.21	1.02	–0.53	2.52	–1.03			–0.31	0.28	1.76
(Percent)	(100.0)	(8.9)	(1.4)	(6.1)	(5.7)	(5.2)	(10.4)	(0.6)	(9.5)	(1.4)			(1.5)	(46.0)	(0.9)
Jute															
39. Output	5.20					–1.83					4.05		7.21	12.13	0.10
40. Area	4.01					2.29					3.50		6.00	6.18	1.20
41. Productivity	0.85					–2.82					0.50		0.92	3.29	–1.00
(Percent)	(100.0)					(17.7)					(6.8)		(56.9)	(2.7)	(14.7)
Gross Cropped Area Distribution of annual rainfall (%)															
42. Abundant (more than 75")	4.32	2.58	—	—	4.05	—	3.14	—	—	2.77	—	100.00	12.78	0.19	67.95
43. Assured (45"-75")	26.80	3.19	—	24.85	9.30	81.43	9.73	—	—	68.23	100.00	—	87.22	16.70	32.05
44. Medium (30"-45")	33.49	25.73	32.63	54.25	18.55	18.57	39.56	4.50	73.43	28.24	—	—	—	69.34	—
45. Low (less than 30")	35.40	68.50	67.37	20.90	68.10	—	47.57	95.50	26.57	2.31	—	—	—	13.77	—
46. *Gross irrigated area/gross cropped area (%)*	18.88	42.22	7.79	45.21	9.24	19.89	6.74	12.53	29.48	5.63	16.42	20.96	21.53	26.62	23.33

(Contd.)

Table 5.1 : (Contd.)

Linear Growth Rates 1952/53-1964/65 (% per year) All crops	*India*	*Punjab*	*Gujarat*	*Madras*	*Mysore*	*Bihar*	*Maha-rashtra*	*Raja-sthan*	*Andhra Pradesh*	*Madhya Pradesh*	*Orissa*	*Kerala*	*West Bengal*	*Uttar Pradesh*	*Assam*
47. *Index of moisture availability*	214.62	179.25	140.32	249.16	154.49	301.33	172.04	117.03	202.91	277.12	316.42	320.96	321.53	229.74	323.33
Index of Productivity (based on averages of years 1956-1957 to 1958-1959; India=100.00)															
48. Per hectare	100.00	131.71	64.58	176.21	64.91	119.53	65.08	51.65	118.85	80.55	132.72	126.17	168.75	128.25	174.04
49. Per agricultural worker	100.00	215.99	105.90	111.24	88.71	62.83	88.94	88.24	103.68	94.35	132.72	110.06	144.15	101.11	111.49
50. *Use of Modern Inputs* Consumption of chemical fertilizers (N + P_2O_5 + K_2O), 1965-1966 (kg per hectare of gross cropped area)	5.30	5.22	4.70	14.49	4.63	3.31	4.60	0.82	9.74	1.64	2.99	14.49	7.61	4.52	3.02
51. *Cooperative credit:* loans advanced by agricultural cooperatives to members in 1963-1964 (rupees per hectare of gross cropped area)	19.52	19.22	33.78	56.31	14.34	4.73	30.24	3.56	21.25	13.73	8.31	42.74	10.06	22.17	0.62

(*Contd.*)

Table 5.1: (*Contd.*)

Linear Growth Rates 1952/53-1964/65 (% per year) All crops	*India*	*Punjab*	*Gujarat*	*Madras*	*Mysore*	*Bihar*	*Maha-rashtra*	*Raja-sthan*	*Andhra Pradesh*	*Madhya Pradesh*	*Orissa*	*Kerala*	*West Bengal*	*Uttar Pradesh*	*Assam*
52. Use of mechanical power in agriculture in 1960-1961 (units per thousand hectares of gross cropped area)	2.58	3.36	5.65	18.86	2.31	0.73	3.88	0.66	4.61	0.88	0.28	2.76	0.72	1.18	0.40
53. Composite index of use of modern inputs in agriculture (India=100.00)	100.00	109.06	160.24	430.96	83.45	38.32	130.69	19.89	157.13	45.13	36.61	199.81	74.34	81.53	25.22
Development of Services															
54. Rural literacy rate (%)	19.0	18.4	24.1	24.7	20.0	16.1	21.5	10.9	16.8	12.7	20.1	45.4	21.6	14.3	24.9
55. Number of doctors per million of population	227	382	230	192	209	157	316	133	196	134	127	215	481	127	257
56. Length of surfaced roads (in kilometres) per thousand square kilometres	76.91	93.62	70.22	259.40	194.40	64.04	83.38	44.89	99.17	54.91	52.44	207.20	155.00	75.03	31.20
57. Number of towns per million rural population	7.49	11.65	11.82	13.73	12.61	3.60	9.37	8.59	7.50	7.89	3.77	6.41	6.77	4.15	5.47
58. Composite index of development of services (India = 100.00)	100.00	135.60	119.32	183.80	154.61	71.29	121.47	72.26	100.96	75.65	69.94	172.16	155.04	71.05	89.47

(*Contd.*)

Table 5.1 : (Contd.)

Linear Growth Rates 1952/53-1964/65 (% per year) All crops	*India*	*Punjab*	*Gujarat*	*Madras*	*Mysore*	*Bihar*	*Maha-rashtra*	*Raja-sthan*	*Andhra Pradesh*	*Madhya Pradesh*	*Orissa*	*Kerala*	*West Bengal*	*Uttar Pradesh*	*Assam*
59. *Composite index of agricultural development* (India = 100.00)	100.00	162.54	138.62	228.55	96.96	65.00	104.29	66.06	116.79	73.69	82.95	127.85	93.00	78.62	57.72

Note: Numbers in parentheses show percentages of all-India output produced in the State in the triennium ending 1964-1965.

Sources: Lines 1-9 and 15-41: "Growth Rates in Agriculture" [see text footnote 3]; Lines 10, 11, 54, and 57: Census of India 1961, Paper No. 1 of 1962, Final Population Totals (Delhi, 1962); Lines 42-46: *Indian Agricultural Statistics 1962-63* [see text footnote 5]; Lines 48 and 49: J.G. Anand: *Measurement of the Actually Realised Agricultural Productivities per Acre and per Worker in the Different Crop Regions of India,* in *Agricultural Situation in India: Annual Number 1964*, Directorate of Economics and Statistics, New Delhi, 1964, p. 401-411; Line 50: *Fertilizer Statistics 1965-66,* Fertilizer Association of India, New Delhi, 1967, p. 101; Line 51: "Statistical Statements Relating to the Cooperative Movement in India 1963-64" (Reserve Bank of India); Line 52: "Livestock Census of India, 1961" (Directorate of Economics and Statistics, New Delhi); Line 55: "Stock of Health and Medical Manpower," *Institute of Applied Manpower Research Working Paper No. 6*, New Delhi, 1965 (mimeographed), pp. 17-18; Line 56: *Statistical Abstract of the Indian Union 1965*, Central Statistical Organisation, Delhi, 1966, pp

Growth Rate Comparisons

The growth rate of agricultural production in India during the period 1952-1953 to 1964-1965 (3.42% per year) was higher than the growth rates of both total population (2.15 %) and male agricultural workers (2.64 %) (Table 5.1, lines 10-11).[4] This constituted a reversal of a trend; for several decades before independence, agricultural growth had been much slower than population increase. In the forty-five-years period 1900-1901 to 1944-1945 the population of undivided India (present day India and Pakistan) increased by 38 per cent, while agricultural production increased by only 12.6 per cent, and foodgrain production remained stagnant. As a result the index of foodgrain output relative to population declined by 27 points (Mukherjee and Sivasubramanian, 1958, pp. 1-43). This stagnation made India a net importer of foodgrains in the early 1920s, though the country had been a net exporter up to that time. It also meant a decline of about 25 per cent in per capita availability of foodgrains (Bhattacharjee and Roy, pp. 188-224).

When the rate of population increase in the period 1952-1953 to 1964-1965 is compared with the growth rate of foodgrains, the latter is found to be only slightly higher than the population growth rate. But in the populous States of Uttar Pradesh, West Bengal, Maharashtra, and Gujarat, which had deficits or marginal surpluses of foodgrains even in the early 1950s, population has been increasing more rapidly than food grain output. These four States accounted on the average for two-thirds of the total foodgrain deficit in India in the three years 1961-1963.[5] Accordingly, the explanation for India's recent food difficulties lies (apart from the drought of 1965-1967) in the relatively slow growth of foodgrain output in the country generally, and in a number of the large and populous States particularly.

Expansion of Cropped Area and Increases in Productivity

The growth of total agricultural output results from some combination of the expansion of cropped area and the increase in productivity of cropland, but in the study period productivity increased considerably more than the cropped area (Table 5.1, lines 1-3). Analysis of the annual index numbers of agricultural production, cropped area, and productivity for all India indicates that the rate of expansion of cropped area was relatively rapid at first and slowed down later, while the rate of increase of productivity, which was slow in the early years, picked up considerably. This is shown by the growth rates given in Table 5.2, which have been derived by dividing the study period into two parts of eight years each, 1952-1953 to 1959-1960 and 1957-1958 to 1964-1965.

Expansion of cropped area results from extension of cultivation to new lands (that is, increase in "net area sown") and from increased multiple cropping (that is, an increase in the proportion of "area sown more than once" to "net area sown"). The gross cropped area of India increased by 19 million hectares between 1952-1953 and 1962-1963 (Table 5.3), but only two-thirds of this total, 12.8 million hectares, represented an increase in the net area sown; the balance came from multiple cropping of the existing cropped area. The growth of multiple cropping is closely linked with the extension of irrigation facilities; irrigation is necessary in most parts of India to produce the second (post monsoon) crop. It will be seen from Table 5.3 that increase in the gross irrigated area has been nearly equal to the increase in the area sown more than once.

Greater productivity also results from two additional factors: improvement in per hectare crop yields and substitution of more productive crops for less productive ones; for example, sugarcane for wheat, or groundnuts for the millets, jowar and bajra. In several States substitution appears to be a major ingredient of increased productivity. Gujarat has experienced the highest rate of productivity increase (4.52%), but the high rate is attributable partly to extensive replacement of the less productive jowar and bajra by the more productive groundnuts and cotton. The rate of expansion of the area under groundnuts has averaged 15.4 per cent per year, which is truly phenomenal. It is noteworthy that productivity (average yield per hectare) of groundnuts has declined, while that of jowar and bajra has increased (Table 5.1, lines 33-35 and 21-26). This indicates that some of the substitution of groundnuts for jowar and bajra has taken place on marginal lands of low productivity and has had the effect of lowering the average yield of the expanding crops and of raising the average yields of the contracting crops.

Increase in Foodgrain and Non-Foodgrain Crops

Nearly three-quarters of the cropped land in India is under foodgrains (Table 5.4), which include cereals—rice, wheat, bajra, jowar, and maize—and pulses or beans. The Indian diet consists almost entirely of cereals and pulses. Rice, wheat, and jowar are the most important cereals, and together occupy 42.5 per cent of the gross cropped area; among the pulses, gram is the most important. The non-foodgrain crops include fibres

Table 5.2 : Linear Growth Rates

(% per year)

	First Period 1952/53-1959/60	*Second Period* 1957/58-1964/65
Output	3.55	4.30
Area	1.84	1.02
Productivity	1.38	2.55

Table 5.3 : Expansion of Cropped and Irrigated Areas

(In thousands of hectares)

	1952-1953	1962-1963	Increase Area	Increase Per cent
Gross cropped area	137,675	156,736	19,061	13.84
Area sown more than once	14,233	20,492	6,259	43.97
Net sown area	123,442	136,244	12,802	10.37
Area sown more than once as Percentage of net sown area	11.53	15.04		
Gross irrigated area	23,305	29,598	6,293	27.00
Area irrigated more than once	2,183	3,935	1,752	80.26
Net irrigated area	22,122	25,663	4,541	21.50
Gross irrigated area as percentage of gross cropped area	16.93	18.88		

Sources: *Statistical Abstract of the Indian Union 1965* [See Table 5.1, footnotes]; *Indian Agricultural Statistics 1962-63* [see text footnote 5].

Table 5.4: Distribution or Cropped Area among Selected Crops, 1962-1963

(in thousands of hectares)

Crop	*Cropped area*		*% of total area*	
Food grains				
Rice	34,934		22.29	
Wheat	13,657		8.71	
Jowar	18,021		11.50	
Bajra	10,800		6.89	
Gram	9,242		5.90	
All foodgrains		116,009		74.01
Non-foodgrain crops				
Cotton	7,845		5.00	
Jute	851		0.54	
Tea	334		0.21	
Sugarcane	2,280		1.45	
Groundnuts	6,804		4.34	
All oilseeds		14,796		9.44
All non-foodgrain crops		40,729		25.99
Total		156,736		100.00

Source : *Indian Agriculture Statistics 1962-63* (see text footnote 5).

(especially cotton and jute), oilseeds (groundnuts, linseed, and so on), sugarcane, plantation crops (tea, coffee, and rubber), tobacco, chilies, fruits and vegetables, and a number of others. Obviously, not all the non-foodgrain crops are non-foodcrops. But since the Indian diet depends so heavily on foodgrains, calculations of supply and demand for food are generally made in those terms. Moreover, most non-foodgrain crops are grown for sale, while foodgrains are grown to meet the food needs of subsistence farmers.

The growth of non-foodgrain crops has been nearly twice as high as that of foodgrains in India as a whole—4.79 per cent as compared with 2.75 per cent (Table 5.1, lines 7 and 4)—and has been appreciably higher in ten of the fourteen States. In Madras, the growth rates are similar, and in only three States—Kerala, Andhra Pradesh, and Bihar—is the growth rate of foodgrains higher than that of the non-foodgrain crops. The higher growth rate of non-foodgrain crops can be explained almost entirely by the more rapid expansion of the area devoted to them. Productivity has increased at similar rates for both groups of crops; the figures for all India are 1.79 per cent for non-foodgrain crops and 1.60 per cent for foodgrains (Table 5.1, lines 6 and 9).

Within the foodgrain group, the growth rates of rice and wheat have been higher than those of the inferior grains. These two crops have similar growth rates for output—3.64 per cent for rice and 3.80 per cent for wheat—but the contributions of expansion of area and increase in productivity differ. The productivity of rice has increased more than the area, but the reverse is true of wheat. The relatively low growth rates of jowar and bajra reflect the small change in the area they occupy; on the other hand, the comparatively high rates of increase in productivity of these crops result mainly from withdrawal of the crops from marginal lands. The growth rates are highest in States in which contraction of area under these crops has been most pronounced: jowar and bajra in Gujarat, bajra in Madras and Maharashtra, and jowar in Madhya Pradesh.

Among the four selected non-foodgrain crops, sugarcane has the highest rate of growth of output, almost 8 per cent, and the growth rates for groundnuts and jute are also much higher than the rate for any foodgrain crop. These high rates of growth of output are due primarily to the rapid expansion of the area under the crop; the rates of increase of productivity are not high. On the other hand, cotton, which has had only a modest expansion of area, has the highest rate of productivity increase of any crop—2.25 per cent.

An adequate explanation of the differences in rates of increase of output, cropped area, and productivity of foodgrains and non-foodgrain crops, or of individual crops, would take us far beyond the scope of this study. It would require analysis of resource allocation among competing crops and, therefore, in turn, analysis of crop prices and of inputs at regional and farm levels. But two facts must be mentioned in order to place the observed trends in historical perspective and to relate them to the effects of overall economic growth. First, the faster growth of non-foodgrain crops than of foodgrains only means extension into the post-independence period of a trend that had existed for several decades. Second, the faster growth of non-foodgrain crops and, among the foodgrains, the faster growth of wheat and rice than of other cereals, is in accord with the observed elasticity of consumer demand. Preference for the superior cereals, rice and wheat, and high elasticity of demand for sugar, oil, tea, and other non-foodgrains are to be expected in the early stages of economic development: they show the first effects of even small increases in per capita income. This response is welcome because it reduces the unhealthy preponderance of grains in the Indian diet.

But faster growth of non-foodgrain crops than of foodgrains also represents a shift in resource allocation; it means that some resources, which would have been allocated to production of foodgrains if the growth rates of output of the two groups were equal, are instead given over to production of non-foodgrain crops. The effect is marginal, however. It is roughly proportional to the difference in rates of aerial expansion of the two groups of crops; their rates of productivity increase are similar, and there is no evidence of a marked shift of resources to secure higher rates of productivity increase for either group. But since non-foodgrain crops occupy only a quarter of the gross cropped area of India, a 3 per cent increase in the area under them means a loss of potential increase of only one per cent of the area under foodgrains. If the rates of increase of area for both groups of crops had been identical in this period, the area under foodgrains would have been higher than it actually was in 1964-1965 by only about 5 per cent. Additional output of foodgrains would have been of the same order, since the rates of increase of productivity for both groups have been similar.

Regional Differences in Growth Rates

The growth rate of agricultural output ranges from 5.56 per cent in Punjab[6] to 1.25 per cent in Assam. Only four States—Punjab, Gujarat, Madras and Mysore—have experienced growth rates higher than the all India average of 3.42 per cent (Table 5.1, line 1). If the states are ranked according to the rate of growth of agricultural output and are divided into two groups, "high" and "low", with seven states in each, it is seen that six of the seven States in the high group are in the west and south of India, and five of the seven States in the low group are in the east and north-central parts of the country. Figure 5.1 shows a fairly clear west-east dichotomy in growth rates; most of the States with high rates form part of a belt that extends from Punjab in the extreme north-west to Madras in the south. The exceptions to this pattern are Kerala and Andhra Pradesh, southern States that are in the low-rate group and Bihar an eastern State that is in the high rate group.

In the five States—Rajasthan, Punjab, Kerala, Madhya Pradesh and Assam—the expansion rate of the cropped area has been higher than the all-India average (1.28%), but no geographical implications can be found in the pattern. On the other hand, the rate of increase of productivity has been higher than the all-India average (1.91%) in seven States (Fig. 5.2), and the west-east dichotomy noted in the case of agricultural output is repeated. Most of the States in the high productivity group also have a high growth rate for agricultural output. The only exceptions are Rajasthan, which has a high growth rate for agricultural output but a low rate of productivity, and Andhra Pradesh, which has a low growth rate for agricultural output but a high rate of productivity.

Regional differences in the growth rates of output of individual crops reflect the conditions under which they are grown and also give evidence of the phenomenon of substitution. In the case of rice (Table 5.1, lines 15-17), comparatively high growth rates of 5 per cent or more have been experienced in four major producing States—Madras, Mysore, Andhra Pradesh, and Uttar Pradesh (Punjab and Gujarat are not major producers). The lowest growth rates have been experienced in Assam and West Bengal. The low rate in West Bengal is especially important because this State, with one-seventh of the all-India rice output in the triennium ending 1964-1965, is the largest rice producer. The low growth rate is attributable mainly to the low rate of increase in area, though productivity also has improved less here than in most other States. Stagnation of the area under rice and the rapid increase (6% per year) in the area under jute indicate diversion of resources in favour of jute.

In West Bengal and the other eastern and north-central States of India most rice is not irrigated, and yields are low in comparison with those in the southern States such as Madras, Mysore, and Andhra Pradesh, in which a large part of the crop is irrigated. It would appear that the growth rate of

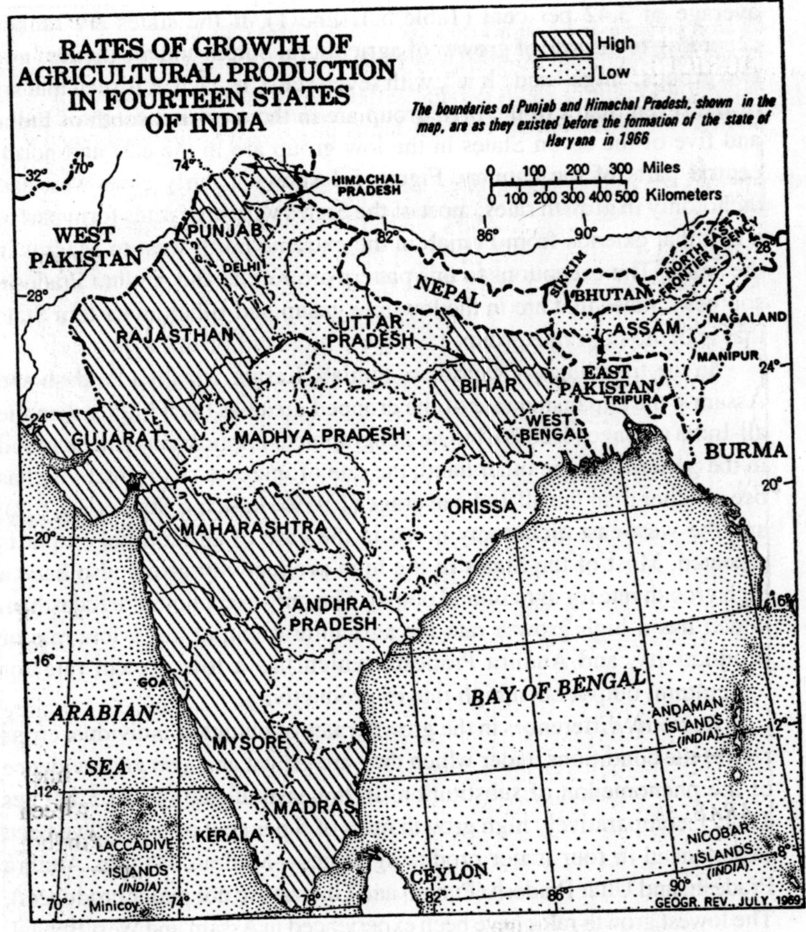

Fig. 5.1 : Rates of Growth of Agricultural Production in Fourteen States of India

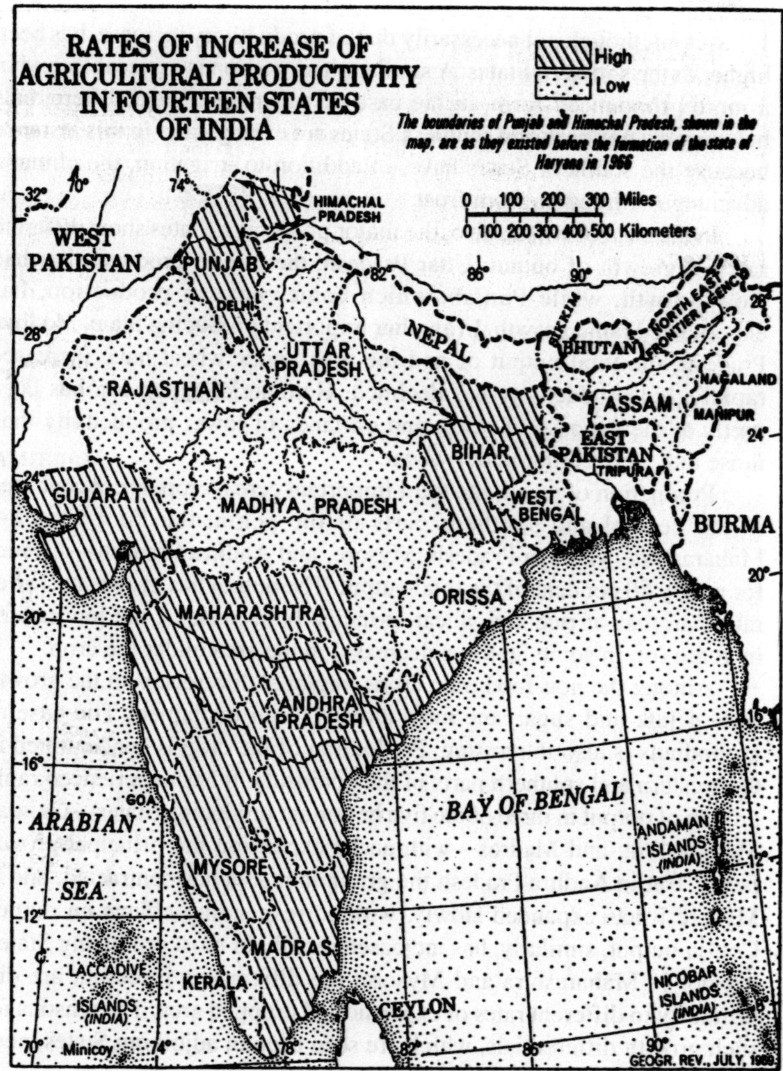

Fig. 5.2 : Rates of Increase of Agricultural Productivity in Fourteen States of India

output, though not necessarily that of productivity increase, has been higher in the southern States. A similar phenomenon is noticeable, and in a more pronounced form, in the case of sugarcane. Yield differentials between the northern and southern States are even greater in this instance because the southern States have, in addition to irrigation, the climatic advantage of freedom from frost.

In the case of wheat, also, the major producing States show different rates of growth of output: Uttar Pradesh, the largest producer, has had slow growth, while Punjab, which comes next in production, has experienced rapid growth. In another important producing State, Madhya Pradesh, the total output of and the area under wheat have increased rapidly, but productivity has declined. Here aerial expansion has been partly at the expense of jowar and on lands of lower productivity than those that were earlier under wheat.

Production of jowar, the third important cereal crop, is concentrated in the central and southern parts of the peninsula. Four States—Maharashtra, Madhya Pradesh, Mysore, and Andhra Pradesh—account for nearly 80 per cent of the total output. The output has grown at a lower rate than that of rice and wheat, principally because of the low rate of increase (or, in some States, a decrease) in the area under the crop.

Among the non-foodgrain crops, regional differences in the growth rate of jute and sugarcane have already been explained. The case of groundnuts is also interesting. Production of the crop is concentrated in the western and southern parts of the peninsula. It has experienced rapid growth of output in three of the five important producing States—Gujarat, Maharashtra, and Madras—with aerial expansion the principal growth factor. But in Andhra Pradesh the groundnut area has contracted, and in Mysore it has expanded slowly, with corresponding effects on output. Cotton output, similarly, has increased rapidly in most producing States, but not in Maharashtra and Mysore; the differences in output are due primarily to different rates of expansion of cropped area. The reasons for such growth differentials, which are seen even in adjoining States, need more detailed analysis than is possible here.

Agricultural Growth Rates, Availability of Moisture, and Selected Economic Variables

The relationship of the agricultural growth rate to the availability of moisture and to certain economic variables has been examined through coefficients of correlation. The coefficients were calculated between the growth rates of agricultural output and of productivity and the variables and composite indices listed in Table 5.5. In addition, coefficients of correlation were calculated between certain of the variables (for example, the proportion of cropped area irrigated and the use of chemical fertilizers) in order to study the relationships among the variables.

Availability of Moisture

The composite index of availability of moisture is based on annual rainfall and the proportion of irrigated land. All cropland was assigned to one of four rainfall zones (Table 5.1, lines 42-46), and the proportion of cultivated land in each zone was then multiplied by the weight assigned to the zone.[7] Finally, the proportion of irrigated land was added to the total. Table 5.6 indicates that the States with high growth rates for agricultural output and productivity are drier than the States with low rates.

In Gujarat, Mysore, and Maharashtra, high growth rates for agricultural output and productivity have been achieved in spite of unfavourable moisture supply. In these States most of the cropped area is in the zone of low rainfall, and less than 10 per cent of it is irrigated. Only in Bihar and Madras do favourable rainfall and high growth rates go hand in hand. On the other hand, several States with low growth rates for agricultural output and productivity—Orissa, Kerala, West Bengal, and Assam—have favourable moisture conditions. The entire cropped area of these States is in the zones of abundant or assured rainfall, and 16 to 23 per cent of it is irrigated. In Madhya Pradesh and Uttar Pradesh, two other States with low rates of agricultural growth, the moisture supply is only slightly less favourable. In Madhya Pradesh, the proportion of irrigated land is low, 5.63 per cent, but almost three-quarters of the State are in the zones of assured or abundant rainfall. Most of the cropped land in Uttar Pradesh is in the zone of medium rainfall, but 26.62 per cent of it is irrigated.

The coefficients of correlation of the index of moisture availability with the growth rate of agricultural output and with the rate of increase of productivity are negative, – 0.58 and – 0.39 respectively (Table 5.5). The correlation between the proportion of cropped area irrigated and the rate of increase of productivity is extremely low, 0.09, and it is not significant. These coefficients confirm the lack of relationship that has already emerged between availability of moisture and agricultural growth rates.

The lack of relationship may come as a surprise to those who are concerned with agricultural development in India, since an assured moisture supply has always been regarded as the prime requisite of

Table 5.5: **Coefficients of Correlation between Selected Variables and Agricultural Growth Rates**

	Coefficient or Correlation
Growth rate of population and growth rate of agricultural output	–0.28
Growth rate of population and growth rate of foodgrain output	–0.51
Growth rate of male agricultural workers and growth rate of agricultural output	0.07
Average productivity per hectare and rate of increase of productivity	–0.18
Average productivity per agricultural worker and growth rate of agricultural output	0.33
Proportion of cropped area irrigated and rate of increase of productivity	0.09
Index of moisture availability and growth rate of agricultural output	–0.58
Index of moisture availability and rate of increase of productivity	–0.39
Proportion of cropped area irrigated and level of use of chemical fertilizers	0.58*
Proportion of cropped area irrigated and index of use of modern inputs	0.55
Level of use of chemical fertilizers and rate of increase of productivity	0.27
Index of use of modern inputs and rate of increase of productivity	0.52
Index of development of services and growth rate of agricultural output	0.48
Index of urbanization and growth rate of agricultural output	0.85*
Index of development of services and index of use of modern inputs	0.72*
Index of development of services and index of agricultural development	0.52
Index of urbanization and index of agricultural development	0.71*

*Significant at 5 per cent level.

Table 5.6 : Percentage of Gross Cropped Area in each Rainfall Zone

State with	Rainfall zone				Gross cropped area irrigated 1962-1963
	Abundant	Assured	Medium	Low	
High rate of growth of output	1.65	15.58	26.73	56.04	17.64
Low rate of growth of output	7.62	40.69	41.86	9.82	19.98
High rate of increase of productivity	1.69	15.96	38.42	43.93	20.45
Low rate of increase of productivity	7.42	39.52	27.69	25.37	16.83

agricultural development. Development plans have emphasized expansion of irrigation and concentration of agricultural-development efforts in areas with assured moisture supplies. More than 40 per cent of the total expenditure on agricultural-development programmes in the three Five-Year Plans was for irrigation (Saran and Chawla, p. 480).

Irrigated areas and areas with an assured moisture supply have been selected for intensive agricultural development programmes, on the ground that farmers will adopt modern, capital intensive production techniques more readily because of greater security of return on investment. Districts with an assured moisture supply were chosen for the Intensive Agricultural District Programme (IADP), which started with seven districts in 1959 and now covers sixteen districts. Since India adopted the "New Agricultural Strategy" in 1966, development efforts have emphasized efficient water management, use of chemical fertilizers, high yielding seed varieties, and pest control on about 25 million hectares of land with adequate moisture. On about half the area quick growing varieties of rice and other cereals are to be substituted for varieties that take longer to mature, so that a second crop can be obtained (Saran and Chawla, p. 475).

Long-term programmes of agricultural development also emphasize maximum expansion of irrigation facilities and the concentration of development resources, especially modern inputs, in the irrigated areas. (Sivaraman, 1967, pp. 433-447) This strategy has been outlined in detail and occupies the central place in the programme of increasing agricultural output recommended in the report of India's Population and Food Problems submitted recently by the [United States] President's Science Advisory Committee, Panel on the World Food Supply (William, pp. 673-711). The Panel recommended heavy concentration of resources in intensive cultivation areas, which could be completely irrigated, holding other areas lightly. The Panel's projections anticipate that intensive cultivation areas will increase from 2 million hectares in 1967 to 42 million hectares in 1986, when they will constitute about 33 per cent of the cropland under foodgrains, but will produce almost 60 per cent of the foodgrains, and will use more than 60 per cent of the chemical fertilizers applied to foodgrains. Average yields in intensive cultivation areas will be about three times the yields in the rest of the area under foodgrain. (William, pp. 704-706). This strategy is backed by considerable experimental evidence which shows that per hectare yield of foodgrains increase with high yielding seed varieties and other inputs, under conditions of assured moisture.

The absence of a relationship between availability of moisture and agricultural growth rates should not be taken to mean that an adequate or assured moisture supply is not required for agricultural development, or that the policies of expansion of irrigation and resource concentration in areas with adequate and assured moisture supply are wrong. But although moisture supply may be a necessary condition for agricultural development, it is not the only requirement, and there is an urgent need to investigate the factors that prevent a number of Indian States with good rainfall and extensive irrigated areas from attaining high agricultural growth rates. Remedial measures aimed at removing the growth-inhibiting factors are just as important as the irrigation programmes that create a higher agricultural production potential.

Growth of Population and of Agricultural Workers

Population growth influences agricultural output in two ways: it increases the demand for agricultural products, and it increases the supply of labour. However, the relationship between agricultural output and labour supply is most easily studied by considering the growth rate of agricultural workers (Table 5.1, lines 10-14). The coefficient of correlation between the population growth rate and the growth rates of agricultural output and of foodgrain output are both negative (Table 5.5); the latter has a value of -0.51, which underlines the difficulties arising in several States in which population has grown rapidly but foodgrain output has not. The low coefficient of correlation between the growth rates of male agricultural workers and of agricultural output (0.07) indicates that factors other than labour supply have had the major influence on agricultural output in this period. The finding is not unexpected, considering the widespread underemployment in Indian to agriculture.

Productivity per Hectare and per Agricultural Worker

The indices of productivity per hectare and per agricultural worker (Table 5.1, lines 48-49) are based on indices of intensity of land use, cropping pattern, and yield per hectare in the period 1956-1959. The influence of the cropping pattern on the index of productivity per hectare is clear from the fact that all States in which rice is an important crop have significantly higher index values than do States in which the area under rice is small. The range of inter-State variation of the index is of the order of 3:1; the highest values are for Madras, Assam, and West Bengal, and the lowest are for Rajasthan, Gujarat, Mysore, and Maharashtra.

Inter-State differences in productivity per agricultural worker are somewhat larger than those in productivity per hectare; the figure for Punjab is three and a half times that for Bihar. Differences of this order, which might appear surprising at first, indicate that large differences in productivity (and income) per worker can exist even in a situation of overall high population pressure. Moreover, the existence of pronounced differences between adjoining States (for example, West Bengal and Bihar, or Punjab and Rajasthan) indicates higher geographical immobility of labour. The coefficient of correlation between productivity per hectare and the rate of productivity is negative, – 0.18, indicating a lack of distributional relationship between the two.

If a high positive correlation had been found between the level of productivity per agricultural worker and the rate of growth of agricultural output, it would have indicated that the capacity to achieve increases in output per worker is greater at higher levels of per capita income. This could have been interpreted as the result of higher levels of savings and investment, or of greater output per worker (which itself is the result of better nutrition and health), or of a number of other reasons. On the other hand, a high negative correlation would have suggested that tensions arise from farmers in poorer States attempting to catch up with their more prosperous neighbours (though one would expect the tension effect to be weak in a situation of pronounced immobility of labour). But, in fact, the actual coefficient of correlation is low (0.33), which indicates that the existing level of productivity per worker has little influence on the growth rate of agricultural output.

Use of Modern Inputs

Three indicators—use of chemical fertilizers, use of mechanical power, and use of cooperative credit—have been selected as indicators of the adoption of modern technology in agriculture (Table 5.1, lines 50-53).[8] The choice of the first-two indicators is obvious, but inclusion of cooperative credit deserves comment. It was selected primarily as a measure of institutional advance: it indicates the successful adoption of cooperative institutions, which have played an important role in the development and modernization of agriculture elsewhere and which are being encouraged by the Indian Government. But the amount of cooperative credit per hectare of cropland is not a good measure of agricultural investment, for several reasons. First, investment in agriculture is different from loans to farmers, since some of the loans are for consumption purposes, while some of the investment is financed from personal savings of the farmers. Second, loans from cooperative societies are only part of the total borrowings of farmers; other sources include the government, moneylenders, relatives, and friends. A survey of rural debt and investment conducted by the Reserve Bank of India in 1961-1962 revealed that loans from cooperatives formed only 18.7 per cent of the total borrowings of farmers (Jakhade, 1967, pp. 540-549). Finally, the figures in Table 5.1 relate only to short-term and medium-term loans, which are used primarily to finance current agricultural operations or short-term investments such as buying a pair of bullocks; they do not include loans for long-term investments such as irrigation wells.

Data on the use of chemical fertilizers relate to nitrogen, phosphate, and potassium fertilizers and are given in terms of kilograms of plant nutrient ($N + P_2O_5 + K_2O$) per hectare of gross cropped area. Data on use of mechanical power in agriculture are derived from the number of tractors and electric- or oil-driven pumps in use on farms, as reported in the Livestock Census of 1961. Each tractor has been considered equivalent to two units, and each pump as equivalent to one unit, in converting the figures into units of mechanical power. Data on cooperative credit, as indicated, relate to short-term and medium-term loans. The composite index of use of modern inputs has been calculated by converting the figures for each indicator into an index (with the all-India average as 100) and then averaging the values. In this way, each indicator has been given equal weight in the composite index.

The figures for individual indicators and for the composite index show large inter-State variations. The range is in the order of 18 : 1 for chemical fertilizers, and it is even larger for the other two indicators and for the composite index. Madras has the highest figures for the three indicators and for the composite index; Rajasthan and Assam have the lowest. Most of the southern and western States have appreciably higher figures than the eastern and north-central States have. These differences reflect, to some extent, the influence of factors such as rainfall, cropping patterns, and development of irrigation. But even more they indicate differences in the acceptance of modern technology. Use of chemical fertilizer, for instance, is higher in Madras, where most of the cropped area is in the zone of medium rainfall and 45 per cent of it is irrigated than in Rajasthan, where most of the land is in the zone of low rainfall and only about 12 per cent is irrigated. Similarly, use of mechanical power is higher in Madras, where groundwater conditions facilitate development of lift irrigation than in Madhya Pradesh, where conditions are less favourable. But such explanations do not adequately explain the large inter-State differences that exist. Low indicator values in the eastern States—Assam, Bihar, West Bengal, and Orissa—and in Uttar Pradesh indicate, primarily, a lag in adopting modern techniques. Also, large inter-State differences in the value of cooperative credit per hectare indicate differences in the willingness and the capacity of farmers to use cooperative credit for agricultural purposes.

The coefficient of correlation between the level of use of chemical fertilizers and the rate of increase of productivity 0.27, is low; but that between the index of use of modern inputs and the rate of increase of productivity is higher 0.52. However, even this last is not significant at the 5 per cent level. The correlations between irrigated land and the use of chemical fertilizers, and between irrigated land and the index of use of modern inputs, are both above 0.5, but again are not significant at the 5 per cent level. However, the index of use of modern inputs has a significant correlation, 0.72, with the index of development of services, which indicates that use of modern inputs is influenced by factors such as the level of literacy of farmers, the existence of good communications, and the number of towns.

Index of Development of Services

The index of development of services (Table 5.1, line 58) is a composite based on four indicators: the rural literacy rate (education), the number of doctors per million of population (medical care), the network of roads in kilometres of roads per thousand square kilometres (communications), and the number of towns per million rural inhabitants (urbanization). It was constructed by first calculating index values for the individual indicators and then averaging the values, in the same way as in the index of use of modern inputs.

The number of towns was selected as an indicator of urbanization in preference to the proportion of urban population to total population; it was felt that not only the size of the urban population but the pattern of its distribution may have an influence on the development of agriculture. An urban population concentrated in one or two cities is likely to have different effects on rural areas than the same population distributed among a number of small or medium-sized towns; the greater number of points for rural-urban interaction may have an influence on diffusion of new ideas and techniques among farmers. It was interesting to test this hypothesis, since the view has recently been expressed that the number of towns in India is unusually small in relation to the size of the rural population and that India should undertake a programme of building 10,000 to 12,000 new market towns with facilities for such activities as marketing and processing of agricultural products, distribution of consumer goods, maintenance of farm implements, agricultural extension services, and the like, which are needed for agricultural development and for the modernization of rural life (National Council of Applied Economic Research, Chapter 1, 1965).

Inter-State variations in the value of the index of development of services are much smaller than was the case in the index of modern inputs; the range is in the order of 3.5 : 1. The southern States and all the western States except Rajasthan have much higher index values than most of the eastern and north-central States do. The important exception is West Bengal, an eastern State, which has one of the highest values in this index.

The coefficient of correlation between the index of the development of services and the rate of growth of agricultural output is less than 0.5 and is not significant at the 5 per cent level. But the correlation between the index of urbanization and the growth rate of agricultural output is high, 0.85, and is significant at the 5 per cent level. The index of urbanization also has a high and significant correlation, 0.71, with the composite index of agricultural development. These coefficients suggest the possible existence of a relationship between the number of towns in a State and its rate of agricultural progress.

Index of Agricultural Development

A composite index of agricultural development (Table 5.1, line 59) based on three factors—the growth rate of agricultural output, the use of modern inputs in agriculture, and the productivity per hectare—has been constructed to give an overall indication of comparative levels of agricultural development in different States. As in the other composite indices, the three constituents are given equal weight. The values of the index show an inter-State variation from 228.55 in Madras to 57.72 in Assam. The States have been ranked by values of the index and have also been divided into two groups, "high" and "low," with seven States in each (Fig. 5.3). It is noteworthy that the west-east dichotomy, to which reference has been made in discussion of growth rates, is even clearer here.

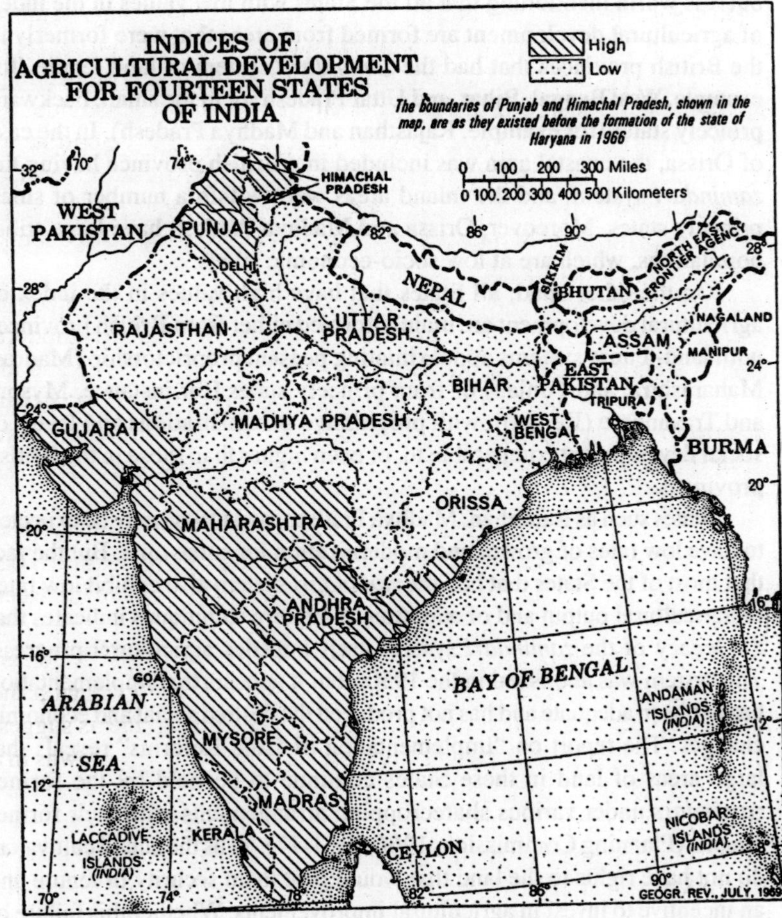

Fig. 5.3 : Indices of Agricultural Development for Fourteen States of India

The coefficient of correlation of the index of agricultural development with the index of development of services is more than 0.5, but it is not significant at the 5 per cent level. However, the correlation of the index of agricultural development with the index of urbanization, 0.71, is significant. The relationship of the index of agricultural development with relevant socio-economic and physical variables needs further study in order to understand the causes of differential progress between States, and in particular of the slow progress in some.

The causes of slow progress will, of course, differ from State to State, but it is worth mentioning that all the States with low values in the index of agricultural development are formed from areas that were formerly in the British provinces that had the *zamindari*[9] system of land tenure (for example, West Bengal, Bihar, and Uttar Pradesh) or in the small, backward princely states (for example, Rajasthan and Madhya Pradesh). In the case of Orissa, the coastal area was included in a British province having the *zamindari* system, and the inland areas were within a number of small princely states. Moreover, Orissa and Madhya Pradesh have large tribal populations, which are at low socio-economic levels.

On the other hand, all States that have high values in the index of agricultural development are mainly formed either from British provinces with land-tenure systems approximating peasant proprietorship (Madras, Maharashtra, and Punjab) or from princely states [for instance, Mysore and Travancore (Kerala)], with progressive administrations and levels of social development comparable to, or even higher than those in the British provinces.

States such as Rajasthan, Madhya Pradesh, and Orissa may be expected to have low rates of growth and modernization for some time. But the fact that most of the States that had the *zamindari* system also exhibit low rates of agricultural output and of adoption of modern techniques indicates that the legacy of the *zamindari* system itself impedes agricultural progress. The system was abolished in the 1950s, but it appears that implementation has not been adequate and has not produced the desired social and economic changes. The report on "Implementation of Land Reforms" reveals that large areas of land in these States continue to be held by the former *zamindars* under various sharecropping arrangements with their former tenants (Planning Commission, 1966, pp. 1-17). Thus the actual cultivators do not have rights to the land that would give them security of tenure and an incentive to invest in agricultural improvements. Whether this failure of land reform is the primary reason for slow agricultural progress in these States or whether there are other reasons needs to be investigated.

A Historical Perspective

In a recent study George Blyn analyzed trends in population, cropped area, and agricultural output in former British India (British Provinces) during the sixty years preceding independence (George, 1966). The analysis comprises the whole of British India except Baluchistan, "for which almost no crop data were available," but it excludes the princely states because of "incompleteness of data." Still, the area covered by the study contained "76 per cent of the population and 51 per cent of the total area of all-India in 1941" (George, 1966, p. 33). A comparison of Blyn's data with the data in this study shows interesting differences and similarities between the trends in the two periods. The growth rates of both population and agricultural output have been appreciably higher in the recent period than before independence. But whereas in the recent period the growth rate of agricultural output has been well ahead of the growth rate of population; agricultural output in the earlier period had not kept pace with population growth. However, two trends noted in the present study—faster growth of output of non-foodgrain crops than of foodgrains, and faster growth of agricultural output in the south than in the east or in Uttar Pradesh (United Provinces in the pre-independence period)—had already appeared in the early years of this century. However, the growth rates of both population and agricultural output have been appreciably higher since independence than they were earlier. The growth rate of agricultural output has been well ahead of the growth rate of population since independence, whereas earlier it was not keeping pace. Of course, comparison of trends in the post-independence period with those in the period studied by Blyn must be confined to the most general terms because of the political changes that have occurred since 1947, including the formation of India and Pakistan, integration of the princely states, and reorganization of the Indian States.

The broad pattern of regional differences revealed by the present study will probably not change much as a result of the more detailed, district-level analysis that will soon be possible. The pattern has historical roots, which suggests the need to investigate the causes of differential progress and, in particular, the causes of slow progress in the eastern and north-central States. The investigation is essential for evolving remedial measures that will enable these States which have a high potential for agricultural growth because of favourable moisture and soil conditions to participate more effectively in agricultural progress.

NOTES

1. A recent publication by the Economic and Statistical Adviser to the Ministry of Food and Agriculture, Government of India, gives linear and compound growth rates for two periods, 1949-1950 to 1964-1965 and 1952-1953 to 1964-1965, and also indicates the relative contributions of expanded cropland and of increased productivity to the growth of output. However, data by States are given only for the period 1952-1953 to 1964-

1965 because "index numbers for the States are available on a uniform basis only from 1952-1953". "*Growth Rates in Agriculture*", Ministry of Food and Agriculture, New Delhi, 1966 [mimeographed].

2. The small Himalayan State of Himachal Pradesh has been omitted from this paper because data for most of the economic variables are not available. Its exclusion reduces the coverage, in terms of gross cropped area, from 99.1 to 98.8 per cent.
3. Data on area, production, and yields of individual crops by districts are found in "*Indian Agricultural Statistics*" 1962-63 Vol. I.. However, data on total agricultural output and growth rates are not available, and growth rates would have to be calculated especially because the boundaries of many districts have changed during the decade of 1950 to 1960.
4. Only male agricultural workers have been considered in this comparison, since data on the number of female agricultural workers are not comparable in the censuses of 1951 and 1961 because of changes in definition. Most female agricultural workers are women of cultivating households who help on the family farms; they are not wage earners. The change in definition of "worker" adopted in 1961 resulted in a far larger number of women being returned as workers than had been the case in 1951. The number of female workers in all-India in 1961 was 52.2 per cent higher than in 1951, and the increases in some States were large (127.7 per cent in Andhra Pradesh and 188 per cent in Madras).
5. From unpublished data supplied in 1968 by the office of the Economic and Statistical Adviser, Ministry of Food and Agriculture.
6. Punjab refers to the State as it was before the creation of the new State of Haryana in 1966.
7. The rainfall zones with more than 45 inches were given a weight of 3; the zone with 30 to 45 inches, 2; and the zone with less than 30 inches, 1. An additional weight of 1 was given for irrigation in all rainfall zones.
8. Improved seed, important as it is as a factor in agricultural output, had to be excluded because of deficiencies of data.
9. *Zamindars* were revenue farmers who acted as intermediaries between the government and the cultivators. They acquired considerable social prestige and political power, and some were regarded as virtual rulers of their areas.

REFERENCES

Bhattacharjee, J.P. and Roy, S.M., "Trend of Consumption of Food and Foodgrains in India", in *Studies in Indian Agricultural Economics*.

Directorate of Economics and Statistics, *Indian Agricultural Statistics*, 1962-63, Vol. 1, New Delhi, 1965.

George Blyn, *Agricultural Trends in India*, 1891-1947, Philadelphia, 1966.

Jakhade, V.M., "Agricultural Production, Credit and Institutional Arrangements", *Indian Journal of Public Administration,* Vol. 13, 1967.

Mukherjee, P.K. and Sivasubramanian, S., "*Agricultural Output and National Income in India*", in *Studies in Indian Agricultural Economics*, (ed. by Bhattacharjee, J.P.; Indian Society of Agricultural Economics, Bombay, 1958).

National Council for Applied Economic Research, *Market Towns and Spatial Development in India*, New Delhi, 1965.

Planning Commission, Government of India, *Implementation of Land Reforms*, 1966.

Saran, R. and Chawla, H.L., "Food Production Policies and Programmes since Independence—A Historical Review", *Indian Journal of Public Administration*, Vol. 13, 1967.

Sivaraman, B., "The Strategy of Food Production", *Indian Journal of Public Administration*, Vol. 13, 1967.

William Holst, "*Evaluation of Population and Food Production Problems of India*", in the *World Food Problem*: *A Report of the President's Science Advisory Committee*, Vols. 2; Washington D.C., 1967.

6

Rural Industrialization

Role of Very Small (Cottage Industries) and Small Scale Rural Industrial Enterprises in Rural Development

Introduction

One of the objects of the Community Development Programme launched in 1952 was to promote rural industrialization. In pursuit of this object, industrial training institutions were opened in rural areas in which industrial skills such as carpentry, masonry and repair of electrical and electronic appliances was given to young men and in cutting, stitching and embroidery on cloth to make garments was given to young women. Artisans in villages were urged to modernize their techniques. The graduates of the schools were expected and did build houses in villages and market towns and repaired the machines mentioned above. Most of the students were sons of artisans. They found employment in market towns and large villages. However, after a few years of working these institutes were closed because most of the students were children of artisans and it was felt that they could learn these skills from their fathers as they could in these institutions. This was a mistake because the institutions would give training in using modern techniques, for which there was great demand for skilled workers in industries, which their fathers could not give. The industrial training institutes for girls are still there mainly in cities and their students find employment in companies, which produce garments for domestic consumption and export.

The Programme was based on the Gandhian concept of a self-sufficient village, which produced its own food, spun and wove into garments the cotton that it produced; pressed its own oil and made soap, for bathing and washing its own cloth. The village depended upon the outside world for sugar, salt, tea or that it did not produce itself.

The Programme, however, failed to achieve its objectives the reasons for this have to be explained.

Gandhiji could talk about such a village because he came from an area, which produced cotton and oil seeds. His birthplace was a small port on the Arabian Sea where making salt from sea-water was an important activity for workers who had specialized in it. However, there are several hundred thousand villages, which do not produce cotton or oilseeds and are not located along the sea. Their residents must buy sugar, oil, soap and salt in exchange for the crops like foodgrains, jute, that they produce. The tribals living in the hilly-forested areas of Madhya Pradesh, inland Orissa, and Jharkhand area of Bihar, a part of West Bengal, Andhra Pradesh, Karnataka, Maharashtra and Gujarat can barely produce food needed for subsistence

What are they to produce in exchange to buy cloth, sugar, soap, salt, and other necessities of life including food? In many of these areas, food has to be dropped from the air, or brought by trucks when the local crops fail. It would be impossible for rural people in coastal Andhra Pradesh or Tamil Nadu to produce their own cotton or oilseeds, because rice and sugarcane in the former and double cropped rice in the latter are the most remunerative crops. The villagers obtain oil, cloth, salt and other needs in exchange for rice and sugar.

What industries can be promoted here in order to give them the purchasing power to buy these foods? Training in industrial skills of carpenters, mason and smiths is useful because it will enable the youth to work as skilled industrial workers in the numerous industrial units located in the region. Training of girls has to concentrate on principles of nutrition and sanitation so that the high infant and maternal mortality rates are reduced.

The Khadi and Village Industries Board with the professed object of implementing Gandhiji's programme, sells cotton, woollen and silk cloth, oil pressed in villages and other products such as honey from producers in villages. However, it obtains its products from areas, which specialize in production of these. Handloom and Handicraft Board also obtains cotton *sarees* from areas, which specialize in production of these. The Silk *sarees* are bought from Srinagar in Kashmir, a suburb of Varanasi in Uttar Pradesh, Dharmavaram in Andhra Pradesh, Kanchipuram a temple town in Tamil Nadu, Mysore city in Karnataka. Similarly, cotton *sarees* are bought in various towns across the country, which specialize in production of these.

All the three boards—the Khadi and Village Industries, the Handloom and the Handicraft—assist millions of handloom weavers to produce cloth and modernize techniques such as teaching them to work on broader looms designed to increase production per day and increase their income. The two latter boards also teach them to adopt modern designs so that the fabrics made by them are attractive for urban consumers in India and in countries in which there are large Indian populations as well as in developed countries. The Handicraft Board works in addition with makers of decorative brassware in Moradabad, carpets in Mirzapur and surrounding villages to improve quality of the carpets and stop use of child labour so that the carpets are acceptable in countries such as the U.S.A. which do not accept carpets in making where child labour is employed.

At the beginning of the 1950s, India had a thriving cotton textile industry. Most of the mills were located in Mumbai, Ahmedabad, Sholapur, Coimbatore and other cities located in areas in which cotton was produced. The mill-owners had made large profits during World War II to meet domestic demand and that of British troops and by export of cloth to neighbouring countries of south, south-east and south-west Asia and east Africa. At the same time, millions of handloom weavers in Tamil Nadu, Kerala and other States were facing threat of unemployment because the cloth made on handlooms could not compete with mill made cloth in price or quality. In order to protect them, the Government of India levied high excise duty on cloth made in mills with no such duty on handloom cloth so that mill-made cloth was not much cheaper than handloom cloth. The employment of handloom weavers was protected, but the less efficient mills in Mumbai, Ahmedabad and other centres were closed. As a result, while production of mill made cloth remained stagnant while the handloom cloth steadily increased. The mill-owners responded by closing their mills and diverted their capital to production of other products or trading in cotton. Some of them installed powerloom clusters because there was low excise duty on cloth made on them.

Later, when use of polyester fibre for making cloth became widespread, progressive owners of mills and powerloom clusters specialized in promotion of cloth made of mixtures of cotton and polyester, wool and polyester, or silk and polyester. The cloth with specified mixtures of the fibres proved very popular because it was cheaper and more comfortable to wear than cloth made of pure cotton, wool or silk. The handloom weavers also switched to production of cloth made of mixtures of cotton and silk fibres. While cloth made from handloom with mixtures of the fibres was used mainly in India, while that made in mills had also a large export market. Still later, some of the more progressive mill owners have concentrated on production of speciality cloth such as cloth for making of jeans. It is noteworthy that powerloom clusters are located in peri-urban areas of cities—Mumbai, Ahmedabad, Sholapur and Coimbatore which were the centres of cotton mills or in cities or towns which were earlier the centres of production of handloom cloth. Thus, powerloom clusters are located in Adampur in Punjab; Panipat in Haryana; Meerut and other towns in Uttar Pradesh; Bihar Sharif in Bihar; Kotah in Rajasthan, Murshidabad in West Bengal, Itchalkarandi in Maharashtra, Mysore city, Hubli and Dharwar in Karnataka and Kancheepuram in Tamil Nadu. All these cities except Mysore city do not produce silk. The silk *sarees* made on handlooms or powerlooms are based on the use of imported silk and polyester which are made in Mumbai and other centres. Powerloom clusters are located also in the peri-urban areas of Delhi and other cities in which they find ready market for their products such as furnishings and bath towels etc.

It is significant that over large areas of the country there are no handlooms or powerloom clusters. The people of hilly-forested areas of Madhya Pradesh, Bihar, Andhra Pradesh, Maharashtra, Gujarat and Rajasthan and the desert or semi-desert areas of Rajasthan obtain cloth from other States.

Rural industrialization in large parts of the country means only training local young men to become efficient electricians, carpenters, masons, smiths and repairmen of motor vehicles so that they can make brick and mortar houses, repair diesel and power operated pumps which supply power for irrigation, tractors and other machines for efficient cultivation and repair of motor vehicles. They will be able to repair also various consumer durables. The increase in agricultural production and industrialization of Punjab is based on the hard work of the farmers and skill of Ramgarhis Sikhs. In all the cities and large towns of Punjab there are concentrations of these artisans. Similarly, in other developed areas, which are large producers of wheat, rice, cotton, sugar, and other foods there are concentration of such artisans. Except in Coimbatore which produces cotton it would be uneconomic to locate powerloom clusters because these areas can obtain their cloth much cheaper from the centres of cloth production than they can produce themselves.

In assisting development of backward areas, it is necessary to train local artisans from whatever caste so that they can repair electric or diesel operated pumps for irrigation and buses and trucks which are the principal means of transport of men, crops, chemical fertilizers and pesticides for improving agricultural production. The large numbers of Moslems of Sherpur Khilchipur (Sawai Madhopur, Rajasthan) who are traditionally smiths or carpenters have found ample opportunities for employment in a large number of petrol pumps and in driving of motor vehicles used by large numbers of tourists who visit the game sanctuary in the cool season. The masons of whatever caste have found employment in construction of the large number of brick and mortar homes that have replaced thatch huts both in the villages and the farms which produce cereals and fodder crops for milch animals in the areas irrigated by surface wells and below tanks in the cool season.

To conclude rural industrialization should mean training in every large village and small town, carpenters, smiths, masons, electricians so that they can repair mechanically driven farm implements and pumps for irrigation and build brick and mortar houses. Rural industrialization does not mean establishing cottage industries in every village through the length and breadth of the country to produce cloth, sugar, salt and other necessities of life.

It is essential that there should be well trained artisans—carpenters, smiths, masons, repairmen of electric and electronic gadgets and motor vehicles in all cities and in rural areas which have adequate and assured supplies of moisture, which have electricity and the farmers use electric or diesel operated pumps for irrigation and improved farm implements including tractors. Their houses have refrigerators, air coolers, and TV receivers. They use natural gas instead of cow dung for cooking. These trained craftsmen provide trained manpower to service and repair these gadgets. They will also assist farmers and agricultural labourers to build brick and mortar houses at costs comparable to their traditional homes. Furthermore, the more enterprising trained workers will establish their own small industry units, which process local materials. Industrial development will be promoted in the areas in which they live. Development of small-scale industries in Ludhiana in Punjab is an example.

The woollen hosiery industry of Ludhiana in Punjab, the sales of which amount to millions of dollars has a large turnover both within India and abroad especially the Soviet Union, has grown without assistance from any government agency; its growth is due entirely to enterprise of private entrepreneurs.

It is economic and feasible to train women in all areas to stitch their own clothes. These trained women have along with male tailors located in Delhi, Mumbai, Lucknow and some other cities have developed garment industries which have large markets within India and abroad.

However, it is neither economic nor feasible to promote industrial development in rural areas and small towns, in all parts of the country, irrespective of availability of raw materials.

The Industrial Policy[1]

In India the strategy of industrialization envisaged a mixed pattern of large-scale modern industries on the one hand, and small-scale and village, largely cottage or household industries (VSIs) basically answering the needs of rural and small town industrialization, on the other. This model was adopted in order to achieve a mix of objectives not necessarily pulling in the same direction. It was envisaged that the VSIs will have both a transitional and a lasting role, acquiring not a dominant but a subsidiary place in India's emerging industrial landscape. This strategy, embodying some features of 'walking on two legs' was designed to reconcile the needs of rapid modern industrialization based largely on imported technology, with the pressing task of large-scale employment generation in our far-flung rural areas, making use of local resources and catering to local needs, and established traditional institutions.

We have obtained mixed results. Any evaluation of the performance of India's industrial sector brings out that along with the growth and diversification of modern industries there has also been impressive gains, by the VSIs in terms of number of enterprises and factories, production, investment, exports and absolute increase in employment (Table 6.1). A number of government policies and promotional agencies along with the general thrust of development of infrastructure as a part of planning have been among the contributory factors to the spread and growth of industries. Despite inadequate and problematic statistics, it is evident that reversing relatively slow growth during the earlier years, the VSI sector has grown faster than the large and medium industries sector, and has increased the farmer's share in the industrial structure. The VSI sector is largely the responsibility of the State governments. The gains and inadequacies as well as other limitations in this sector, therefore, concern the policies, programmes and performance of the States also.

Notwithstanding these achievements, one finds that in terms of employment generation, development of backward regions, innovations for making use of intra- and inter-sectoral linkages, prevention of technological unemployment and for achieving long-term viability, stability and self-sustainability, the achievements of the VSIs remain far from adequate. The data in terms of VSI's contribution to employment

Table 6.1: Rural Enterprises in India (Number and Employment)—1980 and 1990

	Rural Own Account Enterprises		*Rural Establishments*	
	1980*	1990	1980*	1990
Agriculture				
Enterprises (lakh)	10.37 (11.04)**	18.40	1.78 (1.97)**	2.53
Employment (lakh)	17.24	32.40	6.14	10.00
Non-Agriculture				
Enterprises (lakh)	65.71 (75.89)**	94.74	19.79 (23.00)**	31.50
Employment (lakh)	98.74	136.1	91.18	154.60
	Total Rural Own Account Enterprises		Total Rural Establishments	
Enterprises (lakh)	76.08 (86.93)**	113.14	21.57 (24.97)**	34.03
Employment (lakh)	115.98	168.50	97.32	164.60
	1980		1990	
Total Rural Own Account Enterprises and Establishments (lakh)	98.65 (111.90)**		147.17	
Total Rural Employment in Own Account Enterprises and Establishments (lakh)	213.30		333.10	

* Excluding Assam, Bihar, Kerala and Lakshadweep.

** For all the States, including the provisional results for Assam, Bihar, Kerala and Lakshadweep.

and GDP bring out fairly clearly that the growth of industrial output and to a greater extent that of employment have been less than adequate compared to the gigantic tasks facing our country. The problems arising from the rate and pattern of growth of the VSIs are lack of long-term viability of a large number of units set up in response to various planned schemes, absence of technical and organizational innovations to respond to our specific needs, particularly in rural and backward areas. Hence the bulk of rural India persists as industrially backward. This is reflected in the somewhat misleading declaration of a number of districts as 'No industry' districts, ignoring household, traditional industries and the employment provided by them and implicitly identifying industries with 'modern', medium and large industries. The positive results from setting up a large number of industrial estates and units have been limited particularly in the perspective of our development strategy. As has been shown, "even though the proportion of industrial work force based in rural areas to total industrial workforce is considerable and nearly equal to that in urban areas, in terms of its percentage in total work force, the rural sector industrial employment is way behind the urban sector industrial employment.

However, lakhs of units are sick, facing closure and working at less than full capacity. Tax arrears and loan defaults are mounting. They face inadequate and uncertain markets. They are unable to anticipate and cope up with the changes in the market conditions or public policies concerning money, finance, wages, interest, taxation, foreign trade and exchange rate, etc. That is to say, a large number of new industrial units in the small and village industries sector are neither successful as micro entities nor are contributing in their macro aggregate form to the national socio-economic objectives. Liberalization of economic policies does not seem to have shown much sensitivity to the kind of problems of the VSI sector mentioned above.

We may hypothesize certain aspects of the emerging economic structure, policy processes and their political economy, which contributed to the arrival of the VSI sector to the present impasse. The impasse is marked by a paradoxical situation. The public policy support to the VSI is resented by the large, corporate industry and the World Bank. The VSI too complain of its inadequacy, discrimination and pinpricks, like inspector Raj. And socially, the policies for VSI have not proved too successful. In fact, some negative results too have appeared. First, really effective reckonable and on-going support and high priority was obtained by the large and medium industries under our growing corporate sector. Thus the VSI sector has to remain content with a marginal place in public policy and planning (in terms of finance, tax policy, trade policy, infrastructure support, policy consultation etc.). This is probably as true at the Union as at the States level. This is an indication of the similarity of the political economy underpinnings of these policies at the level of both the Union and States. Keeping this in view, one has to examine whether the existing centralization of policies and programmes and the top-down planning and administrative structure could prove equal to the task of decentralized industrialization, particularly in view of the multiplicity of the Central and State level agencies concerned with rural industries. The difficulties on this score may go beyond the question of co-ordination, *e.g.,* whether there should be six separate boards for different non-farm rural industries and that too at the Union level.

It may be further posited that the existing approaches to the growth of rural industries have not been in any real sense based on integrated planning at the regional and sectoral levels nor did they have proper project planning at the micro-level. Such programmes involve a much higher order of micro-macro interface than what one has seen so far. Presently, the impact of specific measures to help the growth of VSI units seem to have been counter balanced by the unplanned influences originating in the macro sphere. For example, credit, input supply, price preference, reservations, etc. gave some benefit to the small units. But the growth of the corporate sector, the MNCs and removal of quantitative restriction on the import of hundreds of commodities capable of causing displacement competition for the VSI sector not only reduced the market and market access, their subsidiaries pocketed the benefits earmarked for the VSI units. The manner in which the small entrepreneur was marginalized and elbowed out on account of the position of the big entrepreneurs, MNCs and imports was repeated *vis-à-vis* the artisans and the informal small-scale industry (SSI) units. In any case, these micro mainly rural small town enterprises rarely fitted in with the regional and industry-wise economic reality and linkages.

An industrial structure saddled with non-viable, sick and limping industrial units cannot contribute to the attainment of the objectives even of industrial growth and would eventually apply brakes to the very process of industrialization. This problem is as relevant at the level of large industries, and national level industrial planning emphasis on efficiency, competitiveness and avoidance of waste is as emphatic at the level of VSI units and the traditional artisan units as at large industries. It is possible that such problems also arise in countries experiencing industrial growth largely through decentralized, private entrepreneurial activities. The market mechanism deals with such cases by forcing bankruptcy and exit. But in our case, public funds, public policy and planning initiative play a large role in the establishment of mainly large and medium and to extent even small new units. Many of the VSI owe a great deal to various public promotional agencies, (like KVIC, KBs, various commodity Boards of the Union government) fiscal and monetary policies and planning at the State and district levels. The opportunity cost of inadequately successful industrial units has to include the costs incurred by these agencies and policies. The dilemma involved in the market option of exit of such policy-propped up units is really acute. The costs of such exit cannot be confined to the promoters and shareholders as these units involve a great deal of social resources and other interests. Hence such exit may jeopardize plan objectives and regional economies, the interests of the suppliers of various inputs, creditors, workers, tax authorities and interrelated firms, in addition to the wastage of the resources directly invested in these units.

The VSIs were expected to provide the basis for rural industrialization. The colonial period led to deindustrialization of India and in particular of her rural economy, which was fragmented, disarticulated and through backwash effects of dualistic growth was denuded of its precious, potentially productive resources. It also disrupted the links between agriculture and industry. Balanced and equitable development requires rural industrialization. Our industrial policy and plan programmes initiated a number of positive and discriminatory programmes for helping the growth of VSIs. The VSIs benefited from the fiscal concessions, cheap and easy credit, arrangements for raw material supply, imparting of training and skills, availability of infrastructure, marketing support and price preference on government purchase. According to some estimates, 'these concessions can add up to as much as 25 to 45 per cent of output value, the excise concessions and price preference being the most important ones'. The forgone revenue on rebate and interest subsidy measures is estimated to have cost the Exchequer in excess of Rs. 160 crore during 1978-79 (The Committee on Tax Measures to Promote Employment). Still, less is known about the share of the rural unorganized segment in these protective and promotional measures. Marshalling available evidence from various studies, particularly those relating to handlooms, matches, *bidi*, carpets and shoe-making, and from various regions, it has been shown that 'most of these lead an isolated and waning existence' and 'the intended help either fails to reach the target groups or is far from adequate and is marked by high leakages either by manipulation of ownership by large enterprises or the exploitative role played by middlemen'. This survey maintains that "most of the rural traditional crafts have been largely by-passed or ineffectively handled by the official programmes". Such long-term, continued miscarriage of the programmes should make one put a serious question mark on the appropriateness of the policy-package, including the clubbing together of the SSIs and the village industries.

In addition to the above, many positive programmes have operated through six boards for promoting different segments of traditional industries and the SIDO. The public sector outlay for these programmes, has gone up from Rs. 24 billion during 1961-66 to Rs. 196.5 billion during the Sixth Plan and is further planned in the Eighth Plan is Rs. 245.8 billion. Bank credit to these small industries has increased from Rs. 3 billion in 1969 to Rs. 66 billion by 1984-85. Many term-lending institutions have also given generous financial support to this sector, though in relative terms the share going to the large and medium sector preponderates.

Only limited information is available regarding the progress of these industries (basically, non-factory sector). Non-factory employment during 1977-87 increased from 17.4 million to 21.4 million. This gives an annual rate of about 2 per cent compared to one per cent yearly during the previous two decades. Nearly 75 per cent of the addition to industrial employment during this period is attributable to non-factory industry.

However, within the small sector, household sector suffered a setback. Between 1961 and 1981, household sector employment declined by 2.2 million. The 17 major household industry groups lost 3.5 million employment opportunities. The biggest decline was in textiles and food processing. The fall in household sector employment in all these groups is concentrated in the traditional industries, notably non-mill spinning, handlooms, *khadi*, hand printing, grain milling, oil crushing, gur-making, and leather and leather footwear and earthenware. Against this, some industry groups like beverages and tobacco and *bidi* making and repair services saw substantial expansion of household industry. In sum, overall employment in most segments of traditional manufacture have remained constant or declined in spite of wide ranging protective and positive interventions by the State and by agencies like KVIC. This experience may suggest that the policies, programmes and agencies may have been victims of 'tokenism', top-downism, technological topism etc. Their mis-appropriateness may have been compounded by lack of voice, inadequate articulation and participation by the rural artisans, craftsmen and potential beneficiaries, while the organized and modern sector, irrespective of size, may have derived disproportionate and undeserved benefits.

An additional and somewhat disturbing feature has been the shifting locational pattern of these industries away from rural areas. The share of rural areas in total employment in non-factory industry has declined sharply. Paradoxically, non-household modern small industries have seen a small shift in favour of rural areas with their share in total non-household, non-factory, industrial employment increasing from a little above 30 per cent in 1961 to almost 35 per cent in 1981.

From the above account, it can be seen that rural industrialization has not made progress commensurate either with our needs or the policy and planning interventions. The large rural-urban average income differentials, the operation of push factors in migration from the rural areas (distress, involuntary migration,) and inadequate linkage between agriculture and industry (seen in sustained industrial growth despite widespread droughts and poor agricultural growth, and *vice versa*) seem to be related to poor performance of rural industrialization programmes.

Many hypotheses have been advanced for explaining the neglect of or slow pace of meaningful rural industrialization and the growing incidence of wasted efforts at fostering rural industrialization, particularly in 'non-industry' and backward regions. Lack of co-ordination, non-suitability and non-viability of projects, particularly lack of their embedding in an integrated meso and micro plans, absence of markets and marketing efforts, or, setting up of marketing networks without creating adequate home market, continued predatory role of merchant and usury capital, particularly *vis-à-vis* household, own-account activities, competition from large, non-rural industries, use of substitutes of inputs of agricultural and rural origin, urban-bias of professional and higher education, inadequate, inappropriate and top-down research and development for rural industries, infrastructure bottlenecks, etc. are in addition to the factors operating at the level of the entrepreneurs and originating from the markets. Absence or inadequacy of efforts as a desirable pattern of industrial growth and structural change reflect in poor project planning, especially in the neglect of the size of the market and the need to create and expand markets, simultaneously with infusion of capital, skills (at concessional prices) and provision of infrastructural support. Uneven and involutionary agricultural growth is also related to slow and uneven growth of rural industries.

None of the above is meant to weaken the proposition that industrialization retains its value as a major means for meeting the diverse and growing needs of the country. However, the validity of this proposition cannot be independent of the pattern of industrialization. The problems bequeathed by the rate and pattern of industrial growth so far and the limitations of the studies of this experience necessitate a fresh look at the whole issue.

Industrial growth in India, impressive in many respects, cannot be said to have made a noticeable impact on reduction of poverty and socio-economic and regional inequities either directly or through a combination of trickle-down and 'pull-up'. Its spread effects too have been limited from the point of view of the rural economy in general and the poor in particular. Its direct employment and income contribution have been far below the level needed for giving access to productive and gainful participation in the economy to millions of Indians. It did not generate re-investible surpluses even for maintaining its own momentum, let alone for transfer to anti-poverty programmes: both the public and organized private sector industries, mainly large and medium industrial enterprises (LMIEs), are guzzlers of resources (savings, foreign exchange, energy, forests, minerals and other natural resources) transferred from the rest of the economy. Millions of project outees— the 'development' refugees— are made to bear a huge cost without any worthwhile compensation. It makes heavy demands on the infrastructure, particularly various sources of energy and means of transport. It did produce major inputs for further industrialization as well as the industrialization and marketization of agriculture in certain regions of the economy (the essence of Green Revolution), but had a doubtful anti-poverty impact, especially owing to the terms on which these supplies were made available to agriculture. Industrial inputs based green revolution led in course of time to reduced employment elasticity of agricultural growth and rising capital intensity and heavy ecological cost. As a result, agriculture and industry still remain inadequately integrated. The alternative of decentralized production of farm inputs in villages and rural towns with labour-intensive technologies using largely local resources would have generated spread effects, given wider base to such a growth process and created a symbiotic farm-industry relationship. Thus, it is little wonder that the growth of industrial investment, output and its diversification largely in urban metropolitan areas, in relatively better-off States and the LMIEs, have not been able to provide productive participation to avoid the inappropriate term often used in this context, *viz.*, employment to affect any worthwhile transfer of work force from the primary sector in order to correct the endemic imbalance in our occupational structure. Thus neither equitable sharing of the fruits of industrial growth nor indigenization of its basic motor power has come about. Low and declining labour absorption in green revolution agriculture as well as organized private industry, mainly LMIEs and increasing capital, foreign debt, high energy and import intensities of efforts at maintaining the tempo of such industrial growth, put a serious question mark on the relevance of continuing with 'more of the same' as far as our industrial development strategy in concerned.

These factors point to the need for searching methods of developing the rural non-farm sector, mainly industries and allied activities, in a big way for improving the level of productive participation and just sharing in the process of development. What is maintained is that the place assigned to 'modern' industrialization and policies followed to attain it have created a wide chasm between the social and economic aspects of industrialization. Even the economic rational and sustainability of this type of industrialization have become highly problematic as is reflected in frequent slow-downs and constant need to offer ever more lucrative incentives and public policy support to the LMIEs.

A brief examination of India's industrial policies and programmes, as seen above, in so far as they impacted the rural industrial enterprises (RIEs) suggest the limitations and inadequacies, of policy interventions.

Rural and small-scale industrial enterprises (RIEs & SIEs) were not clearly distinguished. The concept of RIEs distinct from modern small industrial enterprises (SIEs) remained, by and large, unspecified. The stress on "small is beautiful" was gradually turned into "small is savvy" and "small is possible", as though size or scale is all that mattered. It was hardly realized that all village household units are not rural. Similarly, traditional RIEs may survive largely in their traditional forms, or as stages in the process of transition to "improved village industries". However, it may not be appropriate to treat them as micro, or miniaturized versions of modern industrial enterprises, similar in most respects, except the scale of investment and operation.

In sum, it has to be recognized that while all rural industrial enterprises have to be small all small ones need not be rural. The capital and resource cost of a unit of output and employment of rural enterprises is usually very low and yet intra-rural linkages are very extensive and strong. With an enabling and facilitating macro and micro economic environment helping emerging social capital and conversion of latent demand into effective demand, the rural industries can lead India on a genuine indigenous, sustainable and just path of development.

NOTE

1. The analysis is based on the data given in: *CSO, Economic Census*, 1980 (pp. 4, 7, 11) and 1990 and *Manpower Profile India: Year Book*, 1996. p. 139.

7

Rural Poverty in India

*Regional Dimensions**

Introduction

Rural poverty is the most serious problem in India's economic development. No government in India can survive without indicating its commitment to eradicating poverty among the people. There are large inter-State and intra-State sub-regional variations in rural poverty due to environmental and/or man-made reasons. The percentage of population below poverty line is estimated to have declined steadily from about 55 per cent in the 1973-74 to a projected 18.00 per cent during 2001-2002. There has been sharp decline in 1990s; the rate was 36.0 per cent in 1993-94. The decline is being attributed to the trickle down effect of the rapid growth of gross domestic product achieved during the 1990s.

Two most widely accepted definitions of poverty are discussed. The areas in which large proportions of the rural population suffer from poverty are indicated. It is argued that further progress in reducing poverty will be difficult until productivity and income of the farmers and agricultural labourers in the poverty stricken areas is increased. The nature of the programmes to achieve this objective is indicated. It is argued that the programme will not be effective until they include the food for work programmes in which nutritious and balanced food is distributed to men as part of the wages for work on the programmes. The programmes should aim at enhancing rural infrastructure as well as improving the natural environment. In this way the programmes will achieve the twin objectives of reducing incidence of poverty and reducing the environmental damage that leads to large proportion of the rural population to subsist in poverty.

---

* First published in "*Reinventing Regional Development*", Eds. Surya Kant *et al.* Rawat Publications, 2004.

Two Definitions of Rural Poverty

The two definitions of poverty in use at present :

(i) Those who do not get enough calories from cereals, cooking oil, sugar and other foods to maintain themselves in health. This definition given first by Dandekar and Rath (Dandekar and Rath, 1971) has been accepted by the Government of India, and

(ii) In addition, those who do not have access to clean drinking water, easy access to facilities for curative and preventive health care and suffer, therefore, from various epidemic and endemic diseases. Furthermore, they are ignorant and illiterate for lack of access to or unwillingness to use facilities for education of their children and literacy for adults.

The second definition is used often by the World Bank and other agencies of the UN system. The first narrower definition is used here due to lack of easy access to the broader definition. The regions which are not in need of alleviation of poverty programmes and those which are in need described below have been determined on *a priori* basis. It will hopefully be possible to define them more precisely when data of the decennial census of 2001 which will become available in a few months and are matched with those of the latest rounds of the National Sample Survey. However, it is the contention of the author that decline in rural poverty according to the narrower definition, is accompanied also by a decline in the number of poor using the broader definition.

Programmes for Alleviation of Poverty Pre- and Post-1950s

Food for work programmes have been undertaken by the British government since the 1880s. There were two widespread famines in the country in the last two decades of the Nineteenth century. Millions died from starvation. In addition to organizing food for work programmes in the famine affected areas the government launched a large programme of construction of canals in the following areas :

(i) Undivided Punjab, Sindh, 2 districts of the then Bikaner state, and a large part of western Uttar Pradesh. After western Punjab and Sindh went to Pakistan in 1947, the areas covered by the programmes in India include :

(ii) Punjab, Haryana, almost 20 districts of western U.P. which are irrigated by canals on the Yamuna and the Ganga and 3 districts of northern Rajasthan. The areas under irrigation in Haryana and Rajasthan have increased greatly after construction during 1950s of Bhakra Dam, a 700 ft. high concrete dam on Sutlej River in present Punjab. Furthermore, the governments of Punjab, Haryana and U.P. have encouraged farmers by giving medium term loans to install electricity or diesel oil driven pumps on their surface wells and by constructing deep tube-wells. The latter programme initiated in U.P. in the 1930s and continued in the 1950s and 1960s covers a large area in western Uttar Pradesh and Haryana and a small area also in Punjab.

(iii) Constructing canals in coastal Andhra Pradesh especially in the deltas of Krishna and Godavari rivers.

(iv) Constructing or improving old canals in the delta of the Kaveri River in former Madras presidency (present Tamil Nadu). In both areas the canals were constructed or improved during the British period. The area under irrigation has been increased and irrigation made more intensive in the last 5 decades by improvement of canals and by use of electricity or diesel oil operated pump on surface wells by the farmers.

(v) Construction in the 1930s of a canal on Pykara River to irrigate a large area of land around Coimbatore in Tamil Nadu in which medium staple cotton is the principal crop.

(vi) Renovation or repair of tanks in large areas of peninsular India. A number of princely states notably Mysore, Hyderabad, Travancore and Cochin in the south and Baroda in the west joined in this effort.

(vii) The irrigation area in the former Mysore state (present Karnataka) was increased by renovation and repair of tanks and more important by construction of a dam and a canal on Kaveri River to irrigate a large area located between Bangalore and Mysore city. The irrigated area has been increased further by giving loans to farmers to install electric pumps on their surface wells.

(viii) In Hyderabad, the area under irrigation was increased by constructing dams on numerous small streams. The communities located below the dams depend on them for irrigation of their croplands and for drinking water.

(ix) Western Maharashtra: A large area is irrigated by construction of dams on a number of small streams that flow west from the Ghats to the Arabian Sea. This is a development primarily of the period after independence. This area was drought prone earlier and food for work programmes was undertaken in it from time-to-time.

(x) Coastal Gujarat between Mumbai and Ahmedabad. The area receives adequate rainfall in most years to produce large crops of coarse grains (sorghum or millets) and oilseeds. After establishment of Amul dairy at Anand in central Gujarat and its branches in two other towns production of milk for sale as liquid milk to Mumbai, Ahmedabad and other cities in Gujarat and for manufacture of dairy products—butter, cheese and baby food—for distribution throughout northern and western India has become important.

(xi) A large area in eastern and south-eastern Rajasthan which receives dependable rainfall in the monsoon season and in which large areas are irrigated by tanks or by wells fitted with electricity or diesel oil operated pumps. Coarse grains, oilseeds and cotton are the principal crops.

Altogether these areas together with those in the Gangetic plain in U.P., Bihar and West Bengal comprise about 35 per cent of the total cropped area leaving about 65 per cent of the cropland without irrigation facilities.

These programmes had the desired effect. The areas covered by the irrigation projects not only became self sufficient in foodgrains but had also large surpluses which were sent to other States. Production of medium staple cotton, sugarcane and oil seeds was also concentrated in these areas.

The several major irrigation-*cum*-power generation projects constructed during the period of the First and Second Five-Year Plans of independent India 1951-61 and the programmes to increase irrigated area through repair of tanks and giving loans to farmers to install electricity or diesel oil operated pumps on their wells have further increased the area provided by adequate and dependable irrigation. As a result, the area irrigated by canals, tanks, surface wells, tubewells, etc. increased from just over 17 per cent in 1951-52 to 36 per cent in the mid-1990s. The irrigated areas produce a large percentage of the cereals, cotton, sugarcane and oil seeds, jute and tea produced in the country. Some of these areas were drought prone earlier and were in need of programmes for alleviation of poverty.

The areas in need of alleviation of poverty programmes and those in which there is no need for these need to be separated in order to make the programmes more target oriented and hence more effective.

Areas Not in Need of Such Programmes

(i) Punjab, Haryana, Western Uttar Pradesh and 3 districts of northern Rajasthan. These areas receive irrigation from canals and electricity or diesel operated pumps on irrigation wells and tubewells owned and operated by the State of U.P., Haryana and Punjab. High yield wheat and rice in Punjab; wheat, cotton and oilseeds in Haryana and wheat, oilseeds and sugarcane in western U.P. are the principal crops. The areas produce a large surplus of cereals for distribution through the public distribution system. Medium staple cotton is used by cotton mills to produce fine cloths. There is a number of wheat and rice flour mills, and oil mills for production of cooking oil and sugar mills in U.P. Furthermore, there are several cotton gins and a textile mill in Haryana.

(ii) Coastal Andhra Pradesh including especially the deltas of Godavari and Krishna rivers. Rice and sugarcane are the principal crops. There is a surplus of rice and a significant percentage of the country's sugar is produced in this area. There are a number of sugar and rice mills which provide employment to marginal farmers and agricultural labourers.

(iii) Coastal Tamil Nadu including especially the delta of Kaveri River. The area produces two crops of rice in the year.

(iv) South-west Karnataka especially the area irrigated by a canal from Kaveri River located between Mysore city and Bangalore. High yield rice and sugarcane are the principal crops.

(v) The rice produced in Andhra Pradesh, Tamil Nadu and Karnataka areas mentioned above along with coarse grains (sorghum and millets) produced in unirrigated areas of the State is adequate to meet the consumption needs of the people of the unirrigated areas of these States also. However, there may be deficits in years of deficient rainfall in some unirrigated areas of both Karnataka and Andhra Pradesh especially those which had earlier formed part of dominions of the Nizam of Hyderabad.

(vi) *Kerala:* The State receives rainfall from both the south-west and north-east monsoons. Variability of rainfall is low. Production of rice and tapioca, the principal food of the population is barely sufficient or insufficient in some years for the needs of the population. However, the deficiency can be overcome by purchase of rice from the surplus States because with millions of dollars received annually from the natives of Kerala working in the Gulf countries, the households which do not produce rice for their needs can afford to buy it through private traders. There is no need for distribution of food through the public distribution system.

(vii) *Western Maharashtra :* The valleys irrigated by canals on the small streams that flow west from the Western Ghats to the Arabian Sea. High yield sugarcane and high yield dwarf rice and coarse grains are the principal crops. There is a large surplus of sugar which is sent to other States. Production of rice and coarse grains is adequate for local needs.

(viii) The area around Nasik which specializes in production of vegetables (including onions, tomatoes and potatoes) and fruit (mosambi, oranges and grapes). Fruit and vegetables are sent to cities in Maharashtra, Gujarat and much of north-western India and also to the Gulf countries mainly to meet the demands of Indians working in these countries. In this area also irrigation by electricity or diesel operated pumps on surface wells or deeper tubewells is well developed and enough grains (rice or sorghum) are produced to meet local needs. The drought prone areas of Maharashtra are those located in the south-west and south-east which had formed earlier of the dominions of the Nizam of Hyderabad or formed part of the former British province of Central Province and Berar.

(viii) *Coastal Gujarat* : Local production of rice and coarse grains (sorghum and millets) is sufficient to meet the needs of the population. There is a surplus of cooking oil. Dairying is another source of income for small farmers, as mentioned earlier.

(x) The drought prone areas of Gujarat are Saurashtra and Kutch and the hilly areas inhabited mainly by tribal. Food for work programmes is needed mainly in years when the monsoon rains are deficient.

(xi) *West Bengal and Assam* : Production of rice is enough to meet the consumption needs of the population including that of the Calcutta Metropolitan District in most years. There could be small deficits in years of deficient rainfall or heavy floods during the monsoon season.

Areas in Need of Food for Work Programme

The areas in need of food for work programmes from time-to-time can be divided into two broad macro-regional classes.

Northern India

Central and Eastern U.P. and North Bihar

(i) In the sub-mountain areas of U.P. and North Bihar large areas of inherently fertile lands are covered every year by coarse sand, pebbles and boulders brought down by the monsoon floods. Production in the rest of the States is not adequate to meet the needs of the population, especially in years of deficient or unseasoned rainfall. The areas can be reclaimed by a combination of afforestation in the hills and land reclamation by tractors or machine tools used by the farmers. Food for work programmes have to be undertaken for varying periods before and in many years even after the monsoon. Sikhs from Punjab, have already reclaimed large areas of such lands in north-west U.P. and established highly productive farms which produce wheat, rice and sugarcane. In West Bengal, the government has assisted reclamation of large areas which used to be destroyed every year by monsoon floods of Teesta River by construction of a dam on the river and reclamation of the lands below it by manual and mechanical means. The reclaimed land have been given to the actual cultivators together with short and medium term loans have been given for buying improved seeds, livestock and fertilizers as needed and pumps for irrigation. Ownership rights have been conferred on actual cultivators and those of the intermediary tenure holders such as *zamindars* have been extinguished. As a result of these reforms, production of rice has increased steadily so much so that the deficit has been eliminated. Production of jute has also increased steadily. The governments of U.P. and Bihar should do the same increasing production of cereals through a combination of soil conservation measures in the hills and reclamation in the plains. The cultivators are hardworking and loans provided by the States to buy current inputs would be returned particularly if they are given by the farmers' cooperatives. Medium-term loans given to buy tractors and electricity or diesel operated pumps to the former *zamindars* to cultivate the land left to them for self cultivation will mean better cultivation of the croplands and major increase in the irrigated area and consequent increase in production of cereals (wheat, rice, maize, gram, pulses and oilseeds). Production of mangoes which can be grown in many areas would add further to the value of agricultural output and income of many farmers.

(ii) *South Western U.P. and adjoining Areas of Madhya Pradesh*: Large areas of otherwise fertile land have been rendered infertile because of wind and water erosion. As a result, large cultivable areas are cut by ravines. There is need for reclamation of the land by construction of small check dams on the ravines so that the areas above the dams can be used as pastures for livestock and those below the dams become available for cultivation. The pastures with soil binding grasses and the foliage of the woodlands will strengthen the dams. Grazing in the pastures and cutting of trees for fuel-wood should be controlled, preferably by the cooperatives of farmers. Exploitation of the farmers by money lenders should be prevented because many small farmers become dacoits when they lose their land while trying to repay loans taken from money lenders.

(iii) *Western and Eastern Himalayan Regions* : In Uttranchal in the west and the seven States populated by tribal in the north-east Himachal Pradesh and Jammu & Kashmir which had large deficits earlier are now self-sufficient in most years due to increase in irrigation, although there might be deficits in some years. The States inhabited by tribal are deficient in foodgrains if the local crop of rice is damaged by floods in the monsoon season. Rice and other foods have to be supplied to the people by road and in isolated areas dropped from the air because these States are not connected with the rest of the country by a railway.

Peninsular India

(i) *Coastal Orissa*: Rice is the main crop. Coarse grains and pulses and oilseeds are planted along or after the rice has been harvested. Production in most of the years is adequate to meet the food needs of the people. However, the area is visited often by cyclones during September to December. As a result, large areas are flooded the rice crop is washed away and tens of thousands are rendered homeless. The government of the State, because of red tape and inefficiency has not been able to organize relief quickly by supplying food, medicines, blankets and building materials so that the marooned people survive and do not fall victims to diseases of the respiratory or digestive tracts while they clear their flooded fields or rebuild their homes.

(ii) *Inland Orissa and Chhattisgarh* : These are among the most backward areas of the country. In inland Orissa, there are few roads which connect the area with the rest of the country. Semi-starvation is chronic because the tribal are very backward and their small fields are often washed away during the monsoon. Additional havoc is caused by the cyclones that visit the area from time-to-time between August and December. Despite financial assistance from the Central Government and special releases of building materials to enable people to rebuild their huts and supply of food and blankets by the international Red Cross to the affected population the government of the State is unable to organize relief for months together. As a result, tens of thousands die or are taken ill for lack of food or shelter and outbreak of disease by easily available diseases. The first priority in this area is to organize disaster relief by the government with financial and technical assistance for the Central Government using the supplies provided by it and international relief agencies. Along with the food for work programmes, campaigns have to be organized to prevent spread of diseases of the respiratory and digestive tracks. After a semblance of normalcy has been restored and before the advent of the next monsoon, improved high yielding seeds of rice, chemical fertilizers and pesticides, ploughs and other tools must be supplied to the cultivators so that they can harvest crops of rice or other grams.

The other areas in need of such programmes are :

(iii) The Jharkhand region of Bihar also inhabited mainly by tribal, a large part of Madhya Pradesh all of which are inhabited by tribal.

(iv) Parts of Telengana region of Andhra Pradesh and north-east region of Karnataka.

(v) *Gujarat*: Saurashtra, Kutch and the hilly areas inhabited mainly by tribal in the north-eastern parts of the State.

(vi) Similar areas in south-west Maharashtra some of which had formed part of the dominion of Nizam of Hyderabad.

Food for work programme have to be undertaken for varying periods in years of deficient rainfall in order to avert starvation in all these areas. However, the need for these programmes would be reduced greatly if the programmes include reafforestation in hills and reclamation of flood affected lands by various soil conservation measures in the plains. The forests which provide fodder, fuel and some food to the tribal should be given for management to the tribal instead of being destroyed by forest and mining contractors. The tribal who have been living in these forests for millennia would ensure that check dams which protect their rice fields are quickly restored after the rains. The tribal population displaced by industrial units such as steel mills and thermal and hydro power plants should be settled quickly in new areas and given grants to rebuild their homes and for cultivation of the lands allotted to them. There is no much dissatisfaction among the tribal who are displaced by construction of industrial unit or power plants. The dissatisfaction is due to two reasons: (i) there are long delays in allocation of land and establishing new villages and farms; and (ii) no loans or grants are given to them to rebuild their huts or to buy seed, fertilizers, livestock and implements to cultivate the land allotted to them. Food for work programmes should be undertaken for them until they are well settled in their new villages. Tribal youth should be given training in industrial skills and educated so that they find jobs of skilled and white collar workers in the numerous industrial units located both in Jharkhand and Madhya Pradesh.

The Desert and Semi-desert Areas of Western Rajasthan

These areas are in need of such programmes in two out of three years. In such years, the local pastures are destroyed and the woodlands in the semi-desert areas become thinner because of over-grazing by cattle, sheep and goats. The people migrate from these areas to greener pastures in eastern Rajasthan and adjoining areas of Madhya Pradesh. In the early stages of the drought, before the monsoon rains, food, fodder and water are sent by the State government by roads to feed the people and their livestock. However, if the rains fail, the pastorlists and their herds leave for several months and return only in the cool season.

As a result of the measures detailed above the areas in need for food for work programmes would be reduced progressively because large areas of formerly eroded land or those covered with coarse sands and boulders would become productive. The nature of food for work programme in various areas is described below.

The Nature of Poverty Alleviation Programmes

The most common programmes are food for work programmes in which balanced food (cereals, sugar, cooking oil and powdered milk) is distributed to the workers employed on works such as construction of approach roads to villages, construction and repair of tanks and digging of wells which would supply water for irrigation and for drinking as part of the wages for work. Balanced food is distributed to women with instructions to prepare liquid milk from powdered milk and to boil the milk before feeding the babies or children or drinking for themselves. Instruction in principles of nutrition, child care and keeping their houses and villages (or slums in metropolitan cities) clean should form an essential part of the programmes.

The cost of food and kerosene distributed through the programme forms part of the wages given to the men working on them. Thus, the programmes not only provide remunerative work to small farmers and landless agricultural labourers but also make them healthier. The completed works increase the productive areas by construction of approach roads and increasing sources of water supply for irrigation and for drinking.

Effect of Land Tenure

It is interesting to note that all the areas detailed above which are not in need of poverty alleviation programmes were with the exception of the areas in Rajasthan not under the intermediary tenure holders such as *zamindars*, *jagirdars*, etc. before independence. The farmers paid their land revenues and were provided services directly by the governments of the provinces and some progressive princely states. On the other hand, all the areas in need of poverty alleviation programmes are those in which the farmers were under intermediary tenure holders. Large areas inhabited by tribal in peninsular India formed part of kingdoms of princelings whose kingdoms were too small to provide them with the revenues that would enable them to invest in economic development of the state. The intermediary tenure holders in the Indo-Gangetic plain States from West Bengal to central and south western U.P. were interested more in exploitation of the tenants than in increasing agriculture output. In most of these areas the rights of intermediary tenure holders have been extinguished on paper but not in fact.

The increase in agricultural output experienced in West Bengal has been due partly to abolition of rights of intermediary tenure holders in fact. The farmers, freed from the obligation to pay a proportion of their income from farming have had a strong incentive to increase agricultural output and their income. The State Government has assisted them by providing the seed capital needed to increase agricultural output. Such reforms have been done on paper in Bihar and U.P. but not in most of the areas in fact. On the contrary, attempts to achieve the reforms in practice are resisted so strongly by the former landlords in Bihar that there is literally a class war between them and their tenants in parts of north Bihar. The State Government while claiming to represent the former tenants is too weak to control the violence of the landlords. Furthermore, it has made little effort to provide through various cooperative institutions of farmers the seed capital for increasing agricultural output. In U.P. the rights of the intermediary tenure holders have been extinguished in fact in many areas, but not in others. Furthermore, the State Government has not provided to the farmers the seed capital to increase agricultural output. Part of the reasons for it is that both States are so large and populous that it is difficult for their governments to maintain law and order. In both States, the rights of intermediary tenure holders must be extinguished first and sub-regional structures must be created below the level of the State governments both for providing peace and security to the citizens as also for providing inputs of improved agriculture.

Increase in agricultural output is hampered in the Telegana area of Andhra Pradesh partly by the conflict between the former *zamindars* and their tenants. Agricultural output would increase rapidly once the State governments effectively enforce the rights of the actual cultivators on the areas cultivated by them. Short and medium-term loans should be given to them to buy improved seed and fertilizers for current cultivation. The former landlords should also be given medium-term loans to buy tractors and install diesel oil or electrically operated pumps on surface wells. The increase in agricultural output experienced in Rajasthan during the last five decades has been due in large part to the policy of the State Government to give loans to both tenants for buying inputs of improved agriculture and installation of diesel oil or electric motors on their surface wells and to the former intermediary tenure holders for buying tractors and diesel or electric pumps to irrigate more effectively the lands allotted to them for self cultivation. Such loans given initially by the State Government are now being given through agricultural credit or nationalized banks. The managers of banks enforce repayment to reduce bad debts and the borrowers repay so that they can continue to get loans. The increase in repayment of principal and interest would minimize the draft on the State.

In the areas inhabited predominantly by tribal, short and medium-term loans should be channelled as far as possible through their own associations. This will result both in appropriate utilization of the loans and their repayment on time. In all areas inhabited by tribal, grants need to be given for building huts and clearing the lands for cultivation when they are visited by cyclones or excessive rains in the monsoon season.

Similar grants should be given to assist resettlement of the tribal displaced from their traditional homes for construction of industrial units and thermal or hydro electric power projects. As mentioned earlier, there is much dissatisfaction among the tribal who are displaced.

Conclusion

The foregoing sections have indicated that through appropriate soil conservation and reclamation measures, construction of approach roads, improvement of water supplies and providing advice and loans or grants to small farmers, the areas which are in need of such programmes will be greatly reduced. The latest data available from the National Sample Survey indicate that the proportion of the population which is poor and in need of such programmes has gone down appreciably during the last decade from 36 per cent in 1993-94 to 26 per cent by 1999-2000. The decline is being attributed to trickledown effect of rapid economic growth experienced during the 1990s. Another decade of such growth with welfare should result in further reduction in the proportion of such population.

The planners of the food for work programmes should appreciate that some of the most productive areas located both in north India and in peninsular India were in need of food for work programmes not so long ago. Hence, special emphasis should be given in these programmes to land reclamation, soil conservation and soil upgradation measures so that more and more people are employed in the areas concerned as farmers and as agricultural labourers and the need for such programmes is progressively reduced.

REFERENCES

Bhalla, Surjit S., Crying Wolf Over Proverty. *Economic and Political Weekly*, Vol. XXXVIII, No. 27, 2003.

Dandekar, V.M. and Rath, N., *Poverty in India,* Institute of Political and Social Studies, Pune.

Krishna Anirudh, Falling in Poverty, *Economic and Political Weekly*, Vol. XXXVIII, No. 6, 2003.

8

Integrated Rural and Urban Development

*A Strategy for Spatial Development in India**

Introduction

The principal argument given by the author in this chapter is that integrated rural and urban development should be the centrepiece of the national spatial development strategy and that the strategy should be supported by appropriate policies, programmes and resource allocations under the Five Year Plans. It is explained that the perception of competition between rural and urban development, which has dominated national planning since its inception in the 1950s, however relevant it may have been in the past, is no longer relevant. Persistence of this perception and its consequent policies and resource allocations in successive Five-Year Plans has resulted in giving high priority to rural development and relative neglect of urban development.

The chapter presents the policy background to the argument, describes the principal types of rural-urban interactions, their positive and negative effects, the areas of high interaction, the principal factors contributing to increase in rural-urban interaction, the probable effects of rural-urban interaction and more economic growth than during the 1965-90 era resulting from successful implementation of the economic liberalization policies initiated in July 1991. At the end the author gives a number of recommendations.

The Policy Background

The high priority for rural development is reflected in policy statements and resource allocations in previous Five-Year Plans, manifestoes of

---

* Paper presented at the Fourth Asian Urbanization Conference, Taiwan and printed in the *Proceeding of Fourth Asian Urbanization Conference*, Taiwan, January 1994.

political parties and pronouncements of political leaders. Its latest manifestation was in the paper "Approach to the Eighth Five-Year Plan," prepared by the Planning Commission in May 1990, under the aegis of Janata Party Government, headed by Shri V.P. Singh. It was stated in the paper :

The new mandate rightly stresses the need to correct these distortions and to reorient development policy in such a way that it gives primacy to the immediate and urgent needs of the poor-reserving at least half the public outlays for the benefit of rural areas, and emphasis on village and small scale industries to produce goods and services for mass consumption using labour intensive techniques, reflect these concerns (Planning Commission, 1989 : 5).

It is true that only about one-fourth of India's total population, 23.3 per cent in 1981 and 25.7 per cent in 1991, is urban and that proportion would still be less than 30 per cent even by the end of the century (Table 8.1).

However, more than 70 per cent of the GDP is estimated to be produced in the non-agricultural sectors which are concentrated in urban areas (Planning Commission, 1992, Vol. 1: 54). Mohan has estimated that in 1980-81 the urban population contributed 46.9 per cent of total output to the economy and the rural-urban ratio of value added per worker has increased progressively from 1 : 2.7 in 1970-71 to 1 : 3.34 by 1994-95 (Mohan, 1985 : 637-39). Furthermore, the poor are not confined to the rural areas as Dandekar and Rath concluded in their pioneering and seminal study *Poverty in India.* They found that 30 per cent of the rural population was below the poverty line in 1961-62 but almost half of the urban, population was also (Dandekar and Rath, 1971 : 9 and 11).

It may be expected that the election manifestoes of political parties would emphasize the need for high priority to rural development. The rural areas, with 75 per cent of the population, have the votes which the parties need for being successful in the elections. The emphasis was justified also in the early 1950s when a large proportion of the villages did not have basic services such as approach roads, primary schools, access to health centres, and even adequate water supply facilities. Agriculture was traditional and productivity per worker and per hectare was low. The villagers felt isolated and neglected. However, it is not justified in the 1990s when the basic services mentioned above, are available to most of the villages. As a result of various agricultural development programmes implemented during the previous 4 decades, agricultural production has increased by more than 3 times its level in the early 1950s, with most of the increase coming from increase in productivity. Progress in rural development may be expected to continue in the foreseeable future and could accelerate faster with more efficient implementation of rural development programmes. The emphasis should now be shifted to urban development, neglect of which has two major effects. First, it reduces productivity per urban worker which could be one of the reasons depressing national economic growth. Second, it deprives the rural areas of further progress provided by interaction with the urban areas.

India had a comparatively low rate of increase in GNP per capita (1.9% p.a.) during 1965-90, less than one-third of the rate in China (5.8% p.a.), lower than rates in Pakistan (2.5%) and Sri Lanka (2.9%) and much lower than the rates in the ASEAN countries. Despite India's potential for rapid economic growth because of its wide variety of natural and human resources, the lower rate of GNP could be due, in part, to low productivity of urban workers (Table 8.2).

Large cities with a population of a million or more suffer most from relative neglect of urban development because shortages of housing and of physical and social infrastructures are acute in them. Furthermore, large proportions of their populations are poor and endure conditions of extreme hardship while living in slums and are using grossly inadequate services, ranging from water supply and sanitation to education and health care. There were 23 million-plus cities in 1991: they made up almost one-third of the urban population and more than 8.0 per cent of the total population of the country (Table 8.1). Their number is projected to increase to 39 in 2001 by the National Commission on Urbanization (NCU, 1988: Vol. II, 40-41) and their share of the urban and total population of the country would also increase.

The perception of competition between rural and urban development should change such that rural and urban areas should be viewed as inter-related parts of a settlement system, which should be developed in an integrated manner. This point will be clearer from the discussion in the next section in which the principal types of rural-urban interaction are described along with their positive and negative effects. It should be added that among the 15 major States of the country, the interactions are greater in the States of Punjab, Haryana, Maharashtra, Gujarat, Karnataka, Tamil Nadu and Kerala and the western region of U.P. in which there is a spatially dispersed pattern of urbanization *i.e.* there is a large number of small and medium-sized towns and cities along with one or more metropolitan cities. The effects are much less in the States of Eastern and Central India, notably Bihar, Orissa, West Bengal and Assam and the eastern and central regions of U.P. and Madhya Pradesh. These States-regions have a concentrated pattern of urbanization *i.e.,* their urban population is concentrated in a few large cities and the number of small and medium-sized towns/cities is relatively small.

Table 8.1: India: Trends in Total and Urban Population and Population of Cities, 1951-2001

	1951	1961	1971	1981	1991 (provisional)	2001 (projected)
Total population (million)	361.0	439.2	548.2	683.3	844.3	1029.0
Urban population (million)	62.4	78.9	109.1	159.5	217.2	294.0
Urban/Total population (per cent)	17.3	18.0	19.9	23.3	25.7	28.6
Annual exponential growth rate of urban population (per cent)	3.47	2.34	3.21	3.83	3.09	3.09
Population of cities (million)	27.5	39.9	61.2	94.5	138.8	n.a.
Urban population living in cities (per cent)	44.0	50.6	56.1	59.2	63.9	n.a.
Number of million-plus cities	5	6	9	12	23	39
Population of million-plus cities (millions)	11.7	17.9	27.4	42.1	70.6	n.a.
Proportion of population of million-plus cities to:						
(a) Urban population	17.8	22.6	25.1	26.4	32.5	n.a.
(b) Total population	3.2	4.1	5.0	6.2	8.4	n.a.

Source: 1. Registrar General and Census Commissioner, India: 1991. Percentages have been calculated.

It will be seen that in the States with dispersed urbanization the percentage of urban to total population, is higher than the national average in the majority of districts. On the other hand in States with concentrated urbanization the percentage is lower than the national average in the majority of districts. The best example of concentrated urbanization is West Bengal: almost all its urban population is concentrated in the districts of Calcutta, Howrah, and Hooghly which form part of the Calcutta Metropolitan District and those adjoining CMD while the rest of the State is largely rural.

It can be seen that States with dispersed urbanization are generally at a higher level of economic development than those with concentrated urbanization. The level of economic development of a region is dependent on a complex of factors. It would be useful to investigate if the type of settlement pattern is one of these factors.

Principal Rural-Urban Socio-Economic Interactions

The principal types of interaction are listed below and are discussed at some length in subsequent paragraphs :

- (i) use by villagers of commercial, industrial, social service and recreational facilities located in cities and towns;
- (ii) work in cities and towns by villagers living within commuting distance of them and use of such villages as dormitories by workers in the cities. Travel between rural homes and urban work places could be on foot, by bicycle, motorcycle, bus or train;
- (iii) production by villagers of food including high value perishable foods—milk, vegetables, meat, poultry products, fruit etc.—for urban markets;
- (iv) diversion of agricultural and other rural lands, located on fringes of cities for residential, industrial, commercial or other urban uses. The diversion is greatest on the periphery of large, rapidly growing cities where hundreds of hectares have been diverted to non-agricultural use and other large areas, which have been bought by developers or others for speculative gains, are lying idle;
- (v) rural to urban migration.

(i) *Use by villagers of commercial, industrial, social service and recreational facilities located in cities and towns* : The villagers go to urban places in order to sell their produce, to buy consumer, intermediate or producer goods, to obtain short or medium-term loans from cooperative or commercial banks or to obtain the other services mentioned above. With progressive modernization of the rural economy as a result of improvement in transport and communications, almost universal electrification, spread of modern production techniques there is the rise of a rural middle class, which wants a high standard of living. The consumer goods include increasing number of motor bicycles, television sets, VCRs, gas cookers, refrigerators, air coolers and other durables. The intermediate goods include agricultural inputs, such as improved seeds, chemical fertilizers, pesticides, fuel and spare parts for power driven equipment, cement, steel bars or corrugated iron sheets, needed for construction, repair or renovation of houses and other structures. The producer goods include both traditional, manually operated agricultural implements, such as ploughs as well as power driven equipment, such as tractors, threshers, and diesel or electricity driven pumps for irrigation.

One would expect that villagers would use the commercial and other service facilities located in small or medium-sized towns which are nearest to them. Based on this assumption, Johnson advocated in 1965 building some 10,000 to 12,000 new, small, market towns particularly in States or regions such as Bihar, Orissa, eastern Uttar Pradesh, and eastern Madhya Pradesh, in which the number of such towns was inadequate, as the most important component of the spatial development strategy for India (Johnson, 1965 : 6-15). It is fortunate that no action was taken on the recommendation because its implementation would have meant a colossal waste of scarce public and private resources of finance, manpower and management.

The principal reasons for this reflection in retrospect are the following:

(a) most of the artificially built towns would have failed to grow as service centres; Growth of a town is a natural process, which is determined by a large number of variables, several of which cannot be foreseen;

(b) with improvement in transport and communications, spread of information about prices and concentration of the marketable surplus with larger, more affluent farmers, there is a strong trend among them towards using the marketing and agro-processing facilities of larger market towns, most of which are located at district or divisional headquarters. As regards use of social service facilities, particularly facilities for medical or surgical treatment, villagers with even medium income use the facilities of hospitals, located in State capitals and in mega-cities like Delhi, Bombay, Madras and Calcutta.

The author does not differ, however, with Johnson's emphasis on the need for intermediate urbanization in order to relieve the growth pressure on cities (Johnson, 1965: 11-13). The strategy is also favoured by the Planning Commission in the Eighth Five Year Plan (Planning Commission 1992, Vol. II: 345 and 354-55) and other experts and policy makers (Lewis, 1972: 167-205; National Capital Region Planning Board, 1988 : 18). His main difference is with Johnson's advocacy of building small market towns with population of 5,000-20,000. He feels, along with several others, that the towns or cities, which would serve as effective counter magnets to large metropolitan cities, need to be much larger. Using the data of the 1961 Census, Lewis had indicated a population range of 100,000-300,000 (Lewis, 1962 : 195-97). The Regional Plan NCR 2001 (NCRPB, 1988) implies increasing the population to almost one million. Meerut, which has been selected in the Plan as one of the 8 priority towns for deflecting population from Delhi had a population of almost 850,000 in 1991 and would have a population exceeding one million by 2001. This author would, therefore, emphasize :

(a) assisting growth of existing towns or cities rather than building new towns, and
(b) flexibility in selection of population range of the small and medium sized towns/cities, having in view the regional diversity in topography, climate, soil, population density and other conditions and the sizes of the existing towns/cities.

(ii) *Work by villagers in cities and towns living within commuting distance from them*: Such work increases employment and income thus providing relief from rural unemployment or under-employment and poverty, diversifies consumption among rural households and is also a strong influence for social change. Both, workers from poor landless and artisan families, belonging mainly to the scheduled castes, the scheduled tribes and other disadvantaged sections of rural community, including young men from farmers' families who are not needed for agricultural work or are disinclined towards it, are benefited (Tyagi, 1982 : 157-60). There is less pressure for rural to urban migration because rural living and urban work can be combined and there is less need for expanding housing and infrastructure facilities in the cities. The social change effects are produced by spread of urban consumption patterns and weakening of traditional ties of caste and community: they include reduction in disabilities suffered by the scheduled castes and the scheduled tribes.

Basu and Kashyap have noted a progressive increase in rural non-agricultural employment, based on the data of the Census of India 1981 and of the National Sample Survey. They mention that the share of non-agricultural workers in the rural work force increased from 14.3 per cent in 1961 to 18.6 per cent in 1983. Furthermore, based on their own micro-level studies in 24 regions of India with different agricultural typologies they give details about rural workers in small and medium sized towns (Basu and Kashyap, 1992: A-178 and A-184).

The beneficial economic effects of non-agricultural work by farmers were observed also in a sample survey of farm households located near a small town in Kenya, about 100 km. north-east of Nairobi (Evans and Ngua, 1991: 519-45). Another important finding of the study was that higher and more diversified income, resulting from non-agricultural employment, assisted the farmers in increasing agricultural productivity (per hectare and per worker) by adopting new, improved production practices. With such income, they could take the risks involved in the adoption of improved techniques, which farmers dependent on agricultural income alone were unwilling or unable to take.

(iii) *Increasing production of perishable foods* benefits both farmers and other groups in the villages; it leads also to the establishment of backward or forward-linked industries in major production centres. Production and sale of milk by small, marginal farmers or the landless who keep one or two milk animals, has been an important component of dairy development in Khera district of Gujarat where the well known Amul dairy is located. It is being actively encouraged now by the central government as well as by several State governments under the "Operation Flood" Programme. It may be mentioned that the majority of milk producers in Khera district are women. Payment by the dairy for the milk sold by them, adds to their income, which they can spend on meeting their own needs and those of their children. Furthermore, the payments raise their own status within the household. Production of poultry products, traditionally an activity of scheduled castes and scheduled tribes, has developed during the last four decades into a highly specialized and efficient small industry. Modern poultry farms have been established both near and within metropolitan areas of large cities and at various specialized centres. Production of fruit, which had been an industry with traditional well established centres of production has increased in most of them and has also spread to new centres. The forward linkage industries, such as canning of fruit and vegetables or manufacture of crates and cartons for sending them to markets, and production of butter cheese and powdered milk in the major milk producing regions, generate considerable employment, which is an important spin-off from the production.

There is a great potential for further increase in production of perishable foods for both domestic and international markets. The "Operation Flood" Programme, under which pasteurized milk with specified fat contents is being supplied to the majority of residents of large cities, is an example of the potential for increasing production in the domestic market. Production in the highly competitive international markets is increasing, concentrating on products like mangoes or tropical vegetables in which India has an advantage.

(iv) *Diversion of rural land located on the outskirts of cities for urban uses* has both positive and negative effects. If the land is acquired from small, marginal farmers at low prices and payment of compensation to them is delayed, they become landless and have to work as labourers on construction projects or as domestic servants in the homes of skilled workers, professionals and managers in the new industrial or commercial enterprises. These effects have been noticed in the New Bombay Area (Banerjee-Guha, 1991) and on a much larger scale in the vicinity of the industrial townships located next to the steel and heavy industry plants in the central and eastern States of India—Madhya Pradesh, Bihar, Orissa, West Bengal and Andhra Pradesh. Furthermore, the dispossessed former land-owners, who belong mainly to the scheduled tribes, suffer loss of social status and self esteem. These effects are the principal cause of discontent among the tribal populations of these States and tensions, which frequently erupted in violent conflict, between them and the new comers.

If payment of compensation is timely and adequate (or generous) and is used by the recipients in buying farmland elsewhere, starting non-agricultural enterprises, such as running of buses or trucks, small industries or retail or wholesale shops, education of children, their income increases and level of living improves. These beneficial effects are lost, however, if the funds are squandered in idleness, ostentatious consumption such as large expenditures on marriages, funerals, or other ceremonies, fighting elections or court cases, buying of expensive consumer goods, or in drinking and use of drugs (Tyagi, 1982: 45; Bose, 1972: 190-92). Furthermore, the lands are often kept out of cultivation for long periods, awaiting development of new residential colonies, establishment of factories, markets or training institutions, or for speculative gains by unscrupulous buyers. Finally, the habitation areas of the villages are often reduced to ghettos within the expanding cities, although most of the houses in them are converted from *kutcha* (built of mud and thatch) to *pucca* (built of kiln-baked bricks and mortar) and have electricity, running water and other services (Tyagi, 1982: 46-47).

(v) *Rural to urban migration* reduces under-employment or unemployment in the villages and increases income there through remittances by the migrants to their families. On the other hand, the villagers are deprived of their most productive and dynamic manpower because most of the migrants are young men and women who aspire for more secure and higher income and a better life in the cities than in the villages. Although these aspirations are fulfilled only for a minority and the majority of the migrants can get uncertain, low paid employment in the informal sector of the cities and have to live in squalor and misery in their slums, the possible advantages of migration is enough to induce a steady stream of migrants to the cities. Furthermore, most of them are not seasonal migrants, they go to live in the cities through most of their working life and return to their villages only at the end.

Variations in the number of migrants from year to year depends both on variations in employment opportunities in the cities and economic conditions in the villages. Thus, there would be large migration to a city during the period of its rapid growth due to industrial or other developments. Alternatively, scarcity or famine caused by crop failure, due to drought, floods or other reasons, in a rural region, is generally followed by a large emigration from it (Rao, R.N., 1990 : 24-28).

Migration to large cities at present is and that of the tea gardens of Assam or overseas in the last century, was predominantly from poor and backward districts of eastern U.P., Bihar, Orissa, coastal Andhra Pradesh and Tamil Nadu. The economies of some districts in these regions are often called remittance economies because remittances from migrants are the largest source of income there. However, the fact that the regions have remained backward and poor, despite more than a century of emigration, would indicate that the negative effects of migration has been dominant in these areas.

Migration to the Gulf countries from Kerala, Goa and neighbouring districts of Karnataka from the late 1960s to the 1980s, or of Punjab Sikhs to the UK and the USA in the post-war period, are in a different category altogether. In these cases, the migrant and the areas of emigration and in-migration have all benefited. A study of migration of Punjab Sikhs to Britain brought out the following :

(a) The migrants were mostly industrial workers, who lived in extremely congested houses in British cities and suffered considerable hardship. But their children quickly moved, after education, to well-paid white collar, skilled or professional jobs or started their own small retail stores or other business.

(b) The hard work of the migrants at low wages, contributed to Britain's rapid economic growth during the 1950s and the 1960s.

(c) Remittances from the migrants to their families in Punjab had a major share in investment in the improvement of agriculture that sparked the green revolution in the State (Helweg, 1986: 376-86).

How the migrants make out in the areas of in-migration depends on their background, skills and aspirations. The great majority of Punjab Sikhs who migrated to Britain were peasant proprietors eking out a subsistence living in their home districts. They migrated to Britain in search of prosperity and had, therefore, a strong motivation to educate their children and equip them for white collar jobs so that they would not have to endure the hardship of doing heavy manual labour for long hours in factories and living in crowded rooms that they themselves had to endure. It is not surprising, therefore, that their children moved quickly after education to white collar jobs.

Another example is provided by migrants to Delhi in the period before 1961 and the two decades, 1961-71 and 1971-81 for which data are available from the Regional Plan 2001, National Capital Region (Table 8.3). The proportion from Punjab declined during the period from 16.8 to 6.4 per cent and in Haryana from 22.1 to 12.9 per cent. The proportion of migrants from U.P., on the other hand, increased from 41.7 to 50.1 per cent (Table 8.3). The present migrants from Punjab and Haryana are well equipped for finding remunerative jobs in the city and adapting themselves to urban values and patterns of living. Most of them work as carpenters, masons, electricians, repairmen for electric or electronic appliances, drivers of motor vehicles or as skilled workers in factories. They live in well built brick and mortar houses which have facilities with running water, electricity and surface drainage, although they are located in unauthorized colonies. Most of the migrants from U.P., on the other hand, lack such skills. They come from backward and poor districts of central and eastern U.P. and work in low wage jobs as domestic servants, gardeners, watchmen, messengers etc. Most of them live in slums, which lack the facilities mentioned above. Furthermore, their poorly built dwellings are subject to burning up in Delhi's hot summer or to suffer severe damage in its frequent dust or thunderstorms (Nath, 1993).

Areas of High Rural-Urban Interaction

The areas can be divided into two categories :

(i) *Villages* located within daily commuting distance of cities, particularly large cities;

(ii) *Rural Corridors* where a number of towns and cities are located within a short distance of one another and the intervening villages are being progressively urbanized. The corridors can be delineated roughly on the map showing districts with higher percentages or urban/total population than the national average in 1991. A more precise delineation will become possible when similar figures are published by the Registrar General and Census Commissioner of India for sub-divisions of districts. The following four corridors are well developed already; others are developing and could be called 'incipient'.

Well Developed Corridors

(a) *Coastal Gujarat-Maharashtra* : from Ahmedabad through Vadodra and Surat in Gujarat to Bombay and from Bombay to Pune;

(b) *Coastal Kerala-Karnataka* : from Trivandrum in Kerala to Mangalore in Karnataka, along the west coast of India;

(c) *Punjab-Haryana-western Uttar Pradesh* : from Amritsar Punjab through Haryana to Delhi with spurs going from Delhi, south of Faridabad, west to Gurgaon in Haryana and east-north-east through Ghaziabad and Meerut to Dehra Dun and Bareilly in U.P.; and

(d) *Bihar-West Bengal* : from Dhanbad in Bihar through Asansol, Bardhaman and Bandel to the Calcutta Urban Agglomeration in West Bengal.

Incipient Corridors

The more important incipient corridors are the following :

(a) from Bombay eastward to Nagpur and Chandrapur in Maharashtra;

(b) from Bangalore in Karnataka to Madras in Tamil Nadu;

(c) from Madras west to Coimbatore and south-west to Tiruchirapalli and Madurai in Tamil Nadu;

(d) from Mangalore on the coast of Karnataka east to Vijayawada in Andhra Pradesh, and

(e) from Kanpur to Lucknow in central Uttar Pradesh.

The corridors have developed mainly during the four decades from 1951-91; the principal factors in their development have been the following:

(i) improvement in transport and communications, particularly expansion of highways and feeder roads;
(ii) establishment of new large and small industrial enterprises; and
(iii) modernization of agriculture, near universal rural electrification and subsequent expansion of irrigation by electric pumps which has been a major factor in the modernization.

There is a trend toward the extension of most of the corridors and development of new ones. Thus the coastal Gujarat-Maharashtra corridor is extending at its northern end to include most of former Saurashtra region of Gujarat and at its southern end from Pune to Kolhapur in Maharashtra, Tamil Nadu and Kerala, and could extend in the not distant future to south central Karnataka. The Gujarat-Maharashtra corridor could extend, similarly, to include a large part of Western Maharashtra. The hilly or dry districts within these two sub-regions would then appear as less urbanized, less developed pockets.

Principal Factors contributing to Increase in Rural-Urban Interaction

The most important factors some of which are inter-related are the following:

(i) Rapid urbanization.
(ii) Growth of modern manufacturing industries and service activities and their concentration in and around large cities.
(iii) Improvement in transport and communication leading to increasing travel and transport of goods between villages and urban places by villagers on the one hand and by workers in the urban-based industries and service activities on the other.
(iv) Technological advance in agriculture, leading to increase in agricultural output including output of perishable foods for urban markets. The increase had been aided by the agricultural extension and related Programmes and extension of irrigation through rapid increase in number of electrified wells and tube-wells as well as by extension of canals.
(v) Spread of information through the news and entertainment media—newspapers, magazines, radio and television.

The Prospect : Probable Effects of Economic Liberalization Policies

The prospect for the foreseeable future is for a progressive increase in the range and magnitude of rural-urban interactions. The more important factors contributing to it were listed earlier. The increase would be faster than otherwise, if with successful implementation of the economic liberalization policies, initiated in July 1991, the rate of economic growth increased significantly from the average of 5.3 per cent per annum achieved during 1980-90 (Table 8.2). There would be rapid expansion of modern manufacturing industries and service sector activities. They would be located, as at present, principally in and around large cities and rurban corridors. Their concentration in these locations could be reduced if small or medium sized factories manufacturing components for electrical or electrical appliances, bicycles, motor vehicles etc., were located in other regions also.

Table 8.2 : Growth Rates of GDP and GNP Per Capita in India, China and Selected Countries of South and South-East Asia, 1965-90.

(Per cent per annum)

Country	*Growth Rates*			
	GDP		*GNP Per Capita (U.S. $)*	
	1965-80	1980-90	1990	1965-90
India	3.6	5.3	350	1.9
China	6.8	9.5	370	5.8
Pakistan	5.2	6.3	380	2.5
Sri Lanka	4.0	4.0	470	2.9
Philippines	5.7	0.9	710	1.3
Thailand	7.3	7.6	1,420	4.4
Indonesia	7.0	5.5	570	4.5
Malaysia	7.4	5.2	2,320	4.0
Singapore	10.0	6.4	11,160	6.5

Types of Economy	*GNP per capita in 1990*
Low income	less than $ 610
Middle income	$ 611 – 7619
High income	$ 7620 or more

Source : World Bank, 1992 : 218.

An increasing proportion of the work force, for industry, could be drawn from the neighbouring villages, with the spread of the needed skills among the villagers. This will reduce the pressure of migration from villages to large cities. The pressure would be reduced further, if with improvement of transport and communications, the satellite towns and villages at the periphery of large cities were used as dormitories by workers in the cities much more than at present.

Rapid economic growth would result also in significant reduction in rural and urban poverty, if it is accompanied by an enlightened policy on distribution of its benefits. Two other results would be: (i) increase in size of the middle class, estimated currently at almost 200 million; and (ii) rapid increase in consumption of manufactured consumer goods including consumer durables and perishable foods by both the rural and urban populations. Expansion/improvement of physical and social infrastructures would be more rapid and their operation would be more efficient as private sector resources of finance and management become available to supplement those of the public sector. Generation and distribution of electricity, telecommunications, and construction of highways and operation of passenger road transport are examples of services which are suitable for private sector participation because their output can be priced at levels which would attract participation.

Table 8.3 : Migrants to Delhi by States of their Origin

State	*Before 1961*	*1961-71*	*1971-81*	*Period not known*	*Total*
Haryana	98324 (22.1)	85945 (16.4)	159028 (12.9)	14412	357709 (15.5)
Madhya Pradesh	5585 (1.2)	8860 (1.7)	37709 (3.1)	2496	54650 (2.4)
Punjab	74944 (16.8)	59503 (11.3)	78671 (6.4)	11447	224565 (9.8)
Rajasthan	33341 (7.5)	39885 (7.6)	93936 (7.6)	7603	174665 (7.6)
Uttar Pradesh	185550 (41.7)	260748 (49.6)	616021 (50.1)	54362	1107681 (48.2)
Others (including outside India)	47311 (10.7)	70368 (13.4)	244480 (19.9)	17823	379982 (16.5)
Total	445055 (100.0)	525309 (100.0)	1229745 (100.0)	99143	2299252 (100.0)

Note: Figures in brackets indicate per cent to the respective totals.

Source: National Capital Region Planning Board, Ministry of Urban Development, Government of India: Regional Plan 2001, National Capital Region 1988: p. 138.

Recommendations

Programmes for Progress towards Integrated Rural and Urban Development

The most important Programmes are listed and discussed briefly below:

1. Expansion and improvement of transport infrastructures,

particularly highways and feeder roads. Particular attention should be given to building and maintaining efficient all-weather motorable roads in the central and eastern States where the current network of roads is inadequate and large numbers of villages and small towns remain cut off from the outside world for short or long periods during the rainy season.

2. Improvement of telecommunications by exploiting aggressively the rapid advances in technology that have occurred during the last two decades and still continuing. The objectives should be:

   (i) to provide a telephone within one km. of every village,*

   (ii) to extend progressively to all cities facilities like subscriber trunk dialling (STD), telex and telefax that is available at present only in large cities.

3. Implementing a massive education Programme with the following objectives :

   (i) achievement of functional literacy among all adults by the end of the century (2000);

   (ii) rapid diffusion of marketable skills—technical/ vocational; and managerial—among both rural and urban youth, and

   (iii) multi-faceted social education, which would maximize the positive and minimize the negative effects of rural-urban interaction. Particular emphasis should be given in the Programme to women with suitable changes in its content to meet their particular needs. The Programme for them should have an adequate content of education in home-making, nutrition and child care and prevention of endemic and epidemic diseases. It should also aim at reducing the ignorance of and prejudice against members of other castes and communities.

4. Policies and Programmes aimed at achieving decentralized industrial development. They should be concentrated in the first few years in relatively developed regions, particularly peripheral regions of large cities and rurban corridors. Their extension to other regions, slow at first, should gather momentum progressively in step with improvement in transport and telecommunications and diffusion of marketable skill

---

* The spread of use of call phones since 1994 (Since the author wrote this paper) has reduced the need for provision of landline telephone facilities.

among their people. This strategy of step-by-step development would contribute greatly to the success of the Programmes and minimize their cost to the economy.

5. Increasing production of high value perishable foods and of industries processing them for both the domestic and international markets. This should be an important activity of the Ministries of Food and Agriculture of the Central and State governments. Near universal rural electrification is a major advantage in such expansion. It aids decentralized industrial development also. However, a concerted effort needs to be made to improve supply of electricity by ending the present frequent and prolonged outages of supply and large fluctuations of voltage. The reasons for these deficiencies and the remedial steps needed to correct them have been detailed in reports of the World Bank and other consultants. Significant reduction in the deficiencies would be of great benefit to farmers and small industrial entrepreneurs, because it would save them the high costs of generation of electricity by diesel-operated motors.

6. *Institutional Cooperation*: The legislation for establishment of the institutions for rural development and administration on the one hand and urban local bodies on the other should specify the pattern of interaction between them. In particular, it is necessary to insure that:
   (i) there is no conflict of jurisdiction between the two sets of institutions at the urban fringe relating particularly to diversion of rural lands for residential, industrial, or other non-agricultural uses, and
   (ii) there is adequate and effective cross-representation between the two sets of institutions. Thus the *Zilla Parishads* and *Panchayat Samitis*—elected institutions for rural development and administration at the levels of the district and community development blocks respectively—should have representatives of municipalities located within their areas and the municipalities, should, in their turn, have representatives of the above institutions, as also of market committees, cooperatives and rural banks. The cross-representation will assist greatly in achieving integrated rural and urban development.

7. *Micro-regional Plans*: Preparation of micro-regional plans can be a useful tool for progress towards integrated rural and urban

development. Through them the common problems of rural and urban areas such as unemployment, poverty and deficiency of physical and social infrastructures can be identified and steps taken to alleviate them. Furthermore, policies and programmes can be formulated and implemented for development and conservation of natural resources such as water. The most suitable aerial units for preparation of micro-regional plans are districts and metropolitan areas of large cities.

The Constitutional (Seventy Fourth Amendment) Act 1992 on Municipal Bodies, which was passed by the Parliament in that year but became effective in April 1993, marks a significant advance in this direction by including provisions for preparation of plans for both districts and metropolitan areas. An extract from the Act is given in the Annexure to this chapter. Through it, the State governments are directed to constitute Planning Committees for every district and metropolitan area of the country and to prepare development plans for them; it specifies also the constitution of the committees and the content of the plans. The common interests of rural and urban areas have to be taken into consideration in constituting the committees and the content of the development plans. Both the district and metropolitan planning committees would have as their members, representatives of Panchayats and the municipal bodies. The common interests include spatial planning, sharing of water and other physical and natural resources, the integrated development of infrastructure, environmental conservation and availability of financial and other resources.

District Development Plans : There were about 450 districts in the country according to the Population Census of 1991. Despite the provisions of the Act, simultaneous preparation of development plans for all of them would not be feasible in our view: the funds, and professional personnel, needed for preparation of high quality plans, which keep in view the particular natural and human resources, economic conditions, needs and problems of every district would not be available. Such plans should, therefore, be prepared initially for a limited number of districts and the process should be extended in a phased manner so as to achieve complete coverage of all districts over a period of years. The phasing would ensure that preparation of district plans does not become a routine activity of district level officials and people's representatives, as some earlier attempts at district planning became.

Metropolitan Plans : This limitation does not apply, however, to preparation of metropolitan plans. From the definition of a metropolitan area given in the Act, it is clear that the metropolitan areas of the 23 million-plus cities would be covered. In fact, metropolitan plans have already been prepared for all these cities by Development Authorities (DA's) established by the State Governments. The aerial units for preparation of most of the plans are rather large and include the core cities, their satellite towns/cities besides rural areas. In case of Delhi, a much larger region—The National Capital Region—was designated in 1985 and a planning board was established to prepare a regional plan for it. The plan was prepared by the Board in 1988 and became effective in January 1989. This plan provides the global envelope for preparation of plans of the towns/cities included within the region. Thus, the Second Master Plan of Delhi which covers only the Territory of Delhi and had been prepared by the Delhi Development Authority (DDA) in 1985 was not accepted by the Central Government, which directed the DDA to revise plan to conform to the objectives, strategy, policies, and programmes of the Regional Plan. The revised plan was prepared in 1990 and was immediately accepted and enforced.

As a result of the Act, the States would need to replace the DA's by Metropolitan Planning Committees (MPC's) constituted, as specified in the Act. The principal difference between the two bodies would be that while the DA's are non-statutory bodies and consist entirely (or mainly) of officials, the MPC's would be statutory bodies consisting largely of elected representatives of municipalities and *Panchayats* within a metropolitan area. Secondly, the existing metropolitan plans would need to be revised so as to reflect the views of the MPC's. In addition to the functions specified in the Act for the district and metropolitan development plans, they should give special attention to reducing unemployment and poverty, particularly in the rural areas. This will reduce pressure of migration from villages to towns and cities and from small towns to metropolitan cities.

8. *Need for a national policy on settlements :* There is an urgent need for a national policy on settlements. It should be evolved keeping in view the following :

   (i) demographic, economic and politico-administrative changes of the past four decades and the prospect for further changes during the foreseeable future;

(ii) present and emerging relationships among settlements of different sizes. They include relationships between small or medium-sized service centre towns and the villages served by them, as also among cities and towns of different sizes, and

(iii) realistic acceptance and likelihood of continued concentration of modern manufacturing industries and service activities in large and medium-sized cities, despite the policies of the central and State governments, pursued since the mid-1950s, which discourage such concentration and strongly favour decentralized industrial and economic development.

REFERENCES

Banerjee-Guha, S: Bombay Urban Development Project—A Solution for the Shelter Problem of the Urban Poor? Paper presented at the Third International Conference on Asian Urbanization, New Delhi, 1991 (mimeo).

Basu, D.N. and Kashyap, S.P.: Rural Non-Agricultural Employment in India—Role of Development Process and Rural-Urban Employment Linkages. *Economic and Political Weekly*, Bombay. Vol. XXVII. Nos. 51 and 52. December 19-26, 1992.

Bose, A: *Studies in India's Urbanization 1901-71*. Tata McGraw Hill Publishing Co. Ltd., Bombay and New Delhi, 1973.

Dandekar, V.M. and Rath, N.: *Poverty in India*. Indian School of Political Economy, Bombay, 1971.

Evans, H.E. and Ngau, P.: Rural-Urban Relations, Household Income Diversification and Agricultural Productivity. *Development and Change*, London, Vol. 22.

Helweg, E.W.: Indians in Britain: A Study of the International Relationships of Sending, Receiving and Migrant Societies; in Rao, M.A.S.(ed): *Studies in Migration*. Manohar Publications, New Delhi, 1980.

Johnson, E.A.J. : *Market Towns and Spatial Development in India*. National Council of Applied Economic Research, New Delhi 1965.

Lewis, J.P: *Quiet Crisis in India*. The Brookings Institution, Washington D.C. 1962.

Mohan, R.: Urbanization in India's Future. *Population and Development Review*, New York, Vol. 11. No. 4 (December 1985).

Nath, V. : The Changing Face of a South Delhi Residential Colony, *Urban India*, Vol. xx, No. 1 (2000). The observations are based on the author's experience of living for about 7 years in a South Delhi colony during which he built a house and obtained considerable information on the home districts of carpenters, masons, electricians and drivers of motor vehicles and those repairing electrical and other appliances on the one hand and messengers, gardeners, watchmen etc., on the other.

National Capital Region Planning Board: *Regional Plan 2001 National Capital Region*. New Delhi, 1988.

Planning Commission, Government of India, New Delhi.
(a) Approach Paper to the Eighth Five Year Plan, New Delhi, 1990.
(b) Eighth Five Year Plan, 1992-97.

Rao, Ratna, N.: *Social Organization in an Indian Slum*. Mittal Publications, New Delhi, 1990.

Registrar General and Census Commissioner, India: Census of India, 1991, Series 1. India, Paper 2 of 1991. Provisional Population Totals: Rural-Urban Distribution, New Delhi. 1991. p. 1. The figures for 2001 have been derived by projecting the rate of growth of urban population during 1981-91 to 1991-2001.

Report of the National Commission on Urbanization, New Delhi. 1988.

Tyagi, V.K.: *Urban Growth and Urban Villages: A Case Study of Delhi*. Kalyan Publications. New Delhi, 1982.

ANNEXURE 8.1

The Constitution Seventy-Fourth Amendment Act 1992 on Municipalities

"Committee for District Planning"

243ZD. (1) There shall be constituted in every State at the district level a District Planning Committee to consolidate the plans prepared by the Panchayats and the Municipalities in the district and to prepare a draft development plan for the district as a whole.

(2) The Legislature of a State may, by law, make provision with respect to—

(a) the composition of the District Planning Committees;

(b) the manner in which the seats in such Committees shall be filled;

Provided that not less than four-fifths of the total number of members of such committee shall be elected by, and from amongst, the elected members of the *Panchayat* at the district in proportion to the ratio between the population of the rural areas and of the urban areas in the district;

(c) the functions relating to district planning which may be assigned to such Committees;

(d) the manner in which the Chairperson of such Committee shall be chosen.

(3) Every District Planning Committee shall, in preparing the draft development plan :

(a) have regard to :—

(i) matters of common interest between the *Panchayats* and the Municipalities including spatial planning, sharing of water and other physical and natural resources, the integrated development of infrastructures and environmental conservation;

(ii) the extent and type of available resources whether financial or otherwise;

(b) consult such institutions and organizations as the Governor may, by order, specify.

(4) The Chairperson of every District Planning Committee shall forward the development plan, as recommended by such Committee, to the Government of the State." (pp. 7-8)

"Committee for Metropolitan Planning"

243ZE. (1) There shall be constituted in every Metropolitan area a Metropolitan Planning Committee to prepare a draft development plan for the Metropolitan area as a whole.

(2) The Legislature of a State may, by law, make provision with respect to—

(a) the composition of the Metropolitan Planning Committee;

(b) the manner in which the seats in such Committee shall be filled:

Provided that not less than two-thirds of the members of such Committees shall be elected by, and from amongst, the elected members of the Municipalities and Chairpersons of the *Panchayats* in the Metropolitan area in proportion to the ratio between the population of the Municipalities and of the *Panchayats* in that area;

(c) the representation in such Committee of the Government of India and the Government of the State and of such organizations and institutions as may be deemed necessary for carrying out the functions assigned to such committees:...."

(3) Every Metropolitan Planning Committee shall, in preparing the draft plan :

(a) have regard to :

(i) the plans prepared by the Municipalities and the *Panchayats*, in the Metropolitan area;

(ii) matters of common interest between the Municipalities and the *Panchayats*, including coordinated spatial planning of the area, sharing of water and other physical and natural resources, the integrated development of infrastructure and environmental conservation;

(iii) the overall objectives and priorities set by the Government of India and the Government of the State;

(iv) the extent and nature of investment likely to be made in the metropolitan area by agencies of the Government of India and of the Government of the State and other available resources whether financial or otherwise. (pp. 8-9)

SECTION II
Democracy and Rural Development

9

Panchayati Raj Institutions

The Predecessors of the Community Development and Panchayati Raj Programme

Panchayati Raj Institutions—A Historical Review

It is not well known that the community development and the *Panchayati Raj* Programmes had many distinguished predecessors. Rabindra Nath Tagore is known as a littérateur, a writer of poems, songs and works of fiction in his native Bengali and English. It is less commonly known that he was a pioneer in rural development. A group of villages adjoining Shanti Niketan where he lived and had founded the Vishwa Bharati University, the staff and students of the university spent a lot of time teaching farmers how to increase agricultural output, improve sanitation to improve their health and opened several primary schools and a secondary school for children of the villagers. The villagers responded enthusiastically to these efforts and Shanti Niketan (as the group of villages was called) became an island of prosperity and education in a landscape, which was bleak and desolate for a part of the year.

Then there were the Spencers—American missionaries who had been working in a group of villages in Kerala to increase literacy, education and output of rice and other crops. Again an American missionary Mr. Higginbotham came to India and established an Institute of Agriculture Research in Allahabad in Uttar Pradesh. The staff and students of the university carried out programmes similar to those included in the Community Development Programmes.

An American missionary Mr. S.N. Stokes, a native of Washington State in the U.S.A. was sent to convert people in the Kotgarh area of Himachal Pradesh to Christianity. He was so fascinated by the culture of the local people that he married a Himachal woman and became a Hindu. He saw a great opportunity to improve the economic condition of the local people by teaching them to grow apples because he saw that the climate and soil were similar to those his native Washington. He imported the best available saplings of apples from Washington began to grow them himself. His effort was so successful that he became a rich orchardist.

The long-term result of these efforts has been that the Kotgarh area of Himachal Pradesh is the largest producer of apples in northern India. The local farmers have organized producers' cooperatives which provide them the best breeding stock, chemical fertilizers and pesticides, buy the crop, crate it and send it to wholesalers in markets of Delhi and other cities. Kotgarh apples are available in cities as far as Mumbai.

Another American missionary, Mr. H. Wiser lived for several decades in villages in central U.P. (near Lucknow) teaching farmers in adjoining villages methods of increasing agricultural output and persuading them to send their children to schools. A British group headed by Mr. A. Alexander did similar work in a group of villages around Hoshangabad in Madhya Pradesh. His widow continued the project initiated by him for several years after his death.

Some administrators also carried out programmes similar to the Community Development Programme. Mr. (later Sir) V.T. Krishnamachari who was *Dewan* (Prime Minister) of Baroda for 19 years (1923-42) worked hard to provide drinking water wells and step wells, primary and secondary schools, health centres and even libraries in the villages of his state. Later when he became a member of the Planning Commission, he had a major influence in determining the content of the Community Development Programme. Mr. S.K. Dey, the Administrator of the Community Development Programme (later Minister of Community Development) also sought his advice frequently.

Another distinguished administrator was Mr. F.L. Braine, a senior ICS officer in Punjab in the 1920s to the 1940s. While posted as a Deputy Commissioner (Collector) of Gurgaon a most backward district of Punjab at that time, he carried out a crucial development programme. His emphasis was on education of villagers, increasing literacy and consciousness of good health. He would sing and dance with them and participate in their festivals. His fellow officers considered him 'mad'. They could be half right but he will be remembered long after, the Turtons and Burtons of the *Raj* are forgotten.

Panchayati Raj Institutions 1960s

The establishment of the present *Panchayati Raj* Institutions was first recommended in 1957 by a Committee (Government of India 1957) appointed by the Ministry of Community Development to evaluate progress of community development and national extension service. The principal recommendation of the Committee was that the responsibility for implementation of community development and other related rural development programmes should be transferred from officials to elected representatives of the people. Towards this end, it recommended establishment of the three institutions (Ministry of Community Development and Cooperation, 1957): *Panchayats, Panchayat Samitis* and *Zilla Parishads* at the levels of the village or multi-village level in case of small villages, the community development block or *taluka* and the district respectively. The Ministry of Community Development and Cooperation accepted the recommendation of the committee and the Minister requested the State governments to implement them by establishing these institutions at the earliest. Beginning with Rajasthan in October 1959, the governments of all the States established these institutions in the early or mid-1960s. The political leaders in the central and State governments hailed the step as a major step forward in the direction of 'direct democracy'. It fulfilled also a directive principle of the Constitution of India, which related to establishment of village *Panchayats*.

The three institutions, their mode of establishment and their powers and functions are as follows :

The Panchayat: A body constituted for every village with a population of 1,000-5,000 (up to 10,000 in Kerala) or a group of villages with similar population.

The Panchayat Samiti : A body constituted for every community development block, an area with a rural population between 60,000 (less in mountainous areas) and 150,000 or more in some southern States. The country has been divided into about 5,000 blocks for implementation of the Community Development Programme. The *Panchayat Samiti* was a body consisting of *Sarpanchs* (chairmen) of all the *Panchayats* in its area as its members. It was a rather large body consisting of up to fifty *Sarpanch* members, besides non-voting co-opted members mentioned below.

The *Zilla Parishad* : A body constituted at the district level, in order to oversee Community Development and other rural development programmes within the district. It would distribute the grants given by the State Government for implementation of the community development and other rural development programmes. Since the country had nearly 500 districts in 1951 and about 5,000 blocks every *Zilla Parishad* had an average of 10 blocks within its jurisdiction.

Every MLA was an *exofficio* non-voting member of one or two *Panchayat Samitis* within his constituency. Similarly, every M.P. was an *exofficio* non-voting member of all the *Panchayat Samitis* and *Zilla Parishads* within his constituency.

The *Panchayat* was to be a directly elected body. All adults (men and women) in the village(s) within its jurisdiction were entitled to vote for election of its chairman (*Sarpanch*) and members. The *Panchayat Samiti* and the *Zilla Parishad* were both constituted through indirect elections.

In Maharashtra and some southern States, an older administrative unit the *Taluka* and the community development block were co-terminus.

There was at the level of the *Panchayat Samiti*, a team of extension officers :

(i) An agricultural extension officer for advising farmers on techniques for raising agricultural output and also arranging supplies at the time required of improved seed, chemical fertilizers, pesticides and improved implements.

(ii) A cooperative extension officer for arranging short-term credit through cooperative societies for buying the inputs for current cultivation and medium-term credit for land improvement, digging of irrigation wells or installation of pumps on the wells. Medium-term credit (3-year or more), for the two latter purposes, was given by the Land Mortgage Bank. The cooperative extension officer ensured that credit for current cultivation was provided to the cultivators at the time required by them and that recovery was timely so that the flow of credit was maintained. An officer of Land Mortgage Bank ensured the same for the medium term credit.

(iii) A veterinarian who treated diseases of farm animals and advised villagers on improving livestock and a veterinary dispensary.

(iv) A 6-bed hospital with a doctor, a dispenser and one or more nurses. It had also a lady health visitor who advised the rural women on basics of hygiene, nutrition and childcare. There were also one or more dispensaries in every community development block. This organization provided villagers with curative and preventive health care.

(v) There was a sub-inspector of schools, who supervised working of all the primary and secondary schools in the *Panchayat Samiti* under his supervision. The area of every *Panchayat* had to have at least one primary school. A number of secondary schools were to be located in large villages or small towns to provide secondary school education within their jurisdiction. Every primary school had to have at least one teacher. Every secondary school had a number of teachers. All primary school teachers in its area were to be employees of the *Panchayat Samiti*, which were supposed to work under the direction of the *Sarpanch* and of the *Panchayat* where they were posted.

The *Panchayat Samiti* would oversee working of all the block level extension officers and could report to the State government on unsatisfactory work of any official. They would, however, remain employees of their parent departments and would take technical direction from their superiors in the department.

The district or divisional level officers of the various development departments—agriculture, cooperation, livestock, husbandry, education, preventive health and medical care, engineers for minor irrigation, rural electrification, and buildings and roads were expected to attend all meetings of the *Zilla Parishad* and take suitable action to remove all deficiencies in their working, pointed out by members of the *Zilla Parishad*. The *Parishad* would also distribute to the *Panchayat Samitis* within the district all loans and grants for development works within the district, approved by the State government. The *Panchayat Samiti* would similarly be responsible for distribution of such loans and grants for the *Panchayats* within its jurisdiction and to oversee their proper utilization.

The village *Panchayats* were supposed to levy taxes and to mobilize contribution of labour and/or materials for construction of buildings for primary and secondary school, the office of the *Panchayat* or cooperative society, approach roads to the villages, digging of new drinking water wells or improvement of existing wells or other sources of water supply. The value of loans and grants for these would be equal to the value of contributions by the villagers. Particular emphasis was given to improve drinking water wells, approach roads and construction of primary school buildings in the hamlets of the scheduled castes, the scheduled tribes and other poor sections of rural society[1].

According to the Committee, the Collector was supposed to be the friend, philosopher and guide of the *Panchayati Raj* Institution. He had a senior officer of the State administrative service to assist him in his duties relating to rural development programmes. The officer designated as District Development Officer was also the Secretary of the *Zilla Parishad.*

The Collector was supposed to attend all meetings of the *Zilla Parishad* which had its own chairman called *Pramukh.* He could attend the meeting of any *Panchayat Samiti* that he considered necessary. His duties were to keep the State government informed about the functioning of the *Panchayati Raj* institutions. Thus, he could report to the government any major deficiencies in functioning of any *Panchayat Samiti* or even the *Zilla Parishad.* On receiving his report, the State government would direct him to conduct an enquiry and submit his report for necessary action. He would also enquire into complaints about corruption or unacceptable behaviour of any *Sarpanch.* The State governments have taken these deficiencies into consideration while establishing the new institutions.

The institutions were established by all the State governments in the course of the 1960s but were abolished by most of them during the 1970s because their working was not considered satisfactory by the State governments.[2] They began to be revived by the State governments with greatly increased resources and powers by governments of Karnataka, Kerala and West Bengal in the 1980s. Their establishment has been made mandatory on the State Governments by the 93rd Amendment to the Constitution enacted in 1993. However, they have not been revived in all the State governments. In Bihar for instance, elections to the *Panchayats* were held in 2001 after a lapse of 18 years.

The new institutions have larger grants provided by the State governments. They have been given greatly increased powers of raising taxes and have responsibility for rural development.

Another major difference is that whereas the institutions established in the 1960s were supposed to be non-political and concerned mainly with rural development, the new institutions are recognized to be political institutions. The party in power in a State government tries hard to ensure that its nominees are elected to the maximum number of *Panchayats* and other institutions within the State. Loss of control of a large proportion of institutions is considered by the party in power in the State government as a precursor of loss of power in the next general election.

Furthermore, representation of women and the scheduled castes and the scheduled tribes have been greatly increased in the new institutions. In some States, it has been stipulated that some posts are reserved for these groups for some years.

Panchayati Raj Update[3] reports regularly every month on problems and achievements of these institutions in different States. It is clear from these reports that the working of these institutions in most State is in some way not much better than that of the earlier institutions established in the 1960s. On the other hand, establishment of the institutions has been a major instrument for raising the economic and social conditions and power in village affairs of the scheduled castes and the scheduled tribes and women; they have been a powerful instrument of social integration in a highly stratified society in which inequality in economic and social status and political power of various groups had been the norm.

NOTES

1. These loans and grants had been given by the State Government for implementation of rural development programmes under the Community Development Programme launched in October 1952, which covered the whole country by 1961.
2. A number of committees, including one headed by Mr. Ashok Mehta reported on the reasons for failure of the institutions.
3. *Panchayati Raj Update* is a monthly journal produced by Institute of Social Sciences, Delhi.

REFERENCE

Government of India, Ministry of Community Development and Cooperation, *Committee to Evaluate Progress of Community Development and National Extension Service,* New Delhi, 1957.

10

Planning by Panchayati Raj Institutions (PRIs)*

Planning of development programmes is an essential function of *Panchayati Raj* Institutions. From the *Panchayat* to *Panchayat Samiti* and the *Zilla Parishad*, each of the institutions is expected to take an active part in planning for its area. All the three area units—the village, the block and the district—have been accepted as important units of planning, and during the last ten years, a number of attempts have been made to draw up development plans for these.

However, there is a distinct feeling that much progress still remains to be made in taking forward this process of planning at local levels and ensuring that the *Panchayati Raj* institutions play an adequate and effective role in it. It is the object of this chapter to examine the scope and content of planning by these institutions and to offer some suggestions for making it more fruitful.

The Present Practice

Planning by *Panchayati Raj* institutions forms part of the national planning process: the institutions have to draw up their plans within the framework of the overall objectives, priorities and policies decided at national and State levels. Planning by PRIs relates mainly to programmes which aim at meeting local needs, in which decisions regarding location and size of activity have to be taken on local considerations, and in which success depends primarily upon the initiative and cooperation of the local people. Agriculture and associated fields of animal husbandry, cooperation and minor irrigation, primary and secondary education, sanitation, water supply and basic medical

* Published in Journal of Institute of Public Administration.

care, and local communications are important fields of local planning. On the other hand, large industrial, power, transport and irrigation projects, and facilities for advanced education or health service are outside the field of local planning. The distinction between these two spheres of planning and the fact that the *Panchayati Raj* institutions are concerned primarily with local development programmes is fairly well understood. But even within the area of local planning, the present practice is that priorities for different development programmes, the specific schemes included within each programme and the pattern of each scheme—content, staff, finance, institutional arrangements, etc., are worked out in detail at the State (or even national) levels and decision-making at local levels is concerned largely with selecting locations and beneficiaries. The *Panchayati Raj* institutions, like their predecessors, officials of the community development Blocks and other development departments, have functioned primarily as allocating and distributing agencies deciding where a primary school or a primary health centre should be located and who should get a *taccavi* loan; while the number of schools and health centres to be located in their area and the details of staff, equipment and buildings for these, had been decided at the State level. The typical situation in meetings of a *Panchayat Samiti* or its standing committees is somewhat like this. The B.D.O. (Vikas Adhikari) or the extension officer concerned reads out a circular from the State government which informs (all *Panchayat Samitis* in the State) that a particular scheme is to be implemented and gives the financial pattern and other details of the scheme. The meeting thereupon proceeds to decide which particular villages, persons or groups should benefit from the scheme. There is seldom any attempt to state that the scheme is not suitable for the areas of the *Panchayat Samiti*, that another scheme would be more suitable, or even to attempt to modify the pattern of the scheme in any way. Nor would such attempts be very feasible under the present procedures for sanction and implementation of development programmes.

This practice of deciding patterns of development activity in detail at the State level and leaving the local institutions only the distributive functions has been the subject of considerable argument. Those opposed to the practice have argued that it does not allow plans to be formulated by local people in accordance with their needs and aspirations or the natural resources and development potential of their areas, with the result that less needed activities are often taken up in preference to those which are needed more and would have given better results, that at times money is wasted on unnecessary schemes, and that local people are not sufficiently enthusiastic about development programmes. This, they argue, results in development programmes not having the desired effect in terms of participation of local people and retarded economic development. The protagonists of the practice have defended it on grounds of administrative efficiency, securing a minimum level of development in all areas and ensuring that national and State priorities are reflected in local plans. Allocation of funds between different heads of development and on individual schemes within each head is regarded as the instrument of securing development according to priorities. Working of detailed patterns of each scheme is considered essential for administrative efficiency and avoidance of waste because it is argued effective supervision and assessment of performance would be impossible in the absence of these.

It is also pointed out by many that so long as funds for development activities are provided by the State (or Central Government) and the staffs of *Panchayati Raj* institutions form part of State cadres, the tendency towards detailed planning of programmes at State (and even national) level will continue. They go on to argue that *Panchayati Raj* institutions can have an effective role in planning for their areas only if they have their own staff and raise their own resources. The argument has some force. There is no doubt that when funds are given by the State government, there is a tendency for it to indicate not merely the schemes on which these may be spent but also the manner in which the schemes may be executed. On the side of *Panchayati Raj* institutions also, there is a tendency to regard the schemes as those of the State government, and to execute them according to the instructions of the latter. The immediate history of *Panchayati Raj* institutions, their having been constituted in succession to the C.D. blocks and having inherited the programmes, funds and staff of the blocks and other development departments—strengthens these tendencies. But it must be realized that this situation of funds being given by the State government and technical staff forming part of State cadres, is likely to continue and exercise of initiative in local planning by *Panchayati Raj* institutions has to be achieved within it. The alternative of *Panchayati Raj* institutions having their own staff and raising their own resources will, in the present stage of rural development and growth of these institutions, only result in greatly restricting their role in development, besides reducing staff efficiency. It will reduce these institutions to the position of former district boards.

The tendency towards planning of programmes at State or Central levels has been encouraged by the fact that in much of the rural development activity of the last 12 years, the object has been to provide elementary services and facilities—primary schools, primary health centres, drinking water wells, approach roads, cooperative credit societies—a basic agency for agricultural extension. Creation of these elementary services lends itself very well to 'proliferation of patterns' approach. Primary schools and credit cooperatives are needed everywhere and the local decisions to be taken at the Block level relate mainly to deciding the number and location of these. Therefore, it is an advantage to work out a basic pattern of the primary school or the credit cooperative, which can be adopted throughout the State.

The second reason for adopting the 'programme pattern approach' in the early stages of the Community Development Programme was that until local consciousness of development needs grow, it was necessary to provide a certain leadership from above and take up basic activities, which were clearly the most urgent needs in most areas.

This approach did create imbalances and difficulties in the community development programme. But, since many of these were felt by the State governments themselves, there was a tendency to resolve them through appropriate action between the State government and the Central Ministry of Community Development. Thus, when it was found by State governments that particular activities included in the community development on projects were not suitable for their areas, the Central government was persuaded to give them considerable freedom to decide upon the specific content of the programme within each major field of development activity. But the process was not carried further to district and Block levels, and once the pattern of activity in a field had been decided at the State level, it was applied without major modification to all Blocks of the State.

Need for Shift in Emphasis

But, as a result mainly of the development activity the situation is changing. Firstly, as the need for elementary facilities like primary schools and credit cooperatives has been met, emphasis in rural development programmes is shifting to providing more advanced facilities like secondary schools, cooperative marketing and processing societies and workshops for repair and servicing of agricultural implements. Planning for those more advanced facilities requires much greater attention to local conditions, and it is not possible to apply a uniform pattern to all blocks. Thus, it is not advisable to decide that each block shall have a certain number of secondary schools, marketing societies or centres for training of craftsmen. Block 'A' may need more secondary schools, because it contains a number of small towns in which secondary schools are desired by the people; Block 'B' may be more suitable for location of the training centre for craftsmen because a large factory located within it could provide employment for the trainees of the centre. Location of more specialized facilities like a cooperative ginning factory or sugar mill has to be decided primarily on consideration of specific local factors like availability of raw materials, nearness to markets and advantage of transport. Secondly, experience with development activities has created among the local people much greater awareness of the need for development and of the specific activities needed in their areas. The result is that they are more anxious to participate in the planning process and are more vocal in expression of their needs and aspirations.

These two changes, coming along with strengthening of institutional arrangements—establishment of *Panchayati Raj* institutions and a network of cooperative societies—should give local planning more meaningful content in future.

District as the Primary Unit of Local Planning

Increasing emphasis on provision of more advanced services and facilities will, along with the other factors mentioned below, make the district a more important unit of planning than the community development block. Let us take the examples of education and cooperation again. The community development block was quite a suitable unit for planning a network of primary schools, because the object was to provide every village (or in case of very small villages or hamlets, a group of two or more neighbouring units) with a primary school. But it is not an equally suitable unit for planning location of middle schools, and may have positive disadvantages when adopted as the unit for planning of secondary schools. Similarly, while location of primary credit cooperatives could be planned with the Block as a unit, location of marketing and processing societies has to be planned with a larger area as the unit, because of the need for attention to the specific location factors mentioned above. Making the Block the unit for planning location of the more advanced facilities and deciding that each Block shall have one or a certain number of them will lead to many inappropriate locational decisions.

The need for making the district the principal unit of local planning will also be felt for another reason. Effective local planning will require a considerable measure of decentralization of decision-making from the State to local levels. Such decentralization is for several reasons more feasible at the district level than at that of the Block. First, the district has the full complement of district level officers who can provide the specialist assistance needed for drawing up local plans and making fruitful modifications in schemes drawn up at the State level. On the non-official side also, the *Zilla Parishad* being the apex *Panchayati Raj* institution has the top-level leadership of the district. Secondly, for reasons of administrative feasibility, especially maintenance of effective communication between the State and local levels, the district is more suitable than Block as a unit of local planning. The State development departments will find it more feasible to deal with a limited number of *Zilla Parishads* and district officers than with a large number of *Panchayat Samitis* and Block level extension officers. Thirdly, as conditions within most districts are fairly homogeneous, the need for making further modifications particular to suit the requirements of individual Block is comparatively small, after the pattern of a programme has been decided at the district level. Finally, attention to integrated area development and securing appropriate interaction between towns and villages, which we explain below as important objectives of local planning in the future, will also make adoption of the district as the basic unit of local planning necessary.

Here it is necessary to draw a clear distinction between the unit of planning and the unit of implementation of programmes. The fact that the district is accepted as the unit for planning of a particular programme does not mean that it should necessarily be the unit for its implementation. In some cases, the combination will be useful; but over a large field of development activity covered by the district plan, execution could just as well be done through the *Panchayat Samitis*. Thus, while the district is a more suitable unit than the Block for planning the content of the minor irrigation programme *i.e.,* deciding the emphasis that minor irrigation should receive in the total agricultural production effort in different Blocks, and the specific activities to be taken up in each Block, implementation is best done by the *Panchayat Samitis*. The latter are better equipped than is the *Zilla Parishad* for the tasks of implementation *i.e.,* taking up construction of small tanks, sanctioning loans for construction or repair of wells, or for installation of pumping sets or wells. The decisions regarding the unit of planning and the unit of implementation in respect of each Programme should be taken, keeping in view its nature, the technical staff and other resources required for it, and the structure of *Panchayati Raj* institutions in the State.

Two Aspects of Local Planning

It would be useful to refer to two aspects of local planning which are of growing importance and will demand greater attention from all concerned with local planning in future. Those are:

(i) integrated area development, and
(ii) appropriate interaction between towns and villages.

Integrated Area Development

Integrated area development has been recognized as a major object of the Community Development Programme from its inception. Several of the first community projects were located in areas of major irrigation projects and it was envisaged that agricultural extension, land reclamation, soil conservation and other development activities undertaken through them would enable the cultivators to utilize the irrigation waters earlier and more fruitfully and would accelerate the development of the areas. Some other projects were located in backward areas; location of these was considered the first step in initiating rapid development in these areas. But with rapid expansion of the Community Development Programme, after 1955, emphasis shifted to provision of services and construction of works, and integrated area development was given less attention. This shift in emphasis became necessary perhaps when it was decided to extend the Community Development Programme over the whole country. But the economic development of the last 12 years (1950-62) is now focussing attention again on integrated area development. Location of major industrial, power, transport, irrigation and other projects are bringing about major changes in the economy and social life of several areas of the country. In some other areas like central Punjab, growth of small-scale industry is producing rapid socio-economic changes. Besides these areas of concentrated development, in most others also, growth of commerce and improvement in communications is leading to expansion of towns and increasing interaction between them and the surrounding villages.

These developments are of considerable significance for the rural people. Location of a major project in an area means increased employment for its people and larger demand for agricultural produce including high value farm products like vegetables, milk, fruit, eggs etc. These bring larger income and provide an incentive for increasing agricultural production. They also mean rapid inflow of new ideas, and may accelerate technological change in agriculture and changes in rural levels of living.

It is necessary and important that those concerned with local planning consider how their areas can benefit from the major development projects located within their areas, more adequately. They should concern themselves specifically with the question: what complementary development activities are needed within their area in order that the people can take greater advantage from the major projects. In case of a major irrigation project, such complementary activities are agricultural extension, especially teaching cultivators to change from dry to irrigated farming; reclamation, levelling and preparation of land. Other examples of such complementary development activities are rural electrification and development of small industries in the area of a major power project; development of small ancillary industries and training of craftsmen in the area of a major industrial project. The need for such complementary development activities is recognized. The Planning Commission has gone so far as to say that, "every major project should be regarded as a nucleus for integrated development of the region as a whole. Around the new irrigation projects, for instance, a whole group of schemes aiming at the development of improved agriculture, horticulture, market centres and processing and other industries should be taken up. Similarly steel plants and other large industrial projects provide the basis for the development of small and medium industries and programmes of education and training and other activities" (Planning Commission, p. 149). But in spite of this recognition adequate attention is not being given to taking up complementary development activities. The examples of irrigation projects whose benefits are utilized very slowly, of power projects which do not lead to rural electrification or rural industrialization, and of industrial projects which do not produce enough impact on the economy of the surrounding villages, or of others whose progress is hampered because the local area cannot furnish skilled labour or local cost of living is too high because foodstuffs have to be imported from long distances, illustrate the imbalances which result from inadequate attention to these activities.

The local leaders in *Panchayati Raj* institutions should identify the complementary development needed in their areas consequent on the start of a new project, and press for their inclusion in appropriate development programmes of the State government. They can also play a useful role in making the people of their areas aware of the new opportunities for improving agriculture, starting small industries etc., brought by the project.

Appropriate Interaction between Town and Villages

Let us consider an average district. Its headquarters is a medium-sized town, which performs various services for all or most of the villages and small towns located within it. Frequently, it is also the major commercial centre of the district. The sub-divisional headquarters' towns, important *mandi* towns and other medium-sized towns have similar roles for parts of the district. Within each block, the Block headquarters' town has a similar role in relation to villages of the Block area. In addition, there are in most Blocks, one or more small towns which perform similar functions for groups of 25-30 villages.

One effect of the developments has been that interaction between these towns and the villages served by them has increased, and the towns have a more important role in the economy and social life of the villages (V. Nath, 2007, pp. 67-90). The village people come to the towns more frequently and obtain many more of their requirements from them than they did in the past. The very activities of *Panchayat Samitis*—distribution of *taccavi* loans, distribution of permits for supply of chemical fertilizers, cement or corrugated iron sheets, deciding appeals from decisions of *Panchayats*, various elections—have added to the frequency of these town visits. Many village leaders and affluent cultivators visit such towns almost daily. Most of the towns have expanded considerably in recent years, on account of growth of commerce, resulting from larger agricultural production and higher incomes in the surrounding villages. Their role as service centres for the surrounding villages will become more important in future. As agriculture gets modernized and rural electrification and rural industrialization make progress, they will have an increasingly important role as centres for distribution of new materials and of servicing and repair of power driven implements and machines. This, for the simple reason that facilities for distribution of new materials and repairs and servicing of machines cannot be located in each village, but have to be continued to a few central places.

Yet, very little attention has been given so far to examining the inter-relationship between these towns and their surrounding villages and ensuring that development of the two is complementary and mutually beneficial. Indeed, there are many instances of failure to appreciate this relationship. Location of facilities like primary health centres and secondary schools is decided generally on considerations like availability of local contribution with the result that in many cases these are located not in the small town or large village which is the natural centre of the area to be served by them, but in the village which came forward to pay the required contribution. In many Blocks, the block headquarter town itself is not well located for serving the needs of the Block area.

The first community projects did contain the nucleus of the idea of securing appropriate interaction between towns and villages. They envisaged development of *mandi* centres, improvement of communications between them and the villages, and using them as centres for providing an increasing range of services and dissemination of new ideas to the villages. But these ideas were gradually dropped because other problems were considered more urgent. Moreover, the C.D. and N.E.S. Blocks, which followed the first community projects, had such small budgets that more intensive development activities could not be accommodated within them. But these aspects should be given adequate attention now. The place of the district and Block headquarters towns and the smaller centres within each Block in the development of their areas should be clearly recognized. Location of various service facilities should be so decided as to enable these centres to perform their service role efficiently. Further, the present isolation between the municipalities of these towns and the *Panchayati Raj* institutions should be ended, and the two should be brought into relations of mutual interaction. The latter can be done only at the district level: the Block is too small a unit for this purpose. The recent recommendation of the Sadiq Ali Report (Government of Rajasthan 1964) for providing for association of municipalities with the *Zilla Parishad* in Rajasthan is evidence of recognition of this need. Such association will become especially important when integrated area development is accepted as the object of local planning, and development of both towns and villages is viewed as forming part of it.

Conclusion

The larger field of local planning and a more active role in it for *Panchayati Raj* institutions envisaged above should result in plans becoming more closely related to local needs, potential and resources and in aspirations of local people. They should, as a consequence, evoke greater and more fruitful participation from the people and accelerate their economic progress and social advance. Participation here does not mean merely raising contributions for construction works: the word has been used in a wider sense and includes successful working of institutions, adopting recommended practices and modern techniques in agriculture, and displaying the initiative required for starting new enterprises like small scale industries. Evoking such participation from local people and contribution to their accelerated economic and social progress are the criteria of usefulness of local plans and of success of the local planning process. The success of *Panchayati Raj* institutions as planning agencies will be judged by the contribution their plans make to the achievement of these objectives.

REFERENCES

1. Planning Commission, Government of India, *Third Five-Year Plan.*
2. Government of Rajasthan: *Report of the Study Team on Panchayati Raj,* Jaipur, 1964. (Sadiq Ali Report)
3. Nath V., *Urbanization, Urban Development and Metropolitan Cities in India*. Concept Publishers, New Delhi, 2007.

11

Panchayati Raj

*The Promise and the Prospects**

Introduction

Panchayati Raj with a three-tier structure of democratic institutions at the district, village and intermediate levels was revived or rejuvenated through the central legislation. This development followed three decades of mixed experience with the earlier institutions that were established in different States mainly in the early 1960s. Successful working of the earlier institutions would have contributed significantly to India's progress towards social and economic change and political development. But serious problems in their working, or other reasons, led to disillusionment with them and their supersession in a large number of States during the 1960s or the 1970s. The structural reforms in the institutions, undertaken in recent years in some States, and of the institutions becoming a vital and vibrant component of Indian polity hold the promise of greater success in the 1990s than in the 1960s. This legislation and the reforms are a reflection of the fact that, backed by appropriate statutory safeguards and endowed with adequate resources of finance and manpower, and decision-making powers, the institutions can achieve their enormous potential of contributing to social, economic and political change.

Objectives

Establishment of *Panchayati Raj* Institutions (PRIs) through the legislative process should have four principal objectives:

---

* The article was published in *The Journal of Institute of Public Administration.* A daft of the papèr was also presented at the symposium 'Panchayati Raj' held by Centre for Area Development and Action Research Studies, New Delhi in August 1989.

(i) It should contribute to meaningful participation by the people in local development;

(ii) It should reduce inter-group economic and social disparities and contribute particularly to alleviation of poverty and unemployment;

(iii) It should not affect adversely Centre-State relations, preservation of which forms the basis of our federal polity; and

(iv) It should promote bottom-up planning.

Some Preliminary Points

The context of 1989 and the early 1990s is very different from that of 30 years earlier. However, some of the structural constraints that led to disillusionment with the PRIs and abandonment of several earlier attempts at decentralized planning still remain. But their intensity and influence have weakened enough to warrant hope for more successful working of the new institutions. The differences and constraints are summarized below :

The Differences

(i) Much higher literacy and awareness among the rural people, of both the potential and constraints of rural development programmes and of their own rights in a democratic state. Improvements in transport, greater rural-urban linkages, and experience with the political process over a period of more than four decades, and widespread exposure to communication, media—newspapers, radio and TV—are other factors contributing to the awareness.

(ii) Working experience with rural development programmes—Community Development, Intensive Agricultural Development Programme (IADP), Integrated Rural Development Programme (IRDP), National Employment Programme and others, which have been undertaken during the last four decades.

The experience has demonstrated the potential and constraints on growth of output and income and improvements in levels of living of the rural people. Among the noteworthy successes, perhaps the most important is the IADP and the Green Revolution which have contributed to spectacular increases in agricultural output in some areas (Punjab, Haryana, Western U.P.) and steady increases in output in others' such as the irrigated areas producing rice or other crops. On the other hand, the IRDP and NEP seem to have had negative influence on the under- and -unemployment among rural people.

(iii) Expansion of infrastructures and basic service facilities in most areas.

(iv) Much greater rural-urban interaction, principally through greater participation of the rural people, particularly the youth, in jobs in towns, and greatly increased production by the farmers of perishable foods for urban markets. The interaction is greatest in villages located within 15 km. of large towns.

On the other hand

(v) Little redistribution of rural assets. Land reforms were stopped midstream due to various reasons including strong opposition of large and middle level farmers.

(vi) Number of landless and marginal farmers is much higher than in the 1960s due to increase in population and labour force, without significant increases in the cultivated area, or redistribution of the latter.

(vii) Increase in unemployment—rural and urban; replacement of hidden under-employment by open unemployment due to relatively slow growth in both the rural and urban economies and by adopting capital intensive technology.

(viii) Continuance (or increase) in economic disparities between the large and middle level farmers on the one hand and the marginal farmers and the landless labourers on the other. The large and middle farmers have benefited much more from increase in agricultural output and from most other rural development programmes, than have the small farmers and the landless. The latter have remained the rural poor.

(ix) Greater awareness and discontent among the poor of the increasing economic disparities and unemployment.

(x) The political process is well established, but it is devoid of its post-Independence enthusiasm and idealism. Its means and ends are widely understood, and accepted by the rural public. It is now seen, rightly, as the principal means of obtaining and exercising political power. Obtaining economic benefits through it, including satisfaction of personal greed and increased corruption among politicians is recognized (though not accepted) as an inevitable accompaniment of the process.

(xi) The bureaucracy, state and local, is no longer seen as being independent or impartial. It is *recognized and accepted* as the handmaiden of the political executive. Its inefficiency, delays and greed are also recognized and largely accepted.

The Structural Constraints

Among the constraints two are most important: those arising from the inegalitarian structure of our rural society, and those due to the unwillingness of the State-level political executives and officials to delegate decision-making powers and transfer resources for implementation of development programmes to the PRIs.

1. *Social Constraints*

The political, social and economic inequalities of rural society are well known. The large or middle level farmers, belonging generally to the dominating cultivating castes, are in positions of political power—as *Sarpanchs* of village *Panchayats* and as heads of *Zila Parishads* and intermediate level institutions in most of the States. They have also economic power and social primacy. They controlled the earlier (or existing) *Panchayati Raj* institutions and used them for their personal and class benefits and will, undoubtedly, try to control and use the new ones.

The rural elites have intimate linkages with State and higher-level elites—ministers, MLAs and MPs, most of whom have similar socio-economic backgrounds. But the linkages of leaders of the rural poor with their representatives at the State and Central levels have also increased and could increase more rapidly in future.

The provisions in the central legislation for larger representation in the PRIs for the scheduled castes and scheduled tribes could mitigate the constraint, but could not eliminate it.

2. *State Level Constraints*

Unwillingness (or opposition) of the State level political executive—MLAs and ministers—to decentralize decision-making to the heads of district or lower levels, particularly the heads of the *Zila Parishads* or the intermediate level institutions. Regardless of whether the heads belong to their own or other political parties, they are seen as potential competitors or antagonists and who wants competitors and antagonists?

Unwillingness of State Level Officials to decentralize Decision-making to the PRIs: Within the technical departments, the unwillingness is stated to be due to lack of the specialized technical knowledge, which is essential for efficient and effective working of projects among the elected representatives. They maintain that their own departmental functionaries alone have the knowledge. The stock reply is, "the elected representatives do not have the knowledge needed for making correct decisions because they do not understand technical subjects".

On the contrary, there are trends towards further centralization, among both the political executive and the bureaucracy. The trend extends to the Central government. The proposed amendments in the Constitution of India and enactment by Parliament of the legislations on *Panchayati Raj* and *Nagarpalikas*, which are State subjects under the Constitution, is itself evidence of the centralizing trend.

Paucity of Resources of Finance and Technical Manpower

(i) *Finance*: The taxes with the greatest yield and highest potential for growth with economic development, such as central excise, import and export duties and income tax, are with the Central government. The Central government also raises very large resources through domestic or external borrowings and deficit financing. The State governments have the remaining taxes with high yield and growth potential, notably the sales tax. They also receive large grants or loans from the Central government for meeting their deficits on current or capital accounts. Grants or loans for centrally sponsored schemes are a major constituent of such transfers. Their proportion in the content of State plans has increased from about 44 per cent in 1980 to almost 75 per cent in 1987-88.

The scope for raising resource by the PRIs is limited. For them property tax is the main source of revenue with high yield and potential for steady growth. But these attributes of the tax are important only in urban areas where property values are high; both yield and growth potential are low in the rural areas.

(ii) The PRIs (and *Nagarpalikas*) are not willing to tax heavily their constituents for reasons that are well known. The elites, which control them, do not want to tax themselves, while the poor have low assets and incomes.

Manpower: Technical personnel, including the executives of *Zilla Parishads* are deputed in most States from the revenue or technical departments of the State governments. Creation of separate cadres of officials for these institutions has to be examined in depth and decisions taken, preferably through a consensus between the Central and State governments.

There has been some real decentralization of power and resources to *Panchayat* institutions in recent years in a few States, notably, Karnataka, West Bengal, Andhra Pradesh and Kerala. The experience of these States will be of great interest for the future development of the PRIs. The initial experience with the reforms is encouraging, although an objective assessment of their potential and constraints (success or failure) and the factors contributing to will become possible only after some years of their operation.

The Prospect

These constraints remain, but their intensity and influence have been reduced because of the changes of the last 30 years. The rural elites see the need, indeed the compulsion, of accommodating the interest and aspirations of the scheduled castes, the scheduled tribes and other weaker sections of the community. They realize that accommodation is the only way to avoid confrontation and violent conflicts. The widespread conflicts in rural Bihar, as also those in parts of other States are a pointer in this direction.

The provisions relating to larger representation for the scheduled castes and scheduled tribes in the central legislation could also contribute to greater accommodation between them and the rural elites.

There is greater appreciation with the State governments also of the need for decentralization of decision-making powers and larger transfers of resources to the PRIs. The examples of the four States mentioned above, in which such decentralization has been effected, cannot be overlooked by the other State governments. Increasing proportions of MLAs and ministers in all States will progressively see the need for working through the leaders and members of the PRIs to retain and strengthen their local political bases. They may have to refine their techniques or forge new ones for such working, to achieve their objective.

Successful working of the new PRIs is by no means assured. But the changes of the last 30 years *do hold* the promise of more successful working now than in the 1960s. There will, of course, be large inter-State and intra-State variations in performance of the institutions; they are inevitable in a country of such large size and such regional diversity. But the differences in performance should lead to efforts for structural reforms to remove the weaknesses of the PRIs, which are not doing well, rather than reversal of the whole process of democratic decentralization.

SECTION III
Socio-Economic Structure of Villages in India

12

Village Caste and Community*

I

The Village and the Community

The concept of the community is of fundamental importance for the Community Development Programme. This programme is based on the belief that economic and social advance in rural India can best be secured through rural people working cooperatively as members of communities; and that, for this purpose, it is necessary to strengthen and revitalize the existing communities and to foster the community spirit to the extent that it is deficient. Also, in much of the thinking on community development it is implicit that the "village" is a "community." Concepts like people's participation, or the collective endeavour of a village in undertaking programmes of common benefit, and the development of the three basic institutions—the *Panchayat*, the cooperative society, and the school—are concepts basic to the Community Development Programme and they all assume that the "village" is the "community."

In view of this assumption, it is worthwhile asking: to what extent is the Indian village a community today? This will involve an examination of the nature of the village and of the rural community as well as an analysis of the factors on which the village's role as a unit of community life rested in the past. We shall also discuss how these factors have been affected as a result of the social and economic changes of the last 100 years or more, and whether new units of community life are emerging in rural India.

---

* Published in Turner Roy: *India's Urban Future*, Berkeley, California, pp. 141-154, 1962.

The Village as the Unit of Settlement

For a definition of the term "village" we must go to the Indian census, which says: "It should be borne in mind that the concept of a village is not demographic, but administrative. As a general rule, it represents a parcel of land, the boundaries of which are defined and settled by a Revenue Survey or by a Cadestral Survey. It may be, but need not always necessarily be, a single house cluster with a local name, marking its distinctiveness as a residential locality." (Census of India 1951 part II A, p. 2)

It will be clear from the above definition that the term "village," strictly speaking, does not stand for a social or a settlement unit. It is a term used to express what is primarily a revenue-administrative unit. It is true that in most parts of India this is also a unit of settlement or habitation. The village in these parts conforms to the popular picture of a cluster of houses (or more than one cluster of houses, adjoining) situated amid its cultivated fields which define its boundaries, separate it from other similar units, and give it a distinct identity. It is necessary, however, to emphasize that this picture does not obtain in all parts of the country: that there are important variations from it in several areas and that in some parts of the country the village as a settlement unit does not exist at all.

The identity between the revenue village and the unit of settlement is closest in north-western India and in the "dry" areas of the country generally, e.g.. Punjab, Rajasthan, Western U.P., Bombay, Mysore, and parts of Madhya Pradesh. In these areas, the village is a tightly nucleated unit of settlement, distinctly marked out from other similar units. The main variation from this pattern is that frequently the Harijan Basti is not contiguous with the main village and is located at a small distance from it. But, as we move away from these areas, there is a trend towards a more dispersed settlement pattern, with the village being composed of a "main village" which is usually inhabited by the landholding castes, and one, two, or more "hamlets." In the Gangetic plain, this pattern is already well established in Central U.P. and becomes more marked as we move farther east. Thus over large parts of eastern India (Bihar, Orissa, and West Bengal) the revenue village consists of the main village and a number of small clusters of households (*thollas*), each situated within its own grove of trees, having its own source of water supply, and separated from the others by some distance. Village boundaries are not clearly discernible in these areas, because the clusters which form part of one village are hardly distinguishable from those forming part of the next. A somewhat different situation is found in Madras and parts of Andhra Pradesh. Here the pattern of settlement is generally similar to what would be called the tightly nucleated village type, i.e., a distinct cluster of houses surrounded by cultivated fields. But these "clusters" are not called villages, but "hamlets." The revenue village in these areas consists of a number of such hamlets and generally has a large population, up to 10,000 or 15.000.

The extreme departures from the pattern of the tightly nucleated village are found at the two extremities of the country, Kerala and Himachal Pradesh. In Kerala the unit of settlement is the individual homestead situated within its own compound and agricultural lands. These homesteads extend in almost unbroken lines along the roads and in other areas suitable for settlement. The "village" here is a purely artificial unit created by the revenue administration and has no existence on the ground. Generally, a large population of 5,000 to 15,000 is included in it. In the other parts of the west coast, between Kerala and Bombay City, the settlement pattern can be considered to be intermediate between the homestead type found in Kerala and the "village" type. Villages here are often no more than somewhat more concentrated clusters of homesteads. At the other end of the country, in Himachal Pradesh, where the population is very sparse, the typical unit of settlement is the "hamlet," consisting of a very few houses, sometimes not more than two or three. Himachal Pradesh represents the extreme in this respect, but in hilly and mountainous areas all over the country the "hamlet" type of settlement exists, especially where the population is sparse, and true "villages" begin to appear only in valleys and other areas of more concentrated population.

These examples have been given not to prove that the village is not the unit of settlement over most parts of the country. There is no question about this. They have been given merely to show that this is not universally true and that there are important differences from this pattern in some parts of the country. An adequate appreciation of these differences is of great importance for all policy makers and workers in community development and other rural development programmes, because almost every physical task of development — ranging from agricultural improvement measures, such as irrigation, to location of community facilities, such as schools and *Panchayat* ghars — is vitally affected by them. The planning of rural development programmes has obviously to be very different in Kerala, where each household lives in its own compound, from that in Punjab with its lightly nucleated villages. Certain programmes like the pavement of village streets and drains, so important in Punjab, are scarcely necessary in Kerala. On the other hand, the cost of such a programme as rural electrification is much higher in Kerala, because of the necessity of taking electric lines to every individual homestead The efficiency of Gram Sevaks and other development workers is also influenced by the settlement pattern. In Punjab, the task of the Gram Sevak is relatively easy. Because he has all the families living in a village potentially within his reach, every time he visits the village in Kerala, on the other hand, his work is much more difficult, because for propagation of any programme he has to visit individual homesteads.

The rest of this discussion relates only to areas where the "village" is the unit of settlement, including those areas where the "village" consists of a central unit and one or more hamlets. The feeling of community centering on the village is strongest in those areas, and we feel that by concentrating attention on them we shall be able to see more clearly the factors on which this feeling is based, and also understand its limitations. Areas like Kerala and Himachal Pradesh in which the settlement pattern is very different have been excluded, because the feeling of community centering on the village is very weak or virtually absent in them.

The Village as a Social Unit

The assumption that the "village" is the "community" has a strong basis in historical and even present fact. The people living in a village did not (and do not) have the comparatively superficial or transitory ties which bind the residents of a neighbourhood or a residential suburb in a modern Western city. They had (and still have) intimate economic and social relationships which were (and are) regulated by traditions and institutions which have evolved over centuries The main bases on which these economic and social relationships (and the feeling of community focussing on the village) have rested are three: isolation of the village, this *jajmani* system, and caste and kinship.

The isolation of the village severely limited the contacts of the villagers with the outside world and made it necessary for them to confine their economic and social relationships within the village or within a group of neighbouring villages. Caste and the *jajmani* system provided the social and economic bases on which these relationships rested The two institutions were intimately related and mutually supporting. Caste defined the occupation and the social status of the different individuals and groups living in the village. The *jajmani* system defined their economic relationships and bound the cultivators, on the one hand, and the artisans and other non-agriculturists, on the other, in a system of economic interdependence. The system was organized with the village as the basic unit. Most of the artisans and others who supplied goods and rendered services to the cultivators were resident within the village.

Moreover, the practice of fixed payments in kind at the time of harvest, which constituted the core of the *jajmani* system, represented in fact a sharing of crops by those who rendered services to cultivators As a result, all the residents of the village, both cultivators and non-cultivators, acquired a feeling of direct dependence on the lands of the village, a strong sense of belonging to the village and of sharing in its destiny.

This does not mean, of course, that every village was self-sufficient in every respect or was completely isolated from the outside world. Contacts between neighbouring villages must have been of considerable importance in most areas. Cases of artisans of one village, especially a large village, serving a few neighbouring villages must have been frequent. Marital and other social relationships extended over a number of neighbouring villages, the number of villages and the distances involved being much larger among those groups (e.g., .Jats in northern India) where there are restrictions on marriage within the village. Social scientists who have made village studies in recent years have analyzed the patterns of such inter-village relationships and have also referred to organizations of a specified number of villages (4-20) which had judicial and administrative functions and which must have been well developed in the past. (Lewis, 1954, p. 29-30)[1]

The administrative, economic, and social changes of the last hundred years or so have profoundly affected these three bases on which community feeling centering on the village rested The isolation of the villages has been broken and they have now important administrative, economic, social, and political contacts with the outside world The *jajmani* system has been greatly weakened. In some parts of the country where it existed before, it has practically disappeared. In most others it exists in an attenuated form, with *jajmani* relationships preserved best in the cases of those artisans whose services are most necessary for cultivation (e.g., carpenters) or those whose wares have not been completely replaced by factory-made goods (e.g., potters). Caste has also undergone important changes. Further, the processes which have brought about these changes are operating with ever increasing vigour. This is very clear from the experience of the post-independence years. In this period, as a result of the operation of community development and other development programmes, communications in rural areas have been greatly improved, with the result that the range and magnitude of the villagers' contacts with the outside world have greatly increased. Also systematic efforts are being made to break the mental isolation of villagers and to help them acquire a modern and progressive outlook in the interest of greater production, higher income, and higher levels of living. This is the sole aim of the extension part of the Community Development Programme. Thus, the isolation of the village, both physical and menial, has been effectively broken. The process of substitution of cash transactions for those in kind, which implies breakdown of the *jajmani* system, is being completed at a rapid rate as the villagers are more effectively brought within the orbit of the national market economy. Accordingly, to the extent that the feeling of community centering on the village rested on these two factors—isolation and the *jajmani* system—it is being further weakened at a rapid rate.

The case of caste is different and more complex. The changes of the last hundred years or so have undoubtedly weakened the outward manifestations of caste Thus, they have greatly reduced the rigors of caste taboos and regulations, and weakened organizations, such as the- caste *Panchayats,* which were responsible for enforcing them. Identity between particular castes and occupations has also been affected by the decline of certain occupations (most village crafts), growth of opportunity in others (e.g., trade, and certain service occupation like tailoring), and consequent occupational mobility. Hence the role of caste as a socio-economic-political institution imposing a certain way of life, rules of behaviour, and code of conduct on its members has suffered a decline. But the position of caste as the basic unit of social organization in rural India has not been affected. On the contrary, it is maintained by some sociologists that caste has been strengthened in some ways and is playing entirely new roles which are required and have been made possible by the changed conditions of modern times.[2]

The role of caste in contributing to community feeling centering on the village is rather complicated. The social and economic stability which caste provided was an essential prerequisite of the *jajmani* system: it is doubtful whether the system could have existed in the absence of caste. Therefore, through its support to the *jajmani* system, caste may be seen as an important factor contributing to the feeling of community centering on the village On the other hand, caste itself provides a primary focus for community feeling which is a rival to loyalty to the village. In this connection, the discussion in a recent publication. *Village India.*, is interesting. Srinivas, discussing the social system of a Mysore village, refers to the vertical unity of the village as against the horizontal unity of the caste and says that the village may be described as "a vertical entity made up of several horizontal layers each of which is a caste." Marriott, describing a village in Western UP., analyzes in considerable detail the nature, extent, and limitations of the feeling of community centering on the village and die extent to which the village is a unit. It is interesting to note that both these views, which bring out the limitations of community feeling, centering on the village, are based on field work in parts of the country where the village is a distinct unit of settlement and this feeling is the strongest. In areas, where the settlement pattern is dispersed and the village consists of a number of hamlets, each composed either exclusively or predominantly of members of a single caste, the feeling of community in the sense of belonging to the village is considerably weaker.

The Primary Community

This brings me to the question of the primary community in rural India. After a study of observations made in several village studies which have been published in recent years, and an analysis of experiences with development programmes which required collective effort and contributions from the whole community, I have come to the conclusion that the primary community in rural India is today constituted not by the "village," but by the members of a single caste living within a village. In areas of dispersed settlement where the village consists of several settlement units (*tollas*), the existence of this primary community is very clear, because these *tollas* are organized primarily on the basis of caste. But even in areas where the tightly nucleated village is the settlement unit it is often found that houses of members of different castes concentrate in different sections of the village, the concentration of harijan households in a wing of the village is the most marked. In my view, the multicaste village—most villages in India are multicaste—should more appropriately be called a "secondary community" because the feeling of belonging to it represents the first extension of the primary loyalty to the smaller unit mentioned above. There is considerable support for this view in recent experiences with the Community Development Programme. For example, in many villages participation in such programmes as the pavement of streets and the construction of school buildings and of drinking water wells have been organized primarily on the basis of *tollas*, *mohallas*, or caste groups. This is particularly true where the participation has meant a spontaneous mobilization of local resources of labour, materials, or cash. The whole village might have come together to take a decision for participation in the activity; but the execution of the decision and the actual mobilization of resources has been generally on the basis of the smaller units. This leads me further to think that one reason why development programmes based on the assumption that the village itself is the community meet with considerable difficulties in the field is that, as soon as any such programme is presented to the village, the different primary communities within it begin to think not only of the interest of the village as a whole, but of their own interests, which are often in conflict with the former. Institutions such as panchayats, based on the village as the unit, meet with difficulties for the same reason. The fact has to be faced that the village is a plural society consisting of a number of primary communities, each of which thinks of its own interest at the same time as or even before it thinks of the village.

Conflict between Hierarchical and Egalitarian Concepts

Not only is the village nor the primary community, but its traditional hierarchical organization, in which the status, rights, and obligations of individuals and groups differ, is in fundamental conflict with the egalitarian principles on which India seeks to build new institutions and the new "community." It is necessary to grasp the existence of this conflict and to realize that Indian rural society will have to resolve it and rebuild itself along egalitarian principles. This is no small task, and the difficulties which confront the *Panchayats*, cooperatives, and other institutions requiring cooperative endeavour, can be more readily understood if this fundamental conflict is kept in view. Take the case of the statutory *Panchayats*. Their constitution is based on the two principles that (a) each adult resident in the village has a vote and through it an equal share in the governance of the village, and (b) the entire population of the village shall be governed by the same laws and rules.

Neither of these principles has held for the traditional organization of the village, in which certain groups have had far higher status and far more rights than others, and in which different standards of behaviour and codes of conduct have applied to different groups. The point is so obvious that it is not necessary to elaborate it any further. Therefore, if the village people, the greater part of whose life continues to be governed by the traditional hierarchical organization, have difficulty in grasping the egalitarian principles underlying the statutory *Panchayats* and in working through these institutions, this is not surprising. Similarly, the unsuccessful working of many cooperatives will be found to originate in this conflict between the egalitarian principles which underlie the institution and the hierarchical concepts which govern the rest of village life. In this case, however, the difficulties of bringing the different social and economic groups composing the village into one cooperative society are better appreciated, and it is recognized that separate cooperatives, each catering to the interest of different economic or occupational groups (cultivators, weavers, tanners, carpenters, etc.), are more satisfactory. It is also recognized that it is more feasible to combine the same class of artisans living in adjoining villages in a cooperative society than to combine cultivators and non-cultivators living in the same village. In other words, the bonds of economic life (occupation) with which those of social life (caste) are inextricably mixed are stronger than the community feeling centering on the village.

The hierarchical character of rural life, and the economic and social distances between different sections of the village, arc likely to constitute an even greater difficulty in developing organizations of young men and women. Unlike the *panchayat*, which is a statutory organization, these organizations are voluntary in nature. Moreover, their functions being mainly cultural and recreational, affect those aspects of social life in which deep-seated traditions, emotions, and prejudices play a dominant part. Of the two, the women's organizations will encounter greater difficulties, because the outlook of women is more tradition-oriented than that of the young people But there is no doubt also that the successful working of these organizations would itself prove a powerful factor in social change and in reorienting the pattern of rural social life from the hierarchical to the egalitarian principle.

It is necessary, therefore, to understand clearly the real nature of the task involved in organizing these institutions successfully The task is not merely one of getting rural people to come together to perform certain civic and developmental functions (through *Panchayats*) or economic functions (in cooperatives), or of getting rural women and young people to come together for recreational or cultural programmes. It is really the task of making a fundamental change in the existing basis of social organization of the villages.

Some Future Trends

Toil analysis of the village as a community and the changes to which its social organization has been subjected brings us to the question : what changes in the structure of the village can bc anticipated in the near future, and what kind of a community is likely to emerge, in rural India? This is a large question, an adequate discussion of which is not possible within the scope of this chapter. The following observations may, therefore, be taken as no more than a projection of a few trends which are already observable.

Changes in Physical Structure : Explosion of Villages

The village will undoubtedly remain the unit of settlement in most parts of the country, but there will be important changes in its physical structure and socio-economic composition The physical changes will be especially marked in areas where the tightly nucleated village is the unit of settlement (i.e., the north-west and "dry" areas generally). In most villages in these areas there is acute congestion and shortage of housing, with the result that the villages are under pressure to expand. This pressure is increasing rapidly, because with population growth the demand for housing is increasing and with a rise in living levels people wish to have better, more spacious, and more comfortable houses. The pressure will mount steadily, and there might well be an explosion of villages similar to that which we are seeing today in the case of metropolitan areas like Delhi. The explosion would create a serious land-use situation in many areas. Expansion of villages in most cases can take place only at. the expense of cultivated lands. And, since in most fertile areas there is already intense pressure of population upon cultivated lands, any large scale diversion of these for house-building purposes will aggravate the population pressure still further. Careful land-use planning will, therefore, be necessary.

The expansion of villages will normally mean bringing contiguous areas just outside the village boundaries under habitation. At times this is bound to present serious difficulties, because lands just outside the village may be especially prized for agriculture and, therefore, difficult to obtain; or there may be physical or topographical factors which make such expansion difficult. Consequently, new villages situated at some distance from existing ones will arise. Also there will be a tendency for cultivators to live, homestead fashion, on their fields. This tendency should be particularly marked in areas of well irrigation in which intensive cultivation can be practiced. The factors favouring this tendency are (a) the disappearance or reduced importance of factors such as water supply and need for defense, which favoured nucleated villages in the past, and (b) an appreciation of the advantages, both economic and hygienic, of living on the fields (e.g., more efficient use of farmyard manure, ease of intensive cultivation and production of high-value crops-vegetables and fruit; no need for such facilities as pavement of streets or drains).

The pattern of settlement in these areas is, therefore, likely to become more open and dispersed, with large numbers of new villages and homestead settlements developing side by side with the older, tightly nucleated villages, which would themselves be expanding.

Changes in Socio-economic Composition : Rise of the Service Centres

The socio-economic composition of the villages is also likely to undergo important changes. It is most probable that as the break down of the *jajmani* system becomes complete, more and more artisans and others rendering non-agricultural services will concentrate in the larger villages or small towns. This will have two results:

(1) Progressive agriculturation of the small and medium villages. With the artisans and other non-agriculturists concentrating in the larger villages or small towns, the small and medium villages will become more purely agricultural and thus more nearly homogeneous in both occupational and caste composition.

(2) Growth of the larger villages and small towns into units, which for want of a better name we may call "service centres."

A concentration of artisans in these service centres is essential for technological advance in the crafts and for improvement in the economic and social conditions of the artisans. All the measures needed to achieve these objectives—industrial extension and training of artisans in improved techniques, the provision of common service facilities (e.g., dyeing in fast colours, in the case of handloom weavers), supply of electric power, bulk purchase of good quality raw materials, provision of credit, standardization of product, and efficient marketing) can be provided economically only if the artisans are concentrated in a limited number of service centres instead of being dispersed in every village. Further, innovation, which is necessary for continued technological advance in any industry, can flourish only when artisans are freed from the stagnation imposed by the *jajmani* system, and this can be achieved effectively only when they move from their present locations.

Apart from concentrating the existing artisans, the service centres will supply the large and increasing range of new goods to meet the demands of modern agriculture and rising levels of living. Examples of goods which will be needed in increasing quantities as agriculture is modernized are : improved seed, fertilizers, pesticides and other plant-protection aids, improved implements (including tractors and pumping sets), and such materials as steel, cement, and diesel oil. The supply of these items and the servicing and repair of modern equipment can be arranged efficiently only at service centres. The larger villages and small towns are already centres for the marketing of agricultural produce and the distribution of consumers' goods. Both these roles will assume greater importance as agricultural production, rural incomes, and standards of living rise. Many of the centres will also attract processing industries based upon the agricultural production of the surrounding villages. Some, which have a locational advantage for a particular industry (e.g., availability of raw material or skill in craft), or are caught in the general process of decentralization of industries from the cities, will also develop small or medium-scale industries having a wider market. Facilities for agricultural credit—especially medium-term, long-term, and specialized credit needed for making investments in land or improving agricultural techniques—will also tend to be concentrated at such centres. Further, as cooperative societies for marketing, distribution, and processing grow in importance, these societies will also be located in them.

Social and administrative services already concentrate in the larger villages and small towns. This concentration will continue, and these will be the centres from which all the more advanced services and facilities will be provided to the rural people. While such elementary services as primary education and first-aid medical care can be provided in every village, the more advanced facilities of secondary schools, dispensaries, and hospitals can, obviously, not be thus duplicated. Administrative, recreational, and cultural functions will also follow the concentration of economic and social-service functions in service centres

The above is not a hypothetical picture; it only represents a projection to the near future of the trends which are already visible. Artisans and others providing goods and services to the cultivators already concentrate in larger villages or small towns. Expansion of welfare services is rapidly proceeding to a stage where "service centres" catering to the needs of a number of villages are emerging. The beginnings of these can be seen in many Community Development blocks where a number of facilities are being concentrated in a few large villages which are the natural trade and communication centres for the surrounding villages.

It is difficult to generalize about the size of these centres or about the number of villages or the population that a centre will serve. There will undoubtedly be much variation in these respects in different parts of the country, because of differences in density of population and stage of economic development. In most parts of the country, however, the service centres will have a population ranging between 2,500 and 10,000 (with most falling between 4,000 and 7,500), and will serve a population of 5,000 to 10,000 in their constituent villages. Thus, we visualize that a population of 10,000 to 20,000 (including the population of the service centre itself) will be served by a centre. A normal Community Development block with a population of about 70,000 will, therefore, have three to six such centres, with the block headquarters itself being a bigger centre.

With this development of the service centres, rural society will have two major constituents: (a) a large number of villages, or such smaller units as hamlets or homesteads, and (b) a much smaller number of service centres. The population of the former will be predominantly agricultural, because the artisans and other non-agriculturists will tend to concentrate in the service centres. It will also be more homogeneous socially, because, as explained above, caste and occupation are still closely related in rural India. The villages will, therefore, be predominantly agricultural, with fewer castes and much less social distance between the castes than is the case with villages today. The population of the service centres, on the other hand, will be mixed; besides the artisans and others engaged in service occupations, many cultivators will be living in them. Many of the original cultivator residents of these centres whose lands are close by will continue to live there. In addition, many prosperous cultivators who can afford two establishments will keep their families there (e.g., for the sake of the children's education), while they themselves live on their lands.

The Service Center : Focal Point of the New Community

The service centre with its constituent group of villages will constitute a real community The basis of this community will be functional : the feeling of belonging to it will rest on the wide range of services—economic, social, administrative, cultural, and recreational—which the centre performs for the entire community and on the relationships of mutual dependence (even though based on cash transactions) which will have been established between the artisans and other non-agriculturists on the one hand and the agriculturists on the other It must not be assumed, however, that such a community will be completely or even largely self-sufficient, as the village was very old. For higher social and administrative services, as well as for all economic transactions, the centre will be connected with larger centres—the block headquarters, *mandi* towns[3] and distribution centres—and through them with the wider national life and economy. It will, however, for the reasons explained above be a very real community, the recognition of which will be of immense assistance for planning all rural development programmes.

Such transformations of the structure of the rural society into predominantly agricultural villages on the one hand and service centres on the other, and the emergence of the latter as focal points of the new communities, are essential for an efficient organization of economic functions and for the creation of modern social and administrative purposes. They will also assist in making an effective change from the present hierarchical to the new egalitarian social structure which is the aim of the Community Development Programme. So long as the present economically heterogeneous multi-caste village persists as a basic unit in rural India, the establishment of efficient economic organization and an egalitarian socio-political system will be faced with difficulties. But with the differentiation of the type described above, the change will be easier of achievement. The socio-economic composition of the villages being more homogeneous, social equality will be easier to establish, and, since the relations between agriculturists in the villages and non-agriculturists in the service centres will be primarily cash-based, considerations of caste and social status will be much less important than they are today.

II

Village Caste and Community : A Rajasthan Village*

The village and the caste are the two focii of community feeling in rural India. The average villager feels that he belongs to these two entities. What is happening to these feelings of belonging to the village and the caste in the midst of the rapid social and economic changes, which are coming over rural India? The question is of fundamental importance.

In much of our thinking on rural development, it is assumed that the "village" is the "community". Many of our policies and programmes in this field depend for their success on the existence of a strong feeling of community centering on the village and would by their success, strengthen this feeling further. Programmes requiring popular participation for works of collective benefit like a road or school building, furnish an example.

---

* Published in *Economic Weekly*, Bombay December 8, 1962.

The basic developmental institutions in the village, the *Panchayat* and the co-operative, similarly depend for their success on the existence of a strong feeling of community centering on the village. The feeling of belonging to a caste is to an extent complementary to that of belonging to the village. But it is also competitive; loyalty to caste serves also as a rival to loyalty to the village.

An attempt is made here to answer the question posed above by describing the situation in a Rajasthan village, which the author has had the opportunity to study in some detail for about a year in the early 1960s.

K is a medium-sized multi-caste village with a population of about 2,000 (in 1960), located at a distance of 6 miles from the district headquarter town, which itself is a small town with a population of about 20,000. K is connected with the town by an all-weather motorable road. Until 1955 when the *Jagirs* were resumed, K formed part of the *Jagir* of an important *Jagirdar* of the former Jaipur State. The *Jagirdar* was very powerful in the village, up to the formation of Rajasthan in 1949-50. Thereafter, his power disappeared because Jaipur State ceased to exist; the new Government was committed to abolition of *Jagirdari* and it was accepted by all that its abolition was only a matter of time.

The village has 26 castes, of which Brahmins and *Rajputs* among the high castes, *Jats*, *Malis* and *Meenas* among the cultivating castes, and *Chamaars* among the Scheduled castes are the most numerous. *Chamaars*, forming about one-fourth of the total population of the village, are the largest single caste. However, no single caste is in a dominant position in the village (Table 12.1).

Table 12.1: Caste Composition of Village K*

Caste	Households No	Population No
Brahmin	32	137
Rajput	23	128
Mahajan	14	57
Jat	41	229
Meena	26	145
Mali	·78	380
Gujjar	16	79
Kumhar	21	104
Chamar	88	544
Koli	10	60
Others	72	350
Total	421	2213

* The village has been given a fictitious name 'Maanpur' later in detailed study of Socio-economic change in village India.

Village is Home

The average resident of *K* is very conscious of the fact of his belonging to the village. *K* is his home. He is also keenly aware of membership of his particular caste. Caste is the most important social institution and the main basis of social grouping. The village itself is thought of as an entity composed of seven castes; the smaller castes being ignored in this reckoning. It is recognized that in any matter concerning the whole village, representatives of all the castes must be consulted. Each caste is known by its traditional occupation and social status (place in the social hierarchy), although it is recognized that very important changes have taken place in these respects in recent years; the *Rajputs* have lost their political and social supremacy and that the *Chamaars,* after leaving lifting of dead animals and leather-work, are concentrating on cultivation and are aspiring to become equals of the traditional cultivating castes like the *Meenas* and *Jats.*

***Only One* Abadi**

In order to understand the changes which are occurring in the feelings of belonging to the village and the caste, it will be useful first to recall the bases on which these feelings rested in the past, and then to analyze the changes to which each of these has been subjected. In the present author's view, the feeling of belonging to the village rested on four main bases :

(i) contiguous living;
(ii) isolation and concentration of economic activity within the village;
(iii) the *jajmani* system; and
(iv) caste.

So far as contiguous living is concerned, no marked change has taken place so far. Practically all the village families continue to live within the *abadi* (habitation area) of the village. With increase in population and growing prosperity, a large number of new houses have come up during the last ten years; but all these are located within the village *abadi*. This area is now fully occupied and the villagers have been feeling the need for additional land for housing. A few families whose houses in the village *abadi* are insufficient for their needs have begun to use *baras* (literally "cattle sheds") built near their irrigation wells for residential purposes.

But these *bara* dwellings are additional and supplementary to their main houses in the village. There is as yet no movement out of the *abadi* area; but there will be soon, because the need for additional land is being keenly felt. The new *abadi* lands will have to be at some distance from the existing *abadi*, because the lands contiguous to the *abadi* are all highly productive and well irrigated lands—the best in the village—which the owners are very unwilling to give up. When movement to the new *abadi* areas takes place, the village families will be divided among two, three or more settlement units, and the feeling of belonging to one village, which is continuously strengthened by the fact of living together in a compact settlement, will be weakened. It is not improbable that in course of time each of the new *abadis* develops an identity of its own. However, this is for the distant future.

Isolation and concentration of economic activity within the village are things of the past now. It is hardly necessary to recount the stages in which these changes have occurred over the last 100 years or more, or to mention the social and economic forces, which have brought these about. These are well known. However, it is well to emphasize that these forces have been operating with increasing vigour during the last decade, and especially since the completion of the all-weather motorable road, five years ago (in 1956). To day, the combination of the road, motor transport, and bicycles has brought the village within 20-30 minutes of the town and has made active and daily contact with it possible. One important result of this has been the growth of commuting to work in town. About 50 men of the village have permanent year-round jobs in industries and public works in town or the railway station. Another 100-150 persons work as casual or salaried workers for 4-8 months in the year. These 150-200 workers, representing about one-sixth of the total labour force of the village, go to town almost every day and are in constant touch with happenings in it and the outside world. The merchants, village leaders like the *Sarpanch* and the four students who go to study in the High school, are other frequent visitors to the town. The average cultivator does not go to the town so much: but even he goes often enough—to buy cloth and other essentials, to dispose of his produce and for various miscellaneous purposes.

Contact with Town

Besides the villagers going to town, many town men come to the village. Eight school teachers come daily to teach in the village school: two shopkeepers live in town and come to their shops in the village. Government officials, political leaders, itinerant vendors, are other frequent visitors to the village. The daily newspapers, the postal service and the radio also contribute towards keeping the villagers informed about happenings in the town, in Rajasthan and the world at large. All in all, the village is in constant touch with the town and the average villager is nearly as well informed about news as the town dweller of comparable economic and educational status.

With about one-sixth of the labour force working outside it, the village is no longer the sole theatre of economic activity. Those who work outside feel that they are no longer entirely dependent upon the village for their living but are part of a larger economic system, of which the focus is the town. Even those who do not work themselves know that work is available in town, that it is an alternative or supplement to their agricultural work, and an opportunity for their younger generation which can be availed of when the family holding is no longer sufficient. The village lands are no longer seen as the sole source of sustenance; other sources are seen as actually or potentially important. The consciousness of being part of a nation-wide economic system grows, albeit slowly. The more thinking and better informed villagers realize that the pace of development works, in the town depends upon decisions taken by Ministers and officers in Delhi and Jaipur. The traders and the village leaders who have had much to do with courts and other administrative agencies have had this consciousness for a long time. It is now coming slowly to the ordinary villager.

As a result of this active and continuous contact, there is widespread awareness of the link with the town. However, there is as yet no realization of forming part of a region (like the area of the *Panchayat Samiti* or the *tehsil*) of which the town is the centre. The *Panchayat* members and other informed villagers know that their village forms part of the Sawai Madhopur *Panchayat Samiti*. All of them know that it forms part of the *tehsil* of the same name. But, these institutions only emphasize the link of the village with the town; they do not as yet bring any marked awareness of belonging to the region covered by them or of any link with other villages in the region. The links with other villages depend upon kinship and marital relationships; but the regions[4] for these are different and do not coincide with the above administrative units.

The Jajmani System

The *Jajmani* system has all but broken down. The system even though it had been disintegrating for a long time had continued somewhat longer in this area, than in other parts of the country, because the *Jagirdars* enforced the traditional obligations, especially those involving unpleasant jobs like drawing of water by the *Kumhars* (potters) and cleaning of utensils by the *Nais* (barbers). However, the breakdown of the system was especially rapid after the abolition of *Jagirdari*, when one caste after another repudiated its customary obligations. The biggest blow to the system was given in 1956 by the *Chamaars'* refusal to lift dead cattle and to do leather work. The movement against doing these two jobs had been active among the *Chamaars* of the area since the middle forties. It came to the village immediately after the abolition of *Jagirdari*. Most of the villagers opposed the *Chamaars*: but a few including the *Sarpanch*, who depended upon their votes, supported them. After some time, the villagers acquiesced in this change which had been occurring over the whole area and which they considered inevitable. The dead cattle are now lifted by the *Bhangis* (scavengers), who flay the carcasses and sell the raw hides, but do not do any tanning or leatherwork. The villagers have to depend upon purchases in town for all their requirements of leather goods, chief among which are shoes and *charas*, (leather bucket for lifting water for irrigation). There is not even one cobbler in the village for repairs of leather goods—shoes, *charas* etc. Two other castes, the *Kumhars* and the *Nais*, have left their customary obligations of drawing water and cleaning utensils, though they are carrying on their major traditional occupations of making pots and hair-cutting, respectively.

The *Jajmani* system is being followed in an attenuated form in respect of only four castes: *Kumhars* (potters), *Nais* (barbers), *Khatis* (carpenters) and *Lohars* (smiths). The *Kumhars* supply earthen pots for which there are no factory-made substitutes yet. The other three render services, which are essential, especially for cultivators. But even in case of these castes, the *Jajmani* system is not being followed by all the families in the village. Most of the non-cultivating and a large number of the cultivating families are not following *Jajmani*, but are paying for the goods and services furnished by these castes in cash. Even the families having *Jajmani* relationships, obtain only a part of their requirements in *Jajmani* payments, and pay for the rest in cash.

Caste

Caste acted as a support of the *Jajmani* system: the two were intimately related, and it is doubtful if the *Jajmani* system could have existed without caste. Therefore, through its support to the *Jajmani* system, caste may be seen as a contributor to the feeling of belonging to the village, just as the isolation and the feeling of belonging to the village could be seen as factors contributing to the enforcement of caste discipline. However, the more important role of caste today is as an alternative or rival focus of community feeling, and it is with this role of caste that we are concerned here primarily.

Caste has been weakened in several ways. First, with the growth of individualism, caste organizations have become weaker, especially among the high castes—*Brahmins*, *Rajputs* and *Mahajans*. Many members of these castes feel that they have no caste organization or discipline left any longer. This is an exaggeration however, because there are few cases of serious lapse from the conduct traditionally sanctioned by the caste. The *Rajputs* and to a lesser extent the *Brahmins* have had to suffer a major social and economic comedown in the wake of abolition of *Jagirdari* and to make major adjustments in their attitudes and modes of living. The weakness of the caste organizations among them is due partly to this factor. Among the cultivating and lower castes however, as the following discussion will show, the caste organizations continue to be strong and have been assuming new roles.

Ideas of Social Equality

Second, caste as an arbiter of social status is much less important than before. The lower castes particularly are restive with the inferior status, which the caste system gives them. Ideas of political and social equality have been sweeping the village. There have been (by 1961) two General Elections and four elections to the *Panchayat* and the lower castes have experienced the political propaganda, which accompanies these. They see also that the village level institutions, the *Panchayat*, the co-operative and the school, are all based on egalitarian principles and that they are entitled to the benefits of these institutions as much as the high castes. They see their representatives sitting on the *Panchayat* along with the high castes and realize that one of them could one day be the *Sarpanch* (there is one *Chamaar Sarpanch* in the *Panchayat Samiti* already). This more than anything else convinces them that times have changed and that social equality is not only desirable, but also attainable. They are also becoming increasingly conscious of their economic rights and privileges. This is true especially of the *Chamaars*, who after leaving their leatherwork are depending entirely upon cultivation and labour. They have got rights in land under the recent tenancy legislation and are very anxious to obtain more Government land for cultivation. They know that the Government is giving special concessions to the landless and the scheduled castes in allotment of agricultural lands. They are very keen to avail of these concessions and are quite vocal about their special privileges and "rights".

The high castes also realize that the obvious social inequalities associated with the caste system must go. Some high caste villagers, notably the *Sarpanch*, have made an effort to abolish untouchability and have succeeded to the extent of opening one drinking water well to all castes. They also realize that restrictions on food and drink are not practical in towns, and have seen shopkeepers in the town serving high and low caste alike. However, they are not yet ready to practice commensality in the village.

But while the obvious manifestations of caste are being reduced, caste as a social institution is not getting any weaker, nor is there any diminution in feeling of belonging to one's caste. In fact in some ways, the reverse is true. The caste organization is gathering new strength by acquiring new functions and roles. The role of caste in elections and politics has been commented on by several social scientists and need not be reiterated here. In this area, the most notable recent demonstration of the strength of the caste organizations has been their effectiveness in sweeping away customary obligations: leatherwork for the *Chamaars*; carrying water for the *Kumhars*; cleaning utensils for the *Nais*. No member of the caste concerned in this or surrounding villages dare perform these tasks. The caste organizations are also effective in preventing their members from taking up new occupations for which new opportunities are arising, but which are not sanctioned by them. Thus, there is not a single non-Gujjar who sells milk, or a non-Mali who grows or sells vegetables. The demand for milk and vegetables is increasing with the growth of population in the town and near the railway station. But the supply of these products remains entirely in the hands of castes that have been supplying these traditionally, and in case of milk there is an acute scarcity as supplies have failed to keep pace with the increasing demand.

Rigid Caste Endogamy

It is perhaps unnecessary to mention that there is no instance of inter-caste marriage or other breach of rules of caste endogamy. Any such departure would be inconceivable. What is more significant and disturbing is that association and social intercourse are becoming increasingly caste-wise. The traditional forms of inter-caste association have steadily lost ground and the new forms, mostly sponsored by development staffs, have failed to gain popularity. Feasts on the occasions of marriages and deaths, are the best means for getting together in this area. These are now almost all caste-wise. Large feasts at the homes of rich *Jagirdars* or *Mahajans* which people of all castes attended are becoming infrequent. The *Jagirdars* are gone and large feasts are not encouraged (death feasts are prohibited by law). On the other hand, small feasts to which members of one's own caste alone are invited have become much more frequent; even the small cultivator or labourer can now afford to give a small feast. Festivals like *Dussehra, Teej, Gangore*, which were organized by the *Jagirdar* and in which the whole village participated, have been discontinued. Most of the festivals are now celebrated by the villagers, either in their own homes (e.g. *Diwali*), or in their own temples (e.g. *Janmashtami*) each of which belongs to a particular caste. The only festival, which is now being celebrated by all the villagers together, is the *Jal-jhoolni Gyares*, which comes in September-October. On the other hand the institution of caste-wise *kirtans* has grown. Formerly, *kirtan* was confined to two or three temples of the high castes and was largely the concern of Brahmins. But during the last ten years, *kirtan* parties have sprung up in all temples including that of the *Chamaars* and all these parties are organized caste-wise.

Associations like Youth Club and Community Recreation Centre organized under the Community Development Programme have not become popular. The only institution where members of different castes do meet daily, associate and play together is the school. But the school children are young, and the influence of the school on the associations and recreation patterns of adults will be seen only after 10-15 years when the school children of today grow up.

No Voluntary Community Action

The *Panchayat* and Cooperative are other institutions where persons of different castes come together. But these are not institutions of social intercourse or recreation. They are designed for specific administrative, developmental and economic functions. The institutions have been fairly successful in performing their specific functions. Thus, the *Panchayat* carries out its administrative functions fairly well; and has in the past completed a number of development works like the school building, a drinking water well and the *Panchayat* building. The cooperative is one of the most successful in the district, having a large and successful business in credit and distribution of agricultural supplies. These institutions have a contribution to make in promotion of inter-caste association on an equal footing, but they are not institutions of social intercourse and their working does not furnish any occasion for all or most villagers to come together.

One final fact may be mentioned. K has not had a tradition of voluntary community action. During the time of the *Jagirdar*, all works of collective benefit were carried out under the orders of the *Jagirdar*, often with coercive mobilization of labour and other resources (*Begar*). After the abolition of *Jagirdari*, there has been no other instance of mobilization of resources on a community-wise basis of village-wise benefit except the school building. Monetary contributions for it were collected on behalf of the *Panchayat* by the revenue agency. Two works, pavement of the bazaar and construction of the community centre, are lying incomplete because the requisite contributions are not forthcoming from the villagers. All the village leaders admit that mobilization of contributions for a work of village-wise benefit is extremely difficult. On the other hand, caste-wise mobilization of contributions has been moderately active. Three temples, of the *Chamaars, Malis* and *Jains*, have been completed with contributions from members of the respective castes during the last five years.

Conclusion

The experience of this village leads to two major conclusions :

(i) The feeling of belonging to the village is becoming weaker; but that of belonging to the caste is not becoming weaker and is in fact becoming stronger in some ways. The feeling for the village even though it is local, is secular in character in as much as it transcends caste, kin or other groups, while that for the caste is essentially sectarian.

(ii) The village is being transformed from an integrated socio-economic unit to which all residents had a strong attachment and a feeling of belonging, to a habitation containing a collection of competing castes. This latter stage has by no means been reached; but the trend is in this direction.

The role of caste in the 'community', social and political areas has been explained above. Caste also plays a significance role in assigning occupation to members of a castes group and thus their economics status.

It also directs the mobility of a caste from one occupation to another occupation and into non-traditional and thus non-prescribed occupations. Analysis of caste and occupational mobility from traditional to non-traditional occupations and a shift within the traditional occupations was studied by the author in his field studies in Rajsthan. The findings form part of the chapters on 'Caste and Occupation Mobility' (Chapter 13) and 'From Untouchables to Peasant Proprietors: The Story of the Berwa *Chamaars*' (Chapter 14).

NOTES

1. This is a study of a *jat* village in Delhi State.
2. The role of caste in influencing elections and political alignments is most frequently noted.
3. Markets for agricultural produce.
4. The regions (area) for example in which the marital relations of a caste are concentrated are different for different castes.

REFERENCES

Census of India 1951.

Lewis, Oscar : *Village Life in Northern India;* University of Illinois Press 1958.

Marriott, McKim: *Village India;* Chicago University Press 1955.

Srinivaes, M.N. in *Village India;* ed. Marriott McKim, Chicago Press 1955.

13

Caste and Occupational Mobility*

Caste played and continues to play a very important role in occupational change from the traditional village economy to a market economy in which the economic motive is at least as or more important as the traditional caste based motives. By 1961, a large number of *Brahmin* and *Rajput* young men of Raipur had become *patwaris*, Village Level Workers (VLWs), secretaries of *Panchayat* and cooperative societies, teachers in primary schools, *vaidyas* (practitioners of ancient Ayurvedic system of medicine), clerks in offices of the Rajasthan government and the cement factory. After getting educated up to the middle school or higher secondary school examination, some of the *Brahmin* and *Mahajan* girls had also become teachers in primary schools in their villages. These jobs paid well and since the young men were posted within 30 km. of Raipur, they could visit their families on week-ends and could keep in touch with them through letters. However, no *Brahmin* had taken to trading or become an artisan such as carpenter, mason, smith, driver of motor vehicles, etc. despite the high level of earnings in them. These occupations were literally closed to them.

The *Mahajans* of Raipur could become traders in the Manntown market or like the Brahmin white collar workers after passing the necessary examinations. However, they preferred to remain trader-moneylender-*cum*-non-cultivating owners of their land within their own villages. Besides, relatively high earnings, prestige was a major consideration with staying in the village.

The *Rajputs* of Maanpur were satisfied with remaining non-cultivating owners of their lands that they could retain for self-cultivation. They

---

* This chapter is based on village studies by the author in Sawai Madhopur District of Eastern Rajasthan in early 1960s and a resurvey by a team of researchers deputed by him in 2001.

employed *Chamaars, Meena and Malies* as agricultural labourers or share croppers for cultivation of their lands. Their aspiration was that one or more sons should get educated and become a white collar worker. However, one son must remain to look after the land of the family. This gave prestige to the family and also provided sizeable income. They would marry their daughters to educated *Rajput* young men who were in the Army or were white collar workers or were managing family farms.

The *Meenas* were satisfied with managing their farms better to increase agricultural production. Those with small holdings supplemented their income with unskilled work on repair of the railway tracks or the roads or work in the cement factory. They were interested primarily in producing field crops (sorghum, millet, wheat and oil seeds) but were not interested in producing vegetables, fruit or milk for sale, which was the traditional job of the *Malies*. In addition, they produced wheat, sorghum and oilseeds. The *Gujjars* were helping to meet the demand for milk. Similarly, the increasing demand for meat was met by Hindu *khotiks* and the Moslems.

The *Chamaar* small cultivators were interested in being recognized as a cultivating caste, the equal of the Meenas. They supplemented their income from land like the *Meenas* with unskilled work on repair of the railway tracks or roads. Some of them had become carpenters, masons, smiths, etc. and found well paid jobs in *Maantown* market or in building houses in *Maantown*. The teachers in schools and doctors in hospital could be *Brahmins*, *Mahajans* or *Rajput* while nurses and mid-wives invariably be *Chamaars* or Moslems *i.e.* the women who performed these tasks by tradition. The meat sold in the Maantown market was all goat meat. Beef or meat of camels could not be sold because of the sensibilities of the people in this predominantly Hindu area. Cattle were reared in the woodlands to produce bullocks. The meat of sheeps and goats was sold by *Gujjars* who grazed their herds on the stubble of the cultivated fields and in the forests. This was done primarily to earn some cash and to keep size of their herds within the availability of the pasture. Thus, even in 2001, the economic motive had not become dominant. Caste considerations remained important in choice of new economic activities in the new market economy.

Change in Values

People of all castes including the *Meenas*, *Malies* and *Chamaars* had accepted the fact that education of girls to the primary school level was a good thing. They did not feel that girls educated to primary school level would not work in the fields. Moreover, cultivation of land by tractors and use of other equipment such as mechanical shellers of sorghum and millets or dehuskers of wheat had reduced women's work in the fields. They could, therefore, devote their time to their work as mothers and home-makers. The men realized also that educated women would get prompt treatment for themselves and their children in case of communicable or other diseases of the children or themselves. Furthermore, clean homes and access to clean and more adequate drinking water supply from wells located in the villages or pipe water from overhead tanks meant less disease among their men, children and themselves.

By 2001 most of the *Meenas* still said that they did not accept any bride price, but gave dowry on marriage of their daughters. However the truth of this statement could not be verified. Child marriages had been reduced greatly. The *Brahmins*, *Mahajans* and *Rajputs* married their daughters only when they were 16 or 18 years of age and the young men were 22-25 years old. By this time, both were mature and could not fall easy victims to diseases and death. Widows had always been considered a burden among the high castes, who wanted to keep their number to the minimum, because they were not an economic asset; no high caste woman is! Although, widow remarriage was allowed among all other castes, except the high castes the widows did not have a high social status. Even the Moselems did not accord a high status to their widows. This is primarily because they are not an economic asset. The ban on remarriage of young widows must have relaxed among the high caste; in a recent announcement by one of the *Panchayats* in Madhya Pradesh, special efforts were being made for remarriage of young windows.

A few Moslem widows of Raipur had become tailors so that they could earn some money while sitting at home. A Delhi based NGO, *Dastkar*, had opened a centre in Raipur where Moslem women made quilted bed sheets for export to Europe and embroidered dresses for sale to the tourists. But no Hindu woman took up this activity despite high earnings in it. *Brahmin* widows used to carry milk from Raipur to the Maantown market on their heads to earn a little money to support themselves. They were looked down upon by the rest of the community for being so poor. But these supposedly enlightened people were so stupid that they would not allow their widows to learn a remunerative trade like tailoring. The *Brahmin* women just did not do this skilled work. On the other hand, *Brahmin* cooks who used to cook for marriages in Raipur in

1961 continued this activity in 2001. Some of them had opened shops to sell food and sweets in the Maantown market and were doing very well!

In 1961, almost all the district level officers were *Brahmins*, *Rajputs*, *Mahajans*, *Kayasthas* or Moselems. All the clerks in Collector's office belonged to these groups. Almost all the policemen were either *Rajputs* or *Jats*. The president of the Bar Association was a *Brahmin* lawyer who was also the chairman of the Sawai Madhopur municipal committee. These jobs preferences had changed by 2001 only to the extent that many *Meenas* have become clerks, village level worker, secretaries of *Panchayats* or cooperative societies or traders. Many *Chamaars* had become clerks or junior officers.

Thus, most of the jobs in the new economy had been taken by those for whom the change to these jobs was permitted by tradition. The traditional job preferences or prohibitions had not changed between 1961 and 2001, despite the major economic and social changes that have been described in the subsequent chapter on the village studies in Rajasthan.

14

The Changing Role of Caste

From Untouchables to Peasant Proprietors—The Story of the Berwa Chamaars*

Introduction

It has been mentioned in previous chapters on village, caste and community as well as in later chapters on village studies in Rajasthan that caste has been the most important institution in India for more than 2000 years. Members of a caste have the same occupation, norms of conduct and relationship with members of other castes in the village. Furthermore, there are deep cleavages among the residents of high castes and big landowners on the one hand and residents of the scheduled castes and small marginal farmers on the other. These traditional cleavages have been significantly altered between residents of the villages after the land reform of abolition of *zamindari, jagirdari* and other similar exploitative land tenures, was implemented during the middle 1950s. The *zamindars* mostly *Rajputs* or *Brahmins* lost all the uncultivable land and land that was uncultivated but was cultivable that they had retained as woodlands to graze their animals or to get fuel and fodder and were left with small cultivable areas for self cultivation. The lands taken from them were allotted by the State governments to small, marginal farmers to make their farms viable cultivable units or to members of the scheduled castes so that they could become cultivating owners. After this change in their economic status, members of the scheduled castes, ceased to perform their traditional occupations of flaying hides and skins of dead animals

* This chapter is based on village studies conducted by the author early in 1960s in Sawai Madhopur district of Eastern Rajasthan where he was posted as Collector for two years.

and making leather goods for shoes and for buckets for irrigation wells. They ceased also to do their traditional duties of working for the families of *zamindars* or *jagirdars* on life cycle events such as birth, marriage and death.

They devoted their energy to cultivation of the land that had been allotted to them. They would work as agricultural labourers or labourers on public works, if such work was available, to supplement their income from cultivation. Since they could not draw water from the wells of the high castes, they improved their own wells with financial assistance from the Community Development Administration. Similar assistance was sought and obtained for building primary schools (for boys) in their hamlets or part of the village. Furthermore, 25 per cent of the seats in Parliament and legislatures of most of the States are reserved for the members of the scheduled castes and scheduled tribes. Setting up of three tier *Panchayati Raj* institutions have extended these privileges in the local elected bodies also. Thus, both the land reform of the 1950s and the electoral process have been major influences for social and economic change.

This chapter describes the change in occupation and social status of the *Chamaars* and the migration, which accompanied it among Berwa *Chamaars* of villages in Sawai Madhopur district of Eastern Rajasthan. It gives the regional picture of change with a case study of change in one village Manpur. This village was selected because both types of change—the village *Chamaars* abandoning their traditional occupations and obligations and immigration of *Chamaars*—were represented in it. Besides it analyses through reference to the social forces that have contributed to the change and describes some of its effects. This method of giving first the regional picture and then describing the process of change in one village appears to involve some repetition. But it has the advantage of bringing out on the one hand the general character of change and on the other showing how it occurred and how it has affected the economic activities of the *Chamaars* and social and economic relations within individual village communities.[1]

One of the major social changes in this area has been that the *Chamaars* have left their traditional obligation of flaying carcasses, doing leather work, and rendering certain services to the cultivators and are devoting themselves entirely to cultivation and/or labour. This change began about 20 years ago and had been completed in all villages of this area a few years before the study (in 1961). It has brought a major change in economic activity and social status of the *Chamaars*, transforming them from untouchable, at the bottom of the social scale, to cultivators-*cum*- labourers aspiring for social equality with other cultivating castes. It had also had far reaching repercussion on the social, economic, and political life of the area. The change is a product of the current process of social and political change; but it can also be considered a major event, a landmark, in that process.

The *Berwa Chamaars* [2] are a large group in this area. The number is estimated at ten per cent of the total rural population and is next only to that of the *Meenas.* Until the early 1940s, when this change began, they used to flay carcasses of dead cattle, tan the hides and make leather goods, and do various services (*begars*)[3] for the cultivators and other villagers. They also did agricultural and non-agricultural labour and cultivated small holdings which they owned or took on lease. Tanning of hides and making of leather goods is really the work for the *Rehgars* (lit. tanners and dyers of leather); wherever they lived, they did this work while the *Chamaars* did flaying. But since the *Rehgars* lived only in the large villages, the *Chamaars* did leather work as well. They were bound to the cultivators by contractual obligation embodied in the *Jajmani* system, and received fixed payment in grain at the time of harvest. The *begars* for the cultivators consisted of various labour jobs in the field, in the home and on ceremonial occasions. The *Chamaars* assisted the cultivators in thrashing grain and carrying the thrashed grain and chaff to stores in their homes. They cleaned the cattle shed, and did various jobs connected with cultivation. They were also available for hired labour whenever required; in fact, the *Chamaars* formed the largest component of the agricultural labour force in the area. Their women similarly assisted the cultivators' women in making cow dung cakes and doing such arduous household tasks as grinding grain. *Chamaar* men and women worked at the time of marriage and other ceremonies in the cultivators' homes. The midwives were almost invariable *Chamaar* or Muslim women. The *Chamaars* had certain obligations towards the village also. They had the responsibility of looking after the visiting officials of the revenue department and other department of the State government. They were required to carry their luggage, to bring *charpoys*, bedding, fuel and other supplies for them; to call the cultivators from their homes or fields, when the official wanted to see them, and to remain in attendance for miscellaneous duties. They had also the responsibility of helping the *patwaris*[4] in tasks like measurement of fields. All in all, they were the general purpose servants of the cultivators and of the village, while their women had a similar role in the cultivators' homes.

Non-agricultural labour was another economic activity of the *Chamaars*, but as sufficient employment was not available within the area large numbers went for work outside it. This migration took two main forms: (i) seasonal migration to forests of Madhya Pradesh to make wood charcoal, and (ii) permanent or semi-permanent migration to towns, especially industrial centres like Indore and Ujjain in Madhya Pradesh and Ahmedabad in Gujarat, to work in industries, construction and other such work. The migrants to the forests left homes between November and January, and came back in June, just before the onset of the monsoon. But migration to the industrial centres tended to be more permanent, especially if the migrant was successful in finding permanent employment. It increased in volume in the 1930s and especially in the 1940s, with rapid expansion of employment in industries and public works as a result of World War II.

Accordingly, the *Chamaars* who were flayers of carcasses and workers in leather, as the name of the caste might suggest, but these were only two of either several economic activities and in case of most *chamaar* families not the most important. But these were traditional tasks and the *chamaars'* obligations to the village community; because of their association with these, they were untouchable and thus occupying almost the lowest position in rural society.

All this has changed during the last twenty years. The *Chamaars* have stopped lifting dead cattle, flaying carcasses, making leather goods and doing various *begars* for the cultivators. They have walked out of the *Jajmani* system. Most of them are land-owners and cultivators, though their holdings are small and they have either to take additional areas for cultivation on *betai*, or to supplement their earning from cultivation with agricultural or non-agricultural labour. The social transformation has been even greater. The *Chamaars* feel that since they have given up their 'defiling' and 'servile' tasks, they should be treated as a clean caste. Their ambition is to be recognized as a clean caste of cultivating owners, the equal of the *Meenas.* The people of other castes are also very conscious of the change. They realize that the *Chamaars* have become assertive and unwilling to tolerate social inequality, leave alone untouchability. The *Meenas* and other caste of traditional cultivating owners resent the changes the most, for reasons explained below.

These changes in occupation and social status of the *Chamaars* are not confined to Sawai Madhopur *tehsil*. They have occurred in neighbouring districts of Rajasthan and are of regional occurrence. But in this *tehsil*, they were accompanied by a large migration of *Chamaars*, from villages in which they had been living for generations to other villages and to new settlements of their own. This migration made possible by availability of unoccupied culturable waste land in the foothills, plains and valleys in the eastern part of the *tehsil* has been a distinctive feature of the change in it. It has accelerated and facilitated the change in occupation and made possible attainment of the *Chamaars'* objective of becoming cultivating owners; and it has not brought acute social tension and conflict.

The case description of Manpur is based on the author's field work in the village over a period of more than a year. Data on economic activities of the *Chamaars* were obtained through a household survey. Data on migration of *Chamaars* were collected in all villages of the *tehsil* with the assistance of the *patwaries*.[4] Most of the latter belong to the *tehsil* and have worked in it for a long period, and were quite familiar with the social and economic changes of recent years—including migration of the *Chamaars*. This previous knowledge of migration was an advantage, because both the *Chamaars* and other castes were reticent on the subject of migration. The *Chamaars* were trying to forget their past—their earlier occupation, social position in the old villages, and migration. The *Meenas* and other cultivators, especially of villages from which *Chamaars* had gone, were also not too keen to talk about these happenings[5].

Change in the Area

Before starting description of change in the *tehsil*, it would be appropriate to refer to the riots in 1939 between the *Meenas* and the *Chamaars* in several villages of Lalsot *tehsil* of Jaipur district, located 30 miles to the north of Sawai Madhopur *tehsil*. Influences like spread of ideas of social and political equality and the feeling against untouchability and other disabilities suffered by the scheduled castes, had been working for quite some time, and had been building up. These riots, however, were the first violent expression of these. The riots were suppressed by the police of Jaipur state without much difficulty, but tension prevailed in the area for several months: during this time a number of villages were intensively patrolled and other necessary measures were taken by the police to prevent recurrence of violent outbreaks. But as subsequent events have shown, the riots were the signal for the start of a movement of far reaching significance, which had continued to this day.

The main cause of the dispute between the two castes was the refusal of the *Meenas* to allow the *Chamaars* to give elaborate feasts on marriage and other occasions, erect poles[6] before their houses and to allow *Chamaar* women to wear *Kari* (an ankle ornament) and other silver ornaments or walk through the village street with their shoes on. Thus the stated points of the dispute were items of dress and social practices, which are popular among the *Meenas* (and other cultivating castes) and which the *Chamaars* wanted to adopt. But this desire of the *Chamaars* was regarded by the *Meenas* as an attempt to shake of their position of subservience and social inferiority. It is interesting to note that flaying of carcasses, leather-work or *begar* was not expressly mentioned in the dispute. But the inferiority of the *Chamaars* was based upon these, and allowing them to adopt the dress code and social practices of the *Meenas* would have meant recognition of their claim to social equality. And this would have meant, in turn, acceptance of their right to repudiate their traditional occupation and obligations whenever they wished to. These implications were well understood by both the Meenas and the *Chamaars*. The item of dress and social practice served only as symbols of the social struggle.

The outcome of the riots could be considered to have been favourable to the *Chamaars*. The riots were effectively suppressed, and a large number of *Meenas* were punished for causing violence. What is more important, the *Chamaars* were left with the clear impression that no attempt would be made by the state to enforce their customary obligations to the cultivators or to interfere in any way with their struggle for social equality with the latter.

In Sawai Madhopur *tehsil* proper, the trouble started in 1943-44 in village Surpur, six miles north of Sawai Madhopur town. This is a big village (population in 1961 was about 3,000) with a large population of *Meenas*; it has always been considered to be the leading *Meena* village of the *tehsil*. Moreover, it is surrounded by a number of small villages in which the *Meenas* are predominant. Surpur and all the surrounding villages were *khalse* villages, directly administrated by the Jaipur state. Predominance of *Meenas* and absent of local *jagirdars* or even of large number of people of the high castes, had made the group of the villages a *Meena* stronghold. The points of dispute in this village included refusal of the *Chamaars* to flay carcasses of dead cattle, besides the item of dress and social practices mentioned above. There was some violence, and the *Chamaars* were turned out of the villages by the *Meena* cultivators. But they were assisted by the state in settling down, three miles south of the village, on cultivable waste land which was allocated to them, for settlement and cultivation. The state also helped them to establish a new, well planned village of their own. This clearly shows that the sympathies of the state and its local officers were with the *Chamaars*.

Even before the quarrel in Surpur began, there had been some migration of *Chamaars*, especially from small villages along the Banas River at the northern end of the *tehsil*. But the trouble in Surpur was the signal for quarrel between the *Meenas* and the *Chamaars* and *Chamaar* emigration from small villages in the entire *Meena*-dominated central and northern part of the *tehsil*. The quarrel and immigration was confined, however, to small villages in the *Meena* dominated zone: large villages in the Zone (*e.g.* Raipur), in which people of the high caste were present in large numbers, or villages located in the western part of the *tehsil* in which the *jagirdars* had a strong influence, did not experience these. In the latter the occupational change was accomplished without immigration: the *Chamaars* continued to live in the villages with changed occupation and, gradual change in social status. The rest of the community reconciled itself to the change. However, as the experience of village Raipur (which formed part of a larger study) brought out that strained relations and tensions arising from it continue to this day.

Migration of *Chamaars*

The principal findings are :

(i) Out of a total 2,122 *Chamaar* families living in 199 villages of the Sawai Madhopur *tehsil*[7], 712, or one-third of the total, are living in villages to which they moved during the last 20 years. In other words, one in every three rural *Chamaar* families in the *tehsil* has been affected by the movement.

(ii) But the number of *Chamaar* families reported to have left their villages during this period is only 495; this number is considerably smaller than the figure of immigrant families for the following reasons :

  (a) Increase in the number of families, due to natural increase in population and subdivision of families after arrival in the new villages. The influence of this factor was clearly seen in cases where migration had been entirely from one village *A* to another village *B*. In all such cases the reported number in village *B* was higher than the number of families reported to have left village *A*.

  (b) Net immigration from outside the *tehsil*. While most of the migration has been within the *tehsil*, there has been some immigration from villages outside the *tehsil* also.

  (c) Reporting on the number of families, which had left their villages, cannot be as exact as on the number of families which have arrived; the latter are present in the village and the former are not! From experience in this survey it appears that there is tendency to under-report the out-migration.

(iii) Emigration of *Chamaar* families has been reported from 55 villages, while immigration has been reported in 32 villages. The area of *tehsil* can be divided into three "movement zones" from which there has been the heaviest emigration; it includes the villages of the central plain extending north from Sawai Madhopur town to the Banas River. The second zone of emigration includes the villages to the east and south of Sawai Madhopur town and about 15 villages to the south-east of it (located south of the railway line to Jaipur). This zone contained most of the land available for cultivation, which has been cleared and occupied by the immigrant *Chamaars*. Most of the new *Chamaar* settlements (including the hamlet of Manpur) are located in this zone. The villages in the western part of the *tehsil*, forms the third zone, in which there has been practically no emigration. Most of these villages were under *jagirdars* who had considerable local power, and who did not allow such a movement to develop. Figures on migration in the three zones are given in Table 14.1.

Table 14.1: Migration of *Chamaar* Families

Zone	*Total No. of villages*	*Emigration*		*Immigration*		*Families Present In 1962*		*No of villages Without Chamaar Families*
		No. of Villages Affected	*No. of Families Leaving*	*No. of Villages*	*No. of Families Arriving*	*No. of Villages*	*No. of Families*	
I	93	48	451	8	115	37	504	56*
II	58	1	4	18	523	34	972	24
III	48	6	40	6	74	35	646	13
Total	**199**	**55**	**495**	**32**	**712**	**106**	**2122**	**93**

* 30 Villages were cleared of *Chamaar* families.

(iv) Movement from the old villages has been both by single families and by groups of families. Typically, a few families have left the village and settled down in a new location where they were able to get a sizable area of land for cultivation. In course of

time, they have been joined by other families from their old and neighbouring villages, with the result that the hamlet grew in size. Thus the hamlet of Manpur which had 48 families at the time of this study (1961), had started with only 20 families in 1954. The number of households in most *Chamaar* hamlets range 10 to 30, though a few are larger.

Families Moving

(v) As the following figures will show, most families have moved only short distances :

Less than 5 miles	**195**
Between 5 to 10 miles	**110**
Between 10 to 15 miles	**34**
Between 15 to 20 miles	**89**
From 20 to less than 30 miles	**284**
Total	**712**

Thus about 30 per cent of the families have moved less than five miles and as many 60 per cent have moved less than 20 miles. Even among those, which have moved 20 miles and over, the majority have moved less than 30 miles. The families moving less than five miles have left one village only to settle in the next or the next but to one, where they could get land for cultivation. Movement under such distances can hardly be termed as migration—it would be revealed by statistics of even inter-*tehsil* migration and is more appropriately called a "drift"

(vi) It has been mentioned above, that the movement began before 1943 (*samvat* 2000*)[8] and had continued to this day. The number of families moving in different five years periods is as follows:

1943 (*s.* 2000) and earlier	43	families
1944-45 (*s.* 2001-05)	211	"
1949-53 (*s.* 2006-10	184	"
1954-58 (*s.* 2011-15)	164	"
After 1958 (*s.* 2015)	110	"
Total	**712**	"

The bulk of the movement took place within the 15 years period, 1944 to 1958, when nearly 80 per cent of the *Chamaar* families moved. It began during World War II, after the abrupt rise in prices in agricultural produce and was at its peak during the immediate post-war and post-Independent years. It has decreased generally after 1958, mainly because the cultivable lands have been largely occupied and it is becoming increasingly difficult to get new land for cultivation. The major political change in the area—integration of Jaipur state and formation of Rajasthan State in 1949—has not had marked influence on it, because the policies of both the Jaipur state and the present Rajasthan government have been favourable to it. The attitude of Jaipur state was generally sympathetic toward the *Chamaars* and its local officials helped them in settling on unoccupied cultivable lands. The Rajasthan government had given a preference in allotment of cultivable wastelands to the landless, especially of the scheduled castes. During the 1950s the movement was entirely to wastelands allotted by the Rajasthan government or occupied by the *Chamaars* in an unauthorized way and regularized later. There is still considerable pressure from *Chamaars* for allotment of forest-covered lands in the foothill plains and valleys in the southern part of the *tehsil*. Some small areas, which do not have a good forest cover, are allotted every year. But no large scale allotment is possible now, because further extension of cultivation into the hill slopes and valleys would lead to depletion of forests, accelerate soil erosion and other serious consequences for the agricultural economy of the area. Allotment of these small areas to the *Chamaars* is now encountering increasing competition and resistance from other cultivators and grazers. The landless and the small landholders of less than 10 acres of all cultivating castes are eligible for additional allotment of land. *Meenas*, *Malis*, *Gujjars* and *Jats*, press their claims for allotment. They even claim preference on ground of being residents of the village in which the lands are located. In certain cases, there is resistance from professional grazers, mostly *Gujjars*, whose cattle and buffaloes graze in those wooded areas, and who see in the allotment of these lands for cultivation the end of their grazing activity.

(vii) The *Chamaars* gave two main reasons for their migration :

(a) increasing difficulty in obtaining land for cultivation on *batai* (share-cropping) in the old villages; and

(b) attraction of obtaining land for cultivation in the new villages.

The conflicts arising from cessation of flaying and other *begars* were scarcely mentioned. When asked about conflict in the old villages—the schedule contained a question on this—most of them replied that there was no such conflict, and that they left entirely on their own accord. But the *Meenas* and other residents of the same villages did not have much hesitation in referring to these conflicts giving their details. Secondly, the *Chamaars* were reluctant to discuss their former role of flayers of carcasses, leather workers and servants of the cultivators. They wanted this part of their story to be completely forgotten. They were anxious to emphasize, probably to bolster up their claims for obtaining more land for cultivation, that they were cultivators earlier, are cultivators now, and had moved only because they could not get enough land for cultivation in the old villages and got it in the new. But almost invariably they added that they needed more land. This demand for additional lands always came up in the author's visits to the new *Chamaar* settlements. One reason for this is that most of the settlements have a number of landless families. The success of the first settlers in obtaining land has attracted others but the several latter immigrants have either not been able to get any land at all, or have got only small areas, which are not sufficient for their subsistence, they must rely rather heavily on labour. This is clearly seen in the case of the hamlet of Manpur.

(viii) Seventy-four per cent of immigrant *Chamaar* families (527 out of 712) have been successful in getting land for cultivation while 26 per cent are landless. The area owned by the land-owing families totalled 5,300 acres, an average of a little more than 10 acres per family. The bulk of this area has been obtained through allotment (including regularization of unauthorized possession); a small area totalling about 300 acres was reported to have been purchased. These 5,300 acres are only 3 per cent of the cultivated area of the *tehsil*. That such a small area was sufficient to spark a movement of such magnitude and social significance is a fact of considerable importance for social policy.

(ix) Most of the land has been brought under cultivation after clearing the forests. The *Chamaars* have done enormous labour and spent their meagre capital in cutting trees and bushes, preparing land for cultivation, building *kutcha* houses and cattle sheds, digging drinking water wells, and buying bullocks, seeds, implements and other essentials of cultivation. They have done all this and endured the hardship of living on new settlements, most of which were in the heart of the jungle when started, because of their determination to raise their social and economic status. This determination and the confidence which comes from successful achievement of an objective were noticeable in discussions in all the *Chamaar* settlements visited by the author. These are also responsible for the spirit of going ahead, which appeared to the author to be somewhat more pronounced among the *Chamaars* than among most other castes in this area. Moreover, the *Chamaars* regard their new settlements as their 'villages' and are anxious to build their own wells, temples schools and other community facilities. They have a strong sense of community, of belonging to the new settlements. This feeling had been observed also in other *Chamaar* settlements covered by the research—the hamlet of Manpur and the village Chainpur. It was visible in even small hamlets of 10 or 15 households. The existence of such a strong feeling of belonging together, in settlements which are less than two decades old and to which many families have arrived during the last five to ten years, is due partly to the anxiety of the settlers to avoid encountering the same kind of social disabilities which they suffered in the old villages, and partly from the fact that their relations with people of the surrounding villages are not good. The feelings of mutual indifference and dormant hostility between the *Chamaars* of the hamlet and people of the main village described below in case of Manpur are found in a number of other *Chamaar* settlements also. They originate partly in the opposition of the other castes to the *Chamaars* leaving their traditional obligations, and partly in the fact that the cultivators and the grazers in the villages in which the new settlements are located were opposed to the coming of the *Chamaars*. Their opposition was unsuccessful; but the hostility to the *Chamaars,* who are still regarded as intruders, remains.

(x) Most of the immigrant *Chamaar* families have to supplement cultivation of their own lands, with one or more of the following:

  (a) taking the additional area for cultivation from neighbours;

(b) agricultural or non-agricultural labour near their villages; and
(c) seasonal migration for non-agricultural labour *e.g.* for charcoal-making in the forests of Madhya Pradesh.

Change in Village Manpur—A Caste Study

Manpur is a medium sized, multi-caste village with a population of about 2,200 (1961), situated at a distance of 6 miles from Sawai Madhopur town. It has 88 households of *Chamaars* of which 40 live in the main village and the remaining 48 are in a hamlet of their own about one-and-a-half miles to the east. The hamlet is a distinct entity by itself and could well be considered a separate village; but its inclusion within the administrative area of Manpur makes the *Chamaars* the largest caste in the village. The other prominent castes of the village are *Brahmin, Rajput* and *Mahajan* among the cultivating castes. The distribution of castes having more than 10 households each is given in Table 14.2.

Table 14.2: Caste Composition of Village Manpur

Caste	*Households No.*	*Population No.*
Brahmin	32	137
Rajput	23	128
Mahajan	14	57
Jat	41	229
Meena	26	145
Mali	78	380
Gujjar	16	79
Kumhar	21	104
Chamaar	88	54
Koli	10	60
Others	72	350
Total	**421**	**2213**

The village had formed part of the *jagir* of a very powerful *jagirdar* of the area, who was moreover known for his ultra-conservative attitudes. Secondly, because of its *Rajput* residents, many of whom were in the service of the *jagirdar,* enforcement of traditional *jajmani* obligations to the community and of *begar* for the *jagirdar* were rigorous in this village, as perhaps in any other in this area. Moreover as there were no families of *Rehgars* in it, the *Chamaars* of this village did leather work in addition to flaying of carcasses; they supplied to the cultivators, as part of *jajmani* arrangement, shoes, *charas* and the other requisites of cultivation like leather straps for hitching bullocks to the plough.

In the process of change in the position of the *Chamaars* of Manpur, three events are noteworthy :

(a) Establishment of the hamlet in 1944 by 20 *Chamaar* families coming from villages along the river Banas. These families came after leaving of flaying of carcasses and leather work in their old villages, and settled down here as cultivators-*cum*-labourers;

(b) Cessation in 1952 of traditional *begars* for the *jagirdar* by the cultivators and other castes of the main village; and

(c) Cessation in 1956 of flaying of carcasses and leather work by the *Chamaars* of the main village.

Establishment of the hamlet was a significant event in the process of change in Manpur, because it gave the villagers their first experience with change among the *Chamaars*. Cessation of *begars* for the *jagirdar* was the first step in the process of repudiation of traditional obligations within the main village.

The original families from the Banas village joined in course of time by others mostly from villages located within 5-10 miles of Manpur, as quarrels between the *Meenas* and the *Chamaars* spread out between them. As a result of these additions and divisions of the older families, the number of families in the hamlet increased to 48 by 1961. The leaders of the hamlet stated that the first families moved out of the ancestral villages only because they were experiencing difficulty in obtaining land for cultivation and that there were no quarrels with the Meenas or other cultivators. They explained that they had petitioned the *jagirdar* of Manpur for allotment of 3,000 *bighas* (about 1900 acres) of cultivable wasteland in this area, and that their request was granted; but by the time they could move and occupy the land, only 500 *bighas* (312 acres) were left unoccupied, the remainder having been occupied through encroachments by the cultivators of Manpur and other neighbouring villages. The story is substantially correct and throws light on the attitude of the cultivators to settlement of the *Chamaars* on unoccupied wastelands. The land allotted to the *Chamaars* as well as most of the land further south and east going up to the slopes of the hills (about 2 miles further east from the hamlet) was uncultivated at that time. It was covered with trees and bushes, had abundant grass during the rains, and were used by the villagers for grazing of life stocks and for obtaining fuel and timber. The land vested in the state (or in *jagir* villages like Manpur in the *jagirdar*) but the villagers were allowed the facilities of grazing and removal of forest produce on nominal payment. Moreover the cultivators regarded the land as a reserve for future expansion of cultivation with increase in population, the right to land of their sons and grandsons when their existing holdings were no longer sufficient. Its occupation by the *Chamaars* was, therefore, considered to be an encroachment, which was additionally repugnant, because the *Chamaars* were settling here after repudiating their customary obligations in a bid to become the equals of the cultivators. These attitudes persist and are well brought out in the dispute relating to the cooperative farming society, which occurred about two years before this study.

As part of a programme of encouraging cooperative farming in Rajasthan, a 'drive' to establish cooperative farming societies was launched in the district in 1959. The *Chamaars* of a small hamlet, 3 miles from Manpur, which had been established in the late forties, saw in this drive an opportunity to obtain land for cultivation. About 20 families, most of them landless, joined the cooperative farming society. They were allotted 150 acres of land. The cooperative department of the State government gave a loan of Rs. 10,000 for land improvement, buying bullocks and agricultural implements. The allotment was opposed by the cultivators of 12 neighbouring villages (including Manpur) on the ground that the *Chamaars* had no intention of practicing joint farming, that the society had been formed by them only to obtain land. They argued further that the land could not be allotted for cultivation under the law, because it was grazing land, in which their cattle had been grazing from time immemorial![9] Besides making an application for cancellation of the allotment order, they physically prevented the *Chamaars* from obtaining possession of the land, with the result that there was a scuffle between the two groups and a police case was registered. Finally, in the summer of 1960, the allotment question was decided in favour of the *Chamaars*. But, the *Chamaars* could take up clearance and cultivation of land in earnest only in early 1961. At the time of the study, the *Chamaars* had harvested one *kharif* crop, and were engaged in further clearance and improvement of land. They were also planning to build huts for permanent settlement on it.

The basic hostility of cultivators of Manpur (and other surrounding villages) to the new *Chamaar* settlers, is a major factor in keeping the *Chamaar* of the hamlet away from the people of Manpur. Their hamlet is included within the administrative area of Manpur; they are represented in its *Panchayat* and cooperative society and have some economic relations with its people. But they consider themselves separate and are anxious to have their hamlet recognized as a separate village.

The trouble over *begars* for the *jagirdar* occurred in 1952. The *jagir* had not been resumed till then but *jagir* resumption was already in the air; the law abolishing *jagirs* had been passed by the legislature of Rajasthan and the process of taking over land records and revenue administration work from the functionaries of *jagirdars* had started. Moreover the first General Election (of 1952) had been held, elected *Panchayats* were going to be formed shortly, and new ideas of social and economic change—rights for cultivators, political and social equality—were sweeping the area. The trouble started when some *Mali* and *Meena* cultivators of Manpur refused to give the customary *begars* to the functionaries of the *jagirdar*. The *Malis* used to draw water from wells for them and to supply vegetables, chillies etc., free or at concessional rates: the *Meenas* would bring the bullock carts for their use. This refusal of the cultivators resulted in a quarrel between them and the local *Rajputs*, many of whom were in the service of the *jagirdar*. A case was registered by the police and was sent for trial to the local magistrate. The latter found the servants of the *jagirdar* guilty of obtaining illegal *begars* and awarded them small sentences of imprisonment. This decision was a complete defeat for them. The cultivators and the most other villagers were happy with this decision, as it meant the end of their obligations to the *jagirdar* and the power of the local *Rajputs*. One of their prominent supporters was Ram Singh, who had just then returned to the village after having lived 20 years outside. Even though a *Rajput* himself, he was much opposed to *jagirdari* and all that it stood for (including accessories like *begars*), because he had been deeply influenced by the idea of social and political equality and of giving land to the tillers during his stay outside the village. This action of his made him unpopular with his own caste men but very popular with people of the cultivating castes and the scheduled castes, and contributed to his rise to leadership in the village. He was nominated *Sarpanch* when the *Panchayat* was first formed in 1952; was elected unopposed when the first elected *Panchayat* was formed in 1954, and had continued to be *Sarpanch* ever since.

The *Chamaars* of the main village decided to stop flaying of carcasses and leather work in 1956, soon after the formal resumption of the *jagir*. By this time, the movement for stopping this work had reached an advanced stage in the area—it had been completed in most villages and had been going on in full swing in the rest. Resistance to this decision of the *Chamaars* from the village was rather weak and was soon over. There was opposition from the cultivating owners, *Jats*, *Malis* and *Meenas*, who were the most affected by the decision, and also from the high caste *Brahmins* and *Rajputs*. There was some tension also and a quarrel was feared. The *Sarpanch*, Ram Singh, openly expressed himself in favour of the *Chamaars* and encouraged them in their stand. He also sent a report about tension in the village to the sub-divisional magistrate in Sawai Madhopur. This officer visited the village and warned the villagers against any violence. There was no violence however, the villagers accepted the decision of the *Chamaars* and the tensions subsided after a few days. Ram Singh's attitude was welcomed by the *Chamaars* and other scheduled castes; but was resented by the cultivators and the high castes. The cultivators had been happy with him because of his support to them on the issue of *begars* for the *jagirdar*, and had supported him in his election as *Sarpanch*. But after this incidence they began to be suspicious of his motives and opposed him in the *Panchayat* elections and in other village's affairs. The opposition of the cultivators and the *Chamaar* support to him were important facts in the political life of the village.

Two other steps taken by the *Chamaars* during the next two years completed the social part of the change process. A few months after they quit their traditional activities, they decided that their women would wear *karis* (silver ornaments for the ankles). Several of them got together and got these ornaments made from silversmiths in Sawai Madhopur town. They did this collectively, because they were apprehensive of opposition from the other villagers. But there was no opposition. Soon, after this the *Chamaars* started making their temple *pucca*. The building was completed in 1958, and the winter of that year they installed in it the idol of *Dwarkadhis* (lit. lord of Dwarka, another name of Shri Krishna)[10]. The installation ceremony was on elaborate one and included taking the idol in a procession through the village and a large community feast. The *Sarpanch* Ram Singh was with them at the head of the procession. This was an unprecedented event of the village and one not common in the area until then. The *Chamaars* were very proud: they were installing their idol in the temple in the same way the caste Hindus do. But the cultivators of the high castes were unhappy and angry, because they felt that the *Chamaars* were going too far in their assertion of equality. The *Sarpanch* had sent a request to the police for making security arrangements partly because of these feelings and partly, it appears to the author, to impress upon the villagers his own support for the *Chamaars*. The security arrangements were made and the whole incident passed off peacefully.

The *Chamaars* have since organized a *keertan* (devotional music) party in their temple on the model of similar parties in the caste Hindu temples. They follow *Vaishnavite* worship practices, even though the priest in that temple is a *Chamaar*. On the occasion of *Jaljhoolni Gyares* (a festival coming in the month of September) they take out their idol in a procession to the village tank, just as other castes do. However, it had been agreed between them and the other castes that their procession will start a few hours before the main procession of the village and will have returned to their temple before the latter starts[1].

Effects of the Change

Ever since the *Chamaars* stopped flaying of carcasses, the village *Panchayat* gives a contract for this work. For several years, the contract was being taken by a Moslem, who employed the *Bhangis* of the village to do the work. But in 1961 the contract was taken by the village *Bhangis* themselves for a sum of Rs. 250. Addition of the work has meant a considerable addition to the income of the *Bhangis* (one extended family of six households). The cultivators alleged that it has also made them arrogant because they feel that they are doing a 'dirty' and 'defiling' work which they alone are prepared to do. Some *Mali* cultivators having fertile, irrigated lands in the vicinity of the village *abadi* complained to the author about the damage done to their valuable crops of red hot pepper, sugarcane, and vegetables, by the pigs who roam about everywhere; "these pigs enter our fields and cause so much damage; but the *Panchayat* does not do anything to prevent this and we ourselves are afraid to tell the *Bhangis* lest they get annoyed and stop scavenging and lifting of dead animals."

The cultivators have suffered a considerable economic loss as a result of this change and have also been put to too much inconvenience. They have lost all rights in the carcasses of the dead animals. Under the *Jajmani* arrangement, they used to get a fixed number of shoes, leather straps and other accessories of cultivation, and *charas* (if they had an irrigation well), in exchange for the hides of animals and the grain payment, which they made to the *Chamaars* who also undertook repairs of shoes and other leather goods. Now they receive nothing for the hide and have to buy all their requirements of leather goods in Sawai Madhopur town or in other villages where there are colonies of *Rehgars*. The nearest such village is three miles from Manpur. Moreover, they have to go to the town or to these villages for the smallest repairs. Apart from the unnecessary expense of buying leather goods and paying for repairs, the inconvenience and waste of time involved in going a long distance from the village for the smallest repair job, causes much annoyance to the cultivators. Ram Singh said that in order to remove the repairs difficulty he was trying to get a *Rehgar* to come and settle down in this village. But no one had come to the village till the end of this study[12]. During the busy cultivation season (especially in October-November before irrigation for the *rabi* crop begins), itinerant *Rehgar* families come and camp in the village for a few days and undertake repairs of *charas* and other accessories of cultivation; but at other times no local service is available. The cultivators of Raipur have not yet reconciled themselves to this loss, and depend entirely upon the *Rehgars* for all their requirement of leather goods. The community has suffered an economic loss also. The *Bhangis* do not possess the traditional skill of flaying but are able to get the carcasses on a nominal payment and know that they are doing a job, which nobody else is prepared to do, are not very careful in doing it. Several cultivators of Manpur mentioned that many hides were damaged by them through carelessness in dragging the dead animals or in flaying. The point was also brought up in Raipur, where the *Rehgars* were much more explicit in their complaint.

Some cultivators mentioned to the author that many *Chamaars* of the village regretted their decision of leaving flaying and leather work, because they had lost a good source of income and were not as well off as before. However, experience does not support this view. During the period of more than a year, over which the author had maintained contact with this village, no *Chamaar* ever referred to their past occupation. On the contrary, they were anxious to advance in their new role of cultivators-*cum*-labourers and in several of his discussion with them pressed their claims for allotment of land for cultivation. Secondly, while the possibility cannot be ruled out that an individual family was not as well off as before, the conclusion reached by him on the basis of a sample survey conducted in the village in which data on certain aspects of consumption was collected, was that the *Chamaars* were better off than ever before, and that they were the one group whose economic level had shown the most marked improvement during the past ten years.

Social and Political Effects

One important result of these changes has been a marked reduction in untouchability. Untouchability has not disappeared altogether—it is still practiced by the orthodox; but there is a noticeable relaxation in the attitude and practice concerning it. Most educated young men and political leaders of the village express themselves against practice of untouchability and pay no attention to observe it themselves, especially when they are outside the village. One drinking water well—the best and most popular—is used by people of all castes (except the *Bhangis*), and *Brahmin* and *Rajput* women have no hesitation in drawing water from it at the same time when *Chamaar* women are doing so. *Chamaar* children go to the village school. *Chamaar* members sit as equal on the *Panchayat* and the executive of the cooperative society. The villagers know that some *Chamaars* in the *tehsil* already have *Chamaar Sarapanchs* and that could happen in Manpur also, especially as the *Chamaars* are the largest caste in the village. They are particularly conscious of the fact that the *Sarpanch* Ram Singh could get re-elected in 1960 only on account of the solid support of the *Chamaars*.

The *Chamaars* themselves accept the change in their social position without any noticeable complex. In the meetings of the village *Panchayat* attended by the author, *Chamaar* members participated as equal, did not show any tendency to sit on one side or consider that they are inferior in any way. Whenever he visited the hamlet *the Chamaars* would bring out the *charpoy* and the cotton blanket for him to sit on; and would offer to bring milk or water just like people in other villages.

Reduction in untouchability has been helped by certain changes in religious practices, personal hygiene and consumption among the *Chamaars*. It has been mentioned above, that the *Chamaars* of the main village have rebuilt their temple and installed an idol of Sri Krishna in it with much ceremony, and are very enthusiastic about *keertans* (devotional music) and other aspects of Vaishnavite worship. The *Chamaars* of hamlet have shown similar enthusiasm for building their temple in the summer of 1962. This building—the only *pucca* building in the hamlet—which had cost them nearly Rs. 6,000, was intended also to house the primary school and to serve as their community centre. The idol of the deity had not been installed till the end of this study. When asked about their plans for installation of the idol, their leaders stated that 'the installation ceremony would be accompanied by festivities culminating in a large feast in which, *Chamaars* from a number of surrounding villages would be fed'. They explained that the ceremony and the feast would cost them at least Rs. 2,000 and that they would do it during the winter of 1962-63[13], by which time they hoped to have enough money. They added "we are poor people; we have already spent much and cannot afford to take up the whole burden at one time."

The temple building is a symbol both of their social aspirations and of their feeling of belonging to the new community, the hamlet. They want to worship in a temple of Sri Krishna, to have a proper installation ceremony for the idol, and to have a *keertan* (devotional music) party. They already have an active *keertan* party and are anxious to equip it properly with musical instruments. In one discussion with the author they suggested that he might use his influence with the *Panchayat Samiti* to get a grant for musical instruments for their *keertan* party[14]. The suggestion surprised the author at first; but on going into the matter further, he learnt that the *Panchayat Samiti* had given a grant to *the Panchayat* of Manpur for buying musical instruments for the community centre, that the instruments had been bought, but were often used by the *keertan* party in one of the caste Hindus temples. This had given these people the impression that the *Panchayat Samiti* gave such grants and they wanted similar assistance for their own party.

Corresponding with this emphasis on Vaishnavite religious practice, there are certain changes in attitudes towards consumption of meat and alcoholic drinks, both of which are prohibited in Vaishnavite practice. The *Chamaars* have always eaten meat and taken drink, and both these practices continue. In the sample survey on consumption, for instance, most *Chamaar* households reported occasional consumption of meat. Drinking is also common in them. But the remarks of the two principal leaders of the hamlet are significant as they indicate an interesting change in attitude. They mentioned that they had given up eating meat and drinking[15] themselves and were advocating similar abstinence by other people of the hamlet. When asked the reasons for this they replied, "These things are not 'good', and are taking our people downwards". It is most unlikely that this change in attitude among the leaders will lead to any significant reduction in eating or in drinking among the group; because increasing contacts with urban areas and participation in industrial and other non-agricultural jobs will be influenced against it. It is relevant to mention here that consumption of meat and drinks is quite high among the *Chamaars* of Chainpur (studied by Kamla Nath), who depend mainly upon industrial labour. But the change in attitude of the leaders is of interest, because it indicates an effort to follow the teachings of Vaishnavite religion.

There is also greater attention to personal cleanliness and to keeping their homes and surroundings clean. The hamlet is the cleanest village in the area: the *Chamaar* quarter in Manpur compares most favourably in cleanliness with other parts of the village. As regards personal hygiene, the people of the other castes in Manpur freely admit that the *Chamaars* are now much cleaner than they used to be.

The *Chamaars* are beginning to show a keen interest in education also. There are 27 children from *Chamaar* families of the main village in the village school. In addition, 15 boys from the hamlet go to a primary school in another village, a quarter mile away. The proportion of *Chamaar* children of primary school age (6 to 11 years) going to school is lower than among the high castes, but it is considerably higher than among the *Meenas*, *Malis*, and *Jats*. This is brought out by the following Table 14.3.

Table 14.3: Total Number of Children of Primary School-Going Age (6-11) and the Number going to the School by Caste—Village Manpur

Caste	*No. of Children in Primary School-Going Age (6-11 yrs)*	*No. of Children in Primary (first five) Classes in School*	*Per cent (3/2)*
(1)	(2)	(3)	(4)
High castes			
Brahmin	13	13	100
Rajput	18	11	61.1
Mahajan	9	9	100
Cultivating owner Castes			
Meena	21	5	23.8
Mali	54	4	7.4
Jat	28	4	14.3
Chamaar	84	26+ 15*	48.8

* In other schools
\+ In the village school

The *Chamaars* of the hamlet want a new school to be opened in the hamlet. When asked why they wanted another school when the existing school was so conveniently located, they explained that their school would have a sufficient number of students, because the number of children going to school from their hamlet would double, and children from neighbouring *Chamaar* hamlet would join it.[16] The latter argument is interesting because it shows that they want the school to become an exclusive institute of the *Chamaars.* It gives a significant insight into their desire to build a separate community life of their own. In support of their case for the school, they stated that the *pucca* building, which they had constructed, was eminently suitable for it. They argued that existence of that building was sufficient reason for their getting a school, because many villages had a school without satisfying the conditions laid down by government, of providing a building.

The school was desired partly for reason of convenience, but even more for gaining recognition and prestige. Its establishment would mean, in effect, recognition by government and the *Panchayat Samiti* of the hamlet as a separate entity and themselves as people of status.

The political influence of *Chamaars* had grown steadily as the villagers have become more familiar with democratic process and especially as opposition to *Sarpanch* Ram Singh has increased. As mentioned earlier, he was nominated *Sarpanch* in 1952 and was elected unopposed in the first election of 1954. But in the election held in 1959 there was a contest, though the opposition was rather weak and he was elected without much difficulty. In the latest election, however, the opposition was much stronger and he was elected by a margin of 68 votes (380 votes in favour, 312 against). At the election, most people of cultivating owner castes voted against him; but the *Chamaars* and other scheduled castes voted solidly in his favour, and his victory was due entirely to the latter's support. The high castes' opposition to Ram Singh is due to various personal and factional reasons. Many of them are dissatisfied with his conduct in various cases placed before the *Panchayat.* They are particularly unhappy about his role in one dispute between two *Rajput* families, which had been going on for a number of years and as a result of which there is much bitterness among the Rajputs of the village. Many *Malis*, *Meenas* and *Jats* are for similar reasons are dissatisfied with him. But they (and to a lesser extent the high castes) are angry with him primarily because of his consistent support of the *Chamaars*. Their opposition to him began when he supported the *Chamaars* in their decision to stop flaying of carcasses, and it has grown as he has supported them on various other occasions. The *Chamaars* and other scheduled castes, of course, support him for the same reasons.

The effect of the support pattern is reflected in the working of the *Panchayat.* The *Sarpanch* and the other members of the group are particular to ensure that the *Chamaars* remain pleased with them, and get their due in all matters coming before the *Panchayat.* There are three representatives of the *Chamaars,* two from the hamlet and one from the main village, in the 13-member *Panchayat.* But because of their support of their *Sarpanch* and his group, their influence is much greater than their numbers would suggest.

Nearly three-quarters of the *Chamaar* households own and cultivate land. But most of them have a second source of income also, usually agricultural and /or non-agricultural labour. This is reflected also in the figures on number of workers and jobs. Eighty five per cent of the workers

(262 out of 311) are engaged in cultivation, but the total number of jobs (454) is nearly 50 per cent higher than the number of workers, which indicates that a large percentage of the workers, do more than one job. The most common pattern is for one or more persons in each cultivating households to take up work as a labourer at some time in the year. In most households the young men concentrate on labouring jobs while the women and the older folks devote themselves to cultivation. The latter may also take up agricultural or casual non-agricultural labour for short periods, but sustained non-agricultural work is done mostly by the young men.

The total area owned by the *Chamaars* is 666.5 acres. But since a considerable acreage is taken on lease from other land-owners, of Manpur, and those of a small village adjoining the hamlet, the area cultivated by them is larger—911.5 acres. The *Chamaars* of the main village are better off in land ownership and depend much more on cultivation than do those of the hamlet. The number of landless households is smaller among them and the average area owned per land-owning household is higher. Moreover, since they are able to get a considerable area of land for cultivation on *batai*, from other land owners of Manpur, especially *Brahmins*, most cultivating households have fair-sized holdings.

The average holding of 16.06 acres for *Chamaar* cultivating households is only slightly lower than the average for all cultivators of Manpur. The land is of fair productivity, though nearly all of it is unirrigated. There are several good cultivators among these *Chamaars*. One family in particular, which constructed a small check dam on their land a few years ago with financial assistant from the Community Development Block, are among the best cultivating families in the village. These *Chamaars* can also get agricultural labour on the fields of other cultivators of Manpur quite easily. As a result, they depend upon more agricultural land and much less on non-agricultural labour than do the *Chamaars* of other families. The principal forms of non-agricultural labour in their case are casual labour and seasonal migration to the forests of Madhya Pradesh for making wood charcoal. They are conspicuous by their absence from work involving permanent or more or less continuous employment, such as permanent service in the cement factory and work on the railway, which are important sources of livelihood for the *Chamaars* of the hamlet.

In case of the *Chamaars* of the hamlet, access to a smaller, poorer, agricultural resource on the one hand and nearness to principal sources of non-agricultural labour on the other, combine to produce a much greater dependence upon non-agricultural labour. It has been mentioned in the preceding section that in many of the new *Chamaar* settlements the success of the first immigration in obtaining the land attracted others to join them; but many among the latter were not able to get land. In this hamlet also, most of the landless households are those who have come only during the last few years. Secondly, the holdings of even the land-owners are smaller than those of the *Chamaars* of the main village and since they are not able to get so much land for cultivation on *batai*—they are far from the main village and do not have established relations with its land-owner—their cultivated holdings are smaller still. Finally, the land is unirrigated and of low productivity. It is essentially marginal land, which had not been brought under cultivation earlier by the cultivators of Manpur. Parts of it are subject to erosion or deposition of sand by small *nullahs* (rain torrents) coming down from the hills to the east. Nearly all of it is suitable only for sowing for a single crop (jowar) during the *kharif* season. A small holding of such land is quite inadequate for supporting a family. These people cannot get much agricultural labour also from the main village. They have, therefore, to depend mainly upon non-agricultural labour. But in obtaining the latter, they have an advantage over the *Chamaars* of the main village because the hamlet is one-and-a-half miles closer to the principal sources of non-agricultural employment, the railway station and the cement factory. Moreover many of the non-agricultural workers among them find permanent or semi-permanent employment; very few are casual labourers.[17]

Patterns of Labour

Agricultural Labour

Agricultural labour is done mainly by the women; men prefer non-agricultural work. There are two reasons for this. Firstly, the wages for men in non-agricultural work were 25 to 50 Paise per day higher than those in agricultural work during the period of the study. Secondly, agricultural labour is preferred for the women because it does not involve going out of the village, and is the next best thing to working in the family holding, which is the social objective of these *Chamaars*. They would like their women to work only in the family holdings and not do any work for wages just as the women of the *Meena* cultivators do. But since most households find it necessary to supplement income from cultivation with that from off-firm labour, they prefer that their women do agricultural labour. An interesting result of this attitude was reflected in this study. During the initial stages of the household survey the heads of most households stated that their women were busy only with work in the home or on their family holdings, and did not do any wage labour. Even heads of non-cultivating households reported that their women did not do any labour and spent their time in looking after the livestock; most kept a few animals. But after some months when better rapport had been established with these people and it became known that this statement was not correct, information on work by women was obtained through a recanvass of the question for all the households.

Non-Agricultural Labour

The principal forms of non-agricultural labour are the following :

(a) seasonal migration to the forests of Madhya Pradesh to make wood charcoal;
(b) migration to building stone quarries in the Medak area of Kotah district, located about 25 miles to the south of the village;
(c) labour on the railway;
(d) permanent service in the cement factory, or its quarries; and
(e) casual non-agricultural labour.

Seasonal migration to the forests of Madhya Pradesh has been a distinctive feature of the economic life of the *Chamaars* (and other labouring castes) of this area for several decades. There are many old men both in the main village and the hamlet who can recall going to these forests for 30-40 years and of their parents' going before them. The people going to the forests leave their homes in November- December or January after harvesting the *kharif* crop. They stay in forests for five to eight months and return home in June or early July, just in time for taking of *kharif* cultivation again. They come back in this time even though they have no land, because no work can be done in the forests during the rainy season. Migration is by families. The presence of the women is essential for cooking food or looking after the huts when the family lives in the forests. Moreover, the women and the children work and make a sizable contribution to the family income. An average family, with both husband and wife working usually has a net saving (after meeting expenses of living in the forests) of Rs. 300-400 during one working season.

This migration has played a very useful role in the economy of the *Chamaars*, especially during the recent transitional period. It has helped them absorb the shock of loss of income from leaving their traditional occupation and meet the expenses (*e.g.* of buying bullocks, clearing land, building huts etc.) for starting cultivation in their new settlements.

But in spite of these migration is not looked upon with favour by the *Chamaars* now, and as local employment opportunities increase, more and more of them are turning to these in preference to go to the forests. There are several reasons for the trend. Firstly, life in the forests is hard and not altogether free from danger. Secondly, the work is exhausting and has a bad influence on health; long exposure to charcoal smoke has a tendency to cause lung diseases. Earnings are good; but since the money is paid in advance the workers fritter it away and remain chronically in debt. Finally, the work involves living away from home for long periods, with consequent disturbance to community life. But the migration still serves as insurance against poor times, and in a season in which the *kharif* crop is poor and local employment is scarce, migration increases considerably. Thus, in the migration season of 1961-62, which followed a poor *kharif* crop, the number of persons going to the forests increased to 60 as compared to 36 in the previous season.

Migration to the building stone quarries of Kotah district has started only during the last five years. But it is preferred to migration to the forests because wages are good, averaging about Rs. 2.50 per day and as the quarries are only 25 miles away, it is not necessary for entire families to move. The men go alone and visit their families, which continue to stay in the village, once or twice a week.

Work on the railways is the big source of local employment. But all the persons engaged in it are young men of the hamlet. Wages are fairly good; a young man getting continuous employment makes about Rs. 50 per month. During the last few years, they have been also able to get employment for 6 to 8 months in the year and feel that they will become permanent employees in course of time. Fairly good wages and the facility of commuting to work are the main advantages of this work. The worker does not have to leave his home and can even look after the family land and livestock in his spare time.

Permanent service in the cement factory (or its quarries) is even better than the work on the railway. The minimum wage is Rs. 82 per month; those employed as skilled or semi- skilled workers get much more. But the number of such workers is small, because it is difficult to get employment in the factory.

The casual labourers, most of them from the main village, find employment in odd jobs within the village and in various public works. The public works in progress during the period of this study were laying of transmission lines from a hydro-electric station at Kotah to Sawai Madhopur and other places, construction of an electric substation at Sawai

Madhopur, and construction of a road linking Manpur with a town 20 miles away.

The factory and railway workers and those going to the stone quarries—40 in all—are available for continuous non-agricultural employment. The factory workers are in permanent service already: the others work in their non-agricultural jobs for most of the year, and could work longer if work was available. The leaders of the hamlet indicate that about 50 men could take up full-time, non-agricultural work without detriment to cultivation. They said that they would welcome establishment of any industry which provides such employments. They are an agricultural people, no doubt: every land owning family cultivates its holding and in our discussions they never failed to press their claims for being allotted more land. But they see clearly that their futures lies in non-agricultural work.

Analysis

The influences, which have contributed to the changes described in this chapter, perhaps the most important is the feeling against caste, social inequality and untouchability which began with the social and economic changes of the twentieth century and which was given such powerful impetus by Mahatma Gandhi during the Independence Movement. It will be recalled that uplift of the scheduled castes and abolition of untouchability formed the central planks of the programme of social reform which Mahatma Gandhi placed before the nation during this Movement. The *Chamaars* of this area began to feel the influence of these ideas during the late 1920s and especially during the 1930s when large numbers began to go out of the area for labour in industrial centres and other towns.

But while these influences were creating a certain restiveness among the *Chamaars*, — a symptom of which were the riots in Lalsot village in 1939, — the immediate provocation for change in occupation, through repudiation of traditional obligations and large scale migration appears to have been provided by the economic changes occurring after the entry of Japan in World War II. The sharp increase in prices of agricultural produce and scarcity of foodgrains on the one hand and greatly increased availability of employment at high wages in industrial and other works in towns on the other combined to produce intolerable strains on the *jajmani* system. It will be recalled that quarrels between the *Chamaars* and the *Meenas* and the large scale migration of *Chamaars* started in this area only after 1943, when these economic changes had begun to have effect.

High prices and scarcity of foodgrains also brought to the land owners a sharp realization of the value of land as instrument of production. Earlier, in the two decades of agricultural depression, when produce and prices had been very low, and the cultivators frequently found it difficult to even pay the land revenue, ownership and especially cultivation of land were not so high priced. The average *Meena* or *Jat* cultivating owner had, therefore, no hesitation in giving some of his land for cultivation to *Chamaars* and others and land-owners, especially of the high castes, having difficulty in finding cultivators for their land was quite common. But with high prices of the produce land has acquired a new value and land-owners especially of the cultivating castes were less willing to give it for cultivation on the customary *batai* basis.

This tendency was aided by the growing realization of impending land reforms. The Indian National Congress had propagated, land to the tiller for a long time, and was committed to its achievement through abolition of *jagirdari* and *zamindari* and other measures. The people of this area had known about these ideas. But these began to acquire a real significant for them only in the later War years, when people realized that the end of the War might bring major political and economic changes in the country and that the land reform, including abolition of *jagirdari* and grant of right in land to anyone who was cultivating it at the time, might be the most important among these. The steady rise in population also helped the process, because increasing number of cultivators found that their holdings were sufficient only for the growing number in their own families. It will be recalled that the *Chamaar* leaders of the hamlet of Manpur, and of nearly all the villages covered by the survey of migration had mentioned that they had left their own village because they were having difficulties in obtaining land for cultivation. Even after making allowance for their unwillingness to talk about the quarrel with the cultivators arising from their refusal to do flaying and *begars*, it has to be recognized that difficulty in obtaining land was a contributory factor in the migration of *Chamaars*.

Another aspect of land policy of the new Rajasthan government has been to give preference to the landless, especially for the scheduled castes, in allotment of cultivable wastelands for cultivation. The operation of the policy in this *tehsil*, where large areas of such lands were available, has greatly accelerated the process of occupational change among the *Chamaars*. These lands acted like a powerful magnet drawing the *Chamaars* towards them. It must be made clear, however, that availability of such lands is not essential for the change in occupation of the *Chamaars*, because change had taken place in other parts of this district, in other districts of Rajasthan, and in other States of Northern India in which such lands were not available and no migration took place. But it had enabled the community to absorb the tensions created by the change. A majority of the *Chamaars* has become cultivating owners and is better off than before. The *Meenas* and other traditional cultivators have also more land given to them, and are happy with this result of the change, however, keenly they might resent the other effects. On the other hand, in other parts of the district (*e.g.* the Hinton *tehsil*, 60 miles to the north of Sawai Madhopur) where the pressure of the population on land is high and *Chamaars* have not been able to get much new land for cultivation there is keen competition between them and the other cultivators for the very small area of cultivable wastelands that are available for the allotment, and there is also greater tension.

Abolition of *jagirdari* itself assisted the change in several ways. First, it removed a powerful local influence, which was for preservation of tradition and against change; the *jagirdars* were active in support of *jajmani* system. Secondly, they did not allow any caste to become too assertive or powerful or social tensions to develop within their villages. The attitude of curbing "apishness" which was perhaps necessary for preserving their own position at the apex of the local power structure often worked against the *Meenas*, who were naturally the most powerful caste in the villages. But it also meant discouraging the aspirations of other castes which might disturb the traditional structure of social position and power. The influence of the *jagirdars* in curbing local tensions has been seen very clearly.

During the 1950s the political and administrative changes and special measures for uplift of scheduled castes proved to be noteworthy influences. These did not initiate the change in occupation of the *Chamaars* or their migration, which were already under way. But they were major factors in acceptance by the rest of the community of the *Chamaars* right to give up their traditional occupation to seek a higher social status, and need for improvement in their economic and social condition.

The Political System based on the Adult Suffrage

Every politician understands the importance of the large scheduled caste votes in such a system and is anxious to win it. Among the *Chamaars* themselves, realization of the power of their number grows with every successive election. Moreover, reservation of seats for the scheduled castes in legislatures, *Panchayat* and other bodies have produced a crop of young leaders who understand the mechanism of the political system, are keenly aware of the numerical strength of their caste and are anxious to exploit it.

The establishment of *Panchayats* has made a major contribution in this process. In their absence, the influence of the political system would have been felt only at the time of the general election. But with them, it is felt all the time. The very fact that *Chamaar* members sit as equal with others in the *Panchayats* makes the villagers aware that social equality has come to stay. Moreover, every *Sarpanch* realizes that the scheduled caste vote could be decisive in his election. The *Sarpanch* of both Manpur and Raipur have been elected in the last election on the strength of the scheduled caste vote. There are many others in the area who are in a similar position.

Besides the influence of the political process, the entire educational and propaganda machinery of the State has been directed towards spread of the ideas of social equality, abolition of untouchability and uplift of the scheduled castes. In it, it has the support of the intelligentsias, which forms the bulk of the political leaders, official and the educators in rural areas. The other villagers under influence of the new idea propagated by these educated people are less willing to assert their traditional superiority over the scheduled castes or to observe untouchability, which they are beginning to realize, is an offence under the law.

Finally the fact that the *Meenas*, the principal cultivating owners in the area, do not have a very high social status has helped in the process of improvement of the social status of the *Chamaars*. The *Chamaars* feel that the Meenas are not a high caste that Meenas in other parts of Rajasthan are backward and depressed; but those of this area enjoy a good social status and have risen to the position of the dominant caste only because they own and cultivate land. They have applied the analogy to themselves and gone on to argue: "if we give up our 'defiling' work and get land for cultivation we can also become the equals of the *Meenas:* for, if *Meenas* can be cultivating owners, what is wrong with us ?" But, if the bulk of the cultivators had belonged to a caste with recognized high status (*e.g.* the *Rajputs* or even the *Jats*); it is possible that the social change among the *Chamaars* would have been less easy or less peaceful.

Effects of the Changes

The change had given the *Chamaars* a powerful urge for economic and social advance. They are engaged in a constant endeavour to get more land for cultivation, though further progress in this is slow because of shortage of suitable unoccupied land and increasing competition from the traditional cultivators, especially the *Meenas*. They are also keen to get industrial employment and to climb up the economic ladder through education and learning of new skills. Having a tradition of migration in search of labour, they were the first to go to work in the cement factory and its quarries and form the largest constituent of the labour force in these. Most of them are still unskilled labourers; but the younger men are learning industrial skills, and getting better paid jobs as skilled or semi-skilled workers. They are also quick at availing of the new employment opportunities in public works like the railway. Some enterprising young men are going into contract work, especially building and labour contracts in which they have an advantage because most of the labourers are men of their own caste. The *Chamaars* living in larger villages or in villages nearer the town (*e.g.* Chainpur) are keen to send their boys to school (including high school) with the result that the number of their young men with high school education is increasing slowly but steadily. Many of these young men avail scholarships given by the government for education of the scheduled castes. They are keenly aware that a proportion of the jobs in government service are reserved for the scheduled castes, and look forward to such service as their carreer in life.[18]

Moreover, because of their association with non-agricultural and industrial labour, the *Chamaars* have greater contact with towns than the pure cultivators like the *Meenas* and the *Malis* and are more affected by urban consumption patterns and the way of thinking. The difference in these respects between the industrial *Chamaars* (of Chainpur) and the pure cultivator *Meenas* (of Bijaipur) was noticed only in Manpur where in comparison to *Meenas* and the *Malis* the *Chamaars* of the hamlet, were seen to be much ahead in use of durable, urban type consumption goods like bicycles and wrist-watches. Accordingly, the *Chamaars* are not merely being lifted from being almost the lowest economic and social group in the villages to equality with the cultivating owner castes; but in terms of many indicators of economic progress, they are well ahead of the latter.

The change has also given the *Chamaars* a powerful impetus for social advance. Beginning with the change of name of their caste to *Berwa*, they have made a number of changes in individual or group behaviour—Vaishnavite religious worship, greater attention to personal cleanliness, discouraging women from labour outside the home or the family holding, adoption of customs of the *Meenas* or the high castes in marriages—all of which are motivated by a powerful desire to be accepted as a clean caste by the rest of the community.

These changes in occupation and social conditions of the *Chamaars* have had interesting results on the other sections of the community and the attitude of different castes to these is extremely significant and revealing. The *Chamaars'* repudiation of their traditional occupation and obligations has given the *jajmani* system a blow from which it cannot recover. It has demonstrated that a determined group can repudiate its social status and economic obligations to the community with success, and could even be better off in the process. The lesson has not been lost on the other castes, several of which have followed the *Chamaars* to the extent of leaving their customary obligations to the community while they continue to practice their traditional occupation. Thus the *Nais* (barbers), while they continue to do the barber's work, have stopped cleaning utensils. Similarly, the *Kumhars* (potters), while continue to make pots have stopped drawing water from wells. The stoppage is so complete that it is difficult to get anyone to perform these services even in towns like Sawai Madhopur.

It has been explained earlier that the attitude of the traditional cultivating-owner castes like the Meenas has been hostile to the change. The phase of violent quarrels is over, but resentment against the *Chamaars* persists. The reasons for this are both economic and social. Stoppage of flaying and leather work by the *Chamaars* has caused serious economic loss to them. Moreover, they cannot obtain any longer the *begar* services, which the *Chamaars* rendered. On the other hand, the *Chamaars* are now competitors for allotment of cultivable lands and claim preference on grounds of being landless and a scheduled caste. The Meenas also resent the fact that the *Chamaars*, a large caste numerically, have become a major political force in the area. They have themselves realised the fact only recently; their domination of the *Panchayat Samiti* and a large number of *Panchayats* in the area has become effective only after the 1960 election. The *Chamaars* on their part see the Meenas their opponents and an obstacle to further progress. The memory of having to leave their villages is still fresh, and they encounter opposition from the *Meenas* in land allotment everyday. The sentiments expressed by the *Chamaar* leaders of the hamlet of Manpur (and also of Chainpur) that "the Meena dominated *Panchayat Samiti* will do nothing for us" is widely shared by the *Chamaars* in this area.

In contrast, the high castes, though lacking in any great enthusiasm for the change, have not shown any active opposition to it. They understand the social implications of the change—decline in untouchability, the *Chamaars'* aspiration to social equality with the cultivating owner castes and their adoption of Vaishnative worship and some of the customs of even the high castes. They see all these things happening and the orthodox among them are not happy. On the other hand, the educated young men, who have been influenced by the new ideas of social equality, and have a keen consciousness of the injustice of untouchability and other social disabilities suffered by the scheduled castes, are on the whole sympathetic to the *Chamaars*. Indeed, it is most likely that as these trends continue and the *Berwa Chamaars*, in course of time, make a claim for being recognized as a clean caste, the *Brahmins* and other high castes will not oppose them; the opposition, if any, will come from the *Meenas* and other cultivating castes.

Thus, *Brahmins* are either indifferent or sympathetic. The attitude does not conform to the popularly held stereotype, that the high castes are opposed to abolition of untouchability or social inequality or that the impetus for continuance of these comes from them. This might have been the case in the past, it is not so in this area at present. Moreover, the opposition of the cultivating owner caste is not based on religious or ritualistic conditions: the main reasons for it are economic and social.

The change in the occupation and social status of the *Chamaars* has made a major contribution to social efficiency and in some ways also to social integration. Earlier a large caste, one-tenth of the entire rural population, was condemned to the lowest position of the society; one of its several economic activities (flaying of carcasses) was considered defiling. The number belonging to it was much in excess of the numbers required for doing the work. An idea of the disparity between the numbers in the castes and the numbers required for the work may be had from the fact that while Manpur has 40 households of *Chamaars* (in the main village), the entire work of flaying is now being looked after by 6 households of *Bhangis*—who do it in addition to scavenging! Similarly, while there are 35 households of *Chamaars* in Raipur, the flaying work is now being looked after by just two households of *Bhangis*. The situation in other villages from which *Chamaars* have not moved is similar.

It has been mentioned that the *Bhangis* do not do the work of flaying with care and that there is so much wastage of hides that villages like Raipur which were self-sufficient in leather earlier have to import leather now. If the movement against lifting of carcasses spreads further (it is already of regional occurrence), the problems of disposal of dead animals on the one hand and supplies of leather and leather goods on the other may assume serious proportions. Secondly, it is possible that similar movements may develop among castes practicing other "dirty" occupations, namely *Bhangis* (scavenging) and *Khatiks* (slaughter of sheep). Therefore, if social progress is to be ensured and no caste is to remain condemned to a low social status because of association with a "dirty" occupation, technological change, which takes the 'dirty' aspect out of such occupation, will be essential. The example of scavenging will make the point clear. It is considered to be the dirtiest of all occupations. But there is no stigma against its modern counterpart of working as plumber or sanitary engineer and people from all castes, including the Brahmin, are doing this work in the cities.[19] This is true also of leather work to some extent. There is large number of high caste Hindus among technicians in modern tanneries and among the owners of shoe shops in cities though actual shoe making and tanning are still done by people of *Chamaar* or equivalent castes. It is the author's belief that as the "dirty" aspects of these occupations are eliminated through technological advance, more and more people of high castes will be prepared to enter them and the prejudice against them will decline. Such technological change is no doubt expensive; but the social cost of not making it will be higher. The need of social integration and making all sections of society equal participants in economic and social progress make such technological change imperative.

NOTES

1. As has been mentioned earlier, the author conducted intensive research in three villages of Sawai Madhopur district in eastern Rajasthan on 'Economic Development and Social Change in Village India' in 1961 when he was posted as a District Collector. The villages were resurveyed in 2001. As a result of the changes the *Chamaars* of the area were experiencing major change in their social status and occupation. Similar changes in the position of the *Chamaars* were taking place in several other villages in northern India. For on account of changes experienced by *Chamaars* in an eastern U.P. village, see Bernard S. Cohn: ***The Changing Status of a Depressed Caste***, in Mackim Merriott; ***Village India***, Chicago 1955.
2. The word *Berwa* is used only for *Chamaars* of this and certain neighbouring districts. Apparently it stands for a distinct ethnic group among the large number of such groups which practice these occupations in different parts

of northern India and are given by the generic name of *Chamaar* (from Sanskrit *charmakar*, literally worker in leather). The group, since it has stopped flaying and leather work, resents the use of the word *'Chimera'* preferring to be called *Berwa*. Use of the word *'berwa'* would have been quite appropriate and, in fact, better than *'Chamaar'*. But in this study the word *'Chamaar* has been used in preference to *Berwa* or *Berwa Chamaar*, only because the former brings out more clearly the social changes which form the subject of this study and also aides in understanding the attitudes of the other castes towards the group.

3. *Begar* (literally: forced work). The *Begar* system was part of the feudal way of life, under which different castes were required to perform specific tasks for the *jagirdar,* and the village community. Thus the *Nais* (barber) had the obligation to clean utensils, the *Kumhars* (potters) to draw water from wells, the *Chamaars* to bring fuel, and do field labour and other miscellaneous work. These obligations were in addition to the occupational obligations of the castes.
4. *Patwari* is an officer of the Revenue department who maintains records of land ownership and yearly record of agricultural production etc. The circle of a *Patwari* in this *tehsil* consisted of one to six villages, with a population of between 3,000 and 5,000.
5. In this connection, the author met the *Patwaris* first on one of their monthly meetings in the *tehsil* office. The main fact about the migration of *Chamaars* was discussed in this meeting, and the schedules to be used for collecting information for each village were explained. Two separate schedules were used, one for villages from which *Chamaars* had left (emigration), and the other for villages of in-migration. Both schedules were to be filled for villages which had experienced both emigration and in-migration. The schedules for villages of emigration sought information on the number of *Chamaar* families that had left the village during the last 20 years, the year(s) of leaving, the motives and circumstances of leaving, especially whether it had been the result of quarrel with the cultivators or other castes in the village, and the village or villages to which they had gone (if known). The schedule for villages for in-migration similarly sought information on the number of *Chamaar* families that had arrived in the village during the last 20 years, the year(s) of arrival, the area occupied by them for cultivation, whether obtained through allotment, purchase or unauthorized occupation, and general information on their other economic activities obtained from *Chamaar* leaders and were to be checked and supplemented by discussion with other village leaders and by reference to revenue records, etc. But in village in which no *Chamaar* families were living at the time of the survey, data had to be collected through discussion with the village leaders—the *Sarpanch* and other member of the *Panchayat*, and others. The *patwaris* were requested to complete the schedule at their convenience during the course of a month

and to bring them along at the next monthly meeting. At this meeting, the filled schedules for each village were scrutinized by the author and discussed with the *patwari* concerned. In several cases, extremely useful comments and supplementary information were given by the *patwari* or the land record inspector (a supervisory officer having jurisdiction over the area of about ten *patwaris*) who had been posted in the villages, when the migration of the *Chamaars* actually took place.

In this connection the author's experience may be of some interest. He learnt about the change in occupation and social status of the *Chamaars* soon after his arrival in the district. But the facts about the conflict between the *Chamaars* and the cultivators, and especially about the extent of the migration of *Chamaars* and their settlements in new villages, came to his notice only slowly, over a period of months.

6. A raised platform along the front wall of the house used by the men as a place for sitting and gossiping.
7. The figures exclude Sawai Madhopur town, the cement factory township, and the 'village' comprising the workers' colony of the quarries of the cement factory.
8. *Samvat*, the year of the Bikrami Era. This era was used for most official purposes during the time of Jaipur state; is still used for revenue records by the Rajasthan government, and is in common use in this area. The original figures had to be collected by the years of this era, because villagers count dates invariably according to this era.
9. Under the revenue laws of Rajasthan, land classified as grazing land cannot be allotted for cultivation.
10. All the temples in the village are Vaishnavite temples in which Vishnu (god of preservation in the Hindu trinity), is worshipped in one of his several incarnations. Sri Krishna, the hero of *Bhagavat Gita*, is the most popular incarnation of Vishnu in this area and is worshipped most.
11. This agreement was observed during 1961. The *Chamaars* took out their procession early in the afternoon and had brought it back by about 5 p.m., when the main procession started. The desire of the scheduled castes to take out procession on this festival and the caste Hindus opposition to it have led to several quarrels in villages of this area Thus in 1960, there was a violent quarrel between the high caste Hindus and the *Rehgars* in a large village located about 30 miles to the north of Sawai Madhopur.
12. During the winter of 1961, two Rehgar families from a neighbouring district of Madhya Pradesh came and camped in the village.
13. The installation of the idol was done in January 1963. On this occasion, about 6,000 *Chamaars* were fed in a giant caste feast, which cost about Rs. 3,000.
14. The author was treated to a most delightful recital of *bhajans* (devotional songs) of Raidas and other poet-saints of the Bhakti Movement by the old *Chamaar*, who serves as their priest. Bhakti Movement, a movement for

religious reform was at its height between the 15th and the 17th century. Many prominent religious teachers of North India were associated with it. They emphasized equality of man before God, advocated love of God and Bhakti (devotion to Him) as the sole means of personal salvation: many expressed themselves against the caste system. One of these leaders Raidas (or Ravidas), was a *Chamaar* from Varanasi. He is regarded by the *Chamaars* over large parts of North India as their patron-saint and hero.

15. An instance of a caste giving up drinking in an effort to reform itself came to the author's notice during his visit to the area in July 1963. The *Rehgars* of the area are notorious for heavy drinking at marriages but in May 1963, in a meeting of *Reghars of 18 villages* held in Raipur, it was decided that they will not drink in marriages in future. The meeting was held in Raipur because *Rehgars* of the village have traditionally been *Chaudhris* (recognized leaders) of the caste in the area and initiative for convening it was taken by two *Rehgar* leaders of the village. One of them has extensive political clout including those with a Member of Parliament in New Delhi. When asked what had made them take this initiative they explained, "Our people waste much money on drinking at marriages. Some of them drink so much that they lie unconscious for a night or more. Others laugh at us. They also explained that the decision was being adhered to by the *Rehgars* of all the villages concerned and that the movement was spreading to other villages.

16. The school was opened in July 1963.

17. In 1962, they were expecting to get employment throughout the year, as work on doubling the railway line had started.

18. Several school teachers whom the author met during his visits to villages commented on the eagerness of *Chamaar* and *Rehgar* boys to do well at school.

19. In post-Independence years, Indians have bought several reputed European firms of sanitary engineers. Besides, in cities like Delhi hundreds of people of high castes have set themselves up as sanitary engineers and contractors.

15

Emerging Leadership

*Profiles of Village Leaders**

Introduction

In the growth of new democratic institutions like the *Panchayati Raj* institutions, the people who come to these in the first few years have many important roles. The form and the structure of the institutions—composition, functions and power relations with the State Government and other bodies—are determined by the laws formed by the State Government. But their actual working and the way in which they develop depend in large part on the thinking and action of their members. The *Panchayati Raj* institutions have been established with certain objectives and expectations. They are expected to function as agencies of self-government at various levels and to serve as major instruments of economic development and social advance of the rural people. But whether these expectations are fulfilled and the institutions assume the role advised for them, or they confine themselves to the more limited tasks of mentoring social service or executing certain development programmes or worse become forms for expression of local group or personal rivalries. All this depends very largely upon the understanding of their members of the object and function of the institutions and of their own role in these and their ability to play this role successfully[1]. Accordingly, a study of members of the *Panchayati Raj* institutions is of great importance for understanding of their progress. It is important also for understanding the new trends for rural leadership. These institutions have brought new opportunities for exercise of power and leadership in the

* The observation of the author on which this Chapter is based were recorded during his stay in Sawai Madhopur as District Collector from early 1960 to mid-1962.

rural areas and are developing a new leadership, which is going to be increasingly important.

In recognition of the importance of the study of new leaders, fairly detailed data on some measurable attributes—age, education, caste, economic status etc.—has begun to be collected in Rajasthan (Government of Rajasthan, 1960). This information is valuable in as much as it gives an idea of the social and economic background of these people. But it needs to be supplemented by more detailed studies of selected leaders, to show what kind of persons they are, what influences bring them to the institutions, and what they seek to obtain from them; for themselves and for the people who have sent them there. Appendix 1 of this Chapter contains profiles of 15 selected members of *Panchayati Raj* institutions in Sawai Madhopur district of eastern Rajasthan which throw light on these and related points.

The choice of persons for these profiles has been subjective. It has been influenced by the opportunity, which the author had of knowing members of these institutions and of seeing them at work. But within this limitation an attempt has been made to include the more important types of persons that one comes across in these institutions. Thus, included here are people from the dominant cultivating caste of the area, the *Meenas,* as also those from high castes like the *Brahmin* the *Rajput* and the *Mahajan;* people with purely rural orientation and interests and those with their eyes focussed on the town; people having no interest other than that of representing their village or castes, and those with political offices; old and middle aged men as well as young men. Finally, to complete the picture, one woman and one representative of the Scheduled Caste have also been included. The woman is a co-opted member of a *Panchayat Samiti* but the Scheduled Caste representative is a *Sarpanch* and is a member of *Panchayat Samiti* in his own right as a village leader. Scheduled Castes and women are not adequately represented in the *Panchayati Raj* institutions, and social provision has been made for their representation through co-option.

The collection is not representative in a purely statistical sense: *i.e.* different types of members of these institutions are not represented in it in the same proportions in which they would be found in an average institution like a *Panchayat Samiti*. The majority of members of a *Panchayat Samiti* are cultivators with some urban contacts and often also with some non-agricultural source of income. But these are represented in the study by not more than six profiles. On the other hand, other types like the small town leaders (Lal Chand) and small town businessmen (Sagar Mal) have been included. The latter are not present in a *Panchayat Samiti* in large numbers. But whenever present they are influential, because of their education, wider knowledge and political and other contacts. This being a study of leaders, persons who occupy positions of influence and authority in *Panchayati Raj* institutions, it was considered more important to include in it different types of persons than to make a statistically valid representation of the membership of these institutions.

The observations about each person are based on the author's personal acquaintance with him. He had an opportunity to know each one well, to see him function in various situations in his village and/or *Panchayati Raj* institution and to have informal discussions with him on various issues from time-to-time; these were not structured interviews.

Common Characteristics

When we think of village leaders, the type who readily comes to mind is an older middle aged man, with little or no education, with a basically tradition-oriented outlook, and with his sphere of interest and knowledge limited to his own village or a few surrounding villages. Village leaders of this type (Raj Mal and Harphool in this collection) are no doubt present in *Panchayati Raj* institutions, even in fair number in some but they are not in the majority, and what is more important, their influence is much less than their numbers. Most persons of this type are content to be back-benchers in the institutions, allowing to be guided by others. Further, even young, the literate or barely literate old world types, symbolized by Harphool are definitely on the way out. The average member of *Panchayati Raj* institutions is a young or middle aged man, educated and responsible, well informed and standing midway in outlook, economic interest and social and personal contacts between the village and the town. He has his roots in the village people whom he represents, and he generally belongs to a family, which has been living in the village for generations. But he has also contacts with Block and district level officials and political leaders. Moreover, he has a fair understanding of the economic system—prices, markets, scarcity of products like cement and steel, is well informed about land reform and other laws, which affect the village people, and has detailed knowledge of various development programmes, and of facilities like cooperative credit, *taccavi* loans and grants which are available for their economic benefits.

Most of such leaders belong to the new middle class, which is emerging in rural India. Of the fifteen persons figuring in these profiles, only one (Tara Chand) could be considered rich; all others are only moderately well off, with incomes ranging between Rs. 250-750 per month. None is poor! The cultivators among them are with comfortable holdings: several combine cultivation with other sources of income like money-lending, trade, or ownership of a small processing enterprise like a flour mill. This is true both of persons belonging to the purely cultivating *Meena* caste and of those who belong traditionally to non-cultivating castes; because none of them is an actual tiller of the soil. Some (like Amar Singh) manage their cultivation with the help of hired or attached labourers; others (like Sridher) have given their land on *batai*, still others (like Ram Pratap and Rajaram) who come from joint families look after cultivation themselves. One would be justified in concluding that the time and the energy of the leaders are more useful to their family in the leadership role than in the role of the tiller of soil. There are several reasons why the leader does not cultivate his land himself; two among which are noteworthy. Firstly, it is not considered proper or dignified for a leader like a *Sarpanch* of the *Panchayat* or the *Pradhan* (chairman) of a *Panchayat Samiti* to do agricultural work himself. The entire value system of the village is against his doing such work. Secondly, the business of leadership takes considerable time and money and only those who can afford to spend these can enter it. Attending meetings of the *Panchayat Samiti* or of standing committees of the latter, and joining activities like seminars, training camps and study tours, participation in which is voluntary but expected, take time and require absence from home, sometimes for days together. Even more time is taken in looking after the problems, individual or collective, of the village people. These leaders participate in all activities, which bring their village or an individual villager in contact with the outside world. Leading a delegation of villagers before the Collector or a visiting minister to represent for removal of a grievance or for obtaining an amenity for the village; helping an individual cultivator obtain a *taccavi* loan grant from *Panchayat Samiti* or a permit for scarce material like cement; assisting a villager in a court case or in an appeal before the *Panchayat Samiti*—these are a few of the many things these leaders do. It was observed by the author that except the woman (Ram Devi) and the illiterate *Meena* lad (Harphool), all the persons figuring in these profiles spent a lot of time at a district or *Panchayat Samiti* headquarters towns. They were men about town in very real sense. The cultivator who has to earn his living with his own labour just cannot afford such expenditure of time or money.

Pre-occupation with work of these kinds gives revealing insight into what is perhaps the leader's most important role—that of link between the village and the outside world. The village people have always needed such links. Earlier, these were provided by better educated or urbanized villagers like the traders, richer cultivators, village level official like the *Patwari* and in the *jagir* villages by the *jagirdars* and their servants. Now, this link is provided increasingly by members of *Panchayati Raj* institutions.

Most leaders have come to these institutions because membership confirms prestige and gives opportunity for exercise of power. For some (like Ram Pratap and Raja Ram) membership of the institutions is merely a new expression or formal recognition of the traditional position of influence and prestige, which their family has enjoyed in the village or in the area—a modern symbol of a traditional position. For others (like Jai Singh and Raj Singh) who belong to families of former *jagirdars*, it is an effort to retain some influence and prestige in their former *jagir* villages. But in case of some (like Ram Das) who belong to under privileged castes, it is the symbol of the new, higher status of their caste and their own position as its leaders. In every case, it is the symbol also of personal success. Some of these leaders (like Ram Pratap and Jai Singh) are content to remain *Sarpanchs*, exercising power in their villages or small group of villages and being known as persons of consequence there; but others (like Raja Ram and Tara Chand) have ambitions of higher political offices. Several of them are disappointed that the powers and financial resources of these institutions do not measure up to their expectations, that the reality is much less than what they had been led to believe by the talk about these institutions in the months preceding the 1960 *Panhayat* election. This is particularly true of *Sarpanchs* of the new, small *Panchayats* who are disappointed to find that the funds of the *Panchayats* are very small and the *Sarpanchs* cannot increase it because of the strong opposition to tax among the village people. They cannot expect to get large grants for works, etc., from the *Panchayat Samiti*, because the total amount available for such grants is limited and as a result all *Panchayats* in the *Samiti* area compete for them. They find that after being in office for more than a year they have not been able to take up any construction work in their villages, or show to the village people any other tangible evidence of the functioning of the *Panchayat*. They understand the causes of this difficulty, but feel that the government should have seen it and provided against it while designing the institutions. Those (like Sager Lal and Amar Singh), who have experience of earlier *Panchayats* which had larger area, more funds and also judicial powers, feel that 'nothing much is left in the *Panchayats* now'.

Several of these leaders have good executive ability. In fact, both the quality and quantity of administrative calibre to be found in an average *Panchayat Samiti* in this area will give an outsider a pleasant surprise. But this ability is not finding adequate expression in organizing programmes of rapid economic development or social progress of the village people. Its main expression is in the enthusiasm for running the *Panchayat* office but complete lack of interest in administrative matters, or in discussions of finer points in the Acts and rules. Some (like Suraj Mal and Tara Chand), who are *Pradhans* of *Panchayat Samiti*, tend to function more as executive heads of their institutions than as policy makers giving general directions to their Block Development Officers.

There are several reasons for these phenomena, and they give a revealing insight into the capacity and limitations of these leaders for guiding programmes of economic development. One reason is that most of them have come to their present position in the *Panchayat* or the *Panchayat Samiti* after keen contests and have to contend with strong opposition groups. Several of them have to concern themselves constantly with, to maintain or improve their position; even the others, whose positions are more secured, have to remain vigilant and see that they do things which keep their supporters pleased and their opponents in check. This political compulsion makes it necessary for them to concentrate attention on activities like case hearing in the *Panchayats*, and distribution of grants and loans and for transfer of the staff in the *Panchayat Samitis*. These are the activities for which the supporters seek the leaders' intervention and by taking interest in which they can demonstrate to the supporters both their concern for them and their own effectiveness in the *Panchayats* or in the *Panchayat Samitis.* Thus a *Sarpanch* who obtains a grant for construction of a drinking water well or a community building in his village demonstrates to the village people that he is concerned with the development and is sufficiently influential in the *Samiti* to get the grant sanctioned. If he gets a *taccavi* loan sanctioned for a supporter or an appeal decided in his favour, he similarly demonstrates his willingness and capacity to help the supporter. The *Pradhan* in the *Panchayat Samiti* has a similar compulsion in seeing that position of staff and distribution of grants and loans are favourable to the *Sarpanchs* supporting him. But the same political insight prevents them from taking unpopular actions like levying taxes and collecting contributions for community works and often leads them to give insufficient attention to agricultural extension.

As agricultural development is the most important function of *Panchayati Raj* institutions; the attitude of these leaders towards it needs some explanation. Here it will be useful to make a distinction between the operational aspects of agricultural work such as distribution of loans and supply of materials like chemical fertilizers and cement, and the purely educational and experimental aspects, which relate to propagation of new practices. These leaders are keenly interested in the operational aspects but lack interest in the educational and experimental aspects of agricultural extension. The reasons for it is not difficult to understand when we consider the position of a leader *viz- a- viz* a new practice, which is being advocated in his area by the agricultural extension workers. He finds that the benefits of the new practices are neither collective, nor immediate, nor even certain that they will accrue to individual cultivators. The benefits will accrue after a few months (when the crop is harvested) and only if the cultivators take adequate care of their crop and if the season is favourable. If the leader is a progressive farmer himself, he may take interest in the new practice, to the extent of having a demonstration conducted on his own field; and if it gives good results, of talking about it to friends. But, to the political being in him, which has to keep supporters pleased and opponents in check, interest in the improved practice starts only when it had already been proved successful and when the problems connected with it are not educational, but those of arranging supplies, credit, etc.

The *Meena* representatives are in some ways the most significant persons in these profiles. The whole complex of socio-political changes, described in these studies, has put the *Meenas* in a dominant position in local institutions in this area, and this dominance is likely to continue. Therefore, the working of the institutions and indeed the whole course of their development will be influenced very greatly by the personal qualities, the attitude and the behaviour of the *Meena* representatives. Here, as illustrative of the personality differences which will affect these institutions, let us consider Raja Ram and Ram Pratap on the one hand and Bal Ram and Tara Chand on the other. All four are *Meenas* and they must keep the interests of the *Meenas* in view and their *Meena* supporter pleased all the time. But the difference between the essentially reasonable attitude and action of the former, who will consider the claims of other groups in the village also in view and will try to meet them to the extent possible, and the aggressive casteist approach of the latter, is crucial, because the two approaches evoke very different reactions from the other members of the institutions. The former approach is essential, not merely for harmonious day-to-day working of the institutions but even more for their growth to position of key institutions of local government and development, which is envisaged for them.

Links in the Chain of Political Leadership

It has been mentioned above that these leaders function as links between the village and the outside world as well as in the chain of political leadership, which extends from the State level, through the district and the Block, to the village. The various links in the chain are: the Minister, the Member of the State Legislative Assembly (M.L.A), the *Pradhan* of the *Panchayat Samiti*, the influential *Sarpanch* and member of *Panchayats*. Before the establishment of the *Panchayati Raj* institutions, this leadership chain was incomplete because there was no effective, functional link between State level political leaders like the Ministers and the MLAs and village level leaders like the *Sarpanch* and member of the *Panchayat*. These institutions have supplied the links by creating new area level leaders like the *Pradhans* and the influential *Sarpanchs*. Those people, with active links 'downwards' with the village, function at the area level and they interact with the other area level leaders—the M.L.A., who has linked 'upwards' at the State level. The interaction may be one of mutual support, especially at the time of his election, or the latter might themselves be dreaming of contesting election to the State legislature and be his potential rivals.[2] But the important fact is of interaction, which brings the two sets of area level leaders together, completes the political chain, and makes possible transmission of views, felt needs and problems of the villagers to the highest level of State administration far more affectivity, than was possible earlier.

Leaders and Representatives

The persons figuring in these profiles are representatives of their villages (or larger areas) in democratic institution. But are they "leaders" and if so, to what extent and in which areas of the social life of the village? It is necessary to raise these questions because there are different areas of social life of the village community, which have different leaders, and the fact that a person has been selected for a leadership role in one does not automatically make him a leader in all the others.

In the detailed study of Raipur village, it was found that the young *Sarpanch* of Raipur is not accepted as a leader of the village or even of his own caste for many purposes as do several other leaders figuring in these profiles. It is not possible to enter here into a detailed discussion of the nature of rural leadership or of the different kinds of leadership roles in a village community. But a brief reference to two different leadership roles will serve to illustrate the point. These are: exercise of political power in the village and maintenance of social norms. In the past the first role was played generally by the people having hereditary authority and prestige—the *patels*, the high caste *Brahmins* and *Mahajans* with wealth or large land holdings and the *jagirdars* and their servants in the *jagir* villages. Frequently, village level government servants like the *Patwari* also shared this role. These people served also as the links of the village with the outside-world—for administrative, legal and most economic purposes. The role of maintaining social norms was also played sometimes by these holders of political power—the *jagirdar*, who imposed his authority for maintenance of the *jajmani* system. In his village he was an example of the person who combined the two roles; a better example was the wise *jagirdar*, who was so respected by the village people that they took their inter-caste or inter-personal disputes to him voluntarily. The voluntary aspect was more clearly seen among the *patels*, who were often also the leaders of their caste and were prominent in maintaining social norms within it and in regulation of its relations with other castes. But, equally frequently the second role was played by the people who had no political power, *e.g.* old or middle-aged men of different castes. These persons were respected for their wisdom, cleverness or knowledge of traditional values; inter-personal and inter-caste disputes and cases involving transgression of traditional customs of the caste were referred to them for decision, for they are expected to speak for their caste to or their village when any matter concerning these was under consideration. The role was played at intra-village meetings of caste leaders to settle a dispute in which *e.g.* a woman married to a man has gone to live with another and the aggrieved party has moved the leaders for a settlement of *jhagra*[3].

The village people see their representatives in *Panchayati Raj* institutions pre-eminently in the role of holders of political power—as successors to *patels*, influential wealthy high caste men, and if one might say so, the *jagirdars*. They understand that their position in these institutions gives them political power. But they are equally clear that the other role of maintenance of social norms does not flow to them by virtue of office. An individual member of a *Panchayati Raj* institution may perform this role (Raj Mal does it) in his village and/or (Raja Ram does it conspicuously) among the *Meenas* of the entire *Panchayat Samiti* area.

But this is because of personal qualities and not due to official position; because other holders of similar positions (*e.g.*, Sridhar and Ram Das) are specifically excluded from performance of this role.

It must be assumed that the second role is not important at present. Some aspects *e.g.*, enforcing caste taboos in food and drink may be less important now. But, as we have seen in these studies, other aspects such as regulating changes in occupation and social custom among the scheduled castes and the cultivating castes, are more important, now than they were in the past. Consequently, the leaders who are entrusted with responsibility to maintain social norms have just as important a role in the social life of the village community as have members of *Panchayati Raj* institutions. Recognition of the existence of several leadership roles in a village community, and of the fact that members of *Panchayati Raj* institutions fill only one of these by virtue of their offices is essential for understanding the nature of these new leaders, and their positions in their villages.

Essentials for Leadership in PRIs

In 1961, as well as in 2001, there are two conditions that are essential for leadership in the village and in local institutions. These are brought out by examples of the leaders in the two villages, Maanpur and Raipur, studied by the author in 1961; the villages were resurveyed in 2001. First, the leader should belong to a family with a large land holding or an established position of affluence or prestige in the village. In 1961, late Hari Singh, a *Rajput* with a large land holding in his family and who had been the principal functionary of the former *jagirdar* of the village, was the *Sarpanch* of the Maanpur *Panchayat*. He had been *Sarpanch* since the *Panchayat* was established in 1952. His position was unquestioned for two reasons. First he had the qualities that kept the leaders of various communities (*Rajputs*, *Mahajans*, *Meenas*, *Malis* and the scheduled castes) satisfied and had also established good relations with officials. In 2001, the *Sarpanch* is a successful *Mahajan* businessman. But late Hari Singh's younger brother Mr. Suraj Bhan Singh, an ex-*Sarpanch* of the village, is consulted by leaders of various castes in matters relating to the welfare of all the villages under the *Panchayat*. The leaders of the hamlets of the *Chamaars* and the *Meenas* are also cultivators of more than average landholdings.

The second essential condition for leadership is that he should be convincingly vocal about the needs and problems of the village to the officials and at the same time convince the villagers that he can put forward the demands of all the villagers as well or better than any one else. Late Hari Singh had and Suraj Bhan Singh has these qualities.

In Raipur, the two most respected leaders in 1961 were (i) middle aged *Meena* with a large land holding. He had been a member of the first *Panchayat* established in 1952. The second leader was (ii) middle aged affluent *Mahajan*. The family owned a sizeable landholding and had besides, money-lending as a principal economic activity. He too had been a member and for many years *Sarpanch* of the *Panchayat* established in 1952. The two leaders had mobilized funds, labour and material contributions from the villagers for construction of the buildings of a middle school for boys and a primary school for girls, repair of the approach road to the village, pavement of streets in the habitation area of the village and construction of buildings for the *Panchayat* and the cooperative society-*cum*-store for improved seed, fertilizers and other inputs. They had obtained grants or loans from the community development administration for construction of all these works and also for construction and repair of wells in the hamlets of the *Chamaars* and *Gujjars*, located on the outskirts of the village.

Mr. Sham Lal Sharma, the *Sarpanch* of Raipur in 1961 was very critical of the regime of these leaders; he accused them of corruption, a charge that they reciprocated. But he recognized that he could not mobilize the funds for the works mentioned above that the traditional leaders had done. The maximum that he could do was to maintain these works and at the same time ensure that the *Panchayat* had enough funds for maintaining clean drains in the habitation area of the high castes. The villagers did not allow him to raise taxes to undertake any new development works. Although he was a well-paid clerk in the cement factory, he came from a poor family. Thus he lacked one essential condition for leadership.

In 1961, two essential conditions for position of leadership at the block and district level were also that the leader should be well off enough not to appear to utilize his leadership to enrich himself from the grants or loans that were available for development works in the villages and he should be convincingly vocal about the demands and the difficulties of the villagers to the officials.

The *Pradhan* (chairman) of the Sawai Madhopur *Panchayat Samiti* in 1961 was a middle-aged *Meena* from the central part of the *tehsil* which was the stronghold of the *Meenas*. His family had a large landholding and the *Meena* community had chosen him for being a convincingly vocal representative of the *Meena* caste. Furthermore, he had such personal qualities that the decisions of the *Panchayat Samiti* were seldom overturned by the District Development Officer or the Collector.

In 1961, the MLA of the Sawai Madhopur (unreserved) constituency was a reasonably successful Moslem lawyer. His brother was also a successful lawyer in the Collector's office. Furthermore, he had the backing of the mostly Moslem forest contractors who mobilized men and money for his campaign in return for his ability to get permission to cut forest and other favours from the Collector and the State Government.

He was succeeded in the election of 1962 by a Rajput ex-*Jagirdar*, a traditional leader from a reasonably affluent family. Furthermore, he had the ability to approach the *Meenas*, *Malis* and the *Chamaars* and to convince them that he would further their interests with the State government.

These conditions have remained unchanged in 2001, no matter who occupies the various positions in the *Panchayati Raj* institutions. The *Sarpanch* of Raipur in 2001 is a woman of washermen (*Dhobi)* caste, the lowest in an extremely caste conscious village. She is completely ineffective. She is accused also of corruption because her husband drinks. She was elected because the seat had been reserved for a member of the scheduled caste/scheduled tribe and also reserved for a woman. The SC/ST castes community men could not decide on any one candidate and had put up several women. The *Dhobi* woman won the election primarily as a proxy candidate for whom all high caste voters voted. However, the real leader of the community remains a reasonably affluent *Meena* and two or more reasonably well off *Mahajans* and *Brahmins.*

In Maanpur while the *Sarpanch* is a *Mahajan,* Suraj Bhan Singh, a *Rajput* and the ex-*Sarpanch* are consulted in various matters for their traditional position in the village. The leaders of the hamlets of the *Chamars* and the *Meenas* are also farmers with relatively large land-holdings who are convincingly vocal about demands of their constituents.

NOTES

1. For one view of the influence of the attitude and the cultural orientation of the new leaders on the development of *Panchayati Raj* institutions see, Mathur P.C. (1964.)
2. Nine out of the ten *Pradhans* in Sawai Madhopur district took an active part in the general election of 1962. Three of them contested the election themselves; three were aspirants but could not get the backing of the Congress Party for their candidature, and three others were active campaigners for or against particular candidates.

3. *Jhagra*: payment received by husband whose wife has left him to live with another man.

REFERENCES

Mathur, P.C.: The Sociological Dimensions of *Panchayati Raj*, *Journal of the Indian Institute of Public Administration*, New Delhi, January-March, 1964.

Government of Rajasthan, Evaluation Organization: *Panchayat Election in Rajasthan*, Jaipur 1960.

ANNEXURE 15.1

Profiles of Village Leaders of Sawai Modhopur District

Ram Pratap—Young Cultivator

Ram Pratap 40 is the *Sarpanch* of the newly created *Panchayat*. He belongs to a prosperous, influential, and respected land-owning-cultivating *Meena* family. The family has the biggest landholding in the village and has enjoyed the position of being its most prosperous and influential family for a long time. It is also well known and respected, in its own caste, in the entire of the *Panchayat Samiti*. The family now consist of three brothers and own about 150 acres of good agricultural land in the village. One brother devotes himself entirely to cultivation while the other two spend time also in village's affairs and local politics. Ram Pratap is the middle brother. The eldest brother is the chairman of new *Nyaya (judicial) Panchayat* which has jurisdiction over seven *Panchayat* circles and about 30 villages.

Ram Pratap is not new to local politics: he represented his village as member of the former *Panchayat* for 3 years. But he has more authority and influence in his present position of *Sarpanch*. He is head of his own *Panchayat*, and as a prominent member of the cultivating caste group, which dominates the *Panchayat Samiti* and is one of the most influential members of that body. An added source of power: he is related to and is a close associate of the *Pradhan* of the *Samiti*.

Like many other young or middle-aged leaders of his caste, Ram Pratap has rural and urban, agricultural and non-agricultural interests; in fact he stands between town and village in many ways. He has been educated, up to the primary standard.[1] While his principal economic interest is in cultivation and money lending in the village, he also has a small retail shop in town. He goes to town often in connection with his business and political affairs. He is well acquainted with ways of commerce and of small town politics. His position in the *Panchayat Samiti* is making him increasingly acquainted with district and State level politics. However, he is by no means an urbanite: his primary interests are in the village and its affairs, and he comes to the town as a representative of his village and caste, not *vice versa*.

He is quiet and unassuming by temperament; but he had the confidence which comes from belonging to a substantial and respected family. He is not given to speech-making or throwing his weight about. Because of his position in his caste group and his relationship with the *Pradhan*, he is influential in the *Panchayat Samiti*. His attitude towards officials is one of cooperation and tolerance. As he belongs to a family of hereditary *patels*, he knows official attitude and way of working quite well, and he is quite familiar with both the strength and weakness of the administration of the village, block and district levels. His relation with the *Vikas Adhikari* (Block Development Officer) and staff of the *Panchayat Samiti* are quite cordial.

Ram Pratap's position in the *Panchayat* is an expression primarily of the position of influence and respect which family has enjoyed in this village for a long time; his position in the *Panchayat Samiti* is an expression of the preponderance of his caste in the area. The family was respected and this man is judged to be a worthy member of the family and, therefore, considered quite suitable to lead the *Panchayat* and to represent the village in the *Samiti*.

Ram Pratap considers the *Panchayat Samiti* to be a continuation of the Community Development Block, which did good things for villages in the area; he feels that through his position in the *Samiti* he can get things done for his village and for members of his caste. However, he has been able to accomplish this objective only to the limited extent of getting loans for some cultivators. His village and *Panchayat* circle have not got any funds for works programmes so far. He understands that this is due to shortage of funds within the *Samiti* and is not happy about the working of the *Samiti* on this account. But he is very dissatisfied with the new small *Panchayat* like the one he heads. He feels that these have neither power nor resources nor important functions. His *Panchayat* consists of six small villages with a total population of about 2,500. Such sources of income as share of land revenue and sale of *abadi* lands—sources which brought substantial revenue to the former *Panchayats*—bring in very little money now. The *Panchayat* has not levied any taxes and had practically no money. The judicial function, which is the most important function of *Panchayat* in the eyes of the villagers, has been transferred to the new *Nyaya Panchayats*. As an example of his *Panchayats* lack of power, Ram Pratap cited the instance of ill-treatment of the peon of the *Panchayat* by the people of another village of the *Panchayat* circle. The man was not allowed to enter the village when he went there on *Panchayats* work. Explaining the background of the incident, Ram Pratap mentioned that these people wanted the headquarters of the *Panchayat* to be located in their own village and strongly represented anger at its location in Ram Pratap's village. They said that Ram Pratap's village is in one corner of the *Panchayat* circle and is unapproachable during the rains while their own village was in a centre of *Panchayat* circle and was accessible throughout the year. A more important reason was that the two villages had a long-standing feud, and these people did not want the *Panchayat* headquarters to be located in a rival village. But, when their plea was rejected and Ram Pratap's village was finally selected because it was the largest village in the circle, they decided to boycott the *Panchayat* election and the institution itself. In fact, people of this village and some sympathizers from other villages did not vote in the (1960) *Panchayat* election. Their opposition continues, and their attitude towards the new *Panchayat* is one of complete non-cooperation. Ram Pratap complained that the *Panchayat* is powerless to do anything about it.

Ram Pratap is progressively taking more interest and spending more and more of his time in local "political work". He is very often at the district headquarters in connection with some work of *Panchayat Samiti* or the village. Currently he is spearheading the demand of villagers for compensation for lands submerged and houses damaged by construction of the irrigation tank. The tank was constructed several years ago, but compensation has not been paid to the villagers so far. They also suffer great hardship during the rainy season when their village is almost surrounded by water. Ram Pratap feels that his village has a much better chance of getting a liberal settlement in this pre-election year (1961) than it would in other years. He had advocated the case before the local revenue officials; he has seen to it that they visit the spot and appreciate their difficulties; and he has sought the active support of the local M.L.A., and *Pradhan* and had also been to the State capital and seen the ministers. His conduct in this case is an excellent illustration of the growing understanding among village leaders of the methods of obtaining action on their demands in a political democracy.

Bal Ram—Young Cultivator—Politician

Bal Ram is a self-made young man. He belongs to a poor cultivating family of *Chowkidar Meena* caste[2] and has attained his present position, *Sarpanch*, of a large and important *Panchayat* and an important executive of the *Panchayat Samiti* entirely through hard work, ability, and aggressive political campaigning. He is educated up to the eighth class and he has his service experience for several years. He started service with the *jagirdar* of his village and was transferred to the subordinate service of the State when the *jagir* was resumed. He remained in state service for some years, and then resigned it to enter the Meena Reform Movement. His primary economic interest at present is a grain shop in the *Panchayat* headquarters village, a trade of some local importance. His family lives in a nearby village, where they cultivate about 60 acres of land. Bal Ram has helped to acquire the land through allotment and purchase over the years. He is not rich and can barely manage to afford the standard of living and expense of travel, which his political activities require; but he is not poor either. However, his attitude is deeply coloured by the poverty that he has known as a child.

Bal Ram gained his present position as a leader of his caste, *via* the Meena Reform Movement. This movement was aimed at modernization of the *Meenas* by encouraging modern education, and by abolishing a whole cluster of former caste-customs: group dancing at fairs, the use of heavy silver ornaments, distinctive peasant clothes, and a distinctive hair-do by the women, drinking and meat eating, child marriage, easy and frequent divorce, taking *jhagra* money, etc. the movement was an organized articulation of the process of caste modernization; it began rapidly after the disappearance of the princely states. Bal Ram joined the movement in the early fifties after leaving state service. One of the things which prompted him to join this movement and which also accounts partly for his aggressiveness is the memory of the harsh treatment meted out to members of his caste during the time of the former Jaipur state, when they were classified as a criminal tribe. They were kept under surveillance and were often the victims of harsh treatment at the hands of petty police officials. He never suffered such treatment himself; but the sight of others suffering these inequities has left a deep impression on his young mind.

His attitude forms a fascinating study. He represents, at the local level, the militant and aggressive leadership, which has come up among the cultivating castes following disappearance of the *jagirdari* and establishment of the democratic institutions. Leaders like Raja Ram represent the moderate section in the new leadership. He realizes that the basis of his leadership is caste and that he must retain the support of his caste to be elected to any political position. He appeals to caste loyalty in a frank and aggressive casteist fashion.

He is aggressive due partly to his feeling, perhaps unconscious, that as he belongs to the *chowkidar Meena* group, his appeal must be more frankly casteist if he is to identify himself with the group and own their support. His aggression towards official, however, is due partly to his having been in a subordinate position in government earlier. He feels that he can now question and criticize the actions of official, whom he could only obey in the past and would have continued to obey if he had remained in service. However, he understands and respects government procedures and methods. He was in service too long not to have acquired the habit of respecting government orders !

Bal Ram is the leader of his faction in both his *Panchayat* and the *Panchayat Samiti*. He became *Sarpanch* of his *Panchayat* after a keen contest with a *Mahajan* rival who is much richer and whose family enjoys a position of respect in the village. His main supporters were the cultivating and lower castes, while his rival found support among the traders, *Brahmins* and other high castes. The election rivalry and prestige colour the attitudes and behaviour both by and towards him in the village. There are allegations of mismanagement of *Panchayat* funds against him and he does not hesitate to deliver his counter punches whenever he has the opportunity. One result of the opposition has been his inability to impose any taxes. Even his very hard and successful work in getting the village a higher secondary school has not reduced the opposition. On the contrary, it has accentuated it because his rivals have interpreted the effort merely as a move to improving his own political prospects. Their judgment is not too unjust, because the effort did form part of his campaign to get political recognition and support for his claim to get the Congress Party ticket for election to the State legislature. In the *Panchayat Samiti*, he is a leading member of the dominant *Meena* group, and he has fully used the power, which this position gave him in getting *taccavi* loans and other benefits for his supporters. This has created a certain feeling of dissatisfaction among the *Samiti* members who do not belong to his group.

In spite of his partisanship and aggressiveness, Bal Ram could be a good development worker if he devoted his energies to this task. He demonstrated his capacities in the effort he made recently for establishment of the higher secondary school. He was active in mobilizing contributions for construction of the building and even more so in convincing the local officials, the MLA, and finally the ministers in Jaipur, that this was the most important demand of the village. He suggested that they must accept it if they were to win support in the election in this village and a large number of villages in the neighbourhood which would also derive benefit from the school. But his primary interest is in a political carreer. He is trying very hard to get the Congress Party ticket for election to the State Legislature. He values his present position in the *Panchayat Samiti* and the power and the influence that it gives him in his village and the surrounding villages even more so for the opportunity it offers for climbing to higher political positions. He feels that his caste needs "leaders" and he is one of them. Whether he succeeds in his political ambitions or not, will depend on his capacity to devote himself to the task and appeal aggressively to the caste consciousness of his people.

Jai Singh—Young Rajput

A young educated (up to the matriculation standard) *Rajput*, Jai Singh is the *Sarpanch* of a *Naya Panchayat*, which consists of five small villages with a population of about 2,000. He is not an old resident of this village or even of this district. He makes a living by managing cultivation of his lands. Besides he operates a lime-kiln and lends money for additional income. He owes his political positions in the village partly due to his own personal qualities. He is a smart young politician who has successfully used the techniques of mobilizing local opinion behind a single issue to his own advantage. The issue is the location of headquarters of the new *Nyaya Panchayat*. He wants it shifted from a neighbouring village to his own village. His case is not strong: his village is smaller, much less important, and in many ways much less suitable for being the headquarters than the other villages. But he has been successful for his mobilizing, first people of his own *Panchayat* circle, next of a majority of his members of the *Nyaya Panchayat* and finally of *Panchayat Samiti*. This is undoubtedly a major political accomplishment; it helped him in his candidature for *Sarpanch* and now makes him a prominent member of the *Panchayat Samiti*. Also, he wants to establish a grain market in his village. The prospectus for this are not bright, as the village is small, does not have good communications, and has no particular commercial potential. But his desire for development can be understood only as a typical reaction of a young man who has broken urban connections and is keen to re-creature an urban setting in the village where he has come to settle down.

The small village is hardly sufficient to absorb his energies. He is a frequent visitor to the district town and to the State capital, and he maintains active contacts with district officials, local politicians, and member of the *Panchayat Samiti*. He is the young man about town. In an earlier age he would have been a member of the smart set, albeit of a small princely state (a role for which, alas, there is no scope today). His main motive in coming to the *Panchayat* and the *Panchayat Samiti* is to establish his personal prestige and position in his own and surrounding villages and in the district headquarters town. He wants to be known and respected as a person of consequence in the area. His ambition is strictly local and is quite in accord with his *jagirdari* background. He has no great political ambition; though he may not rule out the prospect of becoming an M.L.A. or the *Pradhan* of the *Panchayat Samiti* at some future date.

Sridhar—Educated Young Leader

Sridhar is the *Brahmin Sarpanch* of a large and prosperous village (population 5,000), which has an important grain market. The village was the seat of an important *jagirdar* of the former Jaipur state. Sridhar's ancestors were tutors to the *jagirdar's* sons and enjoyed a position of respect, influence, and authority in the village. Respect for the family has been an important factor in his election to the present position. The other factor has been the support of an old *vaidya-cum*-political worker who has lived in this village for about 25 years. Sridhar's family is not rich; but they are moderately well off. He himself manages the family lands (about 40 acres of good farm land) and has a shop in a flour-mill in a village. The land has been given for cultivation on *batai* while the mill is being looked after by his partner. This economic interest guarantees him a comfortable, middle class living and also leaves him enough time for local politics.

Sridhar is well-educated (matriculation, Hindi *Sahitya Ratna*)[3] keen, and intelligent, with an interest in politics. He is the type who would have been an active fighter for freedom in the pre-Independence days and who joined the *Sarvodaya* movement[4] out of intellectual conviction. He has already worked for the *Bharat Sewak Samaj*[5] and for Harijan uplift; he still has considerable interest in constructive work. A fairly good speaker, he delights in public speaking and debate. He has considerable political ambition and would not mind making politics a career.

Before becoming *Sarpanch*, he was a member of the village *Panchayat* for three years. He was elected *Sarpanch* after a very keen election contest in which there was some tension in the village. His principal rival was an influential *Mahajan* businessman who had been *Sarpanch* for a number of years and who has the support of the businessmen, a numerous and powerful group in the commercial centre. Sridhar won with the support of the cultivators, artisans, *Chamaars*, and people of the other low castes. The election campaign has left a deep rift in the village, which affects the working of the *Panchayat*. The *Mahajans* are against him, and his own attitudes and actions are quite partisan. He has made several complaints against the former *Sarpanch* and his other political rivals. He has also talked about levying taxes on sales in the grain market, a move, which would affect the interest of the traders.

His village has made very good progress—economic and social—in the years following the formation of Rajasthan and abolition of *jagirdari*. A grain market has been established; business has increased enormously; a large number of *pucca* houses have been built, and a number of development works and social service institutions have been started. To some extent progress represented catching up with modern times and realizing the economic potentials of the village, both of which became possible after removal of the restriction on economic progress (*e.g.* on construction of *pucca* houses) which had prevailed in the *jagirdars* time. The village took an active interest in the Community Development work and a number of works and development activities centreed in it. The higher secondary school and the dispensary are the most important institutions to be located in the village during recent years. The villagers have built a very good building for the school at the cost of about Rs. 40,000 and are particularly proud of this achievement. The *Panchayat* has a substantial income because of the grain market and a fair, which is held annually at a local shrine; it has been an active institution.

Sridhar is anxious that this progress should continue. He takes an active interest in the work of *Panchayat* and in development activity generally. He has proposed a number of taxes for increasing the income of *Panchayat*. He is active in campaigning for improvement of existing development institutions and location of new ones. He is currently campaigning for the addition of science wing in the higher secondary school. He would like to see progress in his village and small industry attracted to it. He meets officials and non-officials frequently to overcome some local difficulty or to improve some institutions.

But he faces serious handicaps in working for the development of his village. In the *Panchayat* and the village he has the stiff opposition of the traders and the others who opposed his election. As a result, it is likely that many of the taxes he is proposing will not be levied, and if levied, will not be collected. Contributions for development works cannot be obtained on any large scale for the same reasons. In the *Panchayat Samiti* he finds himself in a hopeless minority, because he does not belong to the cultivating caste group, which dominates its affairs. Moreover, the members of the *Panchayat* Samiti feel, not entirely without justification, that the village received its share of development funds during the time of the Community Development Block; that it is a rich semi-urban, commercial village which can afford to take up works on its own; and that no substantial development funds need be given to it now. Sridhar protests against this attitude of the *Panchayat Samiti* members but his protest has produced no effect so far. Finally, he is not a good executive. He is a thinker and a speaker, not a man of action. Many of his ideas will remain unimplemented because he neither has the personal qualities to implement them, nor the ability to mobilize the required support for them in the *Panchayat* or the *Panchayat Samiti*.

His position as *Sarpanch* and member of the *Panchayat Samiti* gives him considerable authority and influence in the village. This is a great satisfaction for one whose family has enjoyed respect and authority in the village and who would like to see this position reaffirmed. Even more important, it gives him a chance to pursue his political career as he can meet people at the Block, district, and even State level. He spends quite some time in these political contacts and is somewhat of a lieutenant of the local M.L.A. He realizes his handicaps in pursuing a political career; he does not belong to the dominant cultivating caste and is not rich. But he is more conscious of his assets—public speaking ability, intelligence, education and a personal charm, and feels that with these he can be a successful. He has no immediate political objective, but in course of time he would not mind trying for positions like *Pradhan* and M.L.A.

He is somewhat critical about the *Panchayat Samiti*. He feels keenly that this is a show for group and caste politics and *Sarpanchs* like himself who are in the minority cannot do much in it. He speaks openly and frequently against the partisan character of the *Samiti* and is one of the most vocal critics in this area, of the whole system of *Panchayati Raj* institutions.

Ram Das—Chamaar Representative

Ram Das is the only *Sarpanch* of his caste in the *Panchayat Samiti* and one of the few in the district. He heads one of the newly created *Panchayat* with jurisdiction over 5 small villages (population 3,000). The villages are located near a town, and large number of people are engaged in them in non-agricultural occupations—industrial and casual labour, petty trade, and professions. The caste composition of the population is also very mixed, with no one caste predominant. Ram Das's own caste is in a small minority in these villages, and he has been elected with the support of the other castes, which makes his achievement even more creditable.

He represents the advanced group of the young men of his caste who depend upon non-agricultural labour and other non-agricultural occupations and who have been greatly affected by urban contacts. Educated up to the middle standard, he is a small contractor; he has the labour contracts for loading and uploading freight on the railway. His father was a railway employee, and his uncle had a similar labour contract in another part of the country. He was born and brought up in a non-agricultural environment and started life as small contractor-*cum*-businessman. After two failures, he settled down in his present business, which requires management of human beings; he successfully runs a business, which employs a labour force of about 600 men. This large labour force is an important resource for elections ! Besides giving him his own voting strength, it provides him with the manpower so essential in fighting elections.

Although a non-agriculturist, he has some links with agriculture and rural life. Two of his brothers are engaged in cultivation. He wants to get them more land, and he would like to get some land for cultivation himself.

This is not his first entry into local politics. For several years, he was member of the former large *Panchayat* of which his village then formed a part. Two years ago, he contested for the *Sarpanchship* of the *Panchayat*. He was defeated, but he gave his opponent a very stiff fight. He says that he would have won but for the fraudulent practices of his opponent. He has won the present election by a comfortable margin.

Ram Das is very conscious of the fact that his caste, which forms a substantial section of the rural population, is seriously underrepresented in the *Panchayat Samiti*. He would like to see this imbalance corrected at least in part, at the next *Panchayat* election. He is aware of the special measure being taken for social and economic uplift of his caste and the social concessions being given to them; but he feels that what he has done is not enough, that much more should be done quickly. He feels particularly strongly about the *Panchayat Samiti's* reaction to the needs of his caste. He is himself a member of the standing committee which deals with programmes for the underprivileged groups; but he says that during his 10 months in the committee he has been able to get grant for only one drinking water well for Harijans, and even in that he faced strong opposition from other members of the committee. He complained that the *Panchayat Samiti* was dominated by the *Meenas* and would not give a fair deal to his caste; but he emphasized that as long as he is there he would not let them have their own way entirely. "They are afraid of me", he added.

Besides looking after the interests of his caste in the *Panchayat Samiti*, Ram Das takes interest in the affairs of his village and is pressing for funds for development. However, in this also he is not very successful. He said that his village has several needs, of which a drinking water was most urgent. The villagers were prepared to contribute their share of the cost, but funds were not sanctioned by the *Panchayat Samiti*. "The *Samiti* has not even given *Panchayat* a grant for street lighting which it has given to most other *panchayats*", He said the discrimination has coloured his attitude towards the *Samiti* and he is quite critical of its working.

Like many other *Sarpanchs* of new small *Panchayats*, he feels that the institutions have no resources, few functions, and very little powers. His *Panchayat* has levied no taxes. Its meagre income comes mainly from the sale of *abadi* lands, which together with granting permits for construction of houses appears to him to be the only function of the *Panchayat*. He is anxious to get more area converted into *abadi*, because sales of the house sites in the next *abadi* will give the *Panchayat* a good source of income. It will also help meet the need for more houses, the most urgently felt need in his village. He is also trying to get land allotted for a separate colony of Harijans. When asked about the power of *Panchayats*, his first reply was that the judicial function had been taken away; the *Panchayats* had "very little power left". As an example, he mentioned that a rival whom he had defeated in the election for *Sarpanch* has instigated some people of his village. The *Panchayat* has served notices on these people, but was not in a position to do anything further, because it could not displease a fairly powerful section of the village.

As mentioned above, he is a competent and successful businessman; however, in spite of his economic and political success, he has not yet got over the self-consciousness and inferiority complex which one finds in many urbanized young and middle-aged persons of the *Chamaar* caste. He is not aggressive; on the contrary he is shy and has a tendency to withdraw within himself.

He has given no indication yet of having any higher political ambition. His business absorbs most of his time and energy, and since he runs it by himself he has to give it his first attention. But he will probably not be opposed to seeking a political carreer somewhat later. He is young and has already made a bid for *Sarpanchship* of a large *Panchayat*. He is quite aware of the fact that he has several advantages, some money, education, and contacts with officials and non-officials, executive ability— which is highly prized in political life and is so scarce among people of his caste.

Raja Ram—Prosperous Farmer-cum-Businessman

An important executive of *Panchayat Samiti*, Raja Ram comes from an old, respected and prosperous *Meena* family of a large village. Members of his extended family are influential and respected in the entire area of the

Panchayat Samiti. They are also connected through marriage with many leading families of the caste in the area. His nephew is the *Sarpanch* of the village *Panchayat*; other members of the extended family fill important positions in the cooperative society, the *Panchayat* and the *Nyaya Panchayat*. Several *Sarpanchs, patels* and other leading persons of the *Panchayat Samiti* area are related to the family through marriage. They are solid rural people: not rich, but substantial and comfortable. Raja Ram and his two brothers owned a farm of about 100 acres. The land is cultivated by hired labour under the supervision of Raja Ram's brother. The farm is successful, sugarcane being especially remunerative. They attempted pump irrigation some years ago, but without conspicuous success. They are bold but rather conservative farmers and they have not made any major changes or technological improvements in their cultivation. Besides cultivation, they also lend money, and Raja Ram has an interest in a shop in the town.

Raja Ram is educated only up to the primary standard, and although he is quite familiar with urban ways, he is essentially a villager and a farmer. He is a quiet, unassuming, well-mannered person—intelligent, even shrewd, but completely honest. As a result, he commands respect and the complete confidence of *Sarpancha* of his caste in the *Panchayat Samiti*. His present position in the *Samiti* is due as much to his personal qualities as to the position of his family in the area. As he comes from a family of hereditary *patels*, he is familiar with local administration and has an attitude of cooperation and respect for officials. He is friendly with the officers of the *Samiti* and sympathetic towards the lower staff. These attitude and behaviour are in no small part responsible for the smooth functioning of the *Samiti*.

Local politics is a hobby with him. He has been associated with the *Panchayat Samiti* ever since its formation in 1959. Earlier he had been a prominent member of the Block Development Committee of the Community Development Block. He has also interested himself in district and State level politics. He contested election (unsuccessfully) for the State Legislature in 1957 and is counted among the probable local candidates for the next (1962) election.

The main source of his strength is of course the position of his family among the *Meenas,* who have emerged as the dominant social group in the area after abolition of *jagirdari* and establishment of representative institutions. Members of the caste want their own representative in position of prestige and power. Raja Ram, worthy scion of an old and respectable family, fills this need admirably. Since his position rests in the support of people of his caste, he must do things to keep them pleased and must make an appeal to caste loyalties to retain his position. But he is not aggressive and does not encourage caste and community functions unnecessarily. He must favour members of his group and caste; but he would not do anything blatantly unjust. He is essentially a gentleman.

He sees his position in his *Panchayat Samiti* as a position of prestige and power, one which enables him to control financial and other benefits that flow from the State government for developing of rural areas. He and his supporters control the *Panchayat Samiti* fairly effectively and have no difficulty in directing the flow of benefits to villages and the people of their choice. He appreciates the advantages of *Panchayati Raj* institutions and feels that they give the rural people precisely the kind of say that they should have in development programmes. He is interested in their success. But he is quite conscious of their difficulties and weaknesses. His main complaint is that the *Panchayats* and the *Panchayat Samitis* have such meagre resources. He thinks that many of the charges of discrimination levelled against him and his group by their rivals in the *Panchayat Samiti* would disappear if the *Samiti* had more funds and could be more liberal in giving grants and loans.

Tara Chand—A Representative of the Cultivating Caste

Like Raja Ram, described above, Tara Chand is also an important executive of a *Panchayat Samiti*, belongs to one of the oldest, most influential and prosperous *Meena* families of a big village of his *Panchayat Samiti* area. The family owns a substantial acreage of rich farm land, a large portion of which is irrigated, and grows paddy; a highly remunerative crop. Tara Chand and other members of his family personally supervise the cultivation of their land. They are known to be among the wealthiest cultivators in the *Samiti* area. Tara Chand claims that he and other members of the family were instrumental in reviving cultivation of paddy in the village about 20 years ago, when they found that due to an increase in rainfall and sub-soil moisture (the village had been receiving canal irrigation for more than 50 years), their Jowar crop was not doing well. They experimented with paddy and found the result extremely satisfactory: paddy produce has increased considerably in this area during the last 15 years, and Tara Chand's family has made very good money.

After coming into the *Panchayat Samiti* two years ago, Tara Chand had taken an active interest in the agricultural improvement programme. His most important achievement has been repair and renovation of several small irrigation tanks. The *Panchayat Samiti* has a large number of such tanks built, and maintained by the cultivators themselves. Of late maintenance of these tanks has been in arrears and many of them have deteriorated. In 1961, a large sum of money was received for benefit of the schedule tribes, and six tanks located in Tara Chand's village were repaired with it. This work has benefited the land owning cultivators of his village, most of whom belong to his caste. This shrewd peasant sees in the special fund, an opportunity in benefiting the cultivators of his village, including members of his own and extended families. The money was available without too much political pressure, and he quickly took it. Also, with the unerring eye of the shrewd peasant he used it for a work, which would yield benefits quickly and for a long time. This work has brought a solid benefit to cultivators of his village and greatly raised his stock.

Tara Chand is not well educated. He knows Hindi well, but not English. But he is a shrewd businessman and has plenty of commonsense. He is also tough: he has a strong will and is unquestionably the boss in whichever position he is. His supporters, as well as the staff of any institution in which he works, must obey him. He is a good friend but a bad enemy. However, his attitude towards officials is not without respect and understanding: it cannot be but influenced by the tradition of respect for and obedience to official of the revenue department in his family of hereditary *patels*. The working of his *Panchayat Samiti* has not been marked by any serious feuds, but this is because he has been able to have his way in all matters of interest to him and his group.

He has taken an active interest in local and district politics for some time. He is an active party worker, has been an aspirant for legislative offices, and is planning to take an active part in the forthcoming elections. Politics to him is a means of asserting the position of his family in his caste, and of his caste in the Block and the district. His family has been settled in this area for centuries and has enjoyed respect and influence in the village and the surrounding villages for decades. In recent years, they have made good money and have become known as wealthy people. They see political position as a means of asserting themselves. Tara Chand is the symbol of their influence and strength. Also behind him is his group in the villages. They are with him as against other leader of his caste including the present member of his State legislature who also comes from the same village. He is frankly casteist, and his main political appeal is to caste solidarity. He is anxious to exploit fully the caste motive for enlisting support for himself in his political battle. He would also fight for continuation of the privileges enjoyed by members of his caste. But if he were trained to rise above narrow caste loyalty and take up a wider cause, he would prove to be a tough fighter. He is the material from which fighters for great causes are made by the leaders of political movements.

Raj Singh—A Representative of the Old Rural Elite

Raj Singh is a middle-aged *Rajput* and a former *jagirdar*. He belongs to a family of small *jagirdars* but is related to most of the leading *jagirdar* families of this area. He is also an ex-soldier. He was an officer in the Jaipur state army for about 20 years; he was in the Indian army also and saw action during World War II. He came back to settle down on his family land soon after Independence. *Jagirdari* abolition was in the air at the time, and his main object in coming back to his village was to prevent the family land from being lost to the tenants. Cultivation of this land is his main source of livelihood now. Part of the land has been given for cultivation on *batai*; the remainder is being cultivated by him with the help of *halis*. The standard of cultivation is only fair because Raj Singh is not a good manager. However, income from the land together with the pension gives him enough to maintain a middle-class standard of living and especially to pay for the education of his sons, who are studying in schools and colleges in Jaipur. Like other educated Rajputs of the area, he sees education as the only salvation for members of his group, and to see his sons educated and well placed in service is his main objective in life now. He proposes to persuade one of his sons to stay on the land, and expects that the remaining three will be successful in getting good jobs in government and commercial firms.

Raj Singh is educated up to the matriculation standard. He is a quiet and undemanding person, who nevertheless impresses one with his dignity and self-confidence. He has a position of established respect among the *Rajputs* of the area. Few of the former *Jagirdars* are living in the village now, and among those who are, there are few who are educated or have a modern outlook; so his position as a leader of the group in this area is undisputed.

He had taken an active interest in local affairs. He was the *Sarpanch* of the *Panchayat* of his village for several years, and was re-elected in 1960. But he had to give up this position on election to his present post of *Pradhan* of the *Panchayat Samiti*. He is active also in the cooperative movement and holds important position in several cooperative institutions. He is also interested in the affairs of soldiers and former *jagirdars*, and has served on local committees constituted from time-to-time for their welfare. All in all, he is an influential and respected member of his caste, people of his own and surrounding villages and the officers. Of course he has opposition. He was elected *Sarpanch* in 1960 only after a stiff fight and opposition to him; in the *Panchayat* circle and the *Panchayat Samiti*, continuous to be active. He sees that the membership in the *Panchayat*, the *Panchayat Samiti* and the cooperative institutions confers prestige, power and influence. His family and the large *Rajput* ex-*jagirdar* group, to which he belongs, have always exercised power in the area, and the motive on the seeking membership in these institutions is to maintain the position of power and respect. He explains that people of his caste and his village expected that he, as an intelligent, able and affluent member of a former *jagirdar* family should take an active part in this institution. But an element of fear is also mixed with this. "These are institutions of power and if I and others (*Rajput* ex-*jagirdars*) like me do not take interest in them, their power might be used against us", he says. But he is satisfied with position in local institutions and has no ambition with higher political office. He realizes that his caste and group affiliation and moderate personal income are serious handicaps in pursuing a political career. Besides by temperament and training, he is not a politician. He was brought up as a country gentleman and will be content to remain one.

Amar Singh—A Constructive Cultivator Leader

Amar Singh, the *Rajput Sarpanch* of a medium sized village (population 2,500), is in his middle fifties. He belongs to one of the Rajput families, which had rent-free grants from the *jagirdar* of the village. The Rajputs, belonging to the same caste as the *jagirdars*; were the most important people of the village at that time. As Amar Singh's family had little land, they were relatively poor, and had little influence in the village, he has built the position which he enjoys in the village today, largely by himself.

He left the village as a young man about 35 years ago. He remained in the service of a *jagirdar* in a neighbouring district for 20 years, and came back to settle down in the village about 15 years ago. Since his return he has improved his cultivation, increased his holding, and has gradually risen to the position of the leader of the village. He is *Sarpanch* of the *Panchayat* and chairman of the large-sized cooperative society. What is more, he and his group (which includes his nephew and cousins, two leading *Mahajans* and some prominent cultivators) control almost all the important positions in village level institutions. The group controls all but two seats in the *Panchayat*. Amar Singh's nephew is the representative of the village on the *Nyaya Panchayat*. A cousin is secretary of the cooperative society and a member of executive of the Land Mortgage

Bank of the district. The group also represents the village on the district Cooperative Bank and the Cooperative Marketing Society.

Amar Singh has been *Sarpanch* of the *Panchayat* ever since its formation in 1954. At first he was elected unopposed, but then in two elections he had contestants. The contest in 1960 was quite stiff, and he did not win by a comfortable margin. His support is either among the *Rajputs* and the *Brahmins* or among the *Chamaars* and the other low castes. *Malis, Jats*, *Meenas*, *Gujjars* etc. are not very happy with him; they did not vote for him at the last election. The support of the schedule castes rests on the solid work, which he had done for them after coming back to the village. During his stay outside the village he was influenced by the ideology of the Congress Party and wanted to put it into practice on return. At that time the village was still under the *jagirdar*. But he (*Rajput*) expressed himself in favour of abolition of *jagirdari*, and lent active support to abolition of *begar* (forced labour). There were some incidents between the servants of *jagirdar* and the villagers on the issue of *begar* in the early fifties, in which he expressed himself against the *jagirdar*. This annoyed the *jagirdar*, but it gave Amar Singh a standing in the village and especially among the low castes. He has also worked for abolition of untouchability, and on the two occasions when there were conflicts between the *Chamaars* and the rest of the village, he supported the former. The first occasion was provided by the *Chamaars'* decision to stop lifting carcasses and the second by their decision to build a temple and install an idol of Lord Krishna in it. The cultivators and the members of the high castes, including the Rajputs, have not appreciated his role in this case. They are jealous also of the monopoly of positions of the village level institutions, which Amar Singh and his supporters enjoy. Some of them complain that members of this group have used the positions for personal gains: specially, that they have themselves taken most of the *taccavi* loans given by the Community Development Block. Others complain that the grants for construction of the school building and other works have not been properly utilized, and that money received from the government has been used personally for long periods before being spent for public works. The *Meenas* in particular, are so angry with him that they have completely boycotted the cooperative society.

These allegations are not without foundation. Amar Singh and members of his group have undoubtedly obtained *taccavi* loans and other advantages from the Community Development Block. They have also been prominent in obtaining loans from the district Land Mortgage Bank. It is also true that some of the *taccavi* loans have not been properly utilized, and that construction of the works was delayed for long periods. On the other hand, one must give credit to Amar Singh for obtaining for the village almost every grant, loan and other facilities given by the Community Development Block. Almost every public work included in the programme of the Community Development Block—building for the village school, office of the *Panchayat*, office-*cum*-godown of the cooperative society and residence of the V.L.W., two drinking water wells, and pavement of the village *bazar*—was taken up in the village. He obtained funds for theses works from the Block and raised contributions from the village people. His village was judged to be one of the most responsive to development activities in the district in 1958 and was awarded a cash grant of Rs. 2,000 for attaining this destination. Amar Singh then saw the benefits available from the cooperative movement, especially from the new large-sized societies, which began to be established by the cooperative department after 1956. One such society was established in the village in 1957. He worked hard in building it up, and he is mainly responsible for bringing it to its present position: it has the highest loan operations of any society in the district, and is considered to be a 'model'. Even now he works constantly for the society; he particularly sees to it that recoveries are realized in full. He understands that good recovery of loans advanced, is the key to healthy functioning of the society and spares neither effort nor personal popularity to achieve it. Finally, he is the only village leader in this area who has grasped the value of the long-term loans offered by the newly opened Land Mortgage Bank, and the village advances made by the bank to cultivators in this village—the only one in the district—are the result largely of his efforts. Even his critics admit that he was a very competent and constructive worker that the various village institutions would not function well without his interest and effort.

All in all Amar Singh understands the essential nature of the new economic and political institutions very well, and he knows how to use them for the good of his village and himself. He keeps himself well informed about district and State level politics. But he has no political ambition, and is content to pass the rest of his life as a farmer and village leader. He has contacts in town: his daughter is married there, and one son is working there. But his own interest is in the village and in looking after his land.

Like so many others who have been associated with the Community Development Programme for a number of years and were *Sarpanchs* of former large multi-village *Panchayats*, Amar Singh is very dissatisfied with the present *Panchayats* and *Panchayat Samiti*. The *Panchayat* which earlier, had jurisdiction over ten villages and a substantial income, the jurisdiction of the present *Panchayat* is limited to one village and its income is barely sufficient to meet the administrative expenses of keeping a clerk and a peon. The transfer of judicial function to the *Nyaya Panchayat* has robbed it much of its power. The new *Panchayat Samiti* is dominated by the *Meenas* with the result that non-*Meenas* like him are in a minority and have little say in it functioning. Amar Singh, in spite of his associations with the development institutions for a number of years, and his outstanding work for his village, has not been made a member of any standing committee of the *Panchayat Samiti*. Moreover, his village has not received any grant for a construction work for other development activity ever since the formation of the new *Panchayat Samiti*. All this cannot but make him unhappy.

Suraj Mal—Small Town Politician

An educated *Mahajan* about 35 years old, Suraj Mal is an important executive of a *Panchayat Samiti*. He comes from an old family of cultivators-*cum*-moneylenders in a village near the *Panchayat Samiti* headquarters town, and even though he is himself settled in a small business in the town, his links with the village remain active and close. His brothers are engaged in cultivation of the family holding, he himself has taken interest in its improvement. Recently, he helped his brothers obtain a large *taccavi* loan for installation of a pump on the irrigation well. He has also been actively associated with the village *Panchayat*. He was elected its *Sarpanch* in 1960, and gave up the position only on election to his present office in the *Panchayat Samiti*. But, his primary interest is in the town where he lives. He hopes that with the support of the town's people he can realize his ambition to achieve a position in State level politics.

He entered politics as a young man, fresh from college, 15 years ago. At that time, he came under the influence of a leading political figure of the State that aroused his interest in politics and gave him his first political lesson. He has been active in local politics ever since and has filled several important positions in local bodies. He came to politics not as a spokesman of any particular caste, community, or interest group; but only as an individual, with attractive personal qualities. He is a fairly effective street-corner speaker, a good debater and agitator, and a bit of demagogue. He has administrative experience (of local bodies) and has good political contacts at the local and State levels. But he has his limitation also. His profession, even though it gives him time and inclination for political work, does not bring him much money; nor does it bring him into active contact with the people. He does not have the support of any powerful caste group or region. Finally, he is a faction leader, and lacks the qualities, which would win him support from all sides. His ambition is to enter State level politics by winning a seat in the State Legislature, and it is towards this end that he is working all the time.

His position in the *Panchayat Samiti* gives him political influence and power, keeping busy with the game of small town and local area politics, and at the same time keeps himself in the limelight, for consideration for a position in State level politics. He takes active, continuous and detailed interest in the work of the *Samiti*. He spends a lot of time in the *Samiti* office; he tours extensively, takes an interest in the problem of the rural people and makes a sincere attempt to meet them in so far as this is possible within the limited resources and power of the *Samiti*. He has acquired a thorough knowledge of the legislation relating to the *Panchayat* and the *Panchayat Samiti* and various administrative procedures prescribed under it. He knows precisely what the member of the *Panchayat Samiti*, the Block Development Officer and the other staff of the *Samiti* can or cannot do. He is probably better informed about these things than the Block Development Officer himself. But his relations with the B.D.O. and other members of the *Samiti* staff are not good. One reason for this is that his position in the *Samiti* is not secure. His group does not have a comfortable majority in the *Samiti*; the opposition is strong and active and has already made two attempts to unseat him. Therefore, he finds it necessary to keep members of his group and his supporters pleased and his opponents in check. He often interferes in appointments and transfers of *Samiti* staff and violates prescribed procedures and rules in sanctioning loans, grants etc. This brings him in conflict with the Block Development Officer and other members of the *Samiti* staff. A second reason is personal. He is capable of original and at times unorthodox ideas, and he is so carried away by them that he does not mind violating rules and procedures, and even risking administrative unfeasibility in their implementation. This quality, which could be an asset in a business executive—he would probably make a good one, is not without its handicaps in an executive of a *Panchayat Samiti*.

Lal Chand—Small Town Politician

A small town lawyer, Lal Chand, is one of the oldest, most active and prominent political worker in the district. He filled important positions in local political institutions and in the district organization of the Congress Party and was for some years a member of the State Legislature. He is a clever, well-educated, extremely energetic and ambitious person with considerable political acumen and capacity for organization, who would have been successful in business or a profession anywhere.

His interest in local politics is purely professional; he does not represent any caste, economic interest group or village. It arose because his profession allowed him time and opportunity—for political activity. He was excited by political support, saw that the rewards of success were good, and felt that with his ability, ambition and drive, he could make it. But he has not been successful so far. After some years of local political work he was elected a member of his State Legislature in the early 1950s. But he could not advance to a position in the State cabinet—for which he had intense ambition—or even to retain his legislature seat. He now confines his activities to the local level and is at present a member of *Zila Parishad.* But he sees his present position in the institution primarily as a platform for continuing his political activity. It helps him to remain on the local political scene and keep trying for a position in State level politics. But he is little interested in rural development and welfare of the rural people, which are the primary object of the work of the *Zila Parishad.* His position in the institution is not too important; he lost the contest for an important position. But he is an influential member of the body because he is an eloquent speaker—often regarded as extremely effective behind the scene political worker. In one word, he is one of the many small town politicians who have gate-crashed into *Panchayati Raj* institutions and are using these merely as stepping stones to higher political office.

Sagar Mal—Small Town Businessman

Sagar Mal is an energetic, middle-aged businessman, who is *Sarpanch* of a large semi-urbanized village, located near the Block headquarters town. He comes from one of the old and respected business families of his village. Educated up to the middle standard, he is established in a small construction contracts business with work in and around the town.

Sagar Mal has taken an active interest in the affairs of the *Panchayat* and in development activities in the village for almost a decade. He was a member of the *Panchayat* for several years, was elected as *Sarpanch* in 1958, and was re-elected in 1960. This period has been one of rapid development and change for his village. With expansion of commerce and industry in the neighbouring town, the people of the village have been getting jobs in the town and nearby factory in increasing numbers, and outsiders with jobs in the town or the factory have been coming to live in the village. As a result, incomes have gone up, local business (retail distribution, etc.) has expanded; a large number of *pucca* houses have been built, and the village has been deeply affected by urban influences. It is fast becoming a suburb of the town and will before long form part of it. This period had also seen establishment of a number of institutions—a middle school, a primary school for girls, an *ayurvedic* dispensary and an animal husbandry centre—in the village. The village *bazaar* has been paved, and several new drinking water wells have been constructed with grants from the Community Development Block. Agriculture has been improved, and is being gradually reorganized to supply for urban demand for milk, vegetables and fruits.

Sagar Mal has taken an active interest in development of the village. He has obtained grants for works from the Community Development Block and raised contributions within the village. His construction business brings him in close contact with Block and district officers. He is also a good mixer and makes an effort to establish good relations with officers, so essential for success in his business. Many of his critics in the village say that he has used his position as *Sarpanch* of the *Panchayat* to build up these contacts and he has utilized them for furthering his business interests. But even they cannot deny that he has helped the village to get grants for works and to establish the new service institutions.

The *Panchayat* of his village is quite wealthy. It has good sources of income—in cattle fair and in sale of *abadi* lands. Sagar Mal has set up construction business in the town. But it is alleged by some of the Block staff and by his critics in the village that the *Panchayat* accounts are never in order and that Sagar Mal takes an inordinately long time in rendering accounts for grants given to his *Panchayat*. However, there are no allegations against him either of appropriation of funds or of wasting money. Part of the account difficulty arose precisely from his over-enthusiastic interest in development work and anxiety for rapid development. He started several works in quick succession, diverting money granted for one work to another and *vice versa* as need arose, with the result that the accounts got mixed up. It appears also that he did not always keep grants for these works strictly separate from investment in his town construction business.

He has a very active opposition in his village, especially among people of his own and other high castes, and he derives his support chiefly from the cultivators and scheduled castes. In the 1960 election, he was elected with the support of these castes; the high caste vote was largely against him. This opposition is due partly to old family rivalries: people of other old, wealthy and respected high caste families are jealous of his position. Many others are annoyed with him because of his conduct as *Sarpanch*. They allege that many of his decision in cases brought before the *Panchayat*, and other actions as *Sarpanch*, have been partisan or have been actuated more by expediency than by principle.

His influence in the affairs of the Community Development Block has also declined markedly after the constitution of the *Panchayat Samiti* in 1959, and especially after formation of the present *Samiti* in 1961. Before the constitution of the *Panchayat Samiti*, he was among the most influential members of the Committee, which advised the Block Development Officers. He maintained good relations with officials and as his village is close to block headquarters, besides being rich and progressive, it received much more than its share of attention of the Block staff and funds for development. After formation of the *Panchayat Samiti*, however, his influence decreased because the *Samiti* began to be dominated by the *Meenas*. But he was still one of the fifteen *Sarpanchs* comprising the *Samiti*. The present *Panchayat Samiti*, however, has forty five *Sarpanchs*; the dominance of the *Meenas* has increased further, and non-Meenas like him have very little influences in it. Moreover, the *Meena sarpanchas* coming from small village feel,—not without justification—that Sagar Mal's village received more than its share of funds in the past and need not receive any large grant now. As a result, he is dissatisfied with the working of the *Panchayat Samiti*. He realizes that the *Samiti* will continue to be dominated by the *Meenas* and that persons like him cannot have influence in it. He is, therefore, concentrating his energies in building up the *Panchayat*. Fortunately for him, his *Panchayat* is quite wealthy and its case-work and the other activities are enough to absorb his energies.

What does a person like Sagar Mal seeks in membership of the *Panchayat* or the *Panchayat Samiti*? The answer lies in one word: recognition. He belongs to an old and respected family of the village. His position in the *Panchayat* enables him to have an important say in affairs and to reassert and reinforce the family's position in the village. His membership in the *Panchayat Samiti* makes him as a person of some consequence in the local area. But like many others in this profile, Sagar Mal is quite satisfied with confining his political activity to the local level and has no keen ambition for higher political office. He is conscious of his limitations in pursuing a political career—small finances, business community background, limited education, etc—and will probably not seek a political office like a seat in the State Legislature for a long time.

Raj Mal—An Old Village Leader

An old man of about 60 years, Raj Mal, is *Sarpanch* of a large village. He comes from a high caste family of cultivators, which has been living in the village for centuries and is one of the oldest and most respected families in the entire area of the *Panchayat Samiti*. At one time, it was the largest joint family of cultivators in the area and the rulers of the Jaipur state had conferred a special honour on it. The family is now divided; but the members maintain good relations among themselves, and their support is an important source of strength for Raj Mal in his position in the *Panchayat*.

He has fairly large agricultural holding: the land is highly productive, and the standard of cultivation is very high. Besides cultivation, Raj Mal lends money and has an interest in a flour mill in the town. He is well off: indeed, he is one of the rich man of the village.

His village is about the most faction-ridden in the entire area of the *Panchayat Samiti*. It is a large village (population of about 5,000), with a concentration of *Mahajans* and *Brahmins*. Most of the people are educated. Many of them have left the village for government service or the business. Others remain behind and are engaged in some petty trade and money-lending, supplementing their earnings with income from non-cultivating ownership of small areas of ancestral lands. Most of those who have left live in the neighbouring towns and villages and continue to take interest in the affairs of "their own village". The businessmen continue to make contributions for projects of benefits to their caste or the village; they have recently made handsome contributions for construction of two major buildings—a higher secondary school and a primary health centre with a six-bed hospital. Both these institutions were located in this village because it satisfied the condition of local contribution laid down by the State Government. But such outside interest and interference contributes to factional rivalries and quarrel within the village; though the main reason for these is that life in the village does not fully absorb the energies of these intelligent and educated people. The villagers frequently say that there are no large, well organized factions in their village, that there are no long standing disputes or deep seated reasons for quarrels, and that people quarrel simply because they must, or because every educated person feels that his opinion must be heard and accepted. "Every one is a 'leader' (*neta*) in this village", they explain.

Raj Mal has been the *Sarpanch* of the village *Panchayat* for almost a decade. At the time of the latest (1960) *Panchayat* election, he was not too keen to enter the contest; but he was persuaded to do so at the last moment. He won by a comfortable margin. He is a soft-spoken, unassuming, rather shy, frail, old man. But he is neutral between the rival factions and has reputation for being sagacious and completely honest. His values and outlook are completely tradition-oriented, but he represents the best in tradition and faith in God and acting according to the *dharma* (righteousness). The villagers feel that they can trust him to take an impartial and intelligent view on any issue and to execute the decision with honesty. The traditional respect that his family has enjoyed reinforces the villagers' confidence in him. They know his limitations. They realize that he is not a dynamic personality, that he cannot speak eloquently and put the case of their village strongly in the *Panchayat Samiti*, and that he does not possess the energy to organize campaigns for particular causes within the village and to rush up to Sawai Madhopur or Jaipur to obtain support to them from officers, M.L.A.s, or Ministers. They understand very well that with a more vigorous *Sarpanch*, who could do all this and more, development of their village could have been faster and some of their present difficulties could have been removed. For example, they are very badly in need of an approach road: the village is eight miles from the metalled road and is completely isolated during the rains. More energetic *Sarpanch* could have got them a road. There are vigorous and forceful men in the village; but the villagers prefer Raj Mal because he is honest and wise. There is also the feeling that the record of development activity in his time, even though it has not been spectacular, has not been bad. Raj Mal has brought them together in spite of their quarrels and factions, and enabled them to mobilize contributions for major works like buildings for the higher secondary school and the primary health centre.

As *Sarpanch* of the *Panchayat*, Raj Mal devotes his time mainly to resolving small disputes or attending to various administrative and municipal matters like granting permission for building a house or a shop; clearing encroachments; arranging street lighting, or cleaning the village *bazaar*. As this is a large village with a big *bazaar*, this work takes a lot of time. His *Panchayat* has not suffered financial problem because the village is a commercial centre of some importance. In the *Panchayat Samiti*, his primary concern is to represent the interest of his village. He does not belong to the majority group in the *Samiti* and is, therefore, not an important member. But he is always heard with respect, because he represents the biggest village in the *Samiti* area and because his personality inspires respect.

Even though he is a good cultivator himself, Raj Mal is not interested in such modern innovations as use of chemical fertilizers and pesticides. He believes in traditional methods of good farming. He cannot, therefore, be expected to act as an innovator or an unofficial extension worker. His main interest is in the works and programmes of the *Panchayat Samiti* and in obtaining *taccavi* loans for cultivators of the village. Like many other experienced members of the *Samiti*, he feels that funds for loans and grants are limited and committee discussions and procedural 'wrangles' are too many. He realizes that the *Samiti* is dominated by the *Meenas*, who have their own way in everything and that he or others like him—high caste *Sarpanchs* representing large villages—cannot influence its working much. But his attitude is one of quiet acceptance of this situation; there is no bitterness or rancor in it.

Harphool—A Representative of the Old World

Harphool is the sixty years old *Sarpanch* of a newly created *Panchayat* having jurisdiction over six small villages (population about 1500). His own village, which is the headquarters of the *Panchayat*, is a small single-caste village with only 65 households. He is the representative of the majority faction in the village and had won the *Panchayat* election because of influence of the faction in this and other villages of the *Panchayat* circle. His opponent, younger and wealthier, was the leader of the minority faction in the same village.

This is not Harphool's first experience with popular institutions. For nine years he was member of the large *Panchayat* of which his village then formed part. He is also a prominent member of the successful cooperative society of his village. This is the first election contest however; earlier, he has always been returned unopposed. The contest has moreover badly split this small single caste village, which is known for its internal unity and enthusiasm for development works, and there is at present considerable bitterness among the rival factions. One cause of the bitterness is refusal of Harphool's faction to refuse drawing of water from the well located in their part of the village within the *abadi* and having abundant water throughout the year. The women of the families of opponents of Harphool's faction now draw water from another well, located at a distance of about one furlong (quarter of a mile). This causes them considerable hardship and these families are very angry with their opponents.

In the *Panchayat Samiti*, Harphool represents the old world, the traditional rural India; he is old, barely literate, steeped in tradition, and purely a cultivator whose interests are, confining to his fields, his village, and his relations and acquaintances in the surrounding villages. He is one of the few members of the *Samiti* who cultivates his land. He has a holding of about forty acres, of which ten acres are irrigated. The income from this land is just sufficient to give a comfortable living at the village standard. He is by no means rich, but he is comfortable and his satisfaction with life is enviable. Although a shrewd peasant, he is a back-bencher in the *Panchayat Samiti;* but as he forms part of the dominant *Meena* group, he is a member of an important standing committee of the *Samiti.*

He has no knowledge of the *Panchayat Samiti* Act or of the prescribed rules and procedures, and he has to be guided in all these matters by officials or other members of the *Samiti*. But he has plenty of common sense and knows what the interest of his village or his caste is. His primary interest in the *Panchayat Samiti* is to represent his village and his caste and he sees that he can get for them grants and other benefits, which are obtainable through the *Samiti*. In this he has been successful. He has been able to get a grant for repairs to the village tank, the most keenly felt need of his village. But he feels that the formation of the *Panchayat Samiti* has not conferred any material benefits on the village people. He explained, "It is true, we make our own decisions now, in committee. But the money does not reach us in time because the new procedures are elaborate. Moreover there is much less money now. Earlier, there was more money and the B.D.O. and extension officers of the Community Development Block reached us and did their work quickly." This feeling is easily understandable, because his village did rather well during Block times, being the recipient of a number of development works, including a school building, a drinking water well, and paved village streets.

Harphool is not enthusiastic about the new *Panchayat* either. It has very little money, barely enough to pay the allowance of a school teacher who looks after its work part-time, has undertaken no development activity and has very limited power. About the only thing it has done so far, is to give permission for construction of a few *kutcha* houses. "I did not want to start my career as *Sarpanch* with levying taxes on my own people", Harphool explained. He understands that with these limitations, the institutions cannot do more; but he is not too happy with its limited role.

Ram Devi—The Woman Member—An Extra Vote

Ram Devi, the wife of a young *Sarpanch*, is co-opted member of a *Panchayat Samiti* and had occupied this position for about two years. A young woman of about 30, she is educated up to about matriculation standard. She has four children, two of whom are quite young. She is entirely a housewife and her interests are all in the home: she does not do social or community welfare work among the women of her village. In the *Panchayat Samiti*, she is a member of an important standing committee; but her entire participation in the work of the *Samiti* as confined to attending the meetings of the *Samiti* and the standing committee. In spite of her education, her attitude and way of life remains tradition-oriented. She is not a woman of modern ideas, serving as an innovator or leader among the women of her village. Rather, she is an ordinary high caste village housewife confirming to the attitude and way of living of high caste rural women. In the home she represents traditions and orthodoxy and prevents her young husbands from going too far from traditional practices. She is by no means an incompetent person. Quite the contrary, she is a competent housewife and mother. But she is just not up to the role of innovator, informal educator, and community leader that one might expect from educated women in her position. Her function in his *Panchayat Samiti* is merely that of an extra vote for her husband's group: she has no independent opinion on any issue. She is there because two women members have to be co-opted, and as there are very few literate women in their own caste the *Meenas* who dominated the *Panchayat Samiti*, did not mind putting a high caste woman in the position.

NOTES

1. Fifth class of school.
2. Certain castes and tribes were classified as criminal tribes during British times because of their tendency to commit crime. The classification was abolished soon after Independence.
3. A degree in Hindi
4. A movement for national reconstruction and development, based on Gandhian concepts, led by Vinoba Bhave.
5. An association for voluntary service among rural and urban people.

SECTION IV

The Village Studies : Socio-Economic Change in Village India

16

Self-Sustaining Development

A Study of Four Decades of Rural Development in Three Villages of Eastern Rajasthan

Introduction

In 1961, a study was undertaken in three villages of Sawai Madhopur district of Rajasthan where author was posted as the District Collector. The repeat study of the villages was done in 2001, four decades later in order to see the technological economic and social changes that had occurred in the villages during the intervening 40 years.

Sawai Madhopur district, located about 130 km. from the State capital Jaipur, was one of the backward districts of Rajasthan. It borders Madhya Pradesh on the east, Bharatpur district to its north, Jaipur and Tonk to the west and Kotah to the south. Almost two-third of the district as constituted in 1961, formed part of the former princely state of Jaipur until 1948. The remaining one-third formed part of the former princely state of Karauli.

Sawai Madhopur district had an area of 5,000 sq. km. and a population of 98,000 in 2001. These figures relate, however, to the bifurcated southern part of the district. The bifurcation was done in the 1980s for administrative convenience. Sawai Madhopur town and its suburb Maantown, in which the district offices are located, are in the southern half. The northern half was constituted into a separate district Karauli as a result of the bifurcation.

Seventeen per cent of the population in 1991 was urban and the remaining 83 per cent was rural. More than 40 per cent of the population consists of the scheduled castes and scheduled tribes. In the villages studied, however, they form majority of the population. The *Meenas,* who comprise most of the cultivators are classified as scheduled tribe while agricultural labourers or small cultivators-*cum*-labourers belong to the scheduled caste. The high castes—*Brhamins, Rajputs* and *Mahajans* and the non-scheduled tribes—cultivators, *Gujjars* and *Jats*—form about one-third of the population. The district has five Community Development Blocks which are coterminous with the *Panchayat Samitis*. There are 197 *Panchayats* for almost 900 villages. There are no factory industries[1]. However, there are small industrial units, concerned with processing of crops, wheat and oilseeds. In some villages rolling of *beedis* and making glass bangles are traditional cottage industries.

Until its abolition within three to four years of formation of Rajasthan in 1948, *Jagirdari* was the dominant system of land tenure. After its abolition, full and heritable rights in croplands were conferred on the actual cultivators of lands. Jaipur was a progressive state and had evolved a well-developed revenue administration during the 1940s. It also had a stable government for most of the 1950s and the 1960s and there has been political stability in the state during the last four decades also. The government launched an effective programme of rural development in the 1950s and the 1960s; it was the first State Government in the country to establish *Panchayati Raj* institutions.

The initial study revealed the effects of Community Development and other rural development programmes on people of the villages after a decade of their initiation; the repeat study shows effects of the programmes and technological, economic and social changes in the country during the intervening forty years.

The initial study revealed that except the high castes—*Rajput* former *jagirdars*, with relatively large landholdings, some *Mahajans* (trader-*cum*-money lenders) and *Brahmins* whose sons had become white collar workers, all others were poor. Wives of *Meena* cultivators would thank their stars if they could get enough cereals to eat throughout the year and avoid 'hunger' in the lean season, July-September, *i.e.* before the monsoon season crop of sorghum or millet was harvested in October. The scheduled castes—*Chamaar*, small cultivator-*cum*-agricultural or non-agricultural labourers and other scheduled castes were in a similar position.

Because of the poor level of nutrition of the women and the hard work that they did in the fields, maternal, infant and child mortality were high. Consequently they could not bear to hear about family planning. Education of girls or even of boys was considered useless. In the eighth-grade school located in village Manpur with a population of over 2,500 there were 180 boys but only five girls in 1961.

There had been dramatic changes in all these respects during the intervening forty years. By 2001, most of these people had enough cereals to eat; milk, vegetables and fruit in season formed an integral part of their diet. Production of wheat, the principal food-*cum*-cash crop had more than doubled. Production of mustard—the principal cash crop—had increased also. Increase in agricultural output in turn had been due to more intensive cultivation of croplands by tractors and irrigation by diesel oil-operated pump sets. Irrigation has made it possible to grow high yielding varieties of wheat with chemical fertilizers and pesticides, as needed, and a large proportion of it is cultivated as a cash crop.

Even the *Chamaars* and other scheduled castes small farmers-*cum*-labourers had enough cereals to eat and enough income from work in the neighbouring market town to buy milk, vegetables and fruit in season.

All the villagers had easy access to medical and preventive health care facilities from physicians in two large multi-facility hospitals, besides sub-dispensaries and *vaidyas* in two of the three villages. Maternal, child and infant mortality had been reduced greatly. Most of the boys and a large number of girls were being sent to schools. The farmers and the scheduled castes realize that educated boys could get white collar jobs, and would know enough not to be cheated by merchants in the market and get minimum wages from unskilled work, fixed by the Government of Rajasthan.

They realized also that educated girls were better mothers and wives. They kept themselves, their houses and their children clean and were more willing to consult the physicians and *vaidyas* and take medicines for common diseases of the digestive and respiratory tracts. By 2001, most of the people of high castes and a large proportion of the farmers and the scheduled castes lived in brick and mortar homes. The high castes and many *Meena* farmers had piped water in their homes. They cared enough about having clean and adequate water to have spent several lakhs in construction of large overhead tanks outside the villages so that they could have piped water in their homes. Even those who depended upon wells, for drinking water, bathing or washing clothes took care to keep the wells clean.

A large number had black and white or colour T.V. receivers in their homes; almost all of them had radio receivers so that they were well aware of events in the district, the State and the country. For all these reasons, most of the villagers were not poor but had risen to lower middle or middle-income economic status.

Apparently, similar changes have occurred over a large area of Rajasthan as evidenced by major increases in output of wheat, mustard, groundnut and other cash crops. Use of chemical fertilizers and number of tractors has increased over 3 times between 1976 and 1992. Total, male and female literacy has increased steadily. The latter more than doubled between 1991 and 2001.

Thus the major change influences have been :

(i) Phenomenal increase in agricultural output due to adoption of improved agricultural practices which had led to a major increase in income of farmers and change from subsistence to cash economy;

(ii) Major increase in health and productivity of farmers;

(iii) Increase in the proportion of household income from non-agricultural occupations;

(iv) Major increase in education of males but particularly among females and awareness of rights and entitlements due to higher participation of people in local self-government.

The Study

The study described in this chapter was done first during 1961. The repeat study was done during 2001, *i.e.* after a gap of 40 years. The two studies describe technological, economic and social changes in three selected villages during the intervening four decades.

The three villages—Maanpur, Raipur and Bijaipur—studied are located in a rather backward district (Sawai Madhopur) of one of the most backward states (Rajasthan) in India. The first study was done in 1961 when the author was posted as Collector of the district. The villages were located along motorable roads between three to eight km. from his house and office in Maan Town where the district offices are located. Sawai Madhopur town is six km. east of it. The author had strong interest in studying economic activities, social status and inter-caste relations of people of these villages and the effects of the Community Development and other rural development programmes on them. Before appointment to his post as Collector, he had been Director for five years (1953-58) of the Programme Evaluation Organization of the Planning Commission, Government of India that had responsibility for concurrent and in-depth evaluation, through sample surveys, of the impact of Community Development and other rural development programmes on the economic and social conditions of rural people in different States of the country.

Kamla Nath (his wife) participated in the study[2] when she saw the abject poverty of women of two of these villages. The women worked on the family farms; they did more farm work than the men. Both men and women of the small village, Bijaipur, which Kamla Nath had selected for intensive study, bathed in the pond located outside the village. They were too poor to afford use of soap or hair oil. Since livestock also bathed in it, they were not much cleaner after the bath than they were before it. They were so poor that they thanked their stars, if they had enough cereals to eat and could avoid hunger in the lean season of June to September *i.e.* before the monsoon crops of sorghum and millets became available. There was no question of their consuming milk, vegetables or fruit themselves or giving milk to their growing children. Their only source of drinking water was a well located in the village. As a result of their low level of personal hygiene and deficiency of protective foods in their diet, maternal, infant and child mortality was quite high. Consequently, they were very averse to accepting family planning.

Most of them were illiterate because men of the cultivating and the scheduled castes felt that education of girls was useless. The men were afraid that educated women would not work in the fields. Besides, they argued to themselves that since women were *paraya dhan* (the property of the husband) their parents should not spend on their education. Furthermore, girls as old as 9 or 10 years of age took care of their younger siblings, while their mothers worked in the fields. In the 8-grade school located in Maanpur (one of the two large villages), which was two km. from Bijaipur there were 180 boys but only five girls.

But, men of the high castes—*Brahmin, Rajput* and *Mahajan*—wanted that their women should be educated up to primary level. A large number of young men of these castes were working as *patwaris*[3], village level workers, and secretaries of *Panchayats* or cooperative societies or school teachers in villages located not far from their homes. They could come home only during weekends or holidays but wanted that they should be in touch with their families. Some of them were clerks in offices of the Collector, the Superintendent of Police or other offices located in Maan Town. Furthermore, they wanted to marry their daughters to educated men of similar status as the parents and the ones who were working in various white collar jobs mentioned above.

The *Panchayat* of village Raipur in which people of the high caste were concentrated had, with contributions in money, materials or labour from the villagers and grants from the community development department constructed buildings for a primary (5-grade) school for girls and also for a 8-grade school for boys. It had obtained contributions also for improving the approach road to the village and other works described below. People of the high castes had contributed money, while the farmers and people of the scheduled castes had contributed labour or brought materials for these works.

As Collector, the author could observe the rural people and their various problems in a way in which only a Collector can. They came to him for settlement of disputes about rights in land. They approached him with requests for assistance from the State Government. Thus, they would request him to recommend to the State Government remission of land revenue if there was a crop failure. He saw them also as electors to *Panchayati Raj* institutions, which had been established in the State during 1959, barely 18 months earlier. These institutions were established at the level of the village, the Community Development Block and the district.

The village level institution, called the *Panchayat*, had responsibility for overseeing sustainable development of the natural resources (cultivable land, pastures and woodland, and cultivable or other wastelands if any) of the village; overseeing working of school teachers and other workers having responsibility for assisting the economic or social progress of the villages. In the *Panchayats* established under the Rajasthan Panchayat Act of 1953, a *Panchayat* was established for every village that had a population of 5,000-8,000. In case of small villages, five or more villages were grouped together to establish a *Panchayat* with a population of 5,000. Alternatively, a fairly large village, its hamlets and one or more small villages in its vicinity were grouped to include a population of 5,000. In the Sawai Madhopur *Panchayat Samiti,* which had a rural population of about 80,000 in 1951, there were 16 *Panchayats.* The Act was amended in 1960 under which the area of a *Panchayat* was reduced to 1500-2000 population. As a result total number of *Panchayats* increased in the State from 3,000 to nearly 7,400. In the Sawai Madhopur *Panchayat Samiti* the increase was from 16 to 45.

The district was bifurcated in the late 1980s by constituting most of the area in its northern part plus a small area of the adjoining Jaipur district into a separate district Karauli, which before the bifurcation was part of Sawai Madhopur district. Both districts together had a population of about 164,000 in 2001 and population of Sawai Madhopur was 98,000. The population of the five Community Development Blocks in the present Sawai Madhopur district averaged 160,000 in 1991; it averaged 100,000 in 1961.

In village Raipur, in which people of the high castes were concentrated, the *Panchayat* includes the village and its three hamlets. In the other large village Maanpur, since the population of the village and its one hamlet was much below 5,000 in 1961, five neighbouring villages including Bijaipur were included in the area of the *Panchayat*. By 2001, the population within the jurisdiction of both *Panchayats* ranged between 7,000 and 8,000; but no change was made in their jurisdiction.

When the initial study was done, the villagers had already absorbed the effects of abolition, in the early 1950s, of *Jagirdari*—the system of land tenure that had existed in this area for centuries. Full and heritable rights in land had been conferred on the actual cultivators of croplands. The *jagirdars*, whom the farmers used to pay land revenue and for serving whom, men and women of various scheduled castes had clearly specified obligations had now to content themselves with cultivation of the land left to them for self-cultivation. They cultivated the lands with the help of labourers that they employed or on basis of crop sharing with their former tenants. But there was no feeling of rancor among them. They had accepted the change as an integral part of the democratic process, which conferred equal rights on all.

The repeat study has revealed changes in economic and social status, skills, attitudes and aspirations of the people of these villages during the four decades between the two studies, which could not even be imagined in 1961.

In 1961, most of the farmers and people of the scheduled castes were poor, illiterate and barely aware of events outside their immediate vicinity. By 2001, most of them had risen to lower middle income or middle-income status; their higher income was reflected in higher levels of consumption. They were healthier; as a result of more adequate and balanced food, enough cereals and milk, vegetables and fruit in season and easy access to facilities for preventive health and medical care. They were better educated and well aware of events in the district, the State and the country. The farmers with land holdings as small as ten hectares use tractors for cultivation of their croplands and diesel oil operated pump-sets for irrigation. These machines, improved seed, chemical fertilizers and pesticides were available in the Maan Town market. There were facilities also for repair of the machines and sale of spare parts. But the farmers were skilled enough to correct small defects in the machines themselves. Otherwise the use of the machines would be uneconomic. Their levels of skill and aspirations had been transformed. A large proportion of them lived in brick and mortar houses, had piped water and black and white or colour T.V. receivers in their homes. They sent their sons and daughters to schools; men and women of the high castes and the better-off farmers hoped that while one or two sons would remain in the village and look after the land, the others would become white collar workers. They wanted their daughters to be educated so that they could marry such workers; some of them could work as school teachers before they married. Holders of these jobs had relatively high income, security of service and those appointed as *patwaris* or clerks in various offices had much "power"[4].

The Villages

Maanpur is a multi-caste village located eight km. west of Maan Town, along the Sawai Madhopur-Tonk road. Bijaipur is also located along the same road but about five km. from Maan Town. The high castes—*Rajput*, *Mahajan* (traders-*cum*-moneylenders) and *Brahmin* form about one-third of the population of Maanpur. The rest are *Meenas* and various scheduled castes. The total population of Maanpur and its two hamlets of the *Chamaars* and the *Meenas* was about 7,000 in 2001, two and a half times the population in 1961. In 1961, the Meenas used to live to the west of the village, about 1 km. from the Sawai Madhopur-Tonk road.

The increase in population is due mainly to natural increase, although there has been some influx of people from smaller villages both in the main village and the hamlets. The influx is due to facilities available in Maanpur for sale of produce, shopping and for education and primary health and medical care. The population of Bijaipur which is located about three km. from Maanpur and is included within the jurisdiction of Maanpur *Panchayat* is now more than 500; double the number in 1961. Except five households of *Brahmins*, all the others (107) are of *Meenas*. The five *Brahmin* households are offshoot from the one *Brahmin* household that existed in 1961; all the five sons of the original settler having set up separate households.

Mr. Suraj Bhan Singh, our respondent for Maanpur is the younger brother of late Mr. Hari Singh who was *Sarpanch* in 1961. He is 81 but is quite fit. He was *Sarpanch* for several years. At present a *Mahajan* friend of him holds the post. One son of Mr. Suraj Bhan Singh is teaching in the college located in Maan Town; a daughter is taking the bank officers' examination. Another daughter is married to an army officer. The families of Suraj Bhan Singh, late Hari Singh and another brother are living in separate houses, which are kept in very good repair. They have a jeep, a tractor and a diesel operated pump on their irrigation well. Their entire cropland is irrigated by the well run by a pump-set. They sell cereals in excess of their needs and produce milk, vegetables and some fruit in season primarily for the needs of the families. One son of late Hari Singh has been settled in Jaipur for 35 years. Another son, a physician, is practicing in the village. His wife who is an Auxiliary Nurse Midwife (ANM) hails from south India. She assists women of the village and neighbouring villages in maternity cases and advises them on pre-natal and post-natal care of their children and themselves. She advises them also on family planning.

The above details of the families of Suraj Bhan Singh and late Hari Singh have been given in order to illustrate the changes in attitudes and aspirations of *Rajputs* of this village and this district during the intervening 40 years. In 1961, they would educate their sons so that they could become clerks or other white collar workers or join the army. However, they would ensure that at least one son continued to stay in the village and looked after the family's cropland. Supervising cultivation of their cropland gave their families prestige and also provided a dependable source of income.

Although their women still wore the veil, in 2001, they did not expect their daughters to wear it. The aspiration for their daughters was that they should marry white collar workers or farm owners or those working in the army. Both sons and daughters must be married among children of *Rajputs* of the neighbouring villages or those living in the adjoining *taluka* or Jaipur district or in Jaipur city itself. In 1961 educating their children to become professionals such as physicians or lawyers was far beyond their imagination. They could not even think of one of their children marrying a person from south India, ignoring all considerations of caste and economic status of the parental families.

The description of the occupation of children of Shri Sham Lal Sharma of Raipur, a *Brahmin* and of Mr. Fateh Singh, a *Rajput* given later show similar changes in attitudes, aspirations and practices of the *Brahmins* and the *Rajputs* in the area and have been accepted by the older people.

A large number of houses in the village and a number of those in its two hamlets are made of brick and mortar, have electricity and black and white or colour T.V. receivers. There are 56 telephones in the village and a sub-post office. There is a small government dispensary staffed primarily by the ANM in Maanpur; a doctor visits it for a few hours in the week. The villagers can reach the multi-facility hospital, located in village Alanpur on the outskirts of Maan Town, in 30 minutes by bicycle or bus and sooner by their own motor bicycles or scooters. There are 16 doctors in the hospital besides nurses and paramedical personnel. This location was selected for the hospital because enough land for the hospital and residences of the staff was available there. The hospital is ten km. from Maanpur and five km. from Bijaipur. This hospital and the one located just outside Raipur provide medical care to all the people of the district. In 1961, the only medical facility for people of Sawai Madhopur *tehsil* was the small hospital, with two doctors, two nurses and a dispenser located in Sawai Madhopur town, fifteen km. away.

Education Facilities : The Situation in 2001

There is a degree college, a polytechnic and a higher secondary school in Maan Town. These are all located in Allanpur, a suburb of Maan Town, where there is enough land for them. The number of girl students is quite significant in all, except the polytechnic where it is smaller than that of the boys.

There is a secondary school (with ten classes) a middle school (with 8 classes) run by the Department of Education and a private middle school in Maanpur. There are 350 girls and 400 boys in three schools. The two hamlets of the *Chamaars* and the *Meenas* have their own schools. The school in the *Chamaar* hamlet, which was a primary school and was located in a temple in 1961 is a middle school now and has its own building. But it lacks a boundary wall and the people complain that the *Panchayat Samiti* does not give them the money needed to build the wall because they are a scheduled caste and are poor. The *Meena* hamlet has a primary school: they have built eight rooms so that it can be converted into a middle school and run by the Department of Education. The schools are a powerful medium of social change !

The teachers insist that the boys and girls come to them after a bath using soap and hair oil and in uniforms, which are washed at least once in two days and are well pressed. The habit of personal hygiene travels from the students to their parents. Salaries of teachers are quite high (Rs. 7,000 to 10,000) per month). The *Panchayat* supervises efficient running of the schools.

The 1961 attitude, that girl's education is not needed, has not completely gone among the cultivators or the scheduled castes. Nevertheless girls are being sent to school. The *Brahmins*, *Mahajans* and *Rajputs* are very keen to educate their daughters. The principal reason for this is that they want to marry them to government servants and professionals, who want well-educated wives. The progress made in the life style of women is such that girls are driving cars and scooters in the Maan Town market and nobody bats an eyelid. Many women of Raipur are working as teachers and nurses in the hospital located within the game sanctuary and in the neighbouring villages including Bijaipur.

The habitation area of Maanpur and its two hamlets is much larger than it was in 1961. The hamlet of the *Chamaars* has more than 100 houses; in 1961 it had less than 50. About 50 *Meena* households who used to live to the west of the village are living now in a hamlet located along the Maan Town—Tonk Road. Land for the hamlet was allotted to them in 1961. The location is convenient for supplementing their income from farming by unskilled labour in Maan Town market and on maintenance of the railway lines.

There is a primary school in the hamlet of the *Meenas* also. They have constructed an eight-room building for it so that it can be upgraded to a middle school by the Department of Education. Thus, in contrast to one eight-grade school in Maanpur and one primary school in the hamlet of the *Chamaars* in 1961, there are four schools in Maanpur and its hamlets. The large enrolment in all the schools and the large expenditure by the people on construction and maintenance of the buildings show the value that people of all castes attach to education of their children.

Drinking Water Supply

The villagers of Maanpur have, through contributions from all those who would have piped water in their homes (mainly *Rajputs* and *Mahajans*), contributed Rs. 4 lakh for construction of an overhead tank located outside the village.

The State has constructed three tube wells and provided the operators to run the pumps, which lift the water to the tank. Spending such large amounts to construct overhead tanks, and having piped water in their houses demonstrates the importance that these people now attach to having adequate and safe water for drinking, washing and other uses. The *Chamaars* and the *Meenas* of the two hamlets of Maanpur, however, use water of wells located in their hamlets. They too make every effort to ensure that the surrounding of their wells is kept clean. In 1961, all households in Maanpur and Bijaipur had to draw water manually from the wells. In Raipur, however, a few wells in the *Brahmin* locality had hand pumps installed on them.

Since Maanpur is located along the Maan Town-Tonk Road there are eight teashops and four restaurants on its outskirts. The tax paid by the shops makes a sizeable contribution to the income of the *Panchayat*.

A large number of the houses in Maanpur (and Raipur) have hand pumps. There is a well-kept storm water drain in the centre as well as side drains for draining out the waste-water from the houses along the paved main street of Maanpur so that the village is quite clean.

A number of employees of the railway (gang men), post office, and several clerks and others working in the district offices live in the village. Some of them belong to the village while others are outsiders who find the village a cheap place to live because rents are much lower in it than in Maan Town. Thus, the village has become a dormitory for workers in Maan Town.

In Bijaipur our Informer Hira Lal Meena—is a *Panchayat* Development officer in the office of the *Panchayat Samiti*. He was a primary school student in 1961. He became a Village Level Worker (VLW) by 1975, during our second visit to the village. He is a cultivator with a medium-sized land holding. He commutes to work on his motor bicycle. One of his nephews is a Block Development Officer (BDO), two are Lower Division Clerks (LDCs) and one is an Assistant Station Master.

There are 108 households in the village as against 55 in 1961. Except one household of a *Brahmin* all the others were of Meenas in 1961, but by 2001, the number of *Brahmin* households has increased to five due to bifurcation of the one main household of 1961. Rest of the increase has been due to natural increase of the population resident in 1961; there has been some in-migration from very small villages located near it.

The residents of Bijaipur have also constructed the tank and the tube well and hire an operator to run them without any assistance from the State Government. The main street of the village has been paved and has side drains, which take the waste water to a pond located at the end of the inhabited area of the village. As a result, the village is quite clean.

The *Meenas* of Bijaipur whose food consisted only of cereals and oil in 1961 now have milk and cooked vegetables as a regular part of their diet. They buy milk and vegetables from vendors who bring them from the Maan Town market, if they do not have their own. In 1961, the pond located outside the village was the principal place for bathing of men, women and livestock. It has dried up now. There are two-three community hand pumps in the village. The women walk to them to fetch water for drinking, bathing and washing clothes. There are a number of *pucca* houses (made of brick and mortar). Agriculture production has more than doubled. About thirty households (one-third of the total) have motor bicycles; every household has a bicycle. There are 26 tractors and a similar number of pumps for irrigation. Most of the houses have hand pumps within them.

The villagers have erected a temple of *Hanumanji* along the road to Tonk; it has cost Rs. 7 lakh. Its maintenance is self-financing because of large offerings by devotees from Maanpur, Bijaipur and a number of other villagers in the vicinity. The villagers had a well-attended *puja* to inaugurate the temple in May 2000. It included a *katha* (religious discourse) for a month. They had formed a construction committee to oversee construction of the temple.

One boy of the village is a BDO, 6-7 are LDCs. Many families send their children to attend secondary school in Alanpur (Maan Town) so that they can become white collar workers. People prefer to send their young children both boys and girls to the private school in the village in which the teaching is better than in the government run schools.

There is an 8-grade (middle) school in the village: many girls besides boys attend the school. Some boys go to higher secondary school in Allanpur so that they can become white collar workers.

A number of employees of the railway (gang men); post office, and several clerks and others working in the district offices live in the village, because rents are lower in it than in Maan Town. Thus, the village has become a dormitory for workers in Maan Town.

The creamy upper layer of progressive and educated Meenas of Bijaipur (like *Brahmins* and *Mahajans* of Raipur and *Rajputs* and *Mahajans* of Maanpur) has entered white collar service and professions. They have become affluent and have also acquired power because of their professional skills and even more because of their nearness to officials.

Raipur is a multi-caste village, located about eight km. from Maan Town and about one and half km. from the road to the Ranthambhore game sanctuary. A hamlet of the *Gujjars* located outside the village abuts on the road to the sanctuary. The village, which had a population of about 2,800 in 1961, has a population of about 8,000 in 2001. Almost all the increase has been due to natural increase of the population resident in Raipur; there has, however been some in-migration of *Chamaars* from neighbouring small villages. The high castes—*Brahmins*, *Mahajans* and *Kayasthas*—form about one-third of the population; about ten are Moslems; the remainder are cultivators—*Meenas*, *Malies* and *Gujjars* or the scheduled castes—mainly *Chamaars* and *Rehgars* (leather workers and makers of leather goods), *Dhobis* (washermen) and others. The people of the high castes, the Moslems and the affluent *Meenas* and *Malis* live in the village itself; the rest of the *Meenas* and *Gujjars and the Chamaars* live in separately demarcated hamlets.

In 1961, a large number of *Brahmin* and *Mahajan* young men, after getting educated in the 8-grade middle school located just outside the village, were working as *patwaris*, school teachers, VLW's (Village Level Workers), secretaries of *Panchayats* or cooperative societies or clerks in the offices of the Collector or the Superintendent of Police or others located in Maan Town. Most of them were posted in villages in the Sawai

Madhopur *tehsil* from where they could visit their homes during Sundays or other holidays. They would keep in touch with their families through letters. They were, therefore, keen that their wives should be educated up to the primary level.

The village had an eight-grade school for boys and a five-grade primary school for girls. The school, located at the entrance of the village, had been constructed through contributions (in money) primarily by the *Brahmins* and *Mahajans* but also by a few *Meenas* and others. By 2001 the middle school for boys of 1961 is a higher secondary school and the primary school for girls is an eight-grade (middle) school. In addition, two private teachers had opened eight-grade middle schools. All the schools had large enrolment and their buildings were adequate to accommodate the large number of students. A large number of boys and a number of girls were attending the higher secondary school in Allanpur. Some boys were attending the college also. The number of girls in the higher secondary school is quite significant although much smaller than that of boys. Most of the girls belong to the high castes for a reason, which has been explained earlier. A number of boys are studying in professional colleges in Jaipur and Kotah to become professionals such as lawyers, physicians, or engineers. Many of them were working as professionals or in offices in these or other cities. A large number of *Brahmin* and *Mahajan* men are working in white collar jobs in various offices in Maan Town and in various services in the district. Their parents were proud of this fact.

After beginning of the Community Development Programme in 1953, large grants had been received from the Block Development office for repair of the approach road to the village and for improvement of drinking water wells of the *Chamaars* and the *Gujjars* and for construction of buildings for the offices of the *Panchayat*, the cooperative society, the residence of the VLW and a store for improved seed, chemical fertilizers, pesticides and improved implements. The high castes had made contributions in cash, while the farmers and the scheduled castes contributed labour or locally available materials.

The main street of the village along which most of the *Brahmins, Mahajans* and the Moslems lived was paved with side-drains to drain the wastewater. However, the drains were not cleaned efficiently they overflowed often. As a result, the main street was and remains quite dirty. Water from drains enters into another shallow pond at the back of the *Brahmin* street. The pond is surrounded by several houses of the low castes including the house of a *Dhobi* (washer woman), who was the *Sarpanch* of the village.

There are a number of *vaidyas*[5] in the village. Besides a large multi-facility hospital with forty beds, run by Tiger Watch, a foreign non-governmental organization, located about one km. from the village. A husband-wife team of doctors looks after the hospital from day-to-day. This hospital specializes in operations for cataract and other eye diseases. A number of specialists from Jaipur and even from Delhi come to it for performing operations for cataract and other diseases. Thus, the villagers are very well served with facilities for preventive health and medical care.

In 2001, there were more than 50 telephones, many with STD facility and a sub-post office within the village. A large number of houses had electricity and black and white or colour T.V. receivers. The main street had 130 shops which sold a large variety of goods: (i) foodgrains and other provisions, cloth, clothes, shoes and other leather goods, general merchandise and medical drugs; (ii) black and white and colour T.V. receivers, spare parts for tractors and pump-sets, and cooking gas. The villagers needed to go to the Maan Town market only for buying tractors, pump sets and spare parts for them, which are not available in the village, or for getting greater variety or higher quality of goods than those available in the shops in the village. The Moslem quarter has a number of repair shops for bicycles, motorcycles and various machines. Besides a number of Moslem artisans work as repairmen for repair of motor vehicles, tractors, diesel operated pumps, TV receivers and other electrical appliances. They find opportunities also in the tourist hotels because they are the only ones who can cook meat. Some Mahajans or Brahmins of the village who had specialized in preparing festive meals at marriages of the high castes have opened shops of sweet meat in the Maan Town market and are doing very well. However, a few Brahmin widows who carry milk from the village to the market remain quite poor.

Fateh Singh, the game warden in 1961 has now retired. He runs an NGO called Tiger Watch, and has become an international personality. He accompanied President Clinton on his visit to the game sanctuary. The President arrived by a helicopter and five helipads were specially built for his visit. Fateh Singh lives in a sprawling farm-house. He is a millionaire. One of his sons is a doctor working in the hospital built by the Tiger Foundation. He has got himself allotted about 125 hectares of land, some of which he plans to sell to the Oberois for building a hotel. Watching animals and birds in the sanctuary remains a passion with him. According to him, there are 25 tigers in the sanctuary but they are rarely seen. However, there are a large numbers of *sambhar* (heavy two horned deer), *cheetals* (the spotted golden deers) and *Neelgais*; Fateh Sigh has no estimate of their number. There are also a few elephants and a few crocodiles in the numerous ponds in the jungle.

The one km. approach road to Raipur from the main road to Ranthambhore is not in good condition and is full of potholes, despite constant repairs with funds provided by the *Panchayat Samiti* and the *Panchayat*. The village is dirty because of lack of drainage of waste-water from the houses of the *Brahmins* and the *Mahajans*.

Farming Practices and Crop Production

Very few farmers cultivate their lands by bullocks. There are tractors everywhere. Because of deeper ploughing of cropped area, some increase in the cultivated area, irrigation of most of the cropland by wells fitted with diesel operated pumps and use of improved dwarf, high yielding seed varieties of seed, chemical fertilizers and pesticides for wheat, the production from land has gone up about three times. Production of sorghum, millets, gram (chickpeas) and oilseeds (mainly mustard) have increased also due to irrigation and use of tractors. Most of the cultivators grow the coarse grains and some wheat for food. Oilseeds (mainly mustard) and much of the wheat is sold for meeting the cash needs of the families. As a result of increase in the irrigated area and use of tractors on the cropland, production (of cereals, wheat and chickpeas, in the winter and sorghum and millets in the summer), has increased. Total agricultural production is estimated to have increased about three times. The cultivated area has not increased much but yields per hectare have increased greatly because of irrigation, more intensive cultivation of croplands and use of improved dwarf high yield varieties of wheat along with chemical fertilizers and pesticides as recommended by the agricultural extension officers. There is large production also of milk, fruit and vegetables. Sorghum and millets are produced for food; their stalks provide fodder for milch animals. A large number of buffaloes but fewer cows are kept to provide milk. There are only a few bollocks as compared to their number in 1961 because tractors now cultivate most of the land. Landless *Chamaars* and other scheduled castes buy milk, fruit and vegetables in the Maan Town market or Raipur itself by paying for them with wages for the labour. Farmers produce much more milk and vegetables than they used to. Fruit such as papaya, banana and guava are produced in large quantities. In 1961, hardly any fruit was produced. Farmers in villages, such as Allanpur, that are near Maan Town, have sale of milk, fruit and vegetables to shops in the market as their main source of income. Other fruits, which are imported from Jaipur, are bought only by the tourists, the district level officers living in Maan Town and professionals such as lawyers and physicians. All men of Maanpur and the two other villages drink numerous cups of tea in a day. In 1961, only the leaders of the villages drank tea when meeting officers visiting the villages.

The farmers of Raipur operate about 40 tractors. Most of the cultivators who have tractors also have diesel oil operated pumps on their irrigation wells, because supply of electricity by the State Electricity Board is so irregular. Farmers with small holdings who cannot afford to buy their own tractors can rent them from those who have them. The rate of renting (in 2001) was fixed at Rs. 300 per hour. Others lease out their own small plots for cultivation to farmers with large holdings or become sharecroppers on lands owned by *Rajputs*, *Brahmins* and *Mahajans*. This is true also of most of the Meena cultivators of Maanpur and *Meena* or *Jat* farmers of Raipur. The *Gujjars* cultivate land primarily to supplement their income from sale of milk and sale of sheep or goats that they graze in the forests.

Meenas, *Chamaars* and other scheduled castes also do unskilled labour available in the Maan Town market, on the upkeep of the railway tracks, repair of the road to Jaipur or of the railway station itself. These require much unskilled and skilled labour because there is heavy traffic on the railway tracks and on the road and brisk activity in the market. The Maan Town railway station is much larger than it was in 1961 and is quite clean. There are several trains going between Delhi and Mumbai; in 1961, there were only two trains. There is also a direct fast train between Jaipur and Mumbai via Sawai Madhopur besides the two older trains between Sawai Madhopur and Jaipur. The road to Jaipur via Tonk is a tarmac coated, two-lane State highway. Traffic on it of jeeps, buses, trucks and other motor vehicles (passenger cars and motor bicycles or scooters) is heavy. The trucks bring goods needed by the people of the area and carry to Jaipur the surplus cereals, oilseeds and fruit that they produce. There is such large production of guavas that they are sent to Jaipur and even to Mumbai. However, the road is not well maintained and is full of potholes.

Maan Town and its Market

Maan town had no market in 1961 except a few shop outside the railway station. The security considerations during the visit of Queen Elizabeth II in 1961 necessitated the shifting of these shops. The author then

Collector ordered their rehabilitation in another locality in Maan Town now called the Maan Town Market. Maan Town, in 1961 just a residential colony for the district officers was surrounded by large uninhabited land but is now full of houses and shops and is crowded. The officers' colony including the houses of the Collector and the Superintendent of Police are part of this habitation area. The market has 700-800 shops in contrast with 40 shops allotted in 1961. The dealers sell everything: foodgrains and other provisions; milk, fruit, vegetables and medicines, cloth and clothes, shoes and other leather goods, utensils, spare parts for motor vehicles, tractors and irrigation pumps, T.V. receivers and other electrically operated kitchen gadgets. It has facilities also for repair of tractors, irrigation pumps and other farm implements and also of T.V. sets and other electrical gadgets. Since trucks are parked in the middle of the market, traffic within it moves very slow.

There is a big petrol station in the Maan Town market. It sells petrol, diesel oil and kerosene. Many dealers sell cooking gas also. There is a very large gas bottling plant on the way to the game sanctuary. It supplies gas to the whole district and is the main distribution centre for the entire State of Rajasthan.

There is a cloverleaf fly-over on the railway line at the junction station of Maan Town. The bridge has made communication between the districts headquarters and Sawai Madhopur town and villages like Raipur easy. In 1961, one always had to wait at the level railway crossing sometimes up to half an hour to go to Raipur. Next to the fly-over and near the railway line to Mumbai, there is a large, very modern cinema house in which are shown the latest Bollywood movies. In 1961, the 'cinema' was no more than a shed, which showed movies off and on.

The 6 km. road between Sawai Madhopur and Maan Town, which had few houses and farms in 1961, is now lined with brick and mortar houses and, orchards of vegetables and fruit. There are many milch animals in the farms along the road because of extensive pastures to the rear of the road. The population of Sawai Madhopur town has increased slowly but of Maan Town has increased about ten times. Instead of about 5,000 in 1961 it was estimated at about 50,000 in 2001. The Maan Town metropolitan area stretches along the road to Bijaipur and Tonk. Bijaipur is, however, just outside the metropolitan area.

Due to availability of all necessities of life and adequate facilities for education of their children and of access to primary and curative health care, most of the district and sub-division officers are now living in the officers' colony which has a much larger number of houses than in 1961. The offices of the Collector and the Superintendent of Police are two among many in Maan Town.

Maan Town is, however, a very crowded and polluted ghetto. The vacant land in front of the Collector's office and the houses of the Collector and the Superintendent of Police has been walled and is used as a park for holding exhibitions. The officers' club constructed in 1961 is lying out of use and is now surrounded by small workshops and shops. There is a new circuit house in Allanpur with ten rooms, some of which are air-conditioned. The overcrowding in Maan Town has been caused by total violation of the development plan of the town by successive Collectors. They allowed the land in the area to be sold by the *Panchayat Samiti* or the *Nagar Palika* (municipal committee) for lakhs of rupees. As a result the beautiful view of vast stretches of vacant land in front and back of our house that we enjoyed so much when we slept on the terrace in the summer has completely disappeared.

The cement factory has been closed for many years. It closed because its operation was no longer profitable for the owners. No decision has been taken by the Government of Rajasthan to reopen it. It may never reopen. The unskilled and skilled workers who lived in the housing colony of the factory are still living there.

Due to the residence of the officers in Maan Town, supervision of the game sanctuary and delivery of education and health services to the residents of the town and for villagers of the whole *tehsil* has improved somewhat. The roads to Jaipur via Tonk and those in the market and to the game sanctuary, however, are full of potholes due to failure of the State Government and *Nagar Palika* of Maan Town to sanction enough funds to maintain them in good conditions. In 1961, the officers' colony got its electricity from a power generation unit of the cement factory, which kept its supply very regular. Now the Rajasthan State Electricity Board supplies the electricity and there are daily long power cuts.

There has been a major shift of population and business from Sawai Madhopur town to Maan Town. The Sawai Madhopur town market appeared like a sleepy street in the early evening hours of a working day in 2001; while the Maan Town market hums with activity till late at night. Besides a number of lawyers and merchants from Sawai Madhopur town have shifted their residence to Maan Town. Residence in Maan Town provides easy access to the district officers. The merchants find that there is far more business in Maan Town than in Sawai Madhopur.

Growth Poles in Rural India

Are Maanpur and Raipur Villages or Small Towns ?

In 1961, both Raipur and Maanpur were villages with population between 2500 and 3000. Most of the people, including those of the high castes depended primarily on income from land. The high castes got their land cultivated by sharecroppers or by labourers hired by them. Even those whose sons were working as white collar workers, income from land was an important, though secondary, source of income. For *Meenas*, *Malis* and *Jats*, cultivation of their land provided the only source of income. The *Chamaars* supplemented their income from their small plots of land which they had been allotted by the State Government, by agricultural and/or non-agricultural labour and on maintenance of the railway tracks and the Jaipur-Tonk road. Some of them worked as share-croppers on farms of the high castes. Most people of the other scheduled castes also supplemented income from practice of their traditional craft by agricultural labour.

In 1961, the world-view of most of the villagers was distinctly local. They sold any surplus grain that they had after meeting the food needs of the family to traders, who bought it within the villages. For all except the high castes, Jaipur, which was 130 km. from their villages, was too far to be of any interest to them and Delhi, the national capital, might as well be in another country. Even the young men of high castes who worked as white collar workers (VLWs, secretaries of cooperative societies or *Panchayats*, *Patwaris*, school teachers or clerks in various offices) had little interest in events outside the State. They were only vaguely aware of events in the country. Few of them read newspapers or possessed radio receivers.

In 2001, however, both Raipur and Maanpur had populations of 7,000-8,000 and should be classified as small towns, by the Superintendent of Census of Rajasthan in 2001. They had also other attributes of a town—a sub-post office, more than 50 telephones; more than 100 black and white or colour television receivers and piped water in a large number of houses. Most of the houses of the high castes and of *Meenas* with even middle-sized land-holdings are of brick and mortar. The main street of Raipur had 130 shops, while that of Maanpur had 70 shops besides 8 teashops and 4 restaurants. Both villages had one high ten-grade school and two eight-grade middle schools, sub-dispensaries, a resident physician and/or *vaidyas*.

Shops in Raipur and Maanpur markets sell everything—foodgrains and other provisions; cloth, clothes, shoes and other leather goods and furnishing and drugs. Dealers in them sell kerosene and diesel oils—the fuel for tractors, pump sets and other machines. Some of them sell spare-parts for these also. Dealers in Maan Town market located 5 km. from Raipur and 8 km. from Maanpur also sell various consumer goods. They sell also spare parts for the machines and have facilities for the repair of machines as well as building materials and inputs of improved agriculture—improved seeds, chemical fertilizers and pesticides. Some dealers in both the villages sell cooking gas. Farmers can sell their produce in Maan Town or in the villages themselves.

Most of the farmers produce mustard and groundnuts and some wheat for sale so that they can buy various consumer goods and consumer durables mentioned above. The farmers are part of the regional economy because they sell their crops in it and buy various consumer goods from it. The high castes whose sons are working as white collar workers or professionals or whose daughters are married to them are part of the national economy. They are proud of this fact.

The farmers take large short-term loans from cooperative societies for current cultivation and medium term loans from Land Mortgage Banks or from the branches of scheduled banks located in Maan Town or in the villages for buying tractors, pump sets or other machines, building materials for construction of houses and opening of shops. Farmers are keen to get the maximum prices of their crops and the non-agricultural labourers are keen to get the minimum wages fixed by the Government of Rajasthan. Replacement of dowry for bride price among all but the poorest farmers increases the need for cash further. Both Maanpur and Raipur would have attracted people from small villages in their vicinity to sell their produce or buy consumer goods or consumer durables, if they had not been so close to Maan Town. Thus both Maanpur and Raipur have all the characteristics of a small town.

Caste and Occupational Mobility

Caste played and continues to play a very important role in occupational change from the traditional village economy to a market economy. The economic motive although important is not strong enough to override caste considerations. By 1961, a large number of *Brahmin* young men had become *Patwaris*, VLWs, secretaries of *Panchayat* and cooperative societies, teachers in primary schools, *Vaidyas* (practitioners of ancient *Ayurvedic* system of medicine), clerks in offices of the Rajasthan Government and the cement factory. After getting educated up to the middle (eight-grade) school, some of the Brahmin and Mahajan girls had also become teachers in primary schools. These jobs paid well and since the young men were posted within 30 km. of Raipur, they could visit their families on weekends and could keep in touch with them through letters. However, no *Brahmin* had taken to trading or become an artisan such as carpenter, mason, smith, driver of motor vehicles, etc. despite the high level of earnings in them. These occupations were literally closed to them.

The *Mahajans* of Raipur could become traders in the Maan Town market or like the *Brahmins*, white collar workers after passing the necessary examinations. However, they preferred to remain traders-*cum*-moneylenders-*cum*-non-cultivating owners of their land within their own villages. Besides relatively high earnings, prestige was a major consideration with staying in the village.

The Rajputs of Maanpur were satisfied with remaining non-cultivating owners of their lands that they could retain for self-cultivation. They employed *Chamaars*, *Meenas* and *Malis* as agricultural labourers or sharecroppers for managing cultivation of their lands. Their aspiration was that one or more sons should get educated and become white collar workers. However, at least one son must remain to look after the land of the family. This gave prestige to the family and also provided sizeable income. They would marry their daughters to educated *Rajput* young men who were in the Army or were white collar workers or were managing family farms.

The *Meenas* were satisfied with managing their farms better to increase agricultural production. Those with small holdings supplemented their income with unskilled work on repair of the railway tracks or the roads or work in the cement factory. They were interested primarily in producing field crops (sorghum, millet, wheat, chick-peas) and oil seeds but were not interested in producing vegetables, fruit or milk for sale. Producing fruit and vegetables for sale was the job of the *Malis* who in addition, produced wheat, sorghum and oilseeds. The *Gujjars* were helping to meet the demand for milk. Similarly, the large demand for meat is met by supplies from Hindu *Khatiks* (butchers) and the Moslems.

The *Chamaars* although interested in being recognized as a cultivating caste, had become unskilled workers in the repair of railway tracks and roads like the Meenas. Some of them had become carpenters, masons, smiths, etc. who found well paid jobs in Maan Town market and building houses in Maan Town. The teachers in schools and doctors in hospitals could be *Brahmins*, *Mahajans* or *Rajputs* while nurses and mid-wives in hospitals could be mainly *Chamaars* or Moslems; the women who performed these tasks by tradition. The great increase in demand for them in the two large hospitals had not induced women of any other caste to become nurses or midwives.

The high demand for meat had not led any Hindu caste except the Gujjars to increase the size of herds. The meat sold in the Maan Town market was all goat meat. Beef or meat of camels could not be sold because of the sensitivities of the people in this predominantly Hindu area. Cattle were reared in the woodlands to produce bullocks. *Gujjars* who grazed their herds on the stubble of the cultivated fields and in the forests sold meat of sheep and goats also. But this was done primarily to earn some cash and to keep size of their herds within the availability of the pasture. Thus, even in 2001, the economic motive had not become dominant; caste considerations remained important in the choice of new economic activities in the new market economy.

Change in Values: People of all castes including the Meenas, Malis and *Chamaars* had accepted the fact that education of girls to the primary school level was a good thing. They feel that girls educated to primary schools may not work in the fields but had aspirations to marry their educated daughters to white collar or school educated *Meena* boys who like the high caste educated men would like to have educated wives. Moreover, cultivation of land by tractors and use of other equipment such as mechanical shellers of sorghum and millets or dehuskers of wheat had reduced women's work in the fields. They could, therefore, devote their time to their work as mothers and homemakers. The men realized also that their educated wives would get prompt treatment for themselves and their children in case of communicable or other diseases of the children or themselves. Furthermore, clean homes and access to clean and more adequate drinking water supply from wells located in the villages or piped water from overhead tanks meant less disease among their men, children and themselves.

By 2001, most of the *Meenas* still said that they did not accept any bride price, but gave dowry on marriage of their girls. However, the truth of this statement could not be verified. Child marriages had been reduced greatly. The *Brahmins*, *Mahajans* and *Rajputs* married their daughters only when they were 16 or 18 years of age and the young men were 22-25 years old. By this time, both were mature and would not fall victim to communicable diseases. Even the *Meena*, *Mali* and other cultivators wanted that their daughters should be married when they were old enough to look after their homes and children. Although, widows' remarriage was allowed among the *Meenas*, *Malis*, *Chamaars* and all other castes, except the high castes the widows did not have a high social status. Even the Moslems did not accord a high status to their widows. Widow-remarriage was allowed among all castes but was barred by the high castes. Widows had always been a burden among the high castes that wanted to keep their number to the minimum. The ban on remarriage of young widows must have relaxed among the high castes; in a recent announcement by one of the *Panchayats* in Madhya Pradesh special efforts were being made to arrange marriages of young widows.

A few Moslem widows of Raipur had become tailors so that they could earn some money while sitting at home. A Delhi based NGO *Dastkar* had opened a centre near Raipur where Moslem women made quilted bed sheets, for export to Europe and embroidered dresses for sale to the tourists. But no Hindu woman took up this activity despite high earnings in it. In 1961, *Brahmin* widows carried milk from Raipur to the Maan Town market on their heads to earn a little money to support them. They were looked down upon by the rest of the community for being so poor. But these supposedly enlightened people were so stupid that they would not allow their widows to learn a remunerative trade like tailoring. The *Brahmin* women just did not do this skilled work. The *Brahmin* cooks in 1961 use to cook for marriages in Raipur and some of them went to Mumbai and worked as cooks in *Marwari* homes. In 2001 they had stopped going there and had opened food and sweet-meat seller shops in the Maan Town market and were doing very well !

In 1961, almost all the district level officers were *Brahmins*, *Rajputs*, *Mahajans*; a few were *Kayasthas* or Moslems. All the clerks in Collector's office belonged to these groups. Almost all the policemen were either *Rajputs* or *Jats*. The president of the Bar Association was a *Brahmin* lawyer who was also the chairman of the Sawai Madhopur municipal committee. These jobs preferences had changed by 2001 only to the extent that many *Meenas* have become clerks, village level workers, Secretaries of *Panchayats* or cooperative societies or traders. Many *Chamaars* have become clerks or junior officers.

Thus, most of the jobs in the new economy had been taken by those for whom the change to these jobs was permitted by tradition. The traditional job preferences or prohibitions had not changed between 1961 and 2001 despite the major economic and social changes that have been described above.

Perception of Corruption

A perception widely shared by a large number of people relates to prevalence of corruption among officials and clerks in the offices of the Collector, the Superintendent of Police or other district level offices and even in the *Panchayat Samiti* and the *Zilla Parishad*. This impression prevailed (and justifiably) in 1961 also. Furthermore, the people realize that the money to be paid for 'getting things done' is much higher in 2001 than it was in 1961.

Role of Communication Facilities and Traders

Another major change relates to the role of communication facilities and of private traders in promoting rural development. In 1961, radio receivers were owned by a very few relatively affluent farmers or men of the high castes; there were no television receivers. Now about 20 per cent of the households in Maanpur and a similar number in Raipur and some even in Bijaipur have television receivers in their homes; everyone can afford the radio receivers. The receivers provide information and entertainment. Furthermore, they motivate the people to educate their children, have clean drinking water supply, keep their homes and children clean, and have a balanced diet. These supplement and reinforce the advice and the facilities offered by the extension workers, teachers in primary and secondary schools and doctors and nurses in the hospitals.

In 1961, only the VLWs and agriculture extension officers provided information about improved agricultural practices and supply of inputs for crops. Veterinary assistants treated diseases of animals. Now, traders in the Maan Town market supplement the advice given by the VLWs and the extension officers on the choice and dosages of chemical fertilizers and pesticides for different food and cash crops. The traders who sell tractors pump sets provide fuel and facilities for repair of these. After observing the repairmen, most of the farmers have developed the skill to repair small defects in their machines themselves; otherwise the use of the machines would be too expensive.

In 1961, there were no telephones in these villages. The Collector, the Superintendent of Police and a few district or sub-divisional level officers, the MLA and a few professionals mainly lawyers and the two doctors in the Sawai Madhopur hospital were the only people who had telephones in their homes. Now there are more than 50 telephones with STD facility in both Maanpur and Raipur. In 1961, the only Post Offices were in Maan Town and Sawai Madhopur town. Now there are sub-post offices in both Maanpur and Raipur. The isolation of the villages has been broken not only by motorable roads, buses, and trucks and other motor vehicles but also by telephones and other means of communication.

Essentials for Leadership in PRIs

As has been mentioned in the chapter on Village Leadership that the essential qualifications for being a leader are (i) the family's economic status, (ii) communication skills—convincingly vocal in pressurizing the district administration to attend to the villagers' needs, and (iii) have good relations with the villagers as well as the officers.

In Raipur, the two most respected leaders in 1961 were (i) a middle aged *Meena* with a large land holding. He had been a member of the first *Panchayat* established in 1952, and (ii) middle aged affluent *Mahajan* whose family also owned a sizeable land and had besides money lending as a principal economic activity. He too had been a member and for many years *Sarpanch* of the *Panchayat* established in 1952.

The two leaders had mobilized funds, labour and material contributions from the villagers for construction of the buildings of a middle school for boys and a primary school for girls, repair of the approach road to the village, pavement of streets in the habitation area of the village and construction of buildings for the *Panchayat* and the cooperative society-*cum*-store for improved seed, fertilizers and other inputs. They had obtained grants or loans from the Community Development administration for construction of all these works and also for construction and repair of wells in the hamlets of the *Chamaars* and Gujjars, located on the outskirts of the village.

Mr. Sham Lal Sharma, the *Sarpanch* of Raipur in 1961 was very critical of the regime of these leaders; he accused them of corruption, a charge that they reciprocated. But he recognized that he could not mobilize the funds for the works mentioned above, that the traditional leaders had done. The maximum that he could do was to maintain these works and at the same time ensure that the *Panchayat* had enough funds for maintaining clean drains in the habitation area of the high castes. The villagers did not allow him to raise taxes to undertake any new development works. Although he was a well-paid clerk in the cement factory, he came from a poor family. Thus he lacked one essential condition for leadership.

In 1961, two essential conditions for position of leadership at the Block and district level were also that the leader should be well off enough not to appear to utilize his leadership to enrich himself from the grants or loans that were available for development works in the villages and he should be convincingly vocal about the demands and the difficulties of the villagers to the officials.

The *Pradhan* (chairman) of the Sawai Madhopur *Panchayat Samiti* in 1961 was middle aged *Meena* from the central part of the *tehsil* which was the stronghold of the *Meenas*. His family had a large landholding and the *Meena* community had chosen him for being a convincingly vocal representative of the *Meena* caste. Furthermore, he had such personal qualities that the decisions of the *Panchayat Samiti* were seldom overturned by the District Development Officers or the Collector.

In 1961, the MLA of the Sawai Madhopur (unreserved) constituency was a reasonably successful Moslem lawyer. His brother was also a successful lawyer in the Collector's office. Furthermore, he had the backing of the mostly Moslem forest contractors who mobilized men and money for his campaign in return for his ability to get permission to cut forest and other favours from the Collector and the State government.

He succeeded in the election of 1962 by a Rajput ex-*Jagirdar*, a traditional leader from a reasonably affluent family. Furthermore, he had the ability to approach the *Meenas, Malis* and the *Chamaars* and to convince them that he would further their interests with the State Government.

These conditions have remained unchanged in 2001, no matter who occupies the various positions in the *Panchayati Raj* institutions. The *Sarpanch* of Raipur in 2001 is a woman of washermen caste, the lowest in an extremely caste conscious village. She is completely ineffective. She is accused also of corruption because her husband drinks. She was elected because the seat had been reserved for a member of the scheduled caste/ scheduled tribe and also reserved for a woman. The SC/ST castes community men could not decide on any one candidate and had put up several women. The Dhobi woman won the election primarily as a proxy candidate for whom all high caste voters voted. However, the real leaders of the community remain a reasonably affluent *Meena* and two or more reasonably well off *Mahajans* and *Brahmins*.

Working of Panchayati Raj Institutions and Cooperative Societies in the Three Villages

In 1961, *Panchayati Raj* institutions had been established only two years earlier. The posts of *Sarpanch* (Chairman of the *Panchayat*) were occupied mainly by the high castes—a *Brahmin* in Raipur and a *Rajput* in Maanpur. The other members of the *Panchayat* of Maanpur agreed to whatever the *Sarpanch* (late) Mr. Hari Singh and his supporters decided. The co-opted woman members also agreed with him. He had been the representative of the *jagirdar* but had reconciled himself to his position as a non-cultivating owner of the land that had been left to him for self-cultivation. He had sharecroppers or wage labourers to cultivate his land.

He had utilized the grants available from the Community Development department to construct buildings of an 8-grade school and the offices of the *Panchayat* and the cooperative society. This large building served also as a store for improved seeds, chemical fertilizers, pesticides and improved implements. These were distributed to the farmers by a VLW at the rates fixed by the government. The *Sarpanch* also ensured equitable distribution of sugar and kerosene oil, which was distributed through the public distribution system in 1961.

Although a traditionalist, who would not allow the scheduled castes to worship in the temple of the high castes or draw water from their wells, the villagers respected him for his personal honesty and the development works that he had done for the village. Even the *Chamaars* of the hamlet respected him because he had helped them obtain a grant from the government for improving their drinking water well and in opening of a primary school in their hamlet.

The *Sarpanch* of Raipur in 1961 was a young very vocal *Brahmin*. He was educated up to high school and worked as a clerk in the cement factory. He had been elected with the help of some young supporters against the opposition of the traditional leaders of the village—a relatively wealthy *Mahajan* and an affluent middle aged *Meena*. The latter's predecessors had been headmen of the village for more than two generations. The *Sarpanch* accused the traditional leaders of corruption; they returned the allegation. He tried to cultivate the officials, including the Collector by showing them the development works—buildings for a middle school for boys and a primary school for girls, offices of the *Panchayat* and the cooperative society; a building for residence of the VLW and a store for improved seed, chemical fertilizers, pesticides and improved implements.

But the traditional leaders of the village did not respect him, including several people of his own caste because he came from a poor family and was vocal in his criticism of the traditional leaders. He realized that he could not have mobilized the contributions for the various works that the traditional leaders had obtained. He could not even persuade the *Brahmin* and *Mahajan* families to maintain cleanliness in their streets by arranging effective drainage of the side drains. Thus, the drains in the main street which had as many as 130 shops in 2001 (selling everything from provisions to spare-parts for tractors and T.V. sets) often overflowed with waste water.

Hira Lal Meena our informant in Bijaipur is educated and is Panchayat development officer in the office of the BDO; he comes from a family, which has a large landholding. He is well off; his children are in good jobs and he has been active in the construction committee for the big temple of *Hanumanji* for which more than Rs. 700,000 was collected. He represents Bijaipur on the Maanpur *Panchayat* of which Bijaipur is a part.

The *Sarpanch* of the Maanpur *Panchayat* in 2001 was a *Mahajan.* He worked in close collaboration with the traditional leaders including Mr. Suraj Bhan Singh, the younger brother of late Mr. Hari Singh who had also been *Sarpanch* of the village, and the *Mahajans.* He maintained good relations also with the *Meenas* and the *Chamaars* of the two hamlets and also with the Collector and other officials.

The *Sarpanch* of Raipur in 2001 is a *Dhobi* (washerwoman) woman. She comes from the lowest caste in a highly caste conscious village. She became *Sarpanch* because the seat was reserved for a member of the scheduled castes or the scheduled tribes and for a woman. Their leaders could not agree on any one candidate and put up several *Meena* women. The real leaders of the village, as mentioned earlier, remain unchanged by her election. She was getting no cooperation in her work from traditional village leaders—*Brahmins, Mahajans* and *Meenas.* They all feel she is incompetent and her husband is corrupt. They were openly talking about submitting a no-confidence motion against her leadership as soon as she has completed two years of her mandatory tenure. Even the women members of the *Panchayat*, who constituted 33 per cent of the total members and Ward members who represented all castes, were supporting the traditional male village leaders in their efforts to replace the *Dhobin Sarpanch.*

Working of the *Panchayati Raj* institutions and the cooperative societies in both the large multi-caste villages Maanpur and Raipur can be considered satisfactory. The *Panchayats* of both villages had mobilized contributions in labour, materials and money to maintain various works mentioned earlier for the two villages. The contribution of people of the scheduled castes and the scheduled tribes had been in the form of materials and/or labour while that of the people of the high castes had been in money. The post of *Sarpanch* of *Panchayats* of both Maanpur and Raipur remained for almost three decades after 1961 with people of the high castes—*Rajputs* and *Mahajans*. Thereafter, people of the scheduled castes and the scheduled tribe have assumed it. The high castes have accepted this change in the caste of the leaders. The *Panchayats* of both villages have continued to be active in doing welfare work for the villages during 1961-2001. The *Panchayat* of Raipur, however, has not been able to make effective arrangements for drainage of wastewater from the main street, which remains quite dirty.

The *Panchayats* of both Maanpur and Raipur mobilized contributions in money, materials and labour amounting to about Rs. 4 lakh each to construct overhead tanks from which piped water is supplied to a large number of houses in these villages. While the villagers have constructed the tanks the State Government has provided funds for construction of tube wells, water of which is lifted to fill the tanks. It has provided also the operators to work the pumps. Heads of households who get the piped water supply pay a nominal amount for use of the water.

The leaders of Bijaipur have also concrete paved the main street; constructed side drains and ensured cleanliness in the village. Their principal source of drinking water is a tube well from which water is lifted to an overhead tank and supplied to about half of the houses. The remainders draw water from two wells located on the outskirts of the village. The village leaders ensure effective operation of the tube well and cleanliness around the wells. In Bijaipur, however, the overhead tank and the tube-well were constructed by the villagers themselves.

In all three villages, the schools operated by the government have well maintained buildings and the teachers recruited by the Department of Education do their duties efficiently. The *Panchayats* ensure this. This is not difficult because most of the teachers have their homes in neighbouring villages. Furthermore, the monthly pay (Rs. 7,000-10,000 per month) for a primary school teacher is quite attractive for a young man or young woman who has obtained a teacher's certificate after passing their higher secondary school examination.

The willingness of the parents to pay high fees for "quality education" for their children has induced enterprising teachers to open 'private schools' in both Maanpur and Raipur. There are two 'private schools' in Raipur and one in Maanpur. Fees in them are much high than fees in schools run by the Department of Education. But all the private schools have large number of students because 'quality' of education in them is much better than in schools run by the Department.

The working of the cooperative societies can also be considered satisfactory. In both the large villages the loans given by the cooperatives for current crop production range between Rs. 25-30 lakh. Recovery of loans is not a problem. On the contrary, the Maanpur society received a cash prize of Rs. 100,000 from the State Government for timely recovery of the loans. The medium term loans given by the Land Mortgage Bank or by branches of nationalized banks for buying tractors, pump-sets and other machines and for construction or improvements of homes are also repaid in time because the farmers realize that the flow of loans could not be maintained otherwise. Deposits with the branches of five national banks located in Maan Town market or in Raipur and Maanpur range between Rs. 2-4 crore.

The traditional leaders of the village who dominated the *Panchayats* and the cooperatives in 1961 still maintain their leadership position. They did not have any formal positions in 2001 but they remained the decision-making elite. This is because the villagers have confidence in their commitment to work for all the villagers.

All the three villages have better access to facilities for education and preventive health and medical care than most of the other villages of the district because they are located near the district headquarters. For the same reason, they receive more funds for construction of various works and attention of officers of rural development departments than the other villages of the district. Their educated young men have privileged access to white collar service in offices in the district headquarters.

There have been some important changes in attitudes and aspirations. Education of girls, which was considered useless in 1961, was considered desirable in 2001. Dowry for marriages of girls has replaced bride money even among the not so affluent *Meenas*. Giving dowry, a traditional practice of the high castes, has become a status symbol for the middle income and affluent *Meenas*. The amounts of dowry are not small either, from Rs. 150,000 to 300,000 for young men who have secure white collar jobs-from VLWs and school teachers to clerks and junior officers in various offices in Maanpur. It was difficult to imagine in 1961 that changes of such magnitude would occur during the next 4 decades.

Rural electrification was just starting in 1961; the cumbersome and inefficient *charas* system was used for irrigation of small areas of land. Installation of diesel-operated pumps on most of the irrigation wells has meant a large increase in the cultivated area that is irrigated—two-third of the total in Sawai Madhopur *tehsil*. High yield varieties of wheat, use of which has resulted in large increases in output of wheat and income of farmers were not even heard of in 1961.

The growth poles in the village economy are :

(i) Cultivation by tractors and irrigation by diesel operated pumps. These have contributed to some increase in the cultivated area and much increase in the irrigated area. Production of cereals is three-four times higher than that in 1961. Besides since milk, vegetables and fruit in season have become an essential item of food of all except the very poor, they are produced much more than before. Surpluses of these are sold in the Maan Town market and make a significant contribution to the income of the producers. Due to adequate consumption of food and inclusion of protective foods in their diet, health of the people, men, women and children is much better. The principal diseases are those of the digestive and respiratory tracks. Malaria the great killer had been eradicated by the 1950s has made a comeback.

(ii) Labour, mainly unskilled but also skilled, find enough employment in up keep of the railway station, the railway tracks and the State highway to Jaipur via Tonk. The carpenters, masons and smiths find enough work in construction and repair of shops and houses in Maan Town and its market and the hotels. The mechanics of motor vehicles, tractors and irrigation pumps have enough work in upkeep and repair of these. The electricians have enough work in repair of T.V. receivers and electrical appliances used by housewives in Maan Town, in the officers' colony and in houses, which have electricity, in the villages.

(iii) *The market*: There is so much work in it that it has replaced the factory as a source of employment. Besides it has contributed to the villages being part of a cash economy instead of a subsistence economy.

(iv) *The game sanctuary*: It provides jobs for labourers in maintenance of roads to it and employees of the various tourist agencies.

(v) *Health, education and communication facilities*: Improvement in health of the people because of greater availability of medical facilities and improvement in supplies of drinking water. Increase in education of boys and girls has also resulted in consciousness of a higher level of living. The T.V. receivers tell them to live a better life having access to essentials of clean living, such as soap, hair oil, and medicines which cure diseases of men, women and children. They propagate also family planning. The village women report that they have accepted the two/three child norm. One son is a must; two sons are preferred. A large number of "operations" are reported to be performed every year. But the presence of large number of children in all villages indicates that these statements have to be taken with a large pinch of salt.

(vi) The standard of living of the villagers can be considered lower middle income. Most of the small *Meena* farmers and the scheduled caste agricultural laboureres belong to this group. However, that of some *Rajputs*, *Brahmins* and *Mahajans*, whose sons are in white collar jobs in Maan Town or in other cities can be considered to be in the middle-income category. Thus the standard of living of the villagers is now comparable to that of Otalan[6] in 1963 or higher. Many houses have hand pumps besides the community hand pumps for bathing and drinking water. Ponds are used exclusively for bathing and drinking water of milch animals, buffaloes and cows. Both Maanpur and Raipur have paved streets in the villages for drainage of waste water which is absorbed in the tanks outside the villages.

Maanpur and its two hamlets and Bijaipur are located along a tarmac covered metalled road so that motorized transport is available throughout the day. Raipur is within a kilcmetre of an all-weather motorable road. Because of this facility, villagers can go to and return from Jaipur, the capital for redressal of their grievances within a day.

Further, social development will mean absolute decline in practice of untouchability, greater education of women and children of school-going ages and abolition of child marriage which is still widespread. It will mean even greater migration of sons of *Brahmins, Rajputs* and *Mahajans* to Jaipur, Kotah and other cities in Rajasthan and Delhi in search of white collar jobs. At present there are educated men in Raipur and Bijaipur who are sitting idle due to lack of employment opportunities.

(vii) Bride price is stated to have disappeared among the well-to-do *Meena* cultivators. They pride themselves in giving dowry on marriages of their daughters. The amounts of dowry are not small, particularly for the lowest level white collar workers who can get Rs. 10,000-15,000 salary command a dowry of Rs. 100,000-150,000. They are the most desired grooms. However, there must be bride price among the poor cultivators among whom women did much more work on the farm than even the men. Their farm work as well as that of the men is much less, however, than earlier because the small cultivators can hire tractors and pay also for irrigation water. They pay for these by working on the railway station, maintenance of railway tracks and on the road to Jaipur.

Due to much less farm work for women and men, the women devote their time to care of children and keeping their houses clean. The men have time to work at the railway station; such labour makes a valuable addition to their income.

Concluding Remarks

Although one cannot foresee new growth poles in the economy, there is little doubt that increases in income and consumption, improvement in education and health and attendant rise in aspirations of people of all castes will continue during the next two decades. Production of wheat and mustard in the cool season will continue to increase by more efficient use of chemical fertilizers, pesticides and irrigation water. More dependable supply of electricity by the Rajasthan State Electricity Board will greatly reduce the cost of irrigation because the price of electricity would be much lower than the cost of diesel oil. It will increase incomes of farmers and comfort in living and more households can have the comfort of electric lights and fans in their homes.

With rise in income and consumption, increase in education of children and improvement of health of women, children and men, there have been major changes in attitudes and aspirations of people of all castes during the last four decades 1961-2001. Women of all castes have accepted the need for family planning, mention of which was repugnant to them in 1961. Wives of *Meena* farmers with small landholdings realize that their landholding is small and can provide work for only one son; the others would have to work as share croppers and supplement their income by unskilled labour in Maan Town market or repair of the railway track. Wives of *Chamaars* and other scheduled castes realize similarly that even two sons could not find enough work as share-croppers on land or as non-agricultural labourers. With reduction in infant mortality, they are not afraid that most of their children would die in infancy and they would be left childless. However, it is not certain that the realization has led to smaller families so far. Our respondents in the three villages and Mr. Fateh Singh our respondent for the game sanctuary, all have three to five children and are proud of the fact.

Except Mr. Heera Lal Meena a leader of Bijaipur, whose sons are working in Maan Town, some sons of the others are living in Jaipur or in other States. Earlier after getting education up to high school several high caste young men were working as secretary for cooperative society or *Panchayat*, a school teacher or a clerk in some office in Maan Town. Some *Chamaars* had begun to get into such jobs but the *Meenas* were not interested. Now even *Meenas* are aspiring to get these jobs. Furthermore, the high castes are educating their sons to become college graduates or professionals who will get posts with much higher salaries; no matter that they would live at long distances from their homes. Sons of two of our three respondents, former *Sarpanchs* of Maanpur and Raipur are professionals and are living in Jaipur, Kotah and other cities. One son of Mr. Fateh Singh, a *Rajput* and our respondent for the Game Sanctuary is a doctor who works in the hospital maintained by an international non-governmental organization 'Tiger Watch' and located just outside Raipur. Another son is in Mumbai under training for a male nurse. The parents do not mind this. On the contrary, they are happy at their sons' success as professionals. These are typical attitudes and aspirations of the urban middle class.

Since bride price has been replaced by dowry, the *Meena* farmers realize that they could not afford to provide a dowry for more than one daughter.

In 1961, only young men of the three high castes—*Brahmin*, *Mahajan* and *Rajput*—aspired to and did become white collar workers at the lowest level of the *Patwari*, VLW, secretary of cooperative society or *Panchayat*, a school teacher or a clerk in some office in Maan Town. Some *Chamaars* had begun to get into such jobs but the *Meenas* were not interested. Now even *Meenas* are aspiring to get these jobs. Furthermore, the high castes are educating their sons to become college graduates or professionals who will get posts with much higher salaries; no matter that they would live at long distances from their homes. Due to only people of high castes sending their girls to school there was only one five-grade primary school for girls in Maanpur in 1961. By 2001, there were two schools in Maanpur, one run by the Department of Education and one by private trustees. In Raipur also there was a school for girls run by a private teacher, in addition to the one eight-grade school run by the Department. Besides, there is a ten grade school for boys. In 1961, the *Chamaars* of the hamlet of Maanpur had a primary school located in their temple. By 2001, the school had become an eight-grade school and had its own building. A large number of boys and a few girls from Raipur and Maanpur were attending the boys' school in Allanpur.

In 1961, most of the people of this area—all except the *Meenas* with relatively large landholdings, Rajput, former *jagirdars* or those who were their representatives and *Mahajans* or *Brahmins* whose sons had after education got white collar jobs—were poor. By 2001, most of them had risen to lower middle-income status. Inequalities in social status of people of different castes have been greatly reduced. Assumption of posts of *Sarpanchs* (chairmen) by men or even women belonging to the scheduled castes and the fact that some young men of these castes would get posts of clerks or junior officers in the offices of the district have been accepted by people of the high caste without protest.

Other changes in attitudes of great significance are :

(i) realization of the value of education of girls.
(ii) the need for and practice of family planning by a significant percentage of couples in the reproductive age group.
(iii) land reforms of abolition of intermediary tenure holdings although has not been effective in some areas or there is wide opposition to it from former landowners to its becoming effective, but the number of these areas is small. Over large parts of the country, the reform has been effective for more than four decades.

Assumption of Political Power by Cultivating Community

Assumption of political power by cultivating caste has been the norm in most of the States for almost 50 years; the high castes are fully reconciled to the fact. In two States—U.P. and Bihar—which are most populous, political power has been or is with leaders of other backward castes. There is resistance to it only in Bihar.

A perception, widely shared by large numbers of people relates to prevalence of corruption among officials and clerks in the offices of the Collector, the Superintendent of Police or other district level offices and even in the *Panchayat Samiti* and the *Zilla Parishad*. This impression prevailed (and justifiably) in 1961 also. Furthermore, the people realize that the money to be paid for 'getting things done' is much higher in 2001 than it was in 1961.

Role of Communication Facilities

Another major change relates to the role of communication facilities and of private traders in promoting rural development. In 1961, radio receivers were owned by a very few relatively affluent farmers or men in the high castes; there were no television receivers. Now about 20 per cent of the households in Maanpur and a similar number in Raipur have television receivers in their homes. The radio receivers can be afforded by everyone. The information to cultivators, about the need for education of children, having clean drinking water supply, keeping their homes and children clean, having a balanced diet and availing of medical facilities in case of sickness and family planning practices, can be conveyed to all men and women through radio and television receivers. These supplement and reinforce the advice and the facilities offered by the extension workers and teachers in primary and secondary schools, doctors and nurses in the hospitals.

In 1961, in Maanpur information about improved agricultural practices and supply of inputs for crops were provided only by the VLW's and agriculture extension officers. Veterinary assistants treated diseases of animals; the schools opened a few year earlier had few students mainly boys of the high castes. Now the traders in the Maan Town market supplement the advice given by the VLW's and the extension officers on the choice and dosages of chemical fertilizers for different food crops—wheat and especially mustard which are the principal food and cash crops. The traders sell tractors and pump sets and provide fuel and facilities for repair of these. After observing the repairmen, a few farmers have developed the skill to repair small defects in their machines themselves.

In 1961, there were no telephones in these villages. The Collector, the Superintendent of Police and a few district or sub-divisional level officers, the MLA and a few professionals mainly lawyers and the doctors in the Sawai Madhopur hospital had telephones in their homes. Now there are more than 50 telephones with STD facilities in Maanpur as well as in Raipur. In 1961, the only post offices were in Maan Town and Sawai Madhopur Town. Now there are sub-post offices in both Maanpur and Raipur. The isolation of the villages has been broken not only by motorable roads, buses, trucks and other motor vehicles but also by these means of communication. We could not record the effect of use of cell phones which must have become popular among the villagers as everywhere else during the last five years only.

Self-Sustaining Development

Meaning of Self-Sustainable Development

Self-sustaining development has two meanings in our view. First, it should not make undue demands on the natural resources of soil, water or vegetation. Second, it should mean that the improvements in health and productivity of people, education and awareness should be permanent and it should create aspirations to progress higher in the future.

The development described in the foregoing sections satisfies both criteria of self-sustaining development. The farmland is more productive in 2001 than it was in 1961. In 1961, most of the farmland was bare for more than 6 months in the year (after the monsoon season crops of sorghum or millets had been harvested) and was subject to wind or water erösion. Now, two-thirds of the farmland is irrigated and has two crops—gram (chick peas), wheat, mustard or pulses in the cold season and sorghum, millets or groundnut in the monsoon season. The crop rotation followed is such that the nutrients removed by one set of crops are replaced by another set. Thus, stalks of sorghum, millets and vines of mustard and groundnuts replace most of the nutrients removed by high yield wheat. While some of the stalks of sorghüm and millet and husks of wheat are fed to milch animals, the remainder is ploughed in and improves the physical structure of the soil. The vines of mustard and groundnut, which are ploughed in, not only replenish the nutrients in the soil but also improve its physical structure by taking nitrogen from the air. As a result the need for application of chemical fertilizers is reduced. The pastures are looked after better because production of milk is a major source of income for villages located between Sawai Madhopur and Maan Town. The Ranthambhore forest and game sanctuary are protected both by the forest guards and employees of Tiger Watch an international non-governmental organization, the sole object of which is to preserve the natural habitat of tigers and other wild beasts. Much of the cultivable land which had formed part of the *shikar* (hunting) preserves of former *jagirdars* and was under trees has been cleared for cultivation and allotted to *Chamaars* or other landless or appropriated by the *jagirdars* for self-cultivation. There is no evidence yet of fall in the ground watertable due to irrigation of most of the cropland.

Self-sustaining development also means that increase in income and consumption, improvement in health, increase in education of children and awareness of the people should lead to aspirations for further rise in these. This is also true in this area. In 1961, most of the people, all except the better off *Mahajans* and *Meenas* or *Brahmins* whose sons were working as village level white collar workers, were poor. By 2001 most of them had risen to lower middle income or higher economic status. Even the farmers with small holdings and the scheduled castes agricultural or non-agricultural labourers have enough cereals to eat through the year; milk, vegetables, and fruit in season, which few could afford to eat in 1961 are now an integral part of their diet. Their health is much better, because they have access to medical care facilities in the form of two very well equipped multi-facility hospitals, besides dispensaries and *vaidyas* in both the large villages. In addition, Maanpur has a resident physician and an auxiliary nurse midwife. They realize the value of adequate and safe drinking water supply for maintaining good health to have invested lakhs of rupees in construction of overhead tanks and tubewells to lift water to them in order to have piped water in the homes and constructed side drains along the main streets of all the three villages to drain the waste-water. Two villages—Maanpur and Bijaipur—are quite clean because drain water is discharged in ponds located to the rear of the villages.

Their homes and children are much cleaner because the need for manual work by women on the farms is much less than before, thanks to use of tractors for cultivation and mechanical shellers of sorghum and millet and dehuskers of wheat. A significant percentage of houses are made of brick and mortar which are much easier to clean than the mud and thatch hut in which most of the small cultivators and landless labourers lived in 1961 and that needed, in addition, annual repair. Maternal, infant and child mortality has been reduced so much that many couples in the reproductive age group are practicing family planning. In Maanpur most of the middle aged women with two or more children have opted for 'operations' against further pregnancies and the visiting doctor has conducted about 100 operations, during the last four months (prior to our 2001 survey) among couples.

The value of education of children has been realized so much that most of the boys and a large number of girls of school-going ages are being sent to primary or secondary schools. People of the high castes and more affluent Meenas educate their daughters so that they can be wives of white-collar workers. Furthermore, even the poor farmers and landless labourers realize that educated wives keep their homes and children clean and know enough about preventive health care to avoid themselves or their children falling victims to communicable diseases.

Since a large number of high castes and affluent *Meena* households have black and white or colour T.V. receivers and even the poor have radio receivers, they are well aware of events in the area, district, and the State and even in the country. These receivers inform and entertain. They tell them the essentials of good living and create the desire to have the means to achieve it.

There has been a rise in aspirations of people of all castes. The high castes—*Brahmins, Mahajans* and *Rajputs* are educating their sons to go through degree or professional colleges in Jaipur or Kotah so that they can become professionals or officers in the State government who have much higher salaries than they had in 1961. They are educating their daughters so that they can be married to such officers. The parents are proud of the fact, that some of their sons are professionals living in Jaipur or other districts of Rajasthan or in other States. Even the *Meenas* who were not interested in white-collar jobs are now keen that their sons and daughters should be educated so that they can become white-collar workers.

There has been a major rise in level of skills of the farmers. In 1961, improved ploughs donated by CARE (Corporation for American Relief Everywhere) were lying unused in Maanpur because no one could repair some small defects in them. Now the cultivators who have tractors for cultivation and diesel operated pump sets for irrigation can remedy small defects in them themselves. Facilities for repairs to the machines are available with dealers in the market but the repairs would be too expensive, if the farmers could not repair the small defects in the machines themselves.

Will Development, described above in the Villages of Sawai Madhopur sustain in the Future ?

This question can be answered conclusively only during the next two decades when the technological, economic and social changes can be viewed over a longer-term perspective. However, from present indicators they would appear to be so for the following reasons:

The changes have been accomplished by the people themselves. The social service and infrastructure facilities provided and some of them maintained by the government have assisted the economic and social change process. However, using these facilities and ensuring that they are well maintained is entirely the initiatives of the people. In 1961, the cooperative of Maanpur could give short-term loans of a total of less than Rs. 100,000 for current crop production. Recovery was a problem. Now the short-term loans are taken by almost all cultivators and the amount runs into tens of lakhs and recovery is not a problem; the borrowers realize that prompt repayment of the loans is essential to availability of further loans.

Development will be sustained because it is inconceivable that after having come this far, these people would allow them to be returned to their former poverty, illiteracy and ignorance.

It is true that these people located near the district headquarters have privileged access to education and medical facilities located at the district level; high schools, colleges and hospitals. They have privileged access to white-collar work for the same reason. Farmers located in distant villages would not have such access. However, the changes must be occurring ove r a large area in Rajasthan, as shown by a SIDA study (SIDA, 2000).

Progress of Rajasthan

Data available on various indicators of economic and social development in Rajasthan during the last two decades 1981-2001 show that Rajasthan is a prosperous and progressive State.

The State since its formation in the early 1950s been classified as a BIMARU State (an acronyms for States which include Madhya Pradesh, U.P., Bihar, Orissa among others) in which slow economic progress and social change brings down the rate of increase in G.D.P. and other indicators of economic and social progress such as increase in literacy, decline in infant, child and maternal mortality, proportion of people below the poverty line. The following note indicates that on the basis of several indicators of economic and social development during the last two decades it should be classified now as a progressive State.

Growth of Population

The population of the State increased from 44.3 million in 1991 to 56.4 million in 2001 (Table 16.1). The rate of increase 2.5 per cent per annum was as high as in the previous decade. Apparently, the effects, if any, of family limitation by couples in the reproductive age groups have yet to be seen. The rapid growth reflects, however, major improvement in health of the people due to eradication of malaria and control of diseases of the respiratory and digestive tracts as a result of intensive coverage with facilities for medical and preventive health care and improvement in water supply for villages and towns.

Increase in Per Capita Income

Despite the rapid increase in population, per capita income increased by 83 per cent between 1980-81 and 1996-97, the figures for the two years were Rs. 1220 and Rs. 2247 respectively. The growth rate is much above the national average of 70.5 per cent. Among the 17 States with population above 20 million in 2001, the rates were higher than Rajasthan only in Maharashtra, Gujarat and Tamil Nadu, the States which have high levels of industrial development and in which agricultural output has also increased rapidly (Table 16.1). To be included among the States with rapidly increasing per capita income is a creditable achievement, because as explained below the increase has been almost entirely due to rapid increase in agricultural output, there being no other source of significant economic growth.

Agricultural Growth

There has been rapid increase in agricultural output in the following areas:

(i) Areas in north-western Rajasthan which receive irrigation from a canal from the Sutlej river. The irrigated area has increased considerably after construction of the Bhakra Dam on the river in the 1950s. High yield wheat and medium staple cotton are the principal crops.

(ii) The area in eastern and south-eastern Rajasthan which extend from Alwar in the north, through Bharatpur, Jaipur Kotah, Bhilwara and Udaipur in the south receive irrigation from electric and diesel oil operated pumps. Yield of wheat and sorghum which are the principal food crops and output of mustard and ground nut—the principal cash crops—in these areas has increased. Sale of these crops and also of wheat and medium staple cotton in north-western Rajasthan meets all the needs of the farmers for buying various consumer goods—cloth, clothes, shoes and other leather goods and building materials such as cement, corrugated iron sheets and steel rods for making brick and mortar houses. The *Chamaar* landless labourers-*cum*-small farmers have income from cultivation of their small farms, plus non-agricultural labour in the market towns or as share-croppers for *Rajput* or *Mahajan jagirdars*. They have become masons, carpenters and plumbers so that they can earn high wages in building brick and mortar houses and repairing defects in them. Other scheduled castes, which practice their crafts, have enough income from sale of goods that they produce to be above the poverty line.

Table 16.1: Growth Rate of Population 1981-1991 and 1991-2001 and Growth Rate of Per Capita Income 1980-81 to 1996-97

Sl. No.	*India & States*	*Population in 1990-91 (millions)*	*Population in 2000-01 (millions)*	*Growth Rate of Population per cent per Annum*		*Female Literacy Rate (%)*	*Per Capita Income at 1980-81 Prices (Rupees)*		
				1981-91	*1991-2001*	*2001*	*1980-81*	*1996-97*	*Increase (%)*
(1)	(2)	(3)	(4)	(5)	(6)	(7)	(8)	(9)	(10)
1.	**India**	846.4	1027.5	2.01	1.93	54.16	1625	2814	70.5
2.	Uttar Pradesh	132.0	166.0	2.28	2.30	43.0	1278	1628	27.4
3.	Bihar	64.5	82.9	2.10	2.50	33.6	917	1010	10.1
4.	West Bengal	68.0	80.2	2.14	1.64	60.2	1773	2641	49.0
5.	Madhya Pradesh	48.6	96.8	2.41	2.18	50.3	1358	1877	38.0
6.	Rajasthan	44.0	54.5	2.80	2.49	44.0	1228	2247	83.0
7.	Punjab	20.3	24.3	1.89	1.80	63.5	2674	4171	56.0
8.	Haryana	16.5	21.0	2.42	2.47	56.3	2330	3996	71.5
9.	Orissa	31.7	36.7	1.83	1.48	50.1	1314	1595	21.4
10.	Maharashtra	78.9	96.8	2.28	2.04	67.5	2425	4853	100.1
11.	Gujarat	41.3	50.6	1.92	2.03	58.6	1940	3717	91.6
12.	Kerala	29.1	31.8	1.34	0.90	87.9	1568	2274	45.0
13.	Tamil Nadu	55.9	62.1	1.43	1.06	64.5	1448	2876	98.6
14.	Andhra Pradesh	66.5	75.7	2.37	1.30	51.5	1380	2134	54.6
15.	Karnataka	45.0	52.7	1.92	1.59	57.5	1380	2518	64.5
16.	Goa	1.2	1.3	1.47	1.39	75.5	3145	6550	97.8

Note: The 1991 populations of Uttar Pradesh, Bihar and Madhya Pradesh have been reduced to take into account the separation of Uttranchal, Jharkhand and Chhattisgarh respectively from the three States.

Sources: (a) Registrar General India: Provisional Population Totals 1990-91 Paper No. 1 of 1991 and Provisional Population Totals, Paper 1 of 2001, New Delhi, India. (b) For per capita income: E.P.W. Research Foundation: National Accounts Statistics of India 1950-51 to 1996-97, Mumbai, 1998, pp. 84. (c) For Data on agricultural output: SIDA (Swedish International Development Agency, Rajasthan: A Statistical Study, New Delhi, 1998.

Increase in agricultural output is due also to increase in use of chemical fertilizers by 450 per cent during *Kharif* and 300 per cent for *Rabi* cultivation. (SIDA, p. 36). Total consumption of (NPK) fertilizers increased by almost three times, from 7.4 kg. per hectare in 1980-81 to 20.03 kg. per hectare in 1993-94 (SIDA, pp. 198-99).

(i) Cultivation by tractors and performing other operations in the fields by power driven implements.
(ii) Effective crop protection practices.
(iii) Intensive agricultural extension services and transfer of research results from the laboratory to the farms.
(iv) Extensive rural electrification and a state-wide network of roads connecting villages to market towns.

Thus Rajasthan, which was deficit in foodgrains in the 1950s, has a large surplus and besides has large export of oilseeds. The statistical data for the Sawai Madhopur district and the *tehsil* show that the average yield for wheat has increased by two to three times per hectare, three-and a half times for groundnut, two to three times for mustard. The most remunerative cash crop is mustard; it yields Rs. 800 per hectare. However, groundnut yields only Rs. 600 per hectare, whereas for wheat the return amounts to Rs. 1,375 per hectare.

Increase in Tourism

Jaipur, Ajmer, Jaisalmer, Udaipur and Mt. Abu are visited by millions of tourists, for recreation or for worship. Hundreds of thousands of Moslems pilgrims worship at the *Dargah* (burial place) of Khawaja Moinudeen Chishti, a great Sufi saint of fifteenth century. Mt. Abu is visited similarly by hundreds of thousands of Jain pilgrims from southern Rajasthan and northern Gujarat. Jaipur, Udaipur and Jaisalmer are the most visited cities by foreign and domestic tourists. Jaipur and Udaipur are visited by both domestic and foreign tourists for seeing their palaces and museums; Jaisalmer is visited mainly by foreign tourists to have a glimpse of its distinctive palaces and houses in a desert landscape.

Increase in Literacy

Increase in literacy has been noteworthy. The female literacy rate was as low as 20.4 per cent in 1990-91; the lowest among the then existing 15 major States with population above 20 million. It has more than doubled to 44.3 per cent in 2001 (Table 16.2).

Table 16.2 : Progress in Literacy in BIMARU States, 1991-2001

Sl No.	*State*	*Literacy Rate in 1991 (per cent)*			*Literacy Rate in 2001 (per cent)*		
		Total	*Male*	*Female*	*Total*	*Male*	*Female*
1.	Bihar	38.5	52.6	23.5	47.5	60.3	31.6
2.	U.P.	41.7	55.4	26.0	57.4	70.2	43.0
3.	Rajasthan	38.5	55.1	20.8	61.0	76.5	49.3
4.	M.P.	43.4	57.4	28.4	64.1	76.8	50.3

Source: Registrar General of India: *Census of India*, 2001. Paper No. 1 Provisional Population Tables. New Delhi, 2001.

The literacy rate in 2001 was 76 per cent for males and 44.3 per cent for females higher than the rates in U.P., Bihar, Orissa, Assam and Jharkhand. The rates of 2001 put Rajasthan among States with medium literacy. This is a creditable achievement for a State which had a low level of literacy as late as 1990-91.

The increase is due to the following reasons:

The men realize that if they were literate they would not be cheated by merchants who buy their crops or those who sell them various consumer goods. They appreciate also that wives with some education keep themselves, their children and homes clean and seek assistance in case of sickness. They should have adequate and safe supply of drinking water from tubewells or wells fitted with electric or diesel oil operated pumps. Besides with the use of machines—tractors for cultivation, pump sets for irrigation, mechanical shellers for sorghum and millet and dehuskers for wheat—there is much less work in the fields. They have to look after milch buffaloes, ensure that they are cleaned after the buffaloes have been milked and tied in their yards at night.

Social Change

There have been noteworthy social changes during the last 50 years. *Jagirdari*, which was the dominant system of tenure for collection of land revenue and maintaining law and order in most of the areas of the State, was abolished in the early 1950s and full and heritable rights in land were conferred on the actual cultivators of croplands.

This reform, which still rocks the peace and stability of States such as Bihar, was accomplished without protest from the *jagirdars*. They contented themselves with management of the lands left to them for self-cultivation. They employed wage labourers or share croppers for cultivation. Now, most of them have purchased tractors for cultivation and installed diesel oil or electricity operated pumps for irrigation of the irrigable areas.

Primary health centres (mini-hospitals) at district headquarters towns with dispensaries, auxiliary nurses, midwives and *vaidyas* (practitioners of ancient Indian *ayurvedic* system of medicine) ensures that facilities for preventive health and medical care are within easy reach of residents of both large villages and towns.

Untouchability has been abolished by law and has disappeared in the urban areas and most of the rural areas. The *Chamaars*, the largest group among the scheduled castes, have stopped performing their traditional tasks of flaying the hides and skins of dead animals and making leather goods. They have been allotted cultivable lands released by former *jagirdars* and other cultivable lands by the State Government and are making strenuous efforts to be recognized as a clean cultivating caste. They have also stopped performing their traditional tasks at the houses of the former *jagirdars* or for the village. People of the other scheduled castes who carry out their traditional obligations are no longer considered untouchable.

The progress made by the *Chamaars* is such that a few young men have after being educated to B.A. level, joined the Rajasthan or Indian Administrative Service. Others are working as white-collar workers in offices of the Collector, the Superintendant of Police or other district offices after passing the higher secondary school examination. These young men are very assertive of their right to education in schools and colleges and for employment in offices of the State Government. They cite the provision in the Constitution of India relating to reservation of seats for them in educational institutions and in government service. In the rural areas, many are clerks, school teachers or village level officials such as secretaries of *Panchayats* and cooperative societies. Due to the provisions of reservation of seats for them in *Panchayati Raj* institutions, many of them have become *Sarpanchs* (chairmen of *Panchayats*), *Pradhans* (chairmen) or other influential members of *Panchayat Samitis*. Men of the high castes, who dominated these institutions for the first-three decades after their formation, recognize this change inevitable in a democratic society.

Position of Women

There has been equally remarkable change in the position of women. Child marriage, which was widespread even in the 1960s, has been reduced greatly. There has been rapid progress in education of women. Large numbers of girls are being sent to primary (five-grade) and middle (eight-grade) schools, which are located in every large village. The men are not afraid (as they were until the 1960s) that educated women would not work in the fields. The need for their work in fields is much less because of extensive use of tractors for cultivation and of other machines (such as mechanical thrashers of sorghum and millets and dehuskers of wheat) and for various other tasks. Furthermore, the men realize that wives with some education keep themselves, their children and their homes clean and obtain medical assistance in case of sickness. The people of high castes are educating their daughters to high school or higher levels, so that they can marry white-collar workers including professionals and soldiers in the armed forces who have a steady high income and some power. Some of the high caste educated women have become professionals like teachers and bank clerks etc. Their sons are being educated to higher secondary school or college level so that they can become white-collar workers and professionals such as physicians, engineers and architects.

The ability of Rajasthani society to make such far-reaching changes within five decades reflects a resilience which was quite unexpected even in the 1960s. It is the most important reason for the economic and social progress made by the State and the greatest hope for continuing progress in future.

Conditions affecting Rapid Progress

The most important condition affecting rapid economic and social progress has been stable and development-oriented governments. After a few years of unstable governments after its formation in the late 1940s, Rajasthan had a stable, development oriented government for about 20 years, from mid-1950s to the middle of the 1970s. It was succeeded by another government, which stayed in power for more than a decade and continued the development process initiated in the 1950s. In recent years also there has been political stability. The present Chief Minister has been at the helm of affairs for almost a decade. His predecessor was at the helm of affairs for more than a decade. One result of this is that the officers of the IAS and the technical services can perform their duties without too much interference by ministers and MLAs. Corruption among ministers and influential MLAs is much less and their interference with work of the officers is also much less than in several other States.

Another condition affecting rapid progress is almost exclusive emphasis on development of agriculture and rural development. The efforts of the government to promote industrial development have yielded very limited results despite the large number of highly successful Rajasthani industrialists living in Kolkata and other cities. There are, however, highly skilled craftsmen in Jaipur, Jodhpur and Udaipur who make jewellery, leather goods with exquisite designs, textiles and furnishings printed with distinctive Rajasthani designs. These are popular with domestic and foreign tourists.

The last condition affecting economic and social development is the determination of the people to acquire higher levels of income.

The Future

There are indications of presence of a large field of natural gas in western Rajasthan, almost on the border with Pakistan. If a large field is discovered, the scenario for agricultural and agro-industrial development will be totally transformed. With assured supply of power, the farmers who use diesel oil to operate pumps will use electric pumps. There would be large saving in foreign exchange, now spent on import of diesel oil or kerosene used for lighting kerosene oil or petromax lamps in lighting homes. The desert will bloom; the area was well wooded as late as the sixteenth century. The foliage in the area would be restored so that there is adequate pasturage for the large numbers of livestock (cattle, sheep and goats) that are kept by the herders.

The farmers in the small villages in this area who spend a day fetching two buckets of water for their needs, will be assured of clean drinking water from deep wells located near their villages. They will devote themselves to increase production of food in their farms. The periodic shortage of food, water and fodder that are experienced by this area that leads to migration of people and herds and deaths of thousands of livestocks due to scarcity of water and foliage will be a distant memory.

With completion of Indira Gandhi Canal there will be a large increase in the irrigated area and in agricultural output in the areas irrigated by it. The serious problems of large seepage of water due to wind erosion will be greatly reduced by plantation of trees all along the banks of the canal.

The development of industries in Karachi and rapid increase in irrigated area and agricultural output in west Punjab and Sindh with use of natural gas from the Sui field in Baluchistan illustrates the possibilities that would become realities with discovery of gas.

What Next

Increase in the Number of Tourists:

Make the 3 day Delhi-Agra-Jaipur circle a four-day circle by including a visit from Jaipur to the game sanctuary and back within a day. This would be possible if the road from Jaipur to the game sanctuary is improved so much that motor vehicles can easily go to the sanctuary and back in a day. The sanctuary has the unique feature of having tigers and other wild animals and a fort with great historical value.

Make the road to the fort from its base negotiable by elephants as the road to the Amber palace in Jaipur is at present. Restore the original majesty of the palace by repairs to it and repair the quality of the soldiers and other servants of the palace. The place where Queen Padmini and her fellow wives of soldiers committed suicide should be very well maintained. Trained guides should explain in detail the story of the *Pathan* invader Allauddin Khilji, the Raja and Queen Padmini of Ranthambhore. The sanctuary is unique in that it has wild animals, exotic birds and Ranthambhore Fort which has the legend of unfilled desire of a *Pathan* ruler of Delhi to catch a glimpse of a queen of legendary beauty. The road to it can be negotiated easily by jeeps and elephants.

Make Maanpur and Raipur model villages so that families coming from Jaipur by road and those coming from Delhi by train can see village life first hand.

The standard of living is now comparable to that in village Otalan of Punjab in 1961 with the following exception :

(i) Liberation of girls was much grater in Otalan even in 1963 than in the Rajasthan villages even now.
(ii) A large number of young men of both *Jats* and the scheduled castes went to the army. Very few young men from this village go to the army.
(iii) Improvement of supply of electricity by RSEB will greatly reduce cost of irrigation and contribute to increase in production.
(iv) The leaders of the hamlets of the *Chamaar* and the *Meenas* were and continue to be cultivators of more than average landholdings.

The Future

There is little doubt that increases in income and consumption, improvement in education and health and attendant rise in aspirations of people of all castes will continue during the next two decades. Production of wheat and mustard in the cool season will continue to increase by more efficient use of chemical fertilizers, pesticides and irrigation. More dependable supply of electricity by the Rajasthan State Electricity Board will greatly reduce the cost of irrigation and thus the cost of production, increase in income of farmers, increase in comfort of those who have electricity in their homes and saving in foreign exchange.

With rise in income and consumption, increase in education of children and improvement of health of women, children and men, there have been major changes in attitudes and aspirations of people of all castes during the last four decades 1961-2001. Women of all castes have accepted the need for family planning, mention of which was repugnant to them in 1961. Wives of *Meena* farmers with small landholdings realize that their landholding is small and can provide work for only one son; the others would have to work as share croppers and supplement their income by unskilled labour in Maan Town market or repair of the railway track. Wives of *Chamaars* and other scheduled castes realize similarly that even two sons could not find enough work as sharecroppers on land or as non-agricultural labourers. With reduction in infant mortality, they are not afraid that most of their children would die in infancy and they would be left childless. However, it is not certain that the realization has led to smaller families so far.

In 1961, only young men of the three high castes—*Brahmin, Mahajan* and *Rajput*—aspired to and did become white-collar workers. Some *Chamaars* had begun to get into such jobs; but the *Meenas* were not interested. Now even *Meenas* are aspiring to get these jobs. Furthermore, the high castes are educating their sons to become college graduates or professionals who will get posts with much higher salaries than those of workers in the district; no matter that they would live at long distances from their homes.

Mr. Fateh Singh himself is living now with a modern woman from Gujarat who is running a boutique from her house bringing the latest in ladies fashion to Sawai Madhopur elite and the foreign tourists. She had come to work with Dastkar centre located just outside the sanctuary. The tourists love to spend an evening with Fateh Singh in his sprawling farmhouse with most elegant layout for dinner by fireside and listening to stories of his life with the tigers in the sanctuary.

Most of the people of this area, all except some *Rajputs, Mahajans* or *Brahmins* or *Meenas* with large landholdings, were poor in 1961. There had already been major changes in political, economic and social conditions during the previous 15 years (after Independence when the first study was done), which had been accepted by the people. The *Rajputs* and other *jagirdars* had reconciled themselves to their changed status of non-cultivating managers of their land, which had been left to them for self-cultivation. The *Meena* cultivators were happy that they had got full and heritable rights to the land that they had been cultivating. The *Chamaars* had ceased to flay the hides and skins of dead animals or do unpaid work in the houses of the *jagirdars*, which they had been obliged to do earlier. Most of them had got allotted cultivable wasteland, which had become available following abolition of *jagirdari*. They were trying desperately to be recognized as a clean caste, the equals of the *Meenas*. They and the *Meenas* had given up drinking and eating meat so that they could be recognized as a clean cultivating caste, the equivalent of the *Jats* or *Gujjars*.

Sanskritization in occupations and aspirations are very much visible among the *Meenas* and the *Chammars*. Since the *Chamaars* could not draw water from the wells of the high castes or worship in their temples, they had obtained grants from the Community Development department to improve the wells in their hamlets and had built their own temple. Practice of untouchability had been declared an offence and was disappearing in both rural and urban areas. By 1961 representatives of all castes elected to the *Panchayat* of both Maanpur and Raipur sat together to conduct the business of the statutory *Panchayats*. Furthermore, men of all castes drank tea from the same two shops located in Maan Town market. The *Sarpanchs* of both Raipur and Maanpur were from the high castes in 1961. By 2001, although the *Sarpanch* of the Maanpur *Panchayat* was a *Mahajan,* that of Raipur was a woman of the *dhobi* (washerman) caste. People of the high caste or the cultivators did not respect her but there was no petition pending with the Collector requesting her removal. In Maanpur also, there had been periods when a *Meena* occupied the post.

There has been large investment by the State government in appointing agricultural extension and veterinary officers; opening schools, hospitals and dispensaries, providing loans through cooperative societies and branches of nationalized banks located in both Maanpur and Raipur and the Land Mortgage Bank for current cultivation, for improvement of cropland or buying tractors, pump sets and other machines and building houses. At the same time, as their income has increased, the people have themselves made large investments in buying tractors, pump sets, and other machines and improved seed, fertilizers and pesticides. Large investment has been made by the State also in rural electrification and in construction of tubewells for lifting water to overhead tanks, which supply drinking water to large number of homes in all these villages. The villagers have constructed the overhead tanks, which cost about Rs. 4 lakh each in Raipur and Maanpur and somewhat less in Bijaipur. This expenditure shows the value that they now attach to having adequate and safe drinking water.

These changes in lifestyle, attitudes, in political structures and in the desire of the government and political parties to empower people and realization that development of rural areas is an essential component for self-sustainable development exist. We have no doubt that the direction of development in the villages recorded above will proceed at much greater speed than witnessed during the last 40 years because massive development inputs of the past half a century have already started bringing out the desired results and with additional support and investment the area will experience exponential growth.

The above is a micro study of technological change in agriculture, rise in income and consumption of people of all castes, rise in social status of the scheduled castes and changes in inter-caste relations that have occurred over large areas of eastern Rajasthan as well as in adjoining areas of western Madhya Pradesh and over large areas in several other States.

ANNEXURE 16.1

Rajasthan, A State Study (2000)
Swedish International Development Agency (SIDA)

This is a compilation of statistics about Rajasthan and its various districts with detailed explanatory notes on the tables. The coverage is exhaustive because all sectors of the economy from per capita income and incidence of poverty to agriculture and animal husbandry are covered. The social sectors include total population; its growth rate during 1981-91, literacy rates among males and females and health status of the population. There are a large number of small black and white maps, showing boundaries of various districts besides a large number of tables. All the tables have explanatory notes on them. About half of the tables give aggregates about Rajasthan while others give district-wise details on the subject of the tables. The explanatory notes explain that the Rajasthan Government has made successful efforts in several areas such as:

(i) increasing production of milk in northern Rajasthan and organizing milk producers' cooperatives on the pattern of Amul dairy in Gujarat in order to supply milk to Delhi, Jaipur and other towns;

(ii) increasing production of meat by improving breeds of sheep. The owners of both the bovine and ovine animals are given instructions on preventive diseases of cows and sheep and given regular injections to all the stock in case of outbreak of a disease; and

(iii) promoting tourism by successful advertising and increasing facilities for stay of foreign and Indian tourists to places of pleasure and religious tourism—Jaipur, Udaipur and Jaisalmer (pleasure tourism) and Ajmer, Ranakpur and Mt. Abu (religious tourism).

The emphasis in various Five Year Plans has changed from projects aimed at increasing agricultural output to industrial development, improvement of infrastructures especially by building roads and poverty alleviation programmes. Emphasis on increase in agricultural output continues.

Among the cities in Rajasthan, none except small percentages of the populations in Jaipur, Jodhpur and Udaipur have access to piped water supply with the result that easily preventable diseases such as malaria, diarrhoea, dysentery and tuberculosis are common. This, despite a large network of primary health centres at the Community Development Block level, hospitals at district headquarters and a large number of private practitioners in the cities. The most disease prone areas have been indicated.

The literacy rate is very low. In 1991, only 20 per cent of the females and 55 per cent of the males were literate. There is great difference in the literacy rate between urban and rural areas. In urban areas 65 per cent of the population was literate in 1991, in rural areas it was only 39 per cent. However, even these dismal figures indicate a great improvement over the situation in 1951 when only 9 per cent of the population was literate. Despite this progress, the figure for the State is much lower than the all India average of about 40 per cent. However, life expectancy at birth is close to the all India average, so is child mortality. The family planning programme has not been too successful. Average number of births per woman is 4.6 compared to 3.6 for all India.

Rajasthan remains a backward State despite efforts of the government and NGOs to increase agricultural production, literacy, percentage of children going to school and improve health and productivity of the population. This is due primarily to environmental constraints. Two examples illustrate this. Almost half of the area of the State is desert or semi-desert and is visited by severe drought in one or two years out of every three. In the drought years, all efforts of the government are directed towards providing food and water to people in the drought affected areas and fodder for their livestock. Despite large expenditure by the government and large financial assistance from the Central Government, thousands of people and tens of thousands of animals die. More than 10 per cent of the area in the south is hilly and is inhabited by tribal who are very backward. Economic development in this area is difficult and efforts aimed at it have not yielded quick results. Two reasons for this are: bureaucratic delays and misappropriation of funds by officials and the politicians in-charge of expenditure of the programme. The latter is indicated by a recent incident when the tribal attacked those who were in-charge of distributing funds for their development in Rajsamund (*The Economist*, London, January 13-19, 2001, pp. 29-39).

Beginning with a project to reduce incidence of guinea worm in Udaipur division to improvement of water supply in villages of the division in the mid-1980s, SIDA has undertaken a number of projects to promote economic and social development in Rajasthan. This book is a part of the effort.

ANNEXURE 16.2

Women in the Changing Society : A Study of Social and Occupational Change among Women of Three Castes in Three Villages of Sawai Madhopur in Eastern Rajasthan

Kamla Nath

Any study of social change which does not show how women participate in the change process and how change affects them is incomplete. Dr. Nath, the author of the main study of social changes in villages of Sawai Madhopur district in Eastern Rajasthan described in the chapter studied the changes relating to occupation and social status of particular castes and those resulting from the new political experiences of rural people. These and other changes currently in progress are bound to have their influence on the women. They affect the position of women in the home and in the community, their participation in economic activity and in decision-making; they affect customs of marriage, divorce, and remarriage etc. This study is concerned with these and other aspects of social change. This study, though inadequate, helps build up a fuller picture of social change in this area. The initial study was done in 1961. The changes in the areas covered by the study and observed in 2001 resurvey have been described in the Chapter at the appropriate places. The following description and analysis is based on the 1961 findings only.

The study is divided into four major areas:[1]

(i) certain aspects of consumption—notably food, dress and ornaments, and housing;
(ii) attitudes towards education of girls and towards treatment of disease;
(iii) experience with development programmes designed especially for women; and
(iv) marriage and the family—customs relating to marriage, *e.g.*, age at marriage, selection of spouse, dowry and bride price, divorce and widow remarriage; the position of women in the family and the joint family.

Method

For this study we selected three groups—the high caste, *Brahmins* (of

Raipur); the cultivating caste, *Meenas* (of Bijaipur) and the lowest caste, the *Chamaars* (of Chainpur) from three different villages This method of the study, about adoption of three castes from three different villages rather than of selecting a sample of three castes from a multi-caste village like Raipur was preferred in spite of the advantage of the latter method because data on economic activity of different castes and their social inter-relation were already available for example for village Raipur. But the method of selecting two single caste villages and studying only *Brahmins* of Raipur, even though it involved more work, was selected because it depicted more clearly the effects of change influences on living patterns, attitudes, and social custom of the different segments of rural society in this area. The *Meenas* of Bijaipur are as unresponsive to non-agricultural employment as all the *Meenas* of Raipur (or of the area generally). But the *Brahmin* and the *Chamaar* group selected for the study are ahead of their counterparts—the high castes and the scheduled castes—in most villages of this area, both in acceptance of new economic opportunities and adoption of urban patterns of living. As a result, the difference in occupation, patterns of living, and social attitude among the three groups selected for the study are sharper than differences among difference castes in a single village. This sharper differentiation makes possible a clearer perception of the different ways in which change influence are affecting different segments of rural society.

The study collected demographic and detailed household data as well as data on size of holding, cultivation, and economic activities of each member of the household for the two single caste villages while similar data for Raipur had already been collected for the study conducted by V. Nath and is given in Tables 16.3 and 16.4. Data on the major areas of this study were collected in the second phase, based on interviews with women of the sample households and group discussions with them and other women of the castes.

The purpose of the study was not too well understood in the *Meena* and *Chamaar* villages in the beginning, and the women were suspicious that the wife of the District Collector should visit them and ask so many questions. But as the study progressed suspicion gave way to confidence and, especially in the Meena village, to affection and warmth. The affectionate and cheerful meetings with the Meena men and women in visits to their village during the latter part of the survey, and afterwards, was one of the most rewarding aspects of this study.

The *Meenas* of Bijaipur

Bijaipur is a small village of 63 households (population 321) located three miles from the district headquarters, railway station colony and four miles from Sawai Madhopur town. It is easily reached from the colony and Sawai Madhopur town, with which it is connected by a tarred road and a regular bus service. Of the 63 households, 55 are *Meenas,* 3 *Lohars,* 2 *Ranas* and one each of *Kumhar, Khatik* and *Brahmin*. For all practical purpose, it is a *Meena* village

Economic Activities: Nearly all the *Meena* households (53 out of 55) are cultivators. Cultivation is the sole means of livelihood in most households; but in a few households, one or two young men have taken up casual wage labour, mostly at the railway station. Women work on the family holdings and do not normally work for wages. Altogether, labour, agricultural or non-agricultural, is of minor importance in the economy of the group.

The total area cultivated by the 53 cultivating households is 1,014 acres, an average of 19.1 acres per household. Most households (41 out of 53) cultivate between 15 and 30 acres. The landholding position is not unsatisfactory. But since most of the land is not irrigated and grows only foodgrains, the income of most households is low.

The irrigated area—123 acres—gets its water from the village tank across the road from the main entrance to the village. Irrigation water is for the *rabi* crops, principally wheat and barley; the *kharif* crops are not irrigated. The tank is used also for bathing laundering and watering animals. But its water is not used for drinking.

Jowar (sorghum) in the *kharif* and wheat, barley and gram in the *rabi* are the principal crops grown. The best lands are reserved for cultivation of wheat, which is the prized crop. The other *rabi* grains or mixtures of grains (wheat-barley, gram-barley) are sown in lands which do not have enough moisture or fertility for wheat. The unirrigated *rabi* crops depend entirely on the conserved subsoil moisture of the preceding monsoon. In years of low rainfall, the area under wheat is reduced and that under the other *rabi* grain increases, because most fields have sufficient moisture only for the latter.

In other words, the agricultural economy of the village is almost entirely dependent upon production of foodgrains, principally Jowar and wheat, barley and gram. These meet the people's needs for foodgrains and their sale is the only source of cash. This situation is not unusual in small villages of this area in which most of the land is not irrigated. The land of Bijaipur is considered to be quite fertile by the local staff of the Revenue Department; an average *Meena* household, depending solely upon cultivation of about 20 acres of single cropped land to produce grain for both home consumption and sale, can have only a limited cash income[2]. Moreover, since the income comes in lump sums twice a year, a large part of it is spent in clearing past debts, making ornaments and clothes, and meeting expenses of marriages and other ceremonies. As a result, the households have very little disposable cash for the greater part of the year.

The chronic shortage of cash is an important fact in the life of the *Meenas* and one, which sets them off from both the *Chamaar* and the *Brahmin* groups included in this study. The latter depend mainly on wages or salaries and are paid regularly once in a month, or oftener. Many of the differences between the *Meenas* and the other two groups in food and various other aspects of consumption can be adequately understood only if this major economic difference is kept in mind. Of course, the *Meenas* could have higher income by supplementing their earnings from agriculture and wage labour. Their village has an excellent location with reference to the major centres of non-agricultural-employment—the railway station, the cement factory and the Sawai Madhopur town, and one or more young men from each household could work as the earners for a part of the year at least, without undue interference with cultivation. Their failure to avail themselves of this opportunity is due entirely to a basic social attitude. They feel that they are cultivators, and cultivation is the only proper work for them. Non-agricultural labour would be considered by a *Meena* household only if it had no land or if its holding was too small to support it. But even in such cases the first preference is to rent or share-crop additional land. Non-agricultural labour is accepted only if no land is available. Women are not allowed to engage in non-agricultural labour; it is below the dignity of a *Meena* woman. Even agricultural labour for wages on another's land is not considered quite proper, although it is accepted in case of need. The only proper thing for the *Meena* is to cultivate the land, and it is his woman's job to assist him.

Bijaipur, along with the other two villages included in this study, form part of the Sawai Madhopur Community Development Block. Because it was a small village in which there were no serious dissensions, and people cooperated readily with the development workers; it did rather well in the Community Development Programme. The major construction works undertaken with financial assistance from the Block were building of a primary school, a drinking water well and pavement of a large part of the village's central street. This was perhaps the only village in the Block in which the expensive work of paving the village street was undertaken. The primary school was opened during the time of the Community Development Block and is attended by about 25 boys from the village. The paved street gives the village a neat look. It is unfortunate that the attempt to construct the drinking water well was not successful—the well caved in during digging—an additional well located close to the village *abadi* (the inhabited area) is the most keenly felt need of the village. Only one of the other wells in the village is located near the *abadi* and has water throughout the year. The other two are at some distance from the *abadi,* have less water in them and go dry at the height of the summer. The village formerly sent a representative to the *Panchayat* located in a large village 3 miles away. Since December 1960, however, it has been the headquarters of a *Panchayat* comprising four small villages besides Bijaipur. The election in December 1960 of the *Sarpanch* of the new *Panchayat* was keenly contested between two *Meenas* of this village. Its only effect has been to create strong factional rivalries in a village, which had been practically free from them earlier. But the *Panchayat* has not been able to take up any community work or give any other evidence of its being active in the welfare of the village people.

Houses and household goods: The houses lie both sides of a winding street, which extends from one end of the village to the other. Excepting the house of one rich *Meena*, which is *pucca*, all houses are *kutcha*. They have mud walls and floors and roofs of crude baked tiles resting on a frame work of light beams made from branches of tree. The people make the mud bricks, bake the tiles, and build the houses themselves. A house usually consists of three or four rooms built on three sides of a central courtyard. It has also raised platforms (called *pole*) in front, on either side of the entrance door. These platforms serve as a sitting place for the men in the evening; the platform of a popular householder being used as a *hatai*[3]. Cattle are also kept within the house, usually at the back end of the courtyard, some distance from the living rooms. A separate *nauhra* (cattle shed) is the preferred thing; but most families cannot afford it and have to be content with keeping the cattle at the end of the yard or in an enclosure attached to the house. There is another reason also for keeping cattle within the houses. They want to guard against theft or damage to their animals by a hostile neighbour. The rooms are all purpose; everyone serves as living room. Actually, life is not lived in the rooms to any extent. The men, and most women and children, work out in the fields most of the day. In the summers they sleep outdoors, in the yard or outside the house in the village street. The rooms are essentially places for keeping things—grains, *charpoys* and other crude furnitures, bedding and clothing. Only in the winters or on rainy nights during the monsoons, they are used as bedrooms. Food is also cooked in the open for most of the year; a corner of one of the room is used as a kitchen only during the winter or on rainy days.

Many houses have two or more households living in them; they are of course congested. The 55 *Meena* households (and two non-*Meena* households who share houses with them) used a total of 31 occupied dwellings. Only 19 of these were occupied by one household each; all the others had two or more households living in them:

	Dwelling	*Households*
One household per dwelling	19	19 "
Two " " "	4	8 "
Three" " "	6	18 "
Six " " "	2	12 "
Total	31	57 "

One would not expect such congestion in a small village of cultivators. It arises partly from poverty and partly from the fact that village has no place to expand its *abadi.* The lands on all sides of the village *abadi* are irrigated; the best in the village and their owners will not give them up. Another contributing factor is the prevailing practice of giving a room or two within the family house to each married son and daughter-in-law when they want to live separately. Additional rooms within the house will be constructed whenever the family can afford to do this, but the immediate need is met simply by crowding the rest of the family.

The interiors of the rooms are poor; the most conspicuous articles are a few *charpoys*, earthen pots and brass or aluminum pots, one or more iron suitcases, and the little clothing the family owns. Most of the men and women own only three or four ensembles at any one time. Furnitures and objects of interior decoration are conspicuous by their absence. The prevailing drabness is relieved only by cheap pictures or calendars with pictures of Hindu gods and goddesses, film stars or national leaders like Gandhi and Nehru. Stores of grains also kept within the rooms, usually in one or more big earthen cylinders (*kothis). Kothis* are usually decorated with crude designs painted in white lime or red clay; some of the designs were quite attractive, and a few even had small pieces of mirrors fixed to them. The *Kothis* are used for storing milk, curd, cooked food, and money. Several households have large iron cylinders (also called *kothis*) about twice the size of a beer barrel. These are used for storing drinking water at the time of feasts on marriages and other occasions. In recent years, they have become popular as wedding gifts.

The houses, though extremely modest and bare looking, are quite comfortable. The mud walls and tile roofs keep them cool in summer and warm in winter. The *pucca* houses of the *Brahmins* of Raipur are much less comfortable, especially in the summer when they get quite hot. The houses in the *Chamaar* village, with their small, congested rooms and roofs of corrugated iron sheets[4] get unbearably hot in the summer and are the most uncomfortable of all. The women do quite a lot of work in building and maintain the houses.

Dress and Ornaments

The dress of the *Meena* women consists of a *ghagra* (wide, billowy skirt reaching down to the ankles), a *lugari* (big scarf usually about three yards long) and a *kanchili*—a brief, tight, blouse-like garment which leaves the back and midriff of the wearer open, and covers only the breasts and upper arms. Nothing is worn above this garment while the women work in the field or in the house. But on more formal occasions, a long, loose fitting blouse, *kabza* is worn on top of the *kanchili*.

The *ghagra* and *lugari* are made of coarse cotton cloth. The cloth for these garments used to be woven by local weavers and dyed and printed by dyers and calico printers in Sawai Madhopur town or large villages of this area. The locally-woven coarse cloth has been completely replaced by mill-made cloth; but the local dyeing and printing continues. The cloth is dyed almost invariably in dark colours—maroon, deep red, navy blue, or black (dark colours are preferred so that the garments will not show dirt), and printed on simple traditional designs. Traditionally, small variations in design and colour schemes identified different castes, so that it was possible to know the caste of the wearer simply by looking at her clothes. This is no longer the case, mainly because the traditional dress materials have been replaced by mill-made fabrics of great variety in design and colour. *Chamaars* and *Brahmins* have completely replaced locally dyed and printed dress materials with nice fabrics and among *Brahmins* the *ghagra* and *lugari* have themselves been replaced by the *saree* and the blouse. Departures from the traditional garments have been the minimum in case of the *Meenas*.

Traditional colours and designs are invariably worn by women when they are at work in the home or in the field, and it is only on marriages and other festive occasions that garments of fine cotton or rayon are worn.

All women wore silver or silver-coated ornaments. Three pieces, the *khagali* (heavy necklace weighing two pounds or more), *kari* (anklet) and a bangle worn above the elbow, are made of silver. Besides these, they wear a number of silver-coated iron bangles, which cover large portion of both arms. Each woman wears ornaments weighing 6 to 8 pounds. The weight and number of ornaments has increased during the last 20 years, as these people have become relatively prosperous. Earlier, most families could not afford to buy the full complement of ornaments.

There was striking similarity in the dress and ornaments of all *Meena* women, including those of the one rich *Meena* household[5]. As dress and ornaments are the most common indicators of economic differences, greater variation was anticipated: it was expected that the women of the rich households would have more ornaments, or gold ornaments. It was also expected that they would not be working in the fields. But in all these respects the women of the rich household were no different from the other *Meena* women. The only one rich household has demonstrated its wealth by building a *pucca* house. But the interior of the house was very similar to that of all others in the village, and the absence of furniture and urban consumptions goods was equally noticeable in it.

The men wear a white *kurta* (loose-fitting long shirt) a *dhoti*, and a turban. Stout country-made shoes of similar designs are worn by both men and women. Several men were seen wearing silver anklets or gold ear-rings. The girls wear the same dress as the women, and most boys wear the same dress as the men. But the few boys who go to the primary school wore a white or khaki shirt and khaki half-pants—the prescribed uniform.

Food

Meena food is very simple. In fact, lack of variety, inadequate attention to cooking, and deficiency in essential nutrients (fats, animal proteins and the vitamins and minerals supplied by fruit and vegetables) is its chief characteristic. All the households eat *bajra* (barley and gram mixed), *jowar* and wheat. Even the most prosperous household has not switched over to exclusive use of superior foodgrain, wheat. The *rabi* grains are eaten mainly in the summer and in the rainy period—*i.e.,* after the *rabi* harvest, while *jowar* is eaten during the first-half of the year. The flour for *chapattis* (flat pancakes made with flour) is ground by the women at home, in spite of the fact that there are flour mills in several adjoining villages to which they could easily take their grain. *Chapattis,* eaten with a vegetable or pulse or with crushed raw onions; chillies or raw mangoes (in season), constitute the entire meal. The woman of the house tries to finish most of the cooking for the day in the morning before she goes for work in the field. In the summer, the *chapattis* for the entire day are made in the morning, but the curry for the evening meal is prepared only in the evening because curry made in the morning would spoil by the evening. In winter the cooked food will last until the next meal or even until the next day without spoiling; but as people want to eat hot food, *chapattis* are made fresh at every meal and only the curry from the previous meal is used after reheating. The children have to adept to this regimen. No food is prepared for them when they get hungry in the afternoon; they have to be content with munching *chapattis* prepared in the morning until something is cooked in the evening. This creates a serious nutrition problem.

There is no other local production of vegetables, because there are no *Mali* households in the village[6]. Some vegetables are bought in exchange for wheat when a vendor comes to the village. Otherwise pulses—mostly the home produced *moong* and gram—are the mainstay for curries. Onions, raw mangoes, green leaves of gram and *methi* (a leafy fodder crop) are also used in curries. Onions are the staple seasoning: they are used throughout the year. Raw mangoes are a principal ingredient in curries in the early summer, when they are in season. Consumption of other fruits is negligible. A little fruit is bought occasionally in the town.

Consumption of milk is low and highly variable. Most households have one or more milch animals (cows or buffaloes) and have some milk during the monsoon months and two post-monsoon months, when there is grass in the fields and the animals give milk. But during the rest of the year, they are without milk. Milk is not sold in the market. Few households have a surplus to sell, but even if they did, they would not sell it because of the strong prejudice against sale of milk by cultivators.

The shortage of milk is of course reflected in the children's health: there are many cases of debility, and even death, from malnutrition. A number of cases of *sukha* (marasmus, a disease caused by acute protein deficiency in which the child becomes very thin) were seen in the village.

Consumption of fats is very small. *Ghee* and oils are the only fats used in daily cooking. Nine out of the 13 sample families reported consumption of about 2 pounds of *ghee.* Sweet dishes like *halwa* (a pudding) are eaten, mostly at feasts and rarely otherwise. Gur (unrefined brown sugar), eaten raw, is the only sweetening in the daily diet. No consumption of meat, fish or poultry was reported by women of any household: they all claimed to be vegetarian. The *Meenas* were not vegetarians in the past, but the recent Meena Reform Movement, aiming at raising their social status has emphasized abstinence from meat and drink, and now no one would admit these practices. Smoking the *hukkah* (hubble-bubble) and *beedies*[7] is common among the men, but women do not smoke.

In summary, cereals, supplemented by pulses and a few vegetables, constitute almost the entire diet. Consumption of animal proteins is minimal, being confined to a little milk or buttermilk if and when the household has these. Even consumption of fats and sugar is very small. Poverty, social attitudes (*e.g.,* those against growing vegetables and producing milk for sale), and food taboos (*e.g.,* not eating flesh) combine to produce a cereal-dominated diet. The monotony of food and lack of attention to cooking are better understood if two further facts are also kept in view.

(i) the desire to keep cash expenditure for food at a minimum. This stems partly from a serious lack of money, but it also reflects the traditional agricultural way of life: farmers produce their own food and seldom buy food.
(ii) the time spent in cooking has been reduced to a minimum because women work in the fields.

Personal Hygiene and Medical Care

Women bathe about once a week in the winter and twice a week in the summer. They go to the village tank when the men are not around. During the rainy season, they bathe in small *nullaha* (rain water drain). Women wash their hair with black mud taken from the tank once every two or three weeks and apply *ghee* (clarified butter) to their hair afterwards. Clothes are changed every week or two and are washed with or without soap. Women do not generally use soaps for bathing, but in recent years some of the men and especially the boys who go to the school have started using soap. The soap used is generally a washing soap and not toilet soap. There is no use of any cosmetics. Any small ailment is ignored at first, in the hope that it will be cured by itself. But if this does not happen, then, in case of aliments of women and children, the old *Brahmin* woman who is the *Gram Kaki*[8] is consulted. She prescribes traditional home remedies. Alternatively, a barber's wife from an adjoining village is consulted. If the aliment does not disappear with such treatment, one of the two private practitioners in the town is consulted. One of this is a trained *vaidya* but other is only a *pansari*,[9] (seller of herbal medicines) with no formal medicine training. The medicines prescribed by these practitioners are taken half-heartedly; the general belief is that the patient will get well if he/she is destined to. The doctors in the hospital are consulted last of all; only in cases of serious sickness, and often when it is too late. One reason they hesitate to go to the hospital is that it is very crowded and they have to wait a long time before they can see the doctors. There are no *dais* (midwife) in the village. The work of midwife was done by a *Chamaar* woman when the *Chamaars* lived in the village. But since they left a few years ago the village has no midwife within it and relies on the services of a midwife from a neighbouring village. She is untrained and has no conception of sanitation or modern midwifery practices. If there is any delay in her arrival, the other women of the family or the neighbourhood help the mother. But they will not cut the umbilical cord, because this is considered to be midwife's work, which a *Meena* woman should not do. Sometimes, in case of trouble during labour, the man may, on the advice of the midwife, take his wife to the hospital. Such cases were rare.

Very high infant mortality results from such practices in nutrition and medical care. The women in the 13 sample households reported that of the 64 children ever born to them, only 34 were living. Most of the deaths occurred when the children were very young. The main causes of deaths were reported to be "*sukha*" (marasmus,) "diarrhoea", "the evil eyes", and "not known". These attitudes are typically fatalistic and ignorant and are in marked contrast with those of the *Brahmin* and the *Chamaar* groups studied. Even the latter showed a greater readiness to do something about sickness.

Education

The village primary school is attended by about 25 boys. A few of the older boys go to the middle school in a large village, four miles away. No girl goes to school. The reasons given for this were :

(i) "Education of girls is of no use. The work that a girl has to do when she grows up, in the home and in the field can be done very well without education. Education will only make her sophisticated; she will start behaving like a high caste woman and will not be prepared to work in the fields".

(ii) "The presence of girls is necessary in the home, because they have to look after their younger brothers and sisters when the mother is working in the field, and they help the mother in small household tasks when she comes back from work."

(iii) "Sending girls to a boy's school is not good".

Development Programmes for Women

The development Programmes for women (under the Community Development Programme) included organization of cultural and recreational activities through *Mahila Mandals* (women's club); organization of classes to teach useful skills like stitching, embroidery and knitting; extension work in nutrition, personal hygiene, sanitation and child care; and home improvement, especially adoption of such improvements as the smokeless *chulha* (hearth) also called the *magan chulha*[10] for cooking and *jaali*[11] (cupboard with wire gauze doors and sides) for storing food. The activities were organized by the *Gram Sevika* (woman village-level worker) and the Lady Social Education Organizer (LSEO), with local assistance of the *Gram Kakis.* The *Gram Sevika* and the LSEO are trained extension workers, forming part of the staff of the community development block (now called the *Panchayat Samiti*). The *Gram Kaki* (lit. aunt of the village) is generally a middle-aged woman who has a little education, some competence in crafts, and a progressive outlook. She is an honorary worker who is paid an honorarium of Rs. 15 per month and is expected to do extension work among the women while staying in her own home. The institution of *Gram Kaki* is peculiar to Rajasthan, though many other States have, or have had in the past, similar workers under other names.

At the time of this survey the *Panchayat Samiti* took no interest in these activities. The *Gram Kaki* of this village is the old woman of the *Brahmin* household. She is a competent woman who is respected by other women and is consulted for small ailments and on various domestic matters. She is the best informed and most intelligent woman in the village and is without doubt the most suitable person for this job. She has been doing this work for some years. But the development activities have not made much progress. The *Gram Kaki* explained that she had been told by the extension worker to concentrate on two improvements, the *Magan*

Chulha and the *jaali*. She had done this, but neither of the improvements had been accepted.

The *Magan Chulha* is designed to save time and fuel in cooking: it has three openings on which as many dishes can be cooked at the same time. But the village women did not consider it useful, because they rarely cooked more than one dish for a meal. The village women gave two reasons for non-acceptance of the *jaali* due to its cost, and the fact that it occupied space in an already congested house. Some of them explained that they did not need the *jaali* because they did not keep much cooked food for any length of time so the *jaali* is considered to be an unnecessary expense. A sewing class had been organized in the village during the time of the Community Development Block. But the machine had been out-of-order for several months and the women continue to stitch some garments by hand needles while getting the others prepared by tailors in town.

Marriage

Child marriage is the norm. Girls are married off anytime between the ages of 7-10 and the boys by 10-14. Boys who are not married at this age find it difficult to marry later. They or their parents have to pay a heavy bride price or have to be satisfied with a widow or a girl who has been left by her earlier husband or one who suffers from some physical defect.

Gauna or *Saiya,* a ceremony to mark the commencement of conjugal living, takes place 3, 5, or 7 years after marriage, when the girl is 14 to 16 years old. Most marriages are between residents of villages located within 20 miles[12] of each other. There is no marriage within the village, because these people consider children who live in the same village to be brothers and sisters. Three *gotras* (lineages) are avoided in fixing marriages: those of the father, the mother and the father's mother. Their main considerations in choosing a bridegroom for the girl are:

(i) that the family has enough land and a number of cows and bullocks; and

(ii) that the boy is healthy.

The boy's parents similarly want the girl's family to have plenty of land. But an even more important consideration with them is that the girl be healthy and free from physical defects (like blindness or lameness). As the girl has to work in the home and the fields, they want to be sure that she will make a good worker. The boy's education or the girl's beauty is not really considered.

Most marriages are celebrated on the *Akha Teej*[13] day, the popular saying being that one does not have to consult a *Brahmin* for fixing a marriage on this day. The choice of a day at this time of the year is in perfect accord with the prosperity level and work cycle of the cultivators. The *rabi* crop has been harvested, and there is no work to be done in the fields till the onset of the monsoon which is some two months away. The prosperity curve is at its peak, because the *rabi* harvest has been gathered and the *kharif* was harvested only four months earlier. But precisely because a marriage on this day saves expense, its avoidance has become a status symbol.

Dowry and Bride Price

The boy's parents have to incur considerable expenditure at the time of marriage. They must make heavy silver ornaments for the girl. The financial status of the boy's parents is judged by the kind of *manda* (marriage feast) they give and the weight of the silver ornaments. The weight of ornaments considered 'adequate' has increased by a factor of three or four during the course of one generation ! Gold ornaments are a rarity: even a very prosperous *Meena* would give only one or two small ornaments of gold, weighing not more than one or two *tolas*[14] (little more than ten grams) along with silver ornaments. The expenses of the girl's parents are limited. There is no dowry; the only gifts they give are two dresses (silk or cotton), one for the boy and the other for the girl. In most cases they bear the cost of feeding the marriage party and other expenses of marriage; but not in others. All this, as well as the practice of paying *jhagra* to the husband when a woman leaves him to live with another man, indicates the prevalence of bride price in the past. Payment of bride price is not very common now, and *roti-beti* (*i.e.*, giving the daughter in marriage without any monetary consideration and also bearing the expenses of feeding the marriage party) is the more common practice.

Dissolution of Marriage and Widow Remarriage

There is no formal dissolution of marriage or re-marriage of a widow; but sitting in *nata*, a term which applies both to a widow going to live with another man and a woman leaving her husband to live with another man, is common[15]. Similarly, the man is free to leave one woman and take another as wife. A widower, like Hindu widowers of all castes, can remarry. Leaving a spouse to take another is not considered very wrong, and the caste would not think of sanctions against either the man or the woman concerned. The woman who is widowed or is left by her husband goes to live with her parents until another husband is found for her. There is no stigma or shame attached to this, nor do her parents feel that she is a burden to them. She works for her keep while she stays with them. In fact, the economic relation of women to farm work is the key to the entire structure of social relations and customs.

Jhagra: In all cases where a woman is married to one man and goes to live with another, whether this happens before *gauna* or after, the first husband is entitled to receive from the new husband compensation, which is given the extremely significant name *jhagra* (dispute). The amount is decided by the *Panchayat* (prominent persons of the caste, or the village) on an *ad hoc* basis. Usually the amount they fix has some relation to the marriage expenditure of the first husband, especially on ornaments and other gifts for the wife and money payment, if any, to her family. But as the word *Jhagra* indicates, settlements of compensation money is frequently the cause of dispute, and husbands and their families are anxious to avoid a situation in which they have to claim *jhagra* for a woman who has gone away.

The disputes and violence do not remain confined to the parties concerned; families of the girl, the husband and the second man, but are taken up by caste men of their respective villages and even by those of surrounding villages. Very often, the people of the aggrieved party make an attempt to kidnap the woman or any other woman from the second man's village. This practice based on the principle of "blood for our blood: we shall take a woman from the village which has taken away a woman belonging to us", has greatly declined in recent decades; but it appears to have been the accepted practice to settle such cases in the past when enforcement of law and order by the State was not so effective.

The Joint Family

The joint family[16] is not as common as might be expected. Of the 55 *Meena* households in the village, only 11 could be considered joint families. In 10 of these, one married son and daughter-in-law were living with husbands' parents. In the eleventh household, however, two married brothers were living together along with their widowed mother. In the 13 sample households there were only two joint families. At the time of *gauna*, the young wife invariably comes to live in the home of her husband's parents. She generally lives with them for a few years.

Thereafter, quarrels begin between the mother-in-law and the daughter-in-law and the son and daughter-in-law start a separate kitchen, usually in a separate room in the same house. Separation of cooking may or may not be accompanied by separation of cultivation. It is not uncommon for land to be cultivated jointly for several years afterwards. Generally one son and wife do not find it too difficult to live with her parents-in-law; the eldest son and his wife may continue to live with his parents for many years, and if there are no other sons, the only son and his wife may live with his parents as long the latter live. The crisis point in the history of the family comes after the *gauna* of the second son, when two daughters-in-law begin to live together in the same house. It is not possible to sustain joint living long after this event, and in most cases the family breaks up into two or more units within a year or two of the second *gauna.* The one case of two married brothers living together mentioned above, is an exception and is recognized as such by all the villagers. The reasons given for the break up are: 'have to do too much households work' and because 'they were not being given enough to eat by their mother-in-law'; 'they were eating better after separation'. Joint family and joint living are undoubtedly held as ideals. But there is no strong feeling against separate living, which is viewed in an unemotional, matter-of-fact way. It should also be noted that separation does not mean a clean and final break between the households concerned. Cultivation may continue to be 'joint' for several years after separate living has commenced, and even after cultivation has been separated the bullocks may continue to be jointly owned.

The *Chamaars* of Chainpur

Chainpur consists of 61 *Chamaar* households with a total population of 324. It is located opposite the cement factory, about a mile from the district headquarters' railway station colony.

Chainpur was founded in 1945, by the *Chamaars* of village Surpur after their quarrel with the Meenas (described in Chapter 13 on Caste and Occupational Mobility: A Study of *Berwa Chamaars*). During the last 20 years the original families from Surpur have been joined by a number of *Chamaar* families—some from other villages of this area and others from Surpur who had been settled in industrial centres like Indore, Ujjain and Surajpur (Punjab). Several of the latter have come after establishment of the cement factory, which brought industrial labour similar to that which they were doing. Chainpur is regarded as the village of the *Chamaars* of

Surpur; others are considered outsiders, and if anyone is not liked (*e.g.* the contractor with whom they have been having a quarrel for almost two years), he is considered an intruder.

The village looks fairly clean and attractive at first sight because it is well designed. But a closer look reveals that many of the house sites are congested. Congestion has resulted from continual additions to the original houses to accommodate the rapid increase in numbers.

Economic Activity

Work in the cement factory is the principal economic activity: most of the men and about half of the working women are engaged in it.

Annexure Table 16.2.1 : Occupational Distribution of Adults in Village Chainpur, 1961

	Male	*Female*
Total adults	86	86
Total workers	74	50
Permanent workers in factory	46	2
Skilled	18	—
Unskilled	28	2
Workers with factory contractors	10	24
Self-employed	14	0
Other occupation (mainly cultivation supplemented by casual labour)	4	24

Thus, nearly all the men are working either in the factory itself, or on jobs, which derive sustenance from it. Twenty-six woman workers, more than half of the total, get work in the factory. The remainders take up casual labour from time to time in addition to working in their small plots of land. But they also work either for the contractors working for the cement factory or on small building works in the colony.

While the majority of the men are permanent factory workers, only two women are; all others work as casual labourers for a factory contractor. The fact that the man is considered the principal earner (and gets the better-paid job), the woman's earning role is essentially subsidiary. There is also a tendency for women to stop working when the economic level of the household rises. Labour by the women has begun to be regarded as the product of economic want and even though women of large number of households still work the ambition of every household is counter to this.

The minimum pay of a permanent worker in the factory is Rs. 82 per month. Many get more; some skilled workers make as much as Rs. 150

per month; there is constant endeavour, especially among the men, to get a permanent job in the factory.

The skilled or semi-skilled workers in the factory are mostly young men who work as fitters, helpers, wiremen, drivers, packers, etc. Many men work as masons, shopkeepers, and contractors and have income ranging between Rs. 1,000 and 2,000 per year. The entry of the *Chamaar* into these skilled and entrepreneurial occupations is evidence of their willingness and capacity to take advantage of the varied opportunities for profitable work that an industrial environment offers.

Agriculture is not an important source of livelihood for these people. Of the 61 households in the village 14 are landless and depend entirely upon non-agricultural income; the others have very small holdings (one-third of an acre to five acres). Cultivation is looked after by women and the old folks; the young men help on holidays, and if they are casual labourers they help when they are out of work. However, even though industrial labour is their main source of income, the aspiration to possess and cultivate land continues to be strong among the older people. The younger people, while they do not oppose the demand of their elders, do not show similar interests in agriculture or keenness to possess land.

Income

The income of the 16 samples households ranges between Rs. 400 to Rs. 2,700 a year[17]; the average is a little over Rs. 1,400. The income level of the *Chamaars* is somewhat higher than that of the *Meenas.* In spite of this, *Chamaar* women complained about financial insecurity. In some cases, the husband spent money on drinking and gambling and did not give his wife enough money for the home.

Houses

Many houses have roofs of corrugated iron sheet on one or two rooms. The number of houses with such roof is increasing every year and would increase more rapidly if the sheets were easily available. The iron roofs plus congestion make these houses quite uncomfortable during the summer. Many women complained that their houses were as hot as ovens during the summer days. The *Meena* houses with their tile roofs and open courtyards are infinitely more comfortable, but in spite of this advantage, there is a marked preference for corrugated iron sheets and for the same reason as explained above in case of Bijaipur also.

A higher income level than that of *Meenas*, together with the urban influence of the factory had made *Chamaar* homes quite different from

Meena homes. They contain much more furnitures, crockery, brass and aluminum utensils, hurricane lanterns, kerosene cooking stoves, bicycles, and iron clothes boxes were found in most homes. The rooms looked crowded and less neat than rooms in *Meena* homes, and the distinctive *Meena* paintings on the *kothis* and the walls were conspicuously absent.

Dress and Ornament

Women's dress is basically like that of the *Meena* women. There is increasing use of mill-made cloth. Older men still wear *dhoti, kurta* and turban; their dress is indistinguishable from that of the *Meena* men. But the dress of the young men, who worked as semi-skilled or skilled workers in the cement factory, has undergone a marked change from traditional dress to that of urban middle-class men. Similar changes have occurred among the *Brahmin* young men also. The stimulus in both cases is the same—non-agricultural employment outside the village.

The *Chamaar* women were traditionally not allowed to wear silver ornaments and the *Chamaars* asserting the rights of their women to wear these ornaments was a major issue in the quarrel between them and the *Meenas*. But practically all the *Chamaar* women have all their ornaments made of solid silver. Some of the young *Chamaar* women have even brought small gold ornaments. In matters of dress and ornaments the *Chamaar* have not only attained equality with the *Meenas* but have surpassed them and have begun to adopt some of the practices of the high castes.

Food

Tea drinking is much more widespread than in the other two groups. In the majority of households tea is made regularly in the winter and all members of the household take it. Sweets like *halwa* and *dalia* (two types of porridge) are also made frequently and *Chamaars* consume more sugar than do the *Meenas*. Fruit and sweetmeats are brought occasionally. Consumption of milk is small. Most families use just enough milk for tea. Children go without milk and suffer from malnutrition or sheer starvation until they are old enough to swallow solids. The change to industrial occupation and higher income has increased consumption of both meat and drink. Most sample families eat meat twice a month. Drinking is common among men, and many of the women also drink. Expenditure on smoking is also more than among the *Brahmins* or the *Meenas*, one reason being that most of the *Chamaar* women smoke while the *Brahmin* and the *Meena* women do not.

Sanitation, Personal Hygiene and Medical Care

The village is better off than most others in matters of sanitation. Its planned structure, with a wide, straight central streets, is itself an enormous advantage, but the advantage progressively reduced now by increasing congestion in the house sites. The drinking water supply is much better than in most villages of this area. The drinking water well of the village has abundant sweet water; some years ago the villagers built a well-designed parapet wall and platform for drawing water, bathing, and washing clothes. These were built with financial assistance from the Community Development Block. Paving for the main street of the village had also been promised by the Block staff, but the promise has not been fulfilled. However, lack of pavement in the street causes no great hardship, except that the street is muddy for a few hours after a shower.

Women bathe more frequently than the *Meena* women of Bijaipur. Besides, use of soap is more common in this group than among the *Meenas*; its use was reported by all the sample households. Soap is used for washing clothes and for bathing although many of the older women continue to use mud to wash their hair. Several young women use cheap cosmetics like talcum powder, vaseline, and face cream. All these practices constitute a considerable advance over the practices of *Meena* women of Bijaipur.

This group is better served with medical facilities than either of the other two. Factory labourers are members of the Employees State Insurance Scheme, which covers both workers and families. There is greater consciousness of the need for proper treatment of disease, greater readiness to use the facilities available, and what is most important, greater willingness to spend time and money to be treated, than was the case with the *Meenas.* But it appears that sickness is also somewhat more prevalent in this group than in the other two. There were several cases of serious sickness (particularly tuberculosis) among the sample households, and there were many complaints of minor ailments. The general appearance of the women, in spite of their more varied and richer diet, was not as robust as that of the *Meena* women; and the survival rate of children was not much better than that among the *Meenas*. Of the 84 children born to women in the sample households, only 47 had survived. The higher incidence of serious sickness and the less robust physique may be due to the fact that most of the men and many women have to do work which is arduous and involves exposure to coal and cement dust.

Education

Chamaars are more conscious of value of education than the *Meenas.* Most of the boys of school age (6 to 15 years) go either to the primary school in the village or to the higher secondary school across the road[18]. The latter is run by the cement factory for children of its labourers and other staff. Girls in most families do not go to the school. The few girls who go to the village primary school are all from families of skilled workers or self-employed men whose wives do not work. The reasons given for not sending the girls to school were the same as those given by the *Meena* women: girls are needed in the home to look after younger brothers and sisters when mother is away at work, besides, girls' education is of no use. However, as urban contacts increases, education spreads among young men and more of them get skilled or white-collar jobs, education among the girls will increase. As among the *Brahmins*, the competition for such young men as grooms for their daughters will lead an increasing number of parents to provide more education for their girls.

The Development Programme for Women

As Chainpur is located on a main road near Block headquarters, it was much visited during the period of the Community Development Block. A number of construction works were undertaken and a programme of work among women of instructions in crafts and home improvements as in other villages was organized. The earlier activities, while they must have been beneficial at the time, had not left any appreciable impact; when questioned about them, the women showed no particular interest.

Marriage Customs

The marriage customs of the *Chamaars* are very similar to those of the *Meenas*, and changes in them have also been similar. Until about 20 years ago marriage was a simple affair, which involved little expense. But in recent years marriage expenses have increased considerably, and the trend is towards increasingly elaborate and expensive marriages. As among the *Meenas, roti-beti* is the ideal, and taking bride price, or even the expenses of marriage, is not considered good. There is some hesitation in admitting acceptance of money on the marriage of a girl but not its payment on the marriage of a boy. Women in two households reported that they had given dowry and received bride price at different times, depending upon their circumstances at the time. It is clear that the practices of paying bride price and giving dowry are in a transitional stage. The trend is towards replacement of bride price by dowry. But, bride price is still the norm, commonly restored to when the family is poor.

Widow Remarriage and Dissolution of Marriage

Chamaar customs relating to widow remarriage, dissolution of marriage, and *nata* are similar to those of the *Meenas*. Widow remarriage is freely allowed. Dissolution of marriage is similarly allowed although not favoured; women are sought after for marriage and respected after marriage: they are earning members of the household.

Jhagra is also prevalent in this group as among the *Meenas*.

The Joint Family

Joint families are less common than among the *Meenas*. The usual practice is for the son to start living separately from his parents immediately after, or shortly after *gauna*. Among the 16 sample households, there were only two cases of a married son and daughter-in-law living with his parents. One reason for weakness of the joint family is absence of an economic bond. The bond of dependence upon the family land does not operate in this group; even traditionally the joint family was not as strong among the *Chamaars* as among the cultivators and the high castes.

The Attitude of the Enlightened *Chamaar* Youth

The young men who have skilled or semi-skilled jobs in the factory are in some ways the most significant persons in this group. The young men are keenly aware of the low social status of their caste and of the social disabilities from which it suffers. They are conscious of their superiority to the *Meena* agriculturists—in economic status, in level of living, and in knowledge of the outside world. They are also very conscious of the fact that the government wishes to raise their economic and social status and is taking a number of steps with this end in view. These conflicting influences seem to produce an acute aggressiveness among the young men. In interviews they complained constantly—against the factory[19], against the *Meenas*, against individual officials, and against the government in general.

The *Brahmins* of Raipur

Economic Activity

Detailed data on occupation and economic activity had been collected by V. Nath for his study and are given in Annexure Tables 16.2 and 16.3.

Traditionally these *Brahmins* depend upon rent income from land for their living in the village. Being a literary and priestly caste, they did not cultivate the land themselves but gave it on *batai* and subsisted on the rent share. Some families which had fair-sized irrigated holdings were comfortable; but others with small holdings were quite poor. About sixty years ago men from families with small holdings started to migrate to cities to work as cooks or as priests, the next major change was when educated young men became white-collar workers, and this brought to the caste considerable increases in income and in urban contacts with concomitant changes in ways of living. The changes in food, dress, housing and marital custom described below are closely related to this change in occupation.

A sample of 25 per cent (18 out of 69) of the total *Brahmin* households[20] was selected for the study. The sample households had a total of 53 adults and 25 earners. This is a smaller proportion of earners to total adults than in the other two castes, reflecting the fact that *Brahmin* women do not work outside the homes, while *Meena* and *Chamaar* women do. The earners included 13 white-collar workers from 12 households, 3 "farm managers" and 12 persons in other occupations. The latter include cooks for city merchants (5), priests in the village and outside (5), and two persons working as unskilled workers in the cement factory. In a number of households there was more than one earner, and in practically all there was more than one source of income. The annual income of the households ranged between Rs. 750 and Rs. 4,000.

Houses and Household Goods

The central and south-eastern part of the village is the *Brahmin* quarter. Most of their houses are *pucca,* built entirely of stone and lime mortar; some of these are double-storey. The remaining houses are in various stages of transition from the *kutcha* to the *pucca* state. The *Brahmin* quarter of Raipur is quite congested, in marked contrast to the open look of the *Meenas* and the *Chamaar* villages. One reason for this is the pattern of settlement of the *Brahmin* and other high castes in this area. They live in large numbers only in large or middle sized villages, and their houses are clustered in the central portions of these villages possibly as a security measure.

Annexure Table 16.2.2 : Land-holding and Cultivation by Principal Castes Raipur

Caste	*Total No. of Households*	*No of Households Owning Land*	*Area Owned (acres)*	*Net Area Given Out (-) or taken in (+) for Cultivation. (acres)*	*No. of Cultivating Households*	*Area + Cultivated (acres)*	*Total No. of Workers*	*No. Engaged in Cultivation*
I. High Caste Hindus	101	90	463	-220	17	243	155	21
Brahmin	69	64	294	-121	12	173	98	15
Mahajan	24	22	114	-73	3	41	43	4
II. Cultivating Castes	219	192	+1255	450	184	1705	604	494
Meena	110	101	838	+245	96	1083	301	270
Mali	89	77	313	+183	75	496	251	195
Gujjar	20	14	104	+22	13	126	52	29
III. Artisan Castes	38	25	78	-50	9	28	91	5
Khatik	13	11	45	-35	—	10	21	1
Kumhar	10	4	8	—	4	8	37	—
IV. Scheduled Castes	115	88	307	+94	84	401	250	108
Rehgar	61	52	145	+31	52	176	133	47
Chamaar	35	33	143	+67	30	210	83	56
Koli	10	—	—	—	—	—	16	—
V. Miscellaneous Hindu Castes	19	8	16	+11	5	27	45	9
VI. Moslems	43	30	119	-87	10	32	67	2
Faqir	20	14	19	-10	6	9	30	5
Moslem, other castes	18	13	76	-68	1	8	26	1
Total	535	433	2238	+159	309	2436	1212	639

+In 2000 total area cultivated was 3,000 acre; the area increased due to reclamation of forest land.

Annexure Table 16.2.3 : Caste and Occupation—Principal Castes—Raipur 1961

Caste	Total Number of Households	Total Number of Workers	Number of workers engaged in: Cultivators	Agricultural Labourers (Including halis)	Casual Non-Agricultural Labourers	Service: White Collar	Service: Class IV	Service: Skilled Work	Service: Un-skilled Labour	Commerce	Skilled Work: Traditional Craft or Occupation	Skilled Work: Other	Other Occupations (mainly unskilled labour type)	Total Number of Jobs.
(1)	(2)	(3)	(4)	(5)	(6)	(7)	(8)	(9)	(10)	(11)	(12)	(13)	(14)	(15)
I. High Caste Hindus	101	145	21	—	6	52	10	—	2	23	21	11	10	156
Brahmin	69	98	15	—	5	46	9	—	1	2	11	9	9	107
Mahajan	24	33	4	—	1	4	1	—	1	21	—	2	1	35
II. Cultivating Castes	219	604	494	60	67	2	2	4	20	—	5	—	5	659
Meena	110	301	270	19	14	1	1	1	7	—	—	—	1	314
Mali	89	251	195	35	45	1	—	1	13	—	—	—	1	291
Gujjar	20	52	29	6	8	—	1	2	—	—	5	—	3	54
III. Artisan Castes	38	91	5	—	7	1	1	2	1	—	53	17	37	124
Khatik	13	21	1	—	2	—	—	2	—	—	17	17	—	39
Kumhar	10	37	—	—	—	—	—	—	—	—	12	—	37	49
IV. Scheduled Castes	115	250	108	33	98	—	—	1	22	—	77	1	23	363
Rehgar	61	133	47	29	59	—	—	—	17	—	65	—	—	217
Chamaar	35	83	56	4	22	—	—	—	4	—	—	—	19	105
Koli	10	16	—	—	13	—	—	—	1	—	—	—	3	17
V. Miscellaneous Hindu Castes	19	45	9	6	16	—	3	—	1	—	6	—	6	47
VI. Moslems	43	67	2	—	21	1	1	8	1	—	5	30	19	87
Faqirs	20	30	—	—	12	1	1	1	—	—	—	19	13	47
VII Other castes	18	26	1	—	8	—	—	4	—	—	—	10	4	27
Total	535	1202	639	99	215	56	17	15	146	23	167	59	100	1436

+ Total white collar in 2000 were 250.

Most *Brahmin* homes have the look of middle-class urban homes. But the link with agriculture is also clearly observable. Each house has space for storage of foodgrains. If the family has only one cow it will probably be tied in the courtyard in which case fodder is also stored within the house. The interiors of the houses are neat and well scrubbed. Most housewives pride themselves on the neatness of their houses. But the exteriors are not attractive partly because of the presence of stagnant water explained below. As among the *Meenas* and the *Chamaars*, most *Brahmin* houses contain more than one family.

Dress and Ornaments

The traditional dress of *Brahmin* women was not very different from that of *Meena* women. They wore *ghagra, lugari and kanchi or kabza* made from coarse *khaddar* (hand-spun, hand-woven cloth) and dyed and printed locally. The major difference was in colours: the *Brahmin* women generally wore lighter and brighter colours: *e.g.* orange. The more prosperous *Brahmin* families used silk. Mill-made fabrics began to replace local hand-spun and hand-woven cloth earlier and spread more quickly among the *Brahmins* than among the other two groups. During the last 20 years women's dress has changed altogether, and the change has been from basic similarity with the dress of the peasant to that with the dress of the urban middle-class, a change which is in accord with the group's change in occupation and mode of life. The heavy silver ornaments worn by the *Meena* and *Chamaar* women have also been discarded. Perhaps use of these ornaments was less among *Brahmin* women than among the women of the other two castes even earlier. But it has almost disappeared during the last twenty years. The only silver ornament now worn by the Brahmin women are light anklets; all other ornaments are of gold. Similar changes are to be seen in the dress of the men.

Food

The food of the *Brahmins* always contained more of the superior foodgrain—wheat and less of the coarse grain, jowar, bajra and gram, more milk, *ghee,* sugar and spices than did the food of the *Meenas* and the lower castes. Higher social and economic status and the fact that their women did not work outside the home, and that they had more money and time for household work and they have a greater consciousness of the value of good food, especially of milk and *ghee* are the factors responsible for more elaborate cooking. This is a far cry from the crude cooking of the *Meenas! Brahmins* consume more milk than do the other two groups. Two-third of the sample households, 12 out of 18, used milk.

Although the village sends out substantial quantities of milk for sale to the railway station, and the districts headquarters colony, even so milk is not freely available in the village and those who want to buy have to make long term arrangements with *Gujjars* or other suppliers.

Brahmins are strict vegetarians and teetotalers. Smoking is confined to men, but it is not favoured by the young men, majority of them are non-smokers. The younger people use tea; among the older generation there are still people who never take tea. Few families drink tea during the summer. In the summer, cooling drinks like buttermilk, *thandai* (a special drink made from *khus* seeds and sugar) and *sharbat* (some other sweet drinks) are popular.

Vegetables and fruits are much more commonly used by the *Brahmins* than by the *Meenas*. But there is a pronounced deficiency of proteins. The physique of the *Brahmins,* both men and women, is noticeably weaker than that of the *Meenas*. This may be due partly to their sedentary mode of life, but the protein deficiency in the diet is also perhaps a contributing factor.

Personal Hygiene and Medical Care

Urban patterns have also been adopted in personal hygiene and adornment. Most of the younger women use soap and oil and also cosmetics. But several of the older women still retain the old habit of using earth to wash their hair and apply *ghee* thereafter. A daily bath is the rule, and clothes are washed as frequently as is considered necessary. *Brahmins* are aware of the importance of clean water for health. Most housewives screen the drinking water by placing a piece of cloth on the mouth of the jar while drawing the water from the well. The practice is probably of no value as a preventive against spread of water borne diseases. But it shows a certain concern for sanitation.

Sickness receives relatively prompt and adequate attention by the *Brahmins*. There are five *vaidyas* and six qualified medical assistants Compounders) among the *Brahmin* white-collar workers in this village. The services of the doctors in the hospital in Sawai Madhopur are also frequently utilized. But it must not be assumed that sickness receives adequate attention in the modern sense, or that the attitude towards medical treatment is basically science-oriented instead of tradition-oriented. It is still the latter. For example, nearly all the women interviewed, including those in the families of the *vaidyas* and the medical assistants

(Compounders), reported that their deliveries were attended to by the village *dais* (midwives). The most popular among them is an old Muslim woman who is considered very competent. The *dais* follow traditional methods and has no training in modern midwifery practices. Younger women are prepared to use the services of trained midwives if they are available. The young women particularly are conscious of the need for better nutrition and medical care of the children. The effects, of this consciousness are clearly seen in the following figures on survival rate of children :

	No. of Women	*No. of Children Born*	*No. of Children Surviving*
Married for 20 years and more	12	87	47
Married for less than 20 years	6	14	11

Survival rate of children born to older women is not very different from that of children of women of the other two groups; but among the children of young *Brahmin* mothers there is a marked improvement. The ratio of children to mother is also smaller. This survey did not include a study of fertility rates, attitudes towards family planning etc., but the above data point significantly to the kind of changes, which are coming in the group as a result of education.

Education

Many of the older men who later were educated in schools and entered government service began their education at home in Sanskrit. But in recent years as there has been a complete change to school education, the tradition of learning Sanskrit at home is dying out.

Nearly all the *Brahmin* boys of school-going age are in school. They constitute one-fifth of the boys in the village school. In addition, 8 boys are studying outside the village. Education of a girl is comparatively recent development. Most *Brahmin* girls of the primary school-going-age are now being sent to the girls' primary school in the village. The prevailing attitude is that the girls must be educated through the primary stage. The principal reason for educating girls is that the educated young white-collar workers, who receive first preference as bride-grooms, want wives who have had enough education to be able to write a letter. But in the present stage of social advance of the group, a primary school for girls is considered adequate.

The Development Programme for Women

Village has a *Gram Kaki*, a young widow of the goldsmith caste. She has a sewing machine and conducts the prescribed programme of extension work among 20 families. But her work too had no impact among *Brahmin* women so far. She is a woman of a lower caste who has no more education or knowledge of crafts than many of the *Brahmin* housewives.

Marriage Custom

The marriage customs of the *Brahmins* have always been different from those of the cultivating and the scheduled castes. The major differences are in matters of widow-remarriage and marriage dissolution. Both are permitted among the cultivating and the scheduled castes: but they are not permitted among the *Brahmins*. The man has the right to marry a second time while his first wife is living; he even has the right to forsake his wife without formal dissolution of the marriage. The woman has no such rights. These customs, generally associated with the entire Hindu society, are found in this area only among the *Brahmins* and other high castes, the *Rajput* and the *Mahajan*.

Until recently the age of marriage among *Brahmins* was not very different from that among the cultivating and the schedule castes. At present, the most frequent age of marriage is 14 to 16 years for girls and 18 to 22 years for boys. Marriage within the village is allowed, provided it is not within the prohibited *gotras*. Such marriages occur frequently: there were three cases among 18 sample households. *Brahmins* obviously do not share the prohibition against intra-village marriage, which both the *Meenas* and the *Chamaars* have. But the most important changes relating to marriage are that it has become more elaborate and expensive, and the burden of the expense has begun to fall increasingly on the girl's parents. Bride price was looked down upon; but it was prevalent among the poor families, especially in the form of paying the expenses of marriage of the girl's parents. Finally, as in the case of the other two castes even today, the anxiety for marriage was all on the side of the boy's parents. Increasing elaboration of marriage is to be expected with rise in income, because marriage is the occasion on which a newly rich family announces its new prosperity and an established family confirms its continued affluence. But higher standards of education and salaried jobs have also contributed to this. At one time the main criteria in fixing a match for a girl was the economic status, landholding, and reputation of the boy's family, and the boy's health. Families had small holdings and limited incomes and expenditure on marriages remained within responsible limits.

Now, however, the principal criteria for selection of a good match are the boy's education and his job prospects. Boys with good education and good jobs are till not numerous, so there is spirited competition among girls' parents. Larger dowries and elaborate expensive marriages are one result.

Joint Families

Joint families are somewhat more common among the *Brahmins* than among the *Meenas* and the *Chamaars*. Most of the white-collar workers keep their families in the village who have either to live with the extended family or rent a separate house. Space for rent is not easily available and the families have in fact no choice except to be part of the joint family.

The distribution of households by single and joint families was as follows :

- *Single families – 12*: In five of these, the widowed father or mother of the household lived with the married couple.
- *Joint Families – 16*: Married sons were living with their parents in three families and two married brothers were living together in the other three.

Widow Re-marriage and Status of Women in the Family

The family status of a *Brahmin* woman was never equal to that of *Meena* or a scheduled caste woman. She did not work in the fields, nor did she work for wages; Bride price was not looked upon with favour but it was frequently paid by those marrying late. The burden of the marriage expenses was mainly on the boy's parents, and marrying a girl was not a problem for her parents. The socio-economic changes of recent years have not affected the ban on widow remarriage or the husband's right to leave his wife. On the contrary by adding the problem of finding suitable matches for girls and heavy expenses on girls' marriages, they have made the position of women somewhat worse.

Analysis

This study reveals striking differences (in marriage customs and the position of women in the home) between the high castes on the one hand and the cultivating and the scheduled castes on the other. Ban on widow remarriage and on divorce, dowry, and women's subservient position in the home, generally regarded as distinctive customs of Hindu society, are typical only of the *Brahmins.* The practices among the *Chamaars* and the

Meenas are entirely different, the widow is allowed to sit in *nata*; dissolution of marriage is not considered good and is not frequent but it is allowed and the woman exercises the same initiative in this as the man. Dowry is absent, and the prevailing marriage practices point towards the prevalence of bride price in the recent past. The latter has almost disappeared among the *Meenas;* but it is still prevalent among the *Chamaars*. The position of women in the home is also very different from that among the high castes. The woman is not a helpless creature fit only for home, a burden on her parents so long as she is not married and even thereafter occupying a subordinate position in the home during her married life and condemned to a life of despised dependency should she be widowed. Instead, she is respected and feared; she has almost a dominant position in the home. The anxiety for marriage is all on the side of the boy's parents, because they know that if their son passes a certain age without getting married it will be difficult to find a wife for him. Accordingly the boy's parents take the initiative in fixing a marriage; they spend much more than the girl's parents do, and they take all possible care to please the girl's parents both before marriage and after marriage until she comes to live with her husband. The husband himself, after the wife comes to live with him, realizes that she is his partner in the home and in work, that her contribution could make the difference between prosperity and want, and that if anything happens to her, or if she leaves him, he will find it extremely difficult to get another wife.

In our view, the most important reason for these differences is the economic fact that the women of the cultivating and the scheduled castes work outside the home and are economic assets to the family, while high caste women remain in the home and make no contribution to the family income. The entire superstructure of strikingly different social customs and attitudes seem to be built mainly on this single economic fact.

But it is significant that their own customs are regarded by the cultivating and the scheduled castes as the product of ignorance and want; the customs of the high castes are considered the mark of propriety and respectability. With growing prosperity, the trend is towards adopting high caste customs. Bride price is looked down upon, and *roti-beti* is considered proper. The prosperous *Meena* and the well-to-do *Chamaar* wishes to give a dowry as well. Dissolution of marriage is becoming less free and the practice of *jhagra* and the *Meena* habit of kidnapping of women are looked with increasing disfavour. There is change even in the attitude towards work by women. The *Chamaars* of Chainpur, copying the *Meenas*, want their women to work only on their own fields.

The *Chamaar* industrial workers of Chainpur are beginning to look down upon wage labour by women and the more prosperous among them, like the well paid skilled workers and the self-employed men, want their wives to stay at home and devote themselves also entirely to household work; just as the high caste women do. Boys with some education and white-collar or skilled job, whose wives will not have to work, have begun to be sought after. Among the *Chamaars*, giving dowry and sending girls to school have already started, but not among the *Meenas*—mainly because they continue to be predominantly agricultural. The trend towards seeking boys with well-paid jobs and catering to their demands is most pronounced among the *Brahmins.* Among them the criteria of a good match have undergone a complete change in course of little more than a generation. Dowry, always present but quite nominal in the past, has become large and burdensome—the inevitable result of competition for boys with good jobs—and marriage has become a very expensive affair.

But the trend towards adoption of high caste customs does not extend to widow remarriage, and there is no evidence that the cultivating and scheduled castes will adopt high caste practices of prohibiting widow remarriage. Nor would such a movement be very easy. The practice regarding widow remarriage is a vital matter for a caste. It has been a major determinant of social status in the past—the fundamental difference between high castes on the one side and cultivating and lower castes on the other, and it will not be possible to change it so easily. It is not certain that the change will be entirely in the direction of adoption of high caste practice by cultivating and scheduled castes. The high castes themselves are finding their customs increasingly difficult to maintain; there is growing opposition to it from urbanized and educated youth. It is quite possible that while the cultivating and scheduled castes move towards making widow remarriage less easy (*e.g.,* by prohibiting older widows or those with sons and land from remarrying), the change among the high castes may be in the direction of partial relaxation of the ban, especially in the case of young widows.

The social compulsion towards conspicuous and large expenditure on such ceremonial occasions as marriage and death almost forces each family to scrape the bottom of its financial barrel or to go beyond and borrow. This tendency has been commented upon by most writers on social or economic life in rural India, and there is no sign of its diminution. On the contrary, the effect of the economic and social changes of the last twenty years in this area, which have brought prosperity, or at least freedom from indigence, to an increasing number of rural people, has been to spread this tendency wider and to render ineffective the social restraints which had been imposed either from above (*e.g.*, by the *jagirdars*) or by the castes themselves. Expensive marriages and large feasts, which in the past were the prerogative of the wealthy, mostly the *jagirdars* and the rich *Mahajans*, are now being indulged in by an ever-increasing number. Feasts for 400 to 500 guests are common among the *Meenas*, and even those for 800 to 1000 guests are not at all unusual. The more prosperous families in each caste want to imitate the ex-*jagirdars*, the rich *Mahajans*, and the large cultivators; the poorer families imitate the more prosperous ones. In fact, expensive marriages and large feasts have become the accepted method of proclamation of prosperity by individual families and of freedom of traditional restraints by castes. The *Chamaars* now invest heavily in silver ornaments. They have already outdone the *Meenas* in this respect and are trying to imitate the *Brahmins* by making gold ornaments.

Concentration of marriages on the *Akha Teej* day was another restraint exercised by the village community. But marriage on this day is beginning to be disfavoured precisely because it is not possible to give a large feast! Similarly, the small amount fixed by castes for particular marriage ceremonies, followed by all except the very wealthy 20 or 25 years ago, are no longer adhered to. Among the *Brahmins*, among whom this process is best seen, no new norm have been fixed and giving the maximum on each occasion has become the criterion of a good marriage. Marriages among the *Brahmins* have become the most elaborate and expensive, expenditure in some of these reaches Rs. 5,000 to 6,000. Such expenditure is quite out of proportion to the income level of the *Brahmin* group, and the conclusion is inescapable that an unduly large amount of capital is being eaten by it. It constitutes the single most important cause of indebtedness among all castes, from the highest to the lowest. It is a truism that the villager will starve his children but will not stint on ceremonial expenditure and will on the contrary go to any length in order not to lose face on such occasions. In most *Meena* and *Chamaar* households, if the children had no milk, the *Meena* women explained that the cow was dry and they could not afford to stall feed her and get more milk, or the *Chamaar* women explained that they could not afford to buy milk. But the same households were found to be going out of their way in incurring debts to meet expenditure on marriages and death feasts.

The social significance of these ceremonies is great, unquestionably. Marriages and other occasions when relatives and other people of the caste come together have an important social function. They serve as a club for caste gathering, fashion show for the women, matrimonial exchange, all in one. They could well be considered vital to the functioning of the caste as an institution and even to the entire social life of rural India today. The feasts on these occasions constitute the only break from the drabness and poverty of the villagers' daily food. Marriage ornaments are a kind of insurance for the women—insurance as much against adversity as against disregard of her interests by her husband. But even when all this is taken into account, the wastefulness of a feast in which several hundred people are fed at one time, and its crushing burden on the poor family which spends an amount equal to its year's earnings and several years' savings, cannot but be deplored.

So far, neither social education nor legislation has had any effect on this expenditure. No effective social education programme directed at reducing such expenditure has been undertaken. Legislation against death feasts was brought on the status book in Rajasthan some years ago. Its only effect has been to change the name of this feast from *nukta* (death feast) to *gangoj* (feast given after a person has been to a holy place on the Ganges, usually Haridwar) and to add the cost of the trip to that of the feast. The feasts continue as before, only now more people go to Haridwar so that they can justify before the authorities the claim that the feasts was a *gangoj* and not a *nukta*.

The Joint Family

The joint family is somewhat more common among the *Brahmins* of Raipur than among the other two groups. Among, the former the very practical advantages which joint living confers on the service men who are posted away from their homes but cannot afford separate living, favour joint living. Among the *Meenas*, land acts as an influence in keeping families together; but separate living starts even when cultivation is joint and is in any case accepted as normal and inevitable. Among the *Chamaars* the joint family was never as strong as among the other two groups; now it has almost disintegrated. The overall impression conveyed by the findings of this study is that the joint family is a much weaker institution than it is often represented to be in writings on village India. It is by no means comparable in social significance to caste.

Attitude towards Education of Girls

It is interesting to note the effect of occupation on attitudes towards girls' education, and especially the social process through which the need for girls' education begins to be felt. The *Meena* women don't favour education of girls. They feel that education is of no use and will only make the girls unsuitable for their future role in life. The need for education begins to be felt when the change from an agricultural to a non-agricultural way of life takes place in the caste and more specially when a number of young men enter white-collar, skilled or entrepreneurial work, after education and begin to demand that their wives have some education. This change is most pronounced among the *Brahmins* and is the main reason for sending girls to school. But it has also begun to be noticeable among the *Chamaars*.

Consumption Patterns—The Influence of Occupation

The differences in consumption patterns of the three groups are striking. The *Meenas* have changed the least from their traditional patterns in food, dress and ornaments, housing, personal hygiene, etc.; the changes among the other two groups have been much greater. Distance from the town is not a factor in this: the *Meena* village is not farther from Sawai Madhopur than the other two villages, and it is just as close to availability of consumption goods and services. Income and ready availability of cash are factors of some importance. The *Brahmins* have higher incomes; both the *Brahmins* and the *Chamaars* have more cash than the *Meenas,* and for longer periods. But the *Chamaars* are not much richer than the *Meenas*: on the contrary some of them are poor, and a large number, though better off than the Meenas, face greater financial insecurity.

Occupation is the main factor responsible for these differences The *Meenas* remain the least affected by urban consumption patterns because they remain an agricultural group with non-agricultural sources of income contribute very little to their economy. Even with rise in income they do not incline so much towards acceptance of urban consumer goods, as toward peasant ways of conspicuous consumption—large feasts, for example. *Brahmin* consumption pattern tends to be similar to that of the literate, urban middle class, while *Chamaars* have already begun to take on the colour of industrial labourers in this respect.

The marked, almost aggressive dissatisfaction of *Chamaar* young men have been commented upon. Many of these are associated with an industrial way of life, and *Chamaars* have begun to experience them even though they are living in a village and the older people among them are anxious to preserve their agricultural links. On the other hand, this group has achieved the maximum economic and social advance during the last two decades; it is making good use of the economic opportunities opening up for it and will probably do even better in future. Altogether, this appears to be the most interesting group among the three and we feel that a more detailed study of problems and attitudes of the group will be most rewarding.

NOTES

1. The cement factory, which was operational in Maan Town, closed down some time in the early 1990s. It was a major source of non-agricultural employment for two of the villages included in the study several persons from the third village also worked in the factory.
2. See Appendix 2. Kamla Nath also studied a Scheduled Caste village (Chainpur) located two km. from the cement factory and the Collector's house. All the inhabitants were depended on non-agricultural work mostly in the cement factory. This village does not form part of Dr Nath's study.
3. A Patwari is a person who maintains records of rights of ownership in land, land use (cropland, pasture, woodland or wasteland) of every piece of land. He reports to the government through the Tehsildar and the Collector on the state of the crops and is obliged to do any other work that the Collector assigns him.
4. "Power" here means ability to benefit or harm a villager.
5. Practitioners of the ancient (Hindu) ayurvedic system of medicine.
6. The Punjab village studied in 1963 and 1976 was reported in a series of articles published in *Economic and Political Weekly* under the title "The New Village" and is included in this volume in the Chapter 'The New Village'
7. In some studies done on modernization of agriculture have reported that only the tasks done by men have been mechanized but tasks assigned to women, like weeding, hoeing, transplanting of seedlings etc. are still done by hand without help from the men who are using the time gained from mechanization of agriculture towards taking up non-agricultural work or in dabbling in local politics.

Foot Notes

1. It had been intended to include also study of attitude of women towards political process like elections and towards institutions like the *Panchayat* and the *Panchayat Samiti*. Women had been seen to participate in polling for the two elections, the *Panchayat* Election of December 1960 and the General Election of February 1962, in large numbers. The legislation relating to *Panchayati Raj* institutions provides for co-option of women as members of *Panchayats, Panchayat Samitis* and *Zila Prishads,* and in two of the three villages studied Raipur and Bijaipur, women had been co-opted as members of the village *Panchayats*. But preliminary enquiries during the course of this study revealed a marked lack of interest in and

awareness of political process and institutions among women in all the three villages. They knew about the existence of *Panchayats* and *Panchayat Samitis* and that these bodies had women members; they had voted in the *Panchayat* election. But they knew little else and showed no interest in the functioning of these bodies. Even the woman members either did not attend meetings of these bodies or were silent spectators in the meetings, which they did attend. After the preliminary enquiries revealed this situation, a detailed study was not considered necessary.

2. On the basis of the above figures of per acre yields and the prices prevailing in 1961, the gross annual income of such cultivator comes to Rs. 1,200.
3. *Hatai*: A place where men of a few neighbouring houses gather together for gossip.
4. But, in spite of this disadvantage of corrugated iron sheets, these are very much desired for roofing. Sheet roofs are preferred because they do not need to be repaired after each monsoon and replaced after two to four years that tile roofs do. Besides, the labour of making tiles is saved. The number of houses with sheet roofs is small so far; but this is mainly because of non-availability of sheets. There is a keen demand for sheets and if they were available freely, a large number of houses would have sheet roofs.
5. This is true also of *Meena* women of other villages in the area. In the author, V. Nath's visits to homes of prosperous Meena leaders (*e.g.* Ram Pratap, Raja Ram and Tara Chand described in study of Village Leaders), he found that their women were dressed like other *Meena* women of the villages and also worked in the fields. Building *pucca* houses and giving large feasts on marriages, deaths and other occasions are the principal ways in which the prosperous *Meena* shows his wealth.
6. As explained in the study done by V. Nath, only the *Malis* grow vegetables for sale.
7. *Beedi*: small cigarettes made by wrapping tobacco in *beedi* leaves.
8. *Gram Kaki*: (literally aunt of the village). A woman of the village selected for assisting the extension workers of the Community Development Programme for extension work among village women.
9. *Pansari*: A merchant of traditional herbs and drugs.
10. An improved type of hearth originally designed by a Gandhian Institute of Rural Development.
11. *Jaali*: A small cabinet for storing food. It has wire-gauze doors and sides in order to provide adequate aeration.
12. Since marriage parties used to go (and still do) to the bride's village by bullock carts the distance which a bullock-cart could drive during the course of a day was perhaps a factor in setting the limit on the distance within which marriages were fixed.
13. *Akha Teej*: Third day of the waxing moon in the lunar month of Baisakh. It usually comes in the first fortnight of May.
14. One *tola* = approx. 2/5 oz.

15. "He beats me". "The mother-in-law makes me do all the work but does not give me food to eat", were some of the remarks made by the women of Bijaipur who had left their earlier husbands to live with the present ones.
16. The term 'Joint family' has been used here for all families in which two or more related couples are living together. A family in which one or more married sons are living with their parents, or two married brothers are living together, has been considered a joint family; but one in which one widowed parent is living with his/her married son and daughter-in-law has not been considered as a joint family.
17. Figures on incomes of permanent workers in the factory are fairly accurate; those on incomes of self-employed persons and workers with contractors are rough estimates.
18. This impression had been created because students of the factory school had not done well in the matriculation examination of 1960.
19. There was a dispute at the time about payment of bonus to workers between the management of the factory and the workers union.
20. One household consisting of an old widow, who subsists on food received in charity from other *Brahmin* households and a small income from two acres of unirrigated land has been excluded.

REFERENCES

Ministry of Community Development and Co-operation: 'A Committee to evaluate working of Community Development and National Extension Service Programmes': Government of India, Delhi 1957.

Swedish International Development Agency (SIDA): Rajasthan, A State Study (2000).

17
The New Village[1]

Introduction

During the last few years attention has begun to be directed towards differential progress in agriculture in different parts of the country. It is becoming increasingly clear that while in some areas agriculture has begun to display considerable dynamism, its progress in other areas is still very slow. Identification of the factors—physical, economic and social—which contribute to these differences in progress is important for understanding the dynamics of agricultural progress. Case studies of villages of especially rapid or slow progress is a fruitful method of identifying these factors because the sharp contrasts between the two situations bring out these factors prominently. Moreover the case study method by describing change in different aspects of the economy and social life of the selected village makes it possible to bring out the inter-relationship between these. The author had studied three villages in Sawai Madhopur district of Eastern Rajasthan during his stay there as Collector in 1961-62. As mentioned in Chapter 16, Sawai Madhopur is one of the backward district in one of the then most backward States of the country. The villages selected were, however, less undeveloped than the many in the district because of nearness to the town and a cement factory. The author's interest in making a comparative study of more progressive rural areas in one of the fast developing State—Punjab—led him to select Jitpur a village in central Punjab for the study.

This study of a village in Central Punjab, an area which has experienced rapid technological change in agriculture and economic

---

N.B. : Five articles based on the research were published in *Economic Weekly* during 1964-65 and were later printed as a handbook by the *Economic Weekly*.

progress, has been undertaken with these objects in view. It describes the various changes in agriculture experienced by the village, the interaction between these, the shape of the agricultural enterprise and of the village after the improved practices advocated by extension workers have been largely adopted and, finally, the problems which agricultural progress and relative prosperity created. Although the study is focussed on change in agriculture, progress in other directions—health, education, transport and communications and levels of living—has also been described. A major conclusion emerging from the study is that change in agriculture is part of a larger process of social and economic change, as a result of which the complexion of the village and the character of village life are changing rapidly and a 'New Village' is emerging; hence the main heading. It is hoped that this study will be followed by case studies of slow progress in agriculture in north India and studies of both slow and rapid progress in other parts of the country so that the dynamics of agricultural progress are more adequately understood.[2]

This study is based on a three weeks' stay in 1963 in village Jitpur of Ludhiana district of Central Punjab. This is a comparatively large, multi-caste, village with a population of about 1,850. A village of this size was selected in order to observe the effects of change in agriculture and of economic progress on cultivators as well as non-cultivators and especially to see how far the latter had contributed to these changes and had benefited from them.

A major part of the study consisted of discussions with individuals and groups of cultivators about agricultural techniques and seeing the improved practices and devices at work. Several group discussions in which anybody from the village could participate were held. In addition individual interviews were held with the *Sarpanch* of the village *Panchayat*, the Chairman and the Secretary of the service co-operative, the Manager of the seed and fertilizer depot, the Village Level Worker (VLW), the *Patwari*, a few progressive farmers (on their farms), some Harijan leaders, one of the two fabricators of agricultural implements, and one young man who does electrical installation work in the village.

Data on demographic characteristics, land-holdings and economic activity were collected for all households in the village through a household census. More detailed data on agricultural operations of medium-sized cultivators (those having holdings between 8-14 acres) and on employment and earnings of the Harijans were collected on a sample basis. Ten families of medium-sized cultivators and ten of Harijans were included in the sample. The object of the survey of the cultivators was to obtain a closer acquaintance with their farm operations and to obtain an approximate idea of their levels of production and income. It was also useful in seeing how far improvements like use of chemical fertilizers, for which data on consumption for the Block and the village were given by the Block staff, were being followed by these cultivators. The sample survey of the Harijans was intended to obtain a more precise idea of their level of income.

Besides work in this village, several other villages in the Block were visited in order to see other noteworthy developments. One of these villages had a successful co-operative milk producers' society supplying milk to the Government Dairy at the State capital. Another had a number of progressive farmers settled in a garden colony, which is one of several such colonies established in the Punjab in the post-Partition years. Detailed discussions about agricultural progress and extension activities were held with the Block Development Officer and other members of the Block extension staff, and later with the Pilot Project Officer of the 'Package Programme', and a few specialists at the Punjab Agricultural University, Ludhiana. I am indebted to all these people, and especially to the BDO and his staff who had to spend considerable time with me, for their assistance in this study.

The Area and the Period

Ludhiana is one of the more progressive agricultural districts of Punjab. Since, 1960, it has been selected for the Intensive Agricultural Development (Package) Programme of the Ministry of Food and Agriculture. Accordingly, the intensity of agricultural extension effort in it is greater and the resources being made available for agricultural development are much larger than in an average district of the State. However, this more intensive effort began only in 1961; the district had not received any special attention earlier. The changes described in this study are the results mainly of developments which had taken place before the inception of Package Programme, and, as the discussion brings out, are related to the social and economic changes which have occurred all over Central Punjab in the post-Partition years and to development activities undertaken in all parts of the State. But it is well to keep in view the fact that the very selection of Ludhiana as the Package Programme district indicates a relatively high standard of agricultural development and a potential for attaining rapid increases in agricultural production as a result of the Programme.

Secondly, Ludhiana and a number of smaller towns of Central Punjab have seen rapid growth of small-scale industry in recent years. The centre of this development is the town of Ludhiana itself, in which there has been a phenomenal growth of machine tool and light engineering industries. Lately, this development has overflowed to the larger villages, especially those, which have certain advantages like location along the Delhi-Amritsar (Grand Trunk) Road. This growth of small-scale industries has important effects on the rural economy and agricultural techniques, which are discussed below. Moreover, the agricultural changes described in this study and growths of small-scale industry in towns are both part of a larger process of socio-economic change. However, for the purposes of this study, I took care not to select an industrial village. Such villages are still few in number and selection of one of these would have interfered with analysis of agricultural change, which is the main theme of this study. The influence of industrial growth described in this study is the regional effect, which has been felt by all villages in this area.

The selected village is well served with road transport, has electricity and has attained a high level of agricultural productivity. But, it is not exceptional in any of these respects in this area. The majority of the villages in this CD block are within two miles of an all-weather motorable road and the motor transport facilities available to them are almost as good as those available to this village. Electric supply has been extended to 88 out of 107 villages of the Block. As regards agricultural productivity, the average yields of crops reported for this village are comparable to yields reported for the Block. Similarly, in the level of use of fertilizer, which is a good index of acceptance of agricultural improvements, the village is not exceptional. The average figure of 34.0 kg of chemical fertilizers used per acre under crops reported for this village has been attained and exceeded by a number of other villages in this Block and by several Blocks in this district.

The Village and the People

Jitpur is a medium-sized multi-caste village, having 299 households and a population of about 1,850. It is located at a distance of two miles from *tehsil* and Block headquarters town, which itself has a population of only about 6,000 and is not much more than a large village. Jitpur is situated on an all-weather motorable road, which links it with this town on one side, and with a market town (population about 25,000) on the other. There is a regular bus service with 12 buses plying each way on this road. In addition, four three-wheeler Tempos are plying continuously. As a result, a motor transport vehicle is available on this road every ten minutes throughout the day. The village is not suburban in character; Ludhiana, the nearest large city (population over 5 lakh) is about 25 miles from it. But these details about frequency of road transport have been given in order to indicate how quickly and easily the villager can move out of the village. This fact was brought home to me during the first visit to the village. When I reached the village, I was told that a prominent village leader, whom I had expected to meet, had left for the State capital that very morning. I was disappointed at the prospect of not being able to see him. But before I left the village four hours later, the man had returned. The entire trip to the State capital, located about 40 miles away, including his making certain enquiries about his work in the capital had taken just six hours. The rapidity of travel by road, in which this village or the villages of this Block are by no means exceptional, is a very powerful factor in the travel of new ideas to the village and in lessening of the distance—in time, in ways of thinking and in levels of living—between the people of the villages and those of the towns, which in turn is an important factor in technological progress in the villages.

Another first impression may be recorded also, in order to give a perspective of the technological level to which the village has access now. The village has two shops of fabricators of agricultural implements. These are owned by two extended families of *Ramgarhiya Lohars* (smiths), residents of the village. One of these shops is on the approved list of fabricators of agricultural implements for the State Department of Agriculture. It manufactures *rahats* (iron Persian wheels), iron ploughs, buckets, steel trunks and similar articles of sheet steel, besides doing repair work. This shop with its electric motors, a power press, lathes and other power-driven machines is comparable in equipment and technical skill of its workmen to any small manufacturing unit in the neighbouring *tehsil* town or even in Ludhiana. Several young men from *Lohar* (smith) families of Jitpur are working in Ludhiana as skilled workers in small engineering units and the men working in the village have stayed behind, not because they are inferior in skill or capacity to work to those who have gone out, but only because they feel that they can make as much or more money by running the family shops in the village. These men understand machines—electric motors, tractors, trucks, flour mills, almost any machine that is likely to be used in the village—and their presence in the village is a major factor in technological progress. It means that if an electric motor or other power driven agricultural implement like a chaff cutter or sugarcane press goes out of order, it will be repaired quickly and efficiently, and if the repair cannot be done locally or a part needs to be replaced, the cultivator will be suitably advised to get this done from the Block headquarters town or

Ludhiana. He need not be afraid of being left helpless in case of a breakdown or of long expensive delays or heavy repair costs. It means further that the cultivator or his young son has a high standard of technical competence to look up to. The fact that this standard already exists in the village gives an impetus to him and to his young son to handle machines and to correct small defects himself. During subsequent discussions in the village, many cultivators explained that they seldom have any problem with their electric motors; that they could correct small defects themselves and went to the *tehsil* town only in case of a major trouble like a burnt armature. One elderly cultivator went so far as to say that the longer they worked their motors the fewer breakdowns these had.

This level of competence in handling machines is in striking contrast to that found in an average village in many parts of the country, where the village smith or carpenter confines himself to making and repairing the sugarcane traditional agricultural implements and is either incapable of, or does not care to handle, even such non-power-driven improved implements as iron sugarcane ploughs or sugarcane crushers.[3]

The People

The distribution of households by caste is given in Table 17.1. Detailed data on land ownership, cultivation and other economic activities, distribution of population by age and sex, literacy and standard of education are given, caste-wise, in the Annexure.

Table 17.1: Distribution of Households by Caste

	Caste	*No. of Households*	*Population*
1.	*Jat*	105	780
2.	*Ramgarhiya Mistri* (smith, mason, carpenter)	37	205
3.	*Mahajan** (*Brahmin*, *Khatri*, and Arora)	46	289
4.	Harijan (Ramdasia, Balmiki, Julaha)	87	517
5.	Other artisans: *Darzi* (tailor); *Kumhar* (potter); *Nai* (barber); *Jhiur* (water-carrier); *Teli* (oil-presser); *Gujjar* (grazier)	15	92
6.	*Bazigar*	9	48
	Total	***299***	***1,831***

Note: * The term *Mahajan* is used by the villagers for all these three castes of traders-*cum*-white collar workers. It has been retained here for the sake of convenience even though I realize that quite different castes like *Brahmin* and *Khatri* are included in the group. The number of households by individual caste is as follows: *Brahmin*, 27; *Khatri*, 17; Arora 2.

The *Bazigars* are not permanent residents of the village. They live in semi-permanent huts in one corner of the village and are dependent mainly upon casual agricultural or non-agricultural labour. They also rear buffaloes or cattle for sale of milk or animals. They are a semi-nomadic people who stay at the outskirts of large villages and small towns for months at a time. In recent years they have been trying to settle down as cultivators or cultivators-*cum*-labourers and are being assisted in this process by the State Government with allotment of land for cultivation and with financial assistance.

There are sharp differences in land-ownership and occupation among the different castes as will be seen from Table 17.2. The *Jats* are the principal land owner-cultivators: they own and cultivate practically all the lands of the village. Among the other casts, *Mahajans, Mistris* (mason, carpenters and smiths) and 'other artisans' are essentially non-cultivators. The Harijans have agricultural labour as an important source of income; but they have no rights in land. Of the 104 land-owning families in the village, 96 are of *Jats,* and of the 82 families of cultivators, 76 are of *Jats*. These cultivate 96 per cent of the land of the village. The concentration of land-ownership and cultivation in the hands of a single caste could hardly be greater.

Table 17.2 : Land Ownership and Cultivation

(in acres)

	Land Ownership		Cultivation	
	Families	Area Owned	Families	Area Owned
1. *Jats*	96	1,033.0	76	1,065.0
2. *Mistris*	3	11.5	2	9.5
3. *Mahajans*	4	28.5	4	28.5
4. Harijans	1	6.0*	0	0
Total	**104**	**1,079.0**	**82**	**1,103.0**

* Just allotted in a neighbouring village; cultivation not begun.

Further, as the data of the Annexure bring out, the participation of *Jats* in non-agricultural occupations is relatively small. A number of *Jats* have gone out of the village in the Army and elsewhere but among those living in the village, more than 90 per cent are engaged in cultivation.

Mistris, Mahajans and the 'other artisans' depend upon occupations other than cultivation. In the case of *Mistris*, the principal occupations are those of mason, carpenter and smith, the latter including skilled work in machine shops in the village and outside. Out of 56 *Mistris* workers living in the village, as many as 43 are classified as engaged in skilled work. Fourteen of these are masons, 12 are carpenters, and 11 are smiths. The principal occupations of *Mahajans* are petty shop-keeping and white-collar services. Four families take up cultivation of their small holdings. Agricultural and non-agricultural labour is also reported by a few persons, obviously those who are uneducated or are too poor to do anything else. A number of persons among the *Mahajans* are not doing any work. These are old people, who depend upon their pensions and/or remittances from sons in service outside the village.

The 'other artisans' follow their traditional occupations, supplementing earnings from these by labour, agricultural and non-agricultural. Their numbers are sufficiently small (1-3 households each) to enable them to make a meagre living in this way.

The Harijans are the big landless group. A few families have their traditional occupations—scavenging for six families of *Balmikis*, weaving for six families of *Julahas (*weavers*)*—as important sources of income. But the great majority (75 families), who are called *Ramdasias* or Ravidasias[4], depend almost exclusively upon agricultural and/or non-agricultural labour. These people gave up their traditional *Chamaars'* work, *i.e.* flaying of carcasses of dead cattle and making of leather goods, about 40 years ago. But even when they practiced it, it contributed only a small proportion to their incomes, and their main reliance was on labour. Out of 110 Harijan workers living in the village, as many as 91 were reported to be engaged in agricultural and/or non-agricultural labour. Fifteen among these were *sanjhees* (attached agricultural labourers) working for cultivators for an annual payment, given in most cases as a share of produce; 13 are non-agricultural labourers, while the remainders take up casual agricultural or non-agricultural work as one or the other becomes available.

Since the *sanjhees* get a share of the produce, it may be thought that they are share-croppers and not labourers. The impression is strengthened by the fact that some *sanjhees* besides contributing labour pay proportionate share of the land revenue and cost of seed, fertilizer, etc. The annual contract (usually verbal) between the cultivator and the *sanjhee* specifies the items to be contributed by the latter and the crops of which he is to receive a share. (Usually the *sanjhee* gets a share of the grain and cash crops; but is not given any share in fodders or by-products like chaff, cotton sticks, etc.) But the cultivators were emphatic in maintaining that the *sanjhees* were agricultural labourers, that they had no part in decision making in cultivation and that giving them a share of the produce was only another method of paying for their labour. The Harijans themselves did not contest these claims nor did they make any reference to their having had rights in land at anytime in the past.

The remarkable adherence of castes to their traditional occupations and roles in the village may be noted. Ownership and cultivation of land is concentrated in the hands of the *Jats*. The only other participants in cultivation are Harijans; but their role is confined entirely to furnishing labour. The *Mahajans* and the *Mistris*, the two other major castes of the village, have confined themselves to their traditional roles of traders-*cum*-white-collar workers and skilled artisans respectively. This adherence of traditional occupations and roles is in striking contrast to the technological and economic progress, which the village has made in recent years. It shows that economic progress need not involve basic changes from the traditional roles and patterns of economic activity of the different castes. On the other hand, as the following discussion will bring out, this very adherence, voluntary or forced, has provided a major incentive to economic and social progress. The fact that castes like the *Mahajans* and the *Mistris* did not have an opportunity for participation in land-ownership and cultivation within the village, meant that as population increased and aspirations rose with spread of education and increasing contacts with the outside world, these castes sought an escape from the limitation of local economic opportunity in emigration. Each caste chose the occupation(s), for which it was best suited because of its traditional occupation and role in the village. Among the *Jat* cultivators also, young men from families with small holdings sought an escape from declining incomes at home in emigration. As a result, the area acquired an active tradition of emigration, which has been a major influence in economic and social progress. The alternate response of traditionally non-cultivating castes participating in land-ownership and cultivation with varying degrees of combination between cultivation and the traditional occupation of the caste, which is found in villages in many parts of the country, was not made here[5]. Both the social situation and the laws were responsible for this. The land-owning cultivating *Jats* were too powerful and too deeply attached to the land to allow non-cultivators to acquire rights in it. Secondly, acquisition of land by non-cultivators was prohibited under the well-known Punjab Land Alienation Act of 1901.

Emigrants

The figures given in the Annexure include data on those emigrants from the village who are unmarried and those who are married but keep their families in the village. These persons have been included for two reasons.

Firstly, since emigration is an important factor in technological and social change in the village, some data on numbers who have gone out of the village are of interest for this study. Secondly, people of these two categories, even though living outside the village are part of the social, and to an extent the economic, situation of the village. The men with families living in the village send remittances and themselves visit the village as frequently as possible. Most of those from cultivating families continue their interest in land. The unmarried ones have equally strong links and interests. Their parents, uncles and other relations in the village are the only family they have. They look to them for assistance in getting married and in setting up their own homes in future. These two categories of emigrants are best thought of as constituents of village families, who are living outside it. Many of them will come back; others will remain 'men of the village', until they establish themselves sufficiently to take their wives and children with them.

The emigrants included in Annexure total 89. Most of them are *Jats, Mahajans* and *Mistris*; the number of Harijans and other artisans is very small. Emigration from this village (and this area generally) has been mainly from castes, which are socially and economically the most advanced, and the least from groups like the Harijans which were poor and depressed. The largest number of emigrants (42) is in the Army. More than half of these (23) are *Jats;* the remainder being *Mahajans* (10) and Harijans (7). The other occupations of the emigrants are skilled work (22), and white-collar services and professions (32). The *Mahajans* are either in white-collar services and professions or in military service. The *Mistris* are mostly skilled workers though a few are in white-collar services and professions also. They are conspicuous by their absence from the Army. The 11 *Jats,* listed under skilled work, are mostly drivers of buses and trucks. They are about the only people in the village who take up this form of skilled work: the *Mistris* avoid it. This was explained by the villagers with the remark that the *Jats* alone have the physical strength and stamina required for this exhausting work.

The area has a long tradition of military service. The *Jats* and, to a lesser extent, the *Brahmins,* were the first to join such service. The first recruits to the British Indian Army went in the last quarter of the nineteenth Century and there are many men in the village today, who have served in the first or the Second World War. On the other hand the recruitment of Harijans to the Army is a very recent phenomenon. Six of the 7 young men reported as being in military service, joined the service only after the declaration of the Emergency.

Migration to take up white-collar services and professions and skilled work also began several decades ago. The *Mahajans* were prominent in the former and the *Mistris* in the latter. Masons of this village have been going out for work on public works and private house construction for several decades. Before the partition, they used to go for work on the canals in West Punjab, and to towns like Lahore, Lyallpur and Rawalpindi. This tradition continues and several of them are now working in Delhi and towns of the Punjab.

This tradition of emigration has had very important economic and social consequences some of which are related to the main theme of this study. Emigration with its inflow of money, and new ideas especially from persons who came back to live in the village, brought rise in economic level of the families of the emigrants and rising aspirations and widening mental horizons for the whole village. The village people saw that there was opportunity outside, and that it was possible to avail of it instead of enduring a low and declining income at home. In case of cultivators, emigration meant also that the process of sub-division and fragmentation of holdings was less rapid than it would have been otherwise. The relatively comfortable size of holdings, which we note below as a major reason for successful technological change, is the result partly of emigration.

Two aspects of emigration, which deserve special mention, are going to canal colonies of West Punjab and to foreign countries. The canal colonies were a major avenue of emigration for cultivators of this area in the early years of this century, and the area is now full of cultivators who have come back to their ancestral villages after the partition of the Punjab in 1947. This return migration, as explained later, has been a significant factor in agricultural progress. But this particular village did not participate in migration to canal colonies. The explanation given for this was interesting. It was explained that the then Zaildar of the village when asked by Government whether he or any person from his village would like to take land in the canal colonies, had refused the offer. His grandson, a prominent leader of the village, was mildly proud of this attitude of his ancestor, though many others were of the view that this had retarded the progress of the village.

Emigration to foreign countries from villages of this area has been mainly to Malaya, Thailand and East Africa. From this particular village, several *Brahmin* families have settled in East Africa. But the latest phase of such emigration is migration of young men to the UK for taking up jobs as unskilled or semi-skilled workers. Large numbers of young men from Ludhiana and other districts of Central Punjab have been going to the UK during the last few years and during the course of this study I had occasion to experience the ferment which news of employment in UK on "good wages" was causing in the area. Employment vouchers, wage rates, cost of living and living conditions in UK and the possibility of saving money and sending it home, were the talk of the small Block headquarters town. Information on these points obtained from all possible sources—letters and remittances from the young men who had gone to the UK, news picked up at Ludhiana, Delhi and other towns—was pooled and discussed at length by the young men from the villages who gathered at restaurants and other shops in the town. The consensus of opinion was that wages were "good"; but cost of living was high, and one could save money only by living in overcrowded tenements and enduring physical hardship. Since the average young man of this area is quite prepared for these, there was considerable enthusiasm for going abroad, especially among young men with some education who did not want to engage in farming or other ancestral occupations.[7]

Technological Change in Agriculture

Pattern of Landholdings

It has been noted in Table 17.2 that the eighty-two farmer families of the village cultivate a total of 1,103 acres. This gives a crude average of 13.45 acres per cultivating family. The distribution of families by sizes of cultivated holdings is given in Table 17.3.

Table 17.3: Distribution of Families by Sizes of Cultivated Holdings

Below 5 acres	3
5 to 10 acres	22
10 to 15 acres	30
15 to 20 acres	18
20 to 30 acres	4
30 acres and above	5

The largest number of families (70 out of 82) cultivate between 5 and 20 acres. Families cultivating less than 5 acres are very small in number and have only a part-time interest in cultivation Families cultivating above 20 acres are also very few. Several of them are undivided joint families.

On further classification by one-acre divisions, it is found that the largest number of families (21) cultivated between 10 and 11 acres, and that the median cultivated holding is 10.5 acres. The villagers consider those cultivating between 8 and 14 acres as medium sized cultivators. Such cultivators number 38, somewhat less than half of the total. Data on farm operations of the 10 sample cultivators of this group are presented in Table 17.4.

It will be seen that the net disposable income of these cultivating families ranged from about Rs. 1,200 to over Rs. 5,500 per year; the variation being dependent upon the number of workers in the family, the area cultivated, whether irrigation was being done by bullocks or by electric motor and the level of fertilizer use. This income remained with the family after meeting all its needs of food, providing for fodder for livestock including milch animals, and paying all the cultivation expenses (*e.g.* for seed, manures and fertilizers, labour, etc). The value of the foodgrains and other produce (*gur, khandsari* sugar and cotton) retained by the families for domestic use varied from Rs. 1,275 to Rs. 2,360. Each family was keeping besides bullocks, two or more milk-yielding buffaloes and since the milk yields are fairly high (8 kg per buffalo per day or higher) the milk was sufficient for meeting all the milk and *ghee* requirements of the family. Further, all families grew some vegetables and had kept a few poultry birds also. Accordingly, the food needs of the families were met almost fully, and at a fairly satisfactory level of nutrition; and the disposable income was available for expenditure on clothing, repair or extension of the house, education, travel and miscellaneous expenses.

The calculation is not very refined, but it is adequate for the purpose of obtaining an approximate idea of the economic level of the middle cultivator. It is clear from it that this cultivator is considerably above the subsistence level; that he has a small surplus for education, travel and other needs after meeting his elementary needs for food, clothing, housing, etc. Data on the character of housing, facility of electricity and water supply in the house, and possession of durable goods and other general observations in the village also point to a similar conclusion. The main significance of this conclusion is that since the cultivator is not constantly pre-occupied with meeting his barest minimum needs, he can afford to bring a business approach to his cultivation, to take some risks and to make experiments with new practices. The extension staff emphasized that this latter had been one major result of the economic changes of the last fifteen years. As the VLW stated it, "Earlier the sole aim of the cultivator was to feed his family and that of the Harijan who worked for him. Now however, several of them aim at making more money and are looking for changes in practices which would enable them to do so".

Table 17.4: Farm Operations of Ten Sample Medium Cultivators

Sl. No.	Area cultivated (acres)		Motive Power for Irrigation	Persons in the Household	Workers in the Household	Value in Rupees		Cash Expenditure on			Net Disposable Income		Livestock	
	Total	Irrigated				Home Consumption of Products	Sale of Produce	Labour	Electric power	Fertilizers	Total	Per Family Worker	Work Animals Bullocks	Milch Animals Buffaloes
(1)	(2)	(3)	(4)	(5)	(6)	(7)	(8)	(9)	(10)	(11)	(12)	(13)	(14)	(15)
(i)	9	9	Bullocks	8	3	1700	3960	100	—	181	3679	1226	3 +1 camel	3
(ii)	13	13	-do-	5	1	1495*	750†	100	—	92	1158	1158	2	2
(iii)	8	8	-do-	8	1	1280	1410	160	—	64	1186	1186	2 +1 camel	2
(iv)	11	11	-do-	10	3	1275	2650	100	—	197	2353	784	2 +1 camel	2
(v)	14	14	-do-	12	4	1906	2950	100	—	122	2728	682	4 +1 camel	3
(vi)	13	13	Elec. Motor	17	5	1905	3225	—	522	140	2563	513	4	2
(vii)	14	14	-do-	10	3	2360	6925	100	850	437	5538	1846	3	4
(viii)	8	8	Bullocks	6	2	1266	1270	60	—	42	1168	584	2 +1 cow	1
(ix)	14	14	Elec. Motor	10	2‡	1591	3500	100	400	158	2842	1411	4	4
(x)	13	13	Bullocks	8	2	1515	2404	100	—	72	2232	1116	4 +1 cow	2

Note: * Has other dependants also. † Plus Rs. 600, income from carting.
‡ In addition one *sanjhee* kept and paid 1/9 share of production.

Land Use and Cropping Pattern

Data on distribution of the cropped area among principal crops in 1951-52, 1956-57 and 1961-62, as obtained from the records of the Revenue Department, are given in Table 17.5.

These figures do not show any noteworthy change either in the net area sown or in the gross cropped area during this period. But there is an increase of about 200 acres in the irrigated area. In 1961-62, 85.6 per cent of the cropped area of the village received irrigation. Irrigation was almost entirely from wells. Out of 951 acres irrigated in 1961-62, 940 acres were irrigated by wells. The increase in irrigation during this period has been due to increase in number of wells (from 30 to 51) and electrification of a large number (36) of these. The area under canal irrigation is very small, only 11 acres. The distributary of a canal passes through the village; but very few cultivators take water from it. The main reason given for not taking water from the canal is that there is sufficient water in the wells, and cost of lifting it is not too high. The fear of water logging, a major problem in some of the canal-irrigated areas of Central Punjab, also discourages use of canal water.

Table 17.5 : Distribution of the Cropped Area among Principal Crops

(in acres)

	1951-52	*1956-57*	*1961-62*
Total geographical area	1,238	1,239	1,239
Net area sown:	1,132	1,118	1,118
Irrigated	786	771	951
Unirrigated	346	346	167
Gross cropped area:	1,637	1,663	1,639
Irrigated	1,256	1,271	1,440
Unirrigated	381	372	199
Area sown more than once	505	545	521
Percentage of net area sown	44.6	48.7	46.6
Area under crops			
Kharif: Maize	121	188	240
Cotton	—	198	143
Sugarcane	191	99	178
Summer fodders:	295	231	195
Chari	249	155	127
Other	46	76	68
Wheat	474	357	436
Other *Rabi* grains and mixtures	319	276	237
Winter fodders (mainly *berseem*)	92	154	164
Vegetables	4	4	7
Other crops	16	6	11

The figures of Table 17.5 show significant changes in the cropping pattern, with increases in areas under more remunerative and higher yielding crops like cotton, maize and the winter fodder *berseem*, and decreases in those under low-yielding crops like gram, *rabi* grain mixtures (wheat-gram, gram-barley) and the summer fodder *chari*. The area under maize has doubled during this period; cotton, which was not grown in 1951-52, has become an important crop and acreage under *berseem* has also increased. All these crops yield much more than the crops they have replaced. Maize and cotton are higher yielding or are more remunerative than gram or wheat-gram or barley-gram mixtures. *Berseem* similarly yields much more than *chari*. It gives 5, 6 or more cuttings in one season, compared to one cutting of *Chari*. The value of fodder from an acre under *berseem* is estimated about three times that from an acre under *Chari*.

This change in the cropping pattern has become possible because of increased availability of irrigation, and especially because the cultivator has a much larger quantity of water entirely under his control. He can follow an intensive cropping pattern and ensure adequate attention to each of the crops grown by him. During discussions in the village, the cultivators repeatedly referred to the latter fact.

Consolidation and Electrification

All cultivators agreed that the present phase of rapid improvement in agriculture started after consolidation of holdings, which was completed in the village during 1951-52. The advantages of consolidation of holdings for more efficient and intensive cultivation are so well known that it is not necessary to explain these here. However, the case of the *Sarpanch* may be mentioned to illustrate the point. He said, "Before consolidation my family had share in lands falling under 13 wells; but after consolidation all our lands came under one well, though we constructed another well later." Consolidation of holdings was followed by a spurt of development activity, the most important feature of which was extension of well irrigation. The village had 30 wells in 1951-52. By 1961-62 the number had increased to 45. In addition, there were 6 *kutcha*-bore tubewells in the later year, bringing the total number of irrigation units to 51. The village received electricity in 1954; it was among the first villages in the Block to receive it. Electrification was followed by a wave of installation of electric motors on the wells. Eleven motors were installed, within one month, in 1955 when a large *taccavi* loan was sanctioned for this purpose by the State Government. At the time of this study, 29 out of 45 wells had electric motors and one had a diesel engine. In addition, the 6 *kutcha* bore tube-wells mentioned above were also fitted with electric motors. The *kutcha* bore is an interesting innovation because it enables a cultivator to start irrigating his land without constructing a *pucca* well. A tube is inserted in the ground by digging a *kutcha* hole, a pumping set and electric motor are installed on it and irrigation is started immediately but the *pucca* well is constructed after two, three or more years when the cultivator can spare the capital. It was also reported that some farmers in neighbouring villages had two or three such bores in different parts of their farms and used portable motors which they took from one hole to the other. This latest innovation, which saves time and investment, is an indication of the facility which the cultivators have acquired in the technique of irrigation with the help of electric motors.

Installation of electric motors was helped by liberal grants of *taccavi* loans by the State Government. Loans for 8 electric motors totalling Rs. 13,000 were sanctioned during 1955, when the first set of motors was installed and till the time of this study, loans totalling Rs. 26,300 had been sanctioned for 15 electric motors. Thus, *taccavi* loans have financed electrification of half the village wells.

Electrification makes possible lifting of water at a markedly lower cost, besides allowing a saving of time in irrigation. The estimate given in Table 17.6 of the comparative cost of irrigation of one acre of wheat by electric pumping and by lifting water with the help of bullocks was given by one cultivator and is generally accepted. Irrigation with an electric pumping set besides being much cheaper is also much more intensive and adequate. It was explained that with an electric pumping set four watering for the wheat crop were adequate; but with bullocks six to seven watering were required.

Table 17.6 : Comparative Cost of Irrigation with an Electric Pumping Set and Bullocks

Rauni irrigation (first irrigation after preparing the land) of one acre of wheat			
With Electric Pumping Set	(*Rs.*)	With Bullocks	(*Rs.*)
Consumption of electricity for 6 hours (approx.)	2.00	Wages of 2 men for 2½ days @ Rs. 2.50 per man per day	12.50
Wages of 1 man for three quarters of a day @ Rs. 2.50 per day	1.87	Expenses of two bullocks for 2½ days @ Rs. 5 per day	12.50
Total	*3.87*	*Total*	*25.00*
Or say,	4.00		

The effect of electrification of wells has not been so much increase in area under irrigation, as more adequate and intensive watering of the irrigated land. The saving of labour of man and beast, which electrification has brought about, has been utilized by cultivators mainly in the form of more adequate and intensive irrigation of their crops, which along with increased use of fertilizers and other improved practices, has resulted in increased yields. Improvement in the quality of livestock has been another striking benefit. This has resulted both from reduced strain on bullocks—lifting water for irrigation is considered extremely strenuous for the bullocks—and better feeding, which has become possible as a result of larger area under green fodders. Explaining this point, one cultivator said, "Now we have green fodder the year round, with the result that we feed our animals better and also make a saving on the grains which we used to feed them earlier".

More Intensive Manuring

This is possibly the second most important aspect of technological change in agriculture. It consists both in better use of farmyard manure and greatly increased use of chemical fertilizers. The latter, which began only during the early 50s, has shown a rapid increase especially during the last five years (Table 17.7).

Table 17.7: Use of Chemical Fertilizers

	1958-59	*1959-60*	*1960-61*	*1961-62*	*1962-63**
Nitrogenous: Ammonium Sulphate CAN (Calcium ammonium nitrate)	20.00	23.00	24.00	31.00	36.05
Phosphate: Super phosphate	2.00	3.05	2.00	7.04	10.01
Total	22.00	26.05	26.00	38.04	46.06

Note: * Sale of fertilizer between April and November 1963 was about 75 tonnes and it was estimated by the VLW and the BDO that the total for 1963-64 would be between 90 to 100 tonnes because top dressing of *rabi* crops had yet to be done.

This village is not exceptional in the progress of fertilizer use or in the average quantity of fertilizer used per acre. The total fertilizer consumption in the Block itself had increased from 295 tonnes in 1956-57 to 2,141 tonnes in 1961-62 and is expected to reach 4,000 tonnes in 1963-64. The average figure per cultivated acre in the village was 34 kg.

per acre as compared with 25.3 kg for the Block. The highest average of almost 100 kg per cultivated acre was reported from the garden colony village mentioned later.

Use of chemical fertilizers has become an integral part of the agricultural pattern of the village. The VLW mentioned that practically every cultivator in the village was using chemical fertilizers and that a large number was following the dosages recommended by him. One reason for the popularity of chemical fertilizers is that the average cultivator realizes that the increasingly intensive cropping pattern, which he is now adopting, cannot be sustained without their use. He understands that he just does not have adequate farmyard manure for all his crops and must use chemical fertilizers in addition. There is good awareness also of the relative cost and returns from fertilizer use. In one of the discussions, a cultivator mentioned that in case of the wheat crop, the cost of the chemical fertilizer was recovered from the additional chaff, which they got as a result of the higher yield, and the additional grain was their profit. There was general agreement with this view. Another indication of the cultivators' understanding of chemical fertilizers may be had from the speed with which the new fertilizer CAN (calcium ammonium nitrate) had spread. In the early years of the CD Block, the extension staff popularized the use of ammonium sulphate but during the last three years, when there has been a shortage of ammonium sulphate and CAN from the Nangal fertilizer factory has been freely available, they have been propagating use of the latter.

The BDO explained that while ammonium sulphate was still demanded by cultivators for certain crops—it was considered particularly good for groundnut—the majority of the cultivators had already switched over to the use of CAN. They had understood that their crops needed nitrogen, and that CAN supplied it just as efficiently as did ammonium sulphate. They might not know the English word 'nitrogen'; but they had grasped the basic idea that ammonium sulphate, CAN and other manures (like farmyard manure) supplied the same essential element to the soil.

Use of super phosphate for the wheat and groundnut crops is also increasing rapidly. The latest introduction is potash. Its use is being propagated by the extension staff for the wheat crop from this year (1963-64) only, and eight tons of potash had been distributed in the Block area. As the results are considered to be promising, the Block staff feels that the quantity could be increased to about 100 tons next year. The main advantage of potash is that it gives a polished appearance to the grain, which fetches a higher price in the market. The yield is also reported to be somewhat higher with its use.

Better Use of Farmyard Manure

This is linked with consolidation of holdings on the one hand, and use of chemical fertilizers on the other. Consolidation gave a fillip to use of farmyard manure, because as a result of it, all cultivators and most non-cultivators who had livestock were allotted sites for compost pits on the outskirts of the village. This allotment removed the difficulty of land for pits, which many cultivators and non-cultivators like Harijans who kept cattle faced. All these pits are well utilized. In addition many cultivators have pits in their holdings also. Experience with use of chemical fertilizers has aided use of farmyard manure because it has made the cultivators conscious of the value of their own farmyard manure. So long as the cultivators did not buy fertilizers they were not acutely conscious of the monetary value of the farmyard manure which they produced themselves or which they obtained from Harijans and others in the village. But, when they began to buy fertilizers they began to be aware of the value of farm-yard manure also, because they began to compare what a cartload of farm-yard manure could do for their crops in comparison with what a bag of chemical fertilizers did. Moreover, as a larger number of Harijans and other non-cultivators began to have manure from their newly allotted pits, buying and selling of manure (for cash or in exchange for fodder) became more common. In 1963, the price of one cartload of manure, during the *kharif* sowing season (May-June) when most of the farmyard manure is applied to the fields, was more than Rs. 6 per cart, and many cultivators were commenting that this was an all time high.

However, even though there is greater awareness of the value of farm-yard manure, and its use has increased, the practice of burning cowdung has not stopped. The compost Inspector of the Block explained that the cultivators realized that the practice caused a serious loss to agriculture and that the more progressive and prosperous ones would be quite willing to stop it if an alternate fuel was available easily and cheaply, and the problem of heating milk for making *ghee* could be solved. As regards the latter, he explained that cow-dung cakes were essential for heating milk for *ghee* making, because of the slow heat and the particular flavour which they imparted to the *ghee* and which was especially fancied by the village people. This preference may result in some cow-dung continuing to be burnt for heating milk, even after the households switch over to other fuels. But the main problem is obviously that of providing an alternate fuel.

The Problem of Fuel

The present fuel consumption pattern of the village is somewhat as follows:

> The cultivators and the Harijans depend upon home produced fuel—cow-dung and agricultural wastes like cotton sticks. Most *Mahajan* and *Mistri* families, who do not keep milch animals, buy fuel. They buy cow-dung cakes, agricultural wastes, fire-wood, charcoal or kerosene depending upon availability and price of different fuels, and the income and level of living of the family.

Cow-dung cakes are sold mostly by the Harijans and "other artisans". Fire-wood and charcoal are sold in three fuel shops located in the village. As many as ten families have kerosene stoves, which they use for a part of their cooking.

The chief requisite for reducing consumption of cow-dung as a fuel is making available alternate fuels at a cheap price. The families, which are already buying fuel, will buy any fuel which is cheap and easily available. They will gladly use soft coke or fire-wood or even electricity if it is cheap. The cultivators and Harijans will have greater resistance to buying fuel. But even they will buy fuel, if it is cheap and conveniently available. The value of cow-dung for agriculture is realized by the cultivators and it is not considered free. But it is used, because it is there and is cheap. The *gobar* gas plant and more efficient *chulhas*, especially those which can use agricultural wastes like cotton stocks also have good possibilities of being adopted.

Use of Improved Implements

The third notable aspect of technological change is the use of improved implements. Use of improved iron ploughs, chaff cutters and iron sugar-cane presses, which began to be used in the Punjab villages 30-40 years ago have become universal, and newer improvements like furrow-turning and soil-stirring ploughs, bullock carts with pneumatic tyres, chaff cutters and sugarcane crushers driven by electric motors have also been introduced in considerable numbers. The number of implements, including improved implements, at the time of the study is given in Table 17.8.

Table 17.8 : Number of Implements

Ploughs	
Desi (unimproved)	82
Iron (improved)	142
Iron, furrow turning	44
Cotton drills	6
Maize shellers	3
Tractors	—
Chaff cutters	
Manual	70
Bullock-driven	30
Motor-driven	8
Sugarcane crushers	
Bullock-driven	58
Motor-driven	4
Bullock carts with	
Wooden wheels	34
Pneumatic tyres	38

It will be seen from the above that the stage of acceptance of small improvements, *e.g.* iron ploughs or chaff cutters, is long past. Even the bullock cart with pneumatic tyres, which involves considerable investment, is in general use. The cultivator is now at a stage when he is prepared to adopt any improved implement which is distinctly superior to the one he is using already and which he can afford to buy or hire. Secondly, he is prepared to accept any innovation or modification in existing practice, which results in a clear saving of time, labour or money. This last is very well illustrated by the recent change in the practices regarding threshing of wheat and selling of maize.

Wheat has been threshed in Indian villages from time immemorial by bullocks going over piles of harvested wheat placed on the ground. This process involves back-breaking labour by men and bullocks for two or three weeks in April and May. Winnowing is done by throwing the wheat and chaff against the breeze. Both these processes have been replaced in the West by the combined harvesters. These machines are beyond the reach of the Indian cultivator; but during the last few years a number of small mechanical threshers costing between Rs. 2,000 and 3,000 have appeared in the markets of the Punjab. Some of these have begun to be used by cultivators in this area also and it was reported that some cultivators of this village had got their wheat threshed by one such machine the previous year. However, more significant than use of this machine is the new practice of using the chaff cutter (which most cultivators possess) for threshing wheat. In this new process, whole stocks of wheat are fed through the chaff cutter which cuts the chaff into smaller pieces and separates the ears of grain. The mixture is then gone over lightly by bullocks for a few hours and the grain is separated. Another method is to put the ears of grain through the maize-sheller described below. It was reported that nearly 40 per cent of the wheat crop of the village had been threshed in this way during the previous year.

The advantages of the new process are obvious. It results in considerable saving of time and labour during April and May, which are among the busiest months of the year. This is the time when cotton and early summer fodders have to be sown and weeding of sugarcane has to be attended to. The cultivator does not have to do back breaking labour in the hot sun as he had to do in the past, and can devote himself to more fruitful work. The practice has two other advantages also. It reduces risk of loss of grain and chaff from dust-storms and thunder-storms, which are quite common at this time of the year, and yields better, cleaner grain and chaff because these do not get mixed with the dust. Secondly, it does not involve use of any special, expensive equipment, but depends upon use of tools, which the cultivator possesses already. But the most significant point about it, from the point of view of this study, is that it has become popular mainly through the initiative of the cultivators themselves. An extension worker might have evolved the practice and extension staff might have had some part in popularizing it. But it was obviously not evolved at a research station and was not propagated by the extension staff as an important recommended practice.

The mechanical maize-sheller is a simple device, which consists of nothing more than an old mobil oil barrel, fitted with wooden pedals, mounted on a horizontal wooden shaft. It operates with mechanical or bullock power. There are three such machines in the village, one of which is owned by an agricultural implement fabricator and the other two are owned by the two flour mill owners. These people undertake shelling of maize for cultivators at a charge of one *seer* per *maund* (1 kg per 40 kg) of grain shelled. It was reported that about half of the maize crop of the village was being handled by these machines and that five machines would be adequate to handle the entire crop. Here again is an instance of a simple machine evolved through local ingenuity giving substantial benefits—saving of time, labour and a much better product.

One result of these technological advances is that the extension workers and the engineers working on improved implements have acquired a new hope and confidence. I had occasion to visit the agricultural implements workshop attached to the Agricultural University and to see the work being done on evolving improved implements like improved ploughs, a combined seed-*cum*-fertilizer drill and an improved hoe. Many of the improved ploughs and other implements devised at the workshop are improvements on the implements used by the cultivators earlier and have proved to be very popular. From discussions with these people it was clear that they had acquired the confidence that any implement which was distinctly superior to the one used by the cultivator and met all his requirements would be accepted. This confidence is a very important fact.

At this workshop experiment were also being made with small tractors. The main objective of these experiments is to evolve a tractor which meets all the needs of a medium cultivator with a holding of 10 to 15 acres and which sells at a price which this cultivator can afford to pay. The engineers and some of the other specialists at the University were very confident about the success of these experiments. They felt that among the models available abroad there are some which could meet all these conditions and could with suitable modifications is successfully placed in the Punjab market.

Use of Improved Seed

The Punjab cultivator has long been familiar with the use of improved seed of some crops. Improved varieties of wheat like C-591 and of sugarcane like CO-312 were accepted several decades ago and have since been in general use. The most important change in this area during the last ten years has been introduction of longer staple 'American' varieties of cotton. The practice of growing American cotton was brought to the area by refugee cultivators returning from the canal colonies. It spread very quickly in the early 50s when it nearly replaced the shorter staple *desi* varieties. However, it received a setback later, because the price differential in favour of the American variety was reduced and it was found that the American variety was more susceptible to disease. As a result both American and *desi* varieties are now grown in the area. In this village, most of the cotton grown is of the American variety but as the figures in Table 17.5 show, the area under cotton has declined after 1956-57, partly because of damage from disease.

In case of wheat also the older C-591 variety has been largely replaced by a new variety, C-273, which is more resistant to disease, has bolder grain and consequently fetches a better price. The experience with the spread of this new variety is interesting because it brings out the speed with which a new, distinctly superior variety can replace an older one. This variety was introduced by the Department of Agriculture about seven years ago and it is claimed by the extension staff that it almost replaced the C-591 variety in this Block within a period of about four years. When one considers that one season must elapse before the first demonstrations on cultivators' fields can give results, this time span of four years is quite small and shows a high degree of receptivity of cultivators to improvements like improved seed with which they have long been familiar.

Another noteworthy development is that some of the more progressive cultivators are themselves looking for new varieties. One such cultivator had obtained from a cultivator in another Block, seed of a new variety of wheat, which was supposed to give very high yields with intensive application of chemical fertilizers. This new variety has not yet been released by the Department of Agriculture because experiments on it are still in progress. But this cultivator had obtained it himself and during my interview with him, gave quite a sophisticated analysis of the economics of high yields with heavy doses of fertilizer. Another cultivator was experimenting with a new *kharif* fodder evolved by crossing *bajra* with Napier grass which gives very high yields and is also very nutritious.

Use of Pesticides

Use of pesticides is the latest among the improvements advocated by the extension staff, and is not as widespread as use of improved seed or of chemical fertilizers. This is due partly to the fact that the chemicals and equipment like power sprayers needed for spraying the crops are expensive and partly to the fact that chemical pesticides are ineffective in case of some important plant diseases of the area. Thus, there is as yet no chemical cure for the Gurdaspur borer which attacks sugarcane and causes heavy damage to the crop in some years. But, wherever the cultivators can use pesticides cheaply and effectively they are doing so. This is illustrated by the use of pesticides against storage pests. The practice of using BHC on grain kept in storage has been advocated by the extension staff during the last three years and the VLW claimed that it has already been adopted by the majority of cultivators in this village. Some of them mix BHC with the grain in the storage bin while others spray it by hand on the bags.

Livestock Husbandry

The standard of livestock husbandry in the Punjab has always been comparatively high. Some of the best breeds in the country like the Haryana bullocks and Murrah buffaloes come from the Haryana (south-east Punjab) area, which is not far from this district. Moreover, recent technological changes in agriculture and rise in agricultural productivity have also contributed to improvement in the quality of livestock. Mention has been made above of improvement in feeding, resulting from larger areas under green fodders, and of less strain on the working animals as a result of introduction of electric motors for lifting water. The bullocks and buffaloes are now seen in the village would rank among the best in the country.

The villagers are also keenly aware of the value of good breeding. Two pure-bred bulls, a Haryana cow bull and a Murrah buffalo bull, are maintained by the *Panchayat* through the traditional practice of being allowed to roam freely in the fields. Castration is universally done and early, in order to avoid indiscriminate breeding. However, artificial insemination has not become popular, even though this facility, which is available at the veterinary hospital in the Block headquarters town, can be availed of without difficulty. Certain other attitudes, *e.g.* towards treatment of disease and taking up commercial production of livestock products, also indicate that considerable progress has yet to be made before scientific attitude towards livestock husbandry and a commercial outlook towards production and sale of livestock products become widely established.

Treatment of Disease of Animals and Birds and Attitudes towards Sale of Milk and Eggs

The Block headquarters town has a well-equipped veterinary hospital. Similar hospitals are located in other towns at distances of 5-10 miles. Besides, there are sub-centres in the larger villages. With this network of hospitals and sub-centres, facilities for treatment of sick animals and of breeding with animals of pure breeds are within easy reach of most villages. The veterinary doctor in-charge of the hospital explained that the hospital and sub-centres were quite popular with the villagers; that large number of animals were brought to these daily; that he and his assistants were called frequently in case of serious sickness of animals and that programmes of control of epidemic diseases like HS and foot-and-mouth disease were effectively organized from time to time.

While all this would be correct, another experience, which I had, gives a revealing insight into the present attitudes towards treatment of livestock diseases. During my first visit to the village, I was told that the village was going through an outbreak of foot-and-mouth disease, and that a special ceremony, a *jag* (from Sanskrit *yajna* or sacrifice) would be organized the next day to bring it under control. It was explained that a special messenger had been sent to a neighbouring town to obtain a charm (*taweez)* from a well-known practitioner of charms and that the ceremony would consist in collecting in the morning all the cattle of the village at its various gates, passing them through the gates, and sprinkling on them, while they passed, water in which the charm and leaves and fruit of the *neem* tree had been dipped. They added that a large quantity of rice would be cooked at one place and distributed to all the households in the village, and that no fire would burn, *i.e.* no cooking would be done in any individual house, and that no person would be either allowed to come into the village from outside or to leave it, on that day.

The *jag* was duly held the next day; but I was not able to witness it because of the ban on entry of outsiders. The *Sarpanch*, an educated wide-awake man with extensive urban contacts, was a leading figure in organizing the *jag*, and the other village leaders, most of whom are equally educated and wide-awake, took a prominent part in it. Even the young VLW, an excellent extension worker who was otherwise quite progressive in his outlook, appeared to share the villagers' belief in the *jag*. When I mentioned celebration of the *jag* to the veterinary doctor, he admitted that celebration of such *jags* at the time of outbreaks of foot-and-mouth disease was common in the area. He mentioned also that villagers frequently resorted to treatments of this kind when their animals were sick, and that these treatments were often done simultaneously with the veterinary treatment obtained from hospitals.

Dairying and Poultry Farming

The attitudes towards commercial dairying and poultry production also show that the traditional prejudices against these are being overcome only slowly. There is widespread prejudice against sale of milk by cultivators in Punjab and adjoining State of northern India. This prejudice has been weakening in recent years when, with the growth of urban demand for milk, sale of milk has become very profitable. In this area, the city of Ludhiana and other towns obtain most of their milk supply from villages, through vendors who collect milk in the villages and bring it to the towns on bicycles. The Block headquarters town obtains its milk supply in this way. In addition, there is a large and growing demand for milk from the government dairy at the State capital. The dairy obtains its milk supply from milk producers' co-operative societies, several of which are located in villages of this Block.

This village sends milk to the Block headquarters town, the quantity being estimated at between 120 and 150 kg daily. Besides, there is considerable sale of milk within the village itself. Most *Mahajans* and *Mistris* and many Harijans do not keep milch animals and buy milk, the quantity varying with the size and income of the family. Many *Jats* also buy milk when their animals are dry. But commercial milk production is much less than it could be, and the prejudice against production of milk for sale among cultivators is partly responsible for this. It is significant that sale of milk was reported by only 5 people and three of these were non-*Jat*—one *Brahmin* and two Harijans. Some village leaders mentioned that the number of milk sellers was in fact higher and that many cultivators, who were actually selling milk had not reported the sale, because of the stigma attached to it.

A milk producers' co-operative society for supplying milk to the government dairy at the State capital had been formed in the village two years earlier. It had worked for some time, and had then failed. Its failure was attributed by the village leaders to dishonesty and inefficiency of the staff attached to the milk collection centre located in the village. But later, when I discussed this subject again with them after having seen the successful operation of such a centre in a neighbouring village, they agreed that the main reason for the failure of the scheme was lack of interest in commercial dairying among the cultivators.

The same attitude prevails towards production of eggs for sale. The cultivators have no prejudice against consumption of eggs or other poultry products or against keeping some birds for meeting their domestic requirements of these. In fact, the practice of keeping birds for meeting domestic requirements has increased greatly in recent years, as the cultivators have become more prosperous. The VLW estimated that as many as 75 families (mostly of *jat* cultivators) were keeping poultry. But only one person had started commercial production in a small way, by keeping a flock of about 50 birds.

However, both successful dairying and commercial poultry farming were seen elsewhere in the Block. Dairying was seen in the adjoining village, which had a co-operative milk producers' society supplying milk to the government dairy at the State capital. The society has 20 members from the village, and in addition collects milk from non-members in other villages. The supplies range between 400 and 600 kg of milk daily. The members of the society were very satisfied with its working and explained that they received good income from sale of milk. Many of them had steadily increased milk production during the one year working of the society. It was an experience also to see delicate instruments like the Babcock butter-fat tester being operated by an old illiterate member. The Chairman of the society, a young man, educated and very progressive dairy farmer, was extremely enthusiastic about its working. He mentioned that the members of his society had recently bought 60 quality buffaloes from an adjoining district to increase their production of milk. His own herd of about 15 buffaloes was among the best in the Block and two of his buffaloes had received prizes for high milk production. He explained that the average milk yield of a buffalo among the members of the society was 8 kg per day (some of the buffaloes in his own herd yielded 16 to 18 kg per day, at the peak of the lactation period), that one buffalo could yield a net profit of Rs. 75 to 100 per month to its owner and that several members of the society with only 2 or 3 buffaloes were having incomes of Rs. 150 to 200 per month.

Commercial production of poultry was also seen in this village and elsewhere in the Block. This is one of the Blocks selected for intensive development of poultry in the State. As part of the poultry development programme a poultry extension centre and a marketing society were established at the Block headquarters about a year ago. These provide all the assistance and facilities—one-day old chicks to start a new flock, balanced feed, medical assistance, especially inoculation against disease like *ranikhet*, incubators for hatching of eggs and agreements for marketing of eggs and birds—which a farmer needs to start and run a poultry farm. The Block has about a dozen poultry farms with flocks of 100 to 500 birds each, and the number is increasing.

The poultry farmer in this village was an educated young man, the son of a government officer, who had turned to poultry keeping about a year earlier when he was unable to get a suitable white-collar job. He explained that he had obtained one-day old chicks from the government poultry farm at Ludhiana and got technical assistance from the extension staff at the poultry extension centre. He was a member of the poultry marketing society, bought his feed and marketed his eggs through it. During the previous winter he had made good money by selling eggs for hatching to the IADP people at Ludhiana. He mentioned that he could get a net income of Re one per bird and that he was making more money by keeping poultry than he would have made in any white-collar job. He had started with about 300 birds in his own residential house, but was so satisfied with one year's working of his enterprise that at the time of my visit he was building a new, scientifically designed poultry house outside the village, with plans to increase his flock to 1,000 birds.

Later, I had occasion to see several other poultry farms, including one located at the Block headquarters town, which was being managed by the wife of a white-collar worker. This woman was keeping about 400 birds in the yard of her home. She had started keeping poultry about three years earlier, and her initial success had so encouraged her that she had bought her own incubator and had set herself up as a supplier of chicks to new poultry farmers.

Poultry farming is making rapid progress in the Block and in the district. The number of poultry farms has increased during the last three years and will increase even more rapidly now, since it has caught the attention of the people. The main attraction is the high price of eggs in the markets of Delhi and the Punjab towns. The staff of the poultry extension centre and several of the poultry farmers themselves explained that the new scientific method of keeping poultry, which had eliminated the risk of heavy mortality from disease, had made poultry farming quite profitable. Indeed, it has transformed poultry keeping—a neglected branch of animal husbandry to which only the poor scheduled castes or Muslims paid some attention earlier—into a profitable enterprise.

But it is interesting to note that this new development of poultry is mainly in the hands of educated people. Some of them are cultivators; but others like the wife of the white-collar worker mentioned above are non-cultivators. The enterprise requires a certain amount of capital and what is more, strict adherence to certain recommended practices, *e.g.* inoculation of birds at stated periods, balanced feeding, culling etc., which the average farmer still finds too tedious; but which the educated person can adopt easily.

The speed with which commercial poultry farming is spreading leads the author to think that commercial dairying can also make similar progress, if there are comparable advances in technique and similar facilities for marketing etc. are made available. The main requirements for development of dairying are improving the milk yields of animals and more efficient organization of milk collection. As regards the former, one specialist at the Agricultural University was of the view that through systematic breeding and improvements in feeding practices, the milk yields of buffaloes in this area could be increased by 50 to 75 per cent within a few years.

The Problem of Excessive Numbers

In any discussion on animal husbandry in India, the problem of numbers assumes prominence, because the number of cattle is much in excess of the requirements of agriculture and their low quality is considered to be due mainly to this fact. The prevailing practice in many parts of the country is that animals, especially cows and young stock, are turned loose on village pastures and other common lands and fallows, and subsist on whatever grazing is available in these. The situation in this respect is strikingly different in this village today. The number of cattle is not too large and the practice of grazing on common lands and fallows, never widespread, has almost disappeared. The number of livestock at the time of this survey is reported to be:

Table 17.9 : Number of Livestock

Bullocks	262
Cows	89
Young stock	123
She-buffaloes	261
Young stock of buffaloes	197
Goats	109

Thus there were only 131 pairs of bullocks for over 1,100 acres of intensively cultivated, well-irrigated land, which has a high intensity of double cropping. This number is not only excessive; but appears to be barely sufficient for meeting the requirements of agriculture. The only other animals kept in appreciable numbers are milch buffaloes, which are the primary source of milk supply. On the other hand, the number of cows and young stock, which form such a large proportion of cattle in several other parts of the country, is comparatively small. One reason for this is that the cultivators do not attempt to be self-sufficient in their requirements of bullocks by breeding cows and raising young stock. They do not find this practice economical. The prevailing practice is to buy either mature bullocks or young calves of between 1 and 4 years of age, and to bring them up until they are old enough for work. Buying of young calves is preferred to buying of mature bullocks, because these are cheaper. These bullocks and calves are brought mainly in the *mandis* of the Haryana area which are not far from here. Most cultivators do not rear buffaloes either. These are reared by Harijans or other castes like *Bazigars*, for whom it is an important source of income. Even buffaloes, which have gone dry are often given by cultivators to Harijans to keep through their dry periods and are taken back, when they are in milk.

It is clear from this that the cultivator has a very practical attitude towards livestock husbandry. He keeps only those animals, which are most useful to him, and keeps feeding of unproductive animals or even of productive animals through their unproductive periods at a minimum. But the animals, which he does keep, he feeds well. Unlike farmers in many parts of the country, he does not have the attitude of keeping large numbers of animals (and allowing them to starve) just because it does not cost him anything to do so.

This attitude is related to the fact that the practice of allowing the cattle to graze in pastures, etc, has been stopped and there is now almost exclusive reliance on stall-feeding. Growing of fodder crops and stall-feeding of cattle have been prominent features of the farm enterprise in Punjab for a long time; but in villages of this area, these have received further emphasis after consolidation of holdings and electrification of wells. First, with consolidation even the small areas of pastures, which had been available earlier, were eliminated. Secondly, with the growing intensity of cropping, hardly any areas of fallow lands are available for grazing of animals. Thirdly, as explained earlier, with increase in irrigation and in agricultural productivity, cultivators now grow much larger quantities of green fodder.

Therefore, if the present phase of mechanization, *i.e.* electrification of wells, is followed by the further step of introduction of small tractors, the presence of a large number of surplus cattle will not prove an intractable problem. The introduction of tractors will be accompanied by progressive reduction in the number of cattle through the simple process of cultivators selling their existing bullocks and not buying new ones. Buffaloes will continue to be kept however for their milk and their numbers may even increase, if commercial dairy-farming makes progress. The need for farmyard manure will then be met increasingly from the buffaloes. These developments will be similar to those in USA and Western Europe, where the farm-work animal, the horse, has disappeared after introduction of tractors, and there has been a sharp increase in the number of cows of specialized dairy breeds.

On the Eve of a Technological Revolution

The picture which emerges from the above description is that of an agricultural community in which there has been notable advance in methods of utilization of resources. A process of rapid adoption of improved agricultural practices is now well under way. This process began with consolidation of holdings, which was followed by a rapid increase in the number of irrigation wells and electrification of most of these. These developments made possible a more intensive cropping pattern, more adequate irrigation and care of all the crops grown, and increasing attention to adoption of recommended improvements, notably use of chemical fertilizers. Much progress still remains to be made in intensifying agriculture and extending adoption of improved practices to all the farmers. The use of chemical fertilizers for instance, could be increased ten-fold, before the level considered adequate by the agricultural scientists are reached. But a stage has now been reached when adoption of improved practices has become part of the agricultural enterprise of the average farmer; when proved improvements like improved seeds of several crops, and nitrogenous fertilizers are adopted by the majority of the farmers and a new seed variety or a new fertilizer takes only a few years (3 to 5) to get widely accepted. There are farmers in these villages that are not only ready to adopt recommended improvements; but are themselves looking for these in an effort to increase their production and incomes. Their number is small; but their presence has an influence which is far greater than their numbers. Further, beginnings of highly specialized types of commercial farming or livestock enterprises, like commercial poultry production, have already been made.

The area is now ready for larger changes, which would bring about major changes in farming techniques and make farming significantly more specialized and commercial. Expansion of poultry farming and of commercial dairying; much larger and more scientific use of commercial fertilizers and pesticides; large-scale introduction of the small tractors and mechanization of a variety of agricultural operations will be some of these changes. The successful experience with technological change has put the farmers in a mood in which a large number will be ready to adopt the larger and more fundamental changes. The economic level of the upper half of the farmers (those with holdings above 10 acres) makes it possible for them to be receptive to these changes, and there are no problems like that of a large number of unproductive cattle, which would present insuperable obstacles in the adoption of these.

Impact of Change

The Mahajans

The non-cultivator castes in the village are the *Mahajans,* the Artisans and the Harijans. The *Mahajans* need not detain us long. It has been explained earlier that for several decades they have sought their economic destiny outside the village, through joining services and professions after getting education. The economic changes of recent years have not altered this trend significantly.

The majority of the *Mahajan* families of Jitpur are dependent to a greater or lesser extent upon income originating outside the village. Some depend upon pensions; others receive remittances from sons, nephews, etc., working outside the village. Among the 83 workers listed in the Annexure as many as 30 are 'emigrants' with active links with village families. Even among the remaining 53 workers, who live in the village, as many as 13 are in service jobs outside the village. Within the village, the principal occupation of the *Mahajans* is petty shop-keeping. A few have recently taken to mechanical trades like repair of bicycles and flour-milling. But the scope for such petty commerce is rather limited. The village is not a commercial centre and is not likely to become one in the future, because it is located so close to the Block headquarters town. The aspiration of the *Mahajans* has for several decades been to seek employment outside the village after education, and must remain so.

The Artisans

As mentioned earlier, the village has two main groups of artisans: the *Ramgarhia Mistris*—smiths, masons, carpenters—having 37 households, and 'other artisans'—potters, oil pressers, etc.—represented by 15 households. The impact of the changes on these two groups has been markedly different. Most of the *Mistri* families have done well; but the majority of the families of 'other artisans' have benefited little and continue to be among the poorest people in the village.

The families of smiths are among the most progressive and prosperous in the village. The two families of agricultural implements fabricators are doing a flourishing business in fabrication of agricultural implements and in repair work. Two other families have gone into business—owning brick kilns and trucks and taking up small government contracts. They are among the most prosperous people in the village. A large number of young men from families of smiths have got remunerative employment outside the village, in the machine shops in the Block headquarters town and in Ludhiana. The masons are also doing well. As explained earlier, they are very good craftsmen, and as a result of increase in house-building activity, they have managed to get remunerative employment in the village, in the Block headquarters town and in neighbouring villages. The wages of a mason range between Rs. 4-5 per day plus food, so that an average worker can make about Rs. 150 per month. The carpenters have not displayed the same enterprise as the smiths or the masons have. They remain closely connected with agriculture and have repairs of ploughs and other agricultural implements as their major source of income. But even they have benefited from increase in demand for wood-work, resulting from increased construction activity.

In contrast, the 'other artisans' have benefited very little. The potters and the oil pressers continue their traditional occupations and follow the traditional techniques. But since these do not give them full-time employment, they supplement their earnings from these with agricultural and non-agricultural labour. The potters also haul earth for house construction. The traditional craft of the weavers (6 Harijan families) has been steadily declining as mill-made fabrics have replaced the cloth woven by them, and the recent economic changes have only hastened the decline. The only cloth now produced by them is coarse, heavy *khadi* and *khes* (bed-spreads). Weaving of these two types of cloth survives only because these fulfil some of the more specific needs of rural life. The *khes* for instance is useful not only as a bed-spread, but serves also as a cheap and durable cotton shawl, which can be used as much for protection against rain and cold as for bringing straw or green fodder from the fields.

In case of all these crafts, there is neither any marked increase in demand for the products nor any technological improvement. Nor does continuation of the current change of processes hold any prospects of revival in the foreseeable future. The economic redemption of the artisans practicing these crafts lies in change of occupation—taking up white-collar service after education or entering other skilled occupations after learning new skills.

The Harijans

As explained above, the Harijans of Jitpur are primarily a labouring group. The 75 families of *Ramdasias* depend mainly upon labour, agricultural and/or non-agricultural. The six families of *julahas* (weavers) and six of *balmikis* (scavengers) have their traditional occupations as supplementary sources of income. The labourers can be divided into two groups :

(i) *sanjhees* or attached agricultural labourers with cultivators; and
(ii) casual unattached labourers who take up labour, agricultural or non-agricultural, according to as it becomes available.

Among the latter, 18 men work with trucks, loading and unloading bricks. They could also be regarded as attached labourers, more or less, because they do this work for about ten months in the year and take up other work only during the rainy season when this work is not available.

The other economic activities of the Harijans are service (8 workers) and shop-keeping (3 workers). Service is mainly of the unskilled work type, though two young men are skilled workers and one is a white-collar worker. Eleven Harijan young men of the village are included among the emigrants in the Annexure. Seven of these are in military service and the other four are in other services. The families of shop-keepers and service-men living in the village, and of the young men who have gone out for service are the most progressive and prosperous Harijan families in the village. And, with spread of education and rise in aspirations there is a growing tendency among the young people to look up to these occupations as the means to a higher income and better life.

Wages and Employment

The wages of casual agricultural labourers are Rs. 2 per day plus food or less frequently, Rs. 2.50 per day without food. Wages for certain agricultural operations like harvesting of wheat or maize, and making of *gur,* which are paid in kind, are considerably higher. But such work is available only for a few days in the appropriate seasons. The Harijan casual labourers figuring in the sample survey reported having done such work for 15 to 25 days in the year.

The wages of casual non-agricultural labourers are Rs. 2 per day without food, though workers who load and unload bricks from trucks make much more, up to Rs. 4 per day. These workers have also greater security of employment, because this work is available for about ten months in the year.

From the data of the sample household and from discussions with Harijans in the village, it appears that a casual agricultural/non-agricultural labourer can get employment for about 25 days in a month in most months of the year, and that the only slack period when he is unemployed for any length of time is the rainy season (July-August). Assuming a total work year of 250 to 300 days, taking into account the fact that when he does agricultural work he gets food in addition to money wages, and that in specified agricultural operations like harvesting of wheat or making *gur*, he makes much more than Rs. 2 per day, the average annual earnings of a casual agricultural-cum-non-agricultural labourer come to about Rs. 600 per year. There was general agreement among the villagers on this point.

The women do not take up wage labour, agricultural or non-agricultural. The only work for which they get wages (in kind) is picking cotton. The women of the sample household had obtained 15 to 25 kg of cotton in the previous years, and all of it was retained for household consumption. The main contribution of the women to the income of the household is made through the livestock enterprise. This income comes through increment in the value of the animals kept, less frequently from the sale of milk, and is reported to range between Rs. 200 and Rs. 300 per year. Including this income, an average Harijan household with one male earner working as casual agricultural/non-agricultural labourer makes between Rs. 800 to 1,000 per year. The *sanjhees* and those working with trucks are better off. The latter get higher wages. The *sanjhees* have assurance of obtaining all their needs of food and other agricultural produce fairly comfortably, and have also greater financial security, because they can depend upon financial assistance from their employers in times of need.

Most *sanjhees* are given a share of the produce, the proportion varying with the size of holding, especially depending on whether one or more pairs of bullocks are kept, on the productivity of the farm and the need of the owner for labour. In a holding with one pair of bullocks, the share varies from one-fourth to one-sixth of the produce, and in one with two pairs of bullocks, it varies between one-eighth and one-eleventh. If more than two pairs of bullocks are kept, the proportion is correspondingly smaller. Until about 20 years ago, the *sanjhee's* share in the produce was decided as follows: if a cultivator had a pair of bullocks and two workers of his own family, the *sanjhee* got one-fifth of the produce, bullocks and men being counted equally for this purpose. Now-a-days however, this principal is not always adhered to, mainly because the cultivators feel that productivity of land has increased with intensive irrigation, use of chemical fertilizers and other improved practices, and the *sanjhee*, who does not contribute to the cost of these, is not entitled to the same share which he was getting earlier. Therefore, progressive cultivators with high level of productivity generally give the *sanjhee* a smaller share of the produce. Some of them prefer to pay their *sanjhee* in cash. In such cases the payment to the *sanjhee* varies between Rs. 500 and Rs. 600 per year plus food. On the other hand, a *sanjhee* working with a farmer who has not enough workers of his own, or whose cultivation is not efficient, may get a larger share. There was one case in the sample in which the *sanjhee* was getting one-fourth of the gross produce from a cultivator having one pair of bullocks. But as the man was not an efficient cultivator, and production on his farm was low, the *sanjhee* was no better off than the other *sanjhees* included in the sample.

The *sanjhee* gets a share only in foodgrains and other products like *gur* and cotton, but not in fodder crops, agricultural wastes or by-products like cotton sticks. Most Harijans do keep some milch animals for sale or for meeting the milk needs of their families, and do need fodder. They obtain it in two ways—in exchange for farmyard manure, which they have from their animals, and by their women cutting grass growing along field boundaries or as weeds in the fields with standing crops. The cultivators do not object to Harijan women, especially of the families of *sanjhees* and others with whom they have relations, cutting grass in their fields; and the facility of obtaining grass from the employer's fields is one attraction for a *sanjhee* and even for a causal agricultural labourer.

During the interviews with them, the cultivators complained that because of greatly increased availability of agricultural and non-agricultural employment in recent years, they were experiencing difficulty in obtaining labour for agriculture, especially in the months of April-May and September-October, when agricultural work was the heaviest. They also complained that the labourers preferred non-agricultural work to agricultural work in spite of higher wages in the latter because agricultural work was harder and involved longer hours of work. The Harijans agreed that more employment was now available, but explained that there were still some periods in the year like the rainy season, when they had to remain unemployed for some time. They also admitted that they preferred non-agricultural to agricultural work, and for the reasons given by the cultivators. Their main complaint was that increase in agricultural productions in recent years had not benefited them very much. They stated that the wages for casual labour had not risen in proportion to the rise in prices and that in case of *sanjhees* rise in agricultural productivity had been neutralized by reduction in share of the produce.

We now come to the question: how far have the economic changes of recent years benefited the Harijans and what attitudes do they have to these? The answer may be given somewhat as follows :

- The casual agricultural-*cum*-non-agricultural labourers are still essentially at the subsistence level.
- The *sanjhees* and the workers with trucks are better off. The *sanjhees* have participated differently in the increase in agricultural productivity, though their participation would have been larger if their share had not been reduced. The workers with trucks have a new remunerative source of employment.
- The best-off families among Harijans are those in which one or more members are engaged in occupations like shop-keeping or service.

The Harijans are keenly aware of the fact that economic progress in the village has so far failed to lift most of them above the subsistence level and has only increased the economic disparity between themselves and the cultivating-owners. This creates dissatisfaction among them, especially among the young men.

The largest gains to the Harijans have come through changes in social attitudes and improvement of social services. Untouchability, never as rigorous in this area as in other parts of the country (partly because of the influence of Sikh religion) has almost disappeared. Improvement in health services, construction of works like pavements of streets and *pucca* wells in the Harijan quarters, and loans for housing have also benefited them. But the main benefit has come through education. It has been explained earlier that the most prosperous and progressive Harijan families in the village are those of shopkeepers and men in service, or families from which boys have gone out for service. All these people have been able to enter these more remunerative occupations because of education. It appears that spread of education will be the main instrument for economic and social progress of the Harijans and such progress will come mainly through the social process—education, wider outlook, higher aspirations, striving for and getting better paid jobs, mainly outside the village. The recent extension of compulsory primary education, which has brought a large proportion of the Harijan boys into the schools, is a major step in this direction.

Other Aspects of Change

Education

The tradition of modern type school education is quite well established in this area, especially among groups like *Mahajans* and *Ramgarhia Mistris* from which large numbers have been going out in services, professions and skilled work. Among the *jats* too, education has been widespread because of the tradition of emigration and military service. But in recent years education has been spreading rapidly among all groups including the Harijans. The village has two primary schools now, one for boys and the other for girls, which have 285 students. In addition 83 boys and girls go to the three high schools in the Block headquarters town and three boys attend the college located in the *mandi* town. Thus, the total number of students in the village is 371. Their distribution by sex, caste and type of school attended is given in Table 17.10.

Table 17.10 : Distribution of School Students by Sex, Caste and Type of School Attended

Caste	Primary School: Ist 3 Classes M	F	T	Primary School: Class IV & V M	F	T	High School M	F	T	Total M	F	T
Jats	46	31	77	22	9	31	23	9	32	91	49	140
Mistris	16	16	32	8	3	11	6	10	16	30	29	59
Mahajans	13	19	32	4	9	13	15	12	27	32	40	72
Harijans	44	14	58	6	5	11	6	—	6	56	19	75
Other artisans	5	3	8	2	1	3	1	—	1	8	4	12
Bazigars	3	2	5	4	—	4	1	—	1	8	2	10
Total village	**127**	**65**	**212**	**46**	**27**	**73**	**52**	**31**	**83**	**225**	**143**	**368**

Compulsory primary education was introduced in the village three years ago. It has been effectively enforced in case of boys and with the exception of a stray case here and there, every boy of school-going age now goes to school. In case of girls, however, enforcement is not equally strict and there are many girls especially among the Harijans, who do not attend school. The figures in Table 17.10 bring out clearly the effect of enforcement of compulsory education on school-going. The sharp increase in the number of Harijan boys in the first-three classes is particularly noteworthy. The number of Harijan girls going to school has also shown a marked increase though it is still small. Among the *jats* also the number of girls going to school is much less than the number of boys but the effect of introduction of compulsory primary education is clearly seen in the increase in number of girls in the first-three classes as compared with that in the higher classes. Among the *Ramgarhia Mistris* and *Mahajans* on the other hand, the number of girls going to school including high school is comparable to or higher than that of boys. In both these groups, education of girls has become an accepted social practice.

The number of boys and girls in classes 1 to 9 is estimated to be about 66 per cent of those in the age-group 6-15. The percentage of boys and girls of the age-group 6-11 going to school would be higher still because the numbers in primary classes are much higher than those in the post-primary classes. But the village is still far from universal literacy. The percentage of literates among adults (above 15 years) was found to be only 23.8, in this survey. The position of universal literacy will be reached only after a generation when the boys and girls who are now going to school become adults. But a situation has already been reached in which because of large number of boys and girls in schools, presence of a number of educated men in the village, and the growing awareness and knowledge of things even among the illiterates, ignorance has ceased to be a relevant fact in the village life. This is a most significant fact for the education and cultural progress of village India; because it means that the point at which ignorance ceases to be important can be reached considerably before universal literacy has been attained. Literacy and education are important as ends in themselves. But they are equally important as means of banishing ignorance and superstitions, and changing the mental outlook from a basically tradition-oriented one to a change oriented one. Experience here shows that the watershed between ignorance on one side and knowledge on the other can be crossed and a change oriented outlook produced even before the entire population becomes literate.

Health

By far the most significant recent development in the field of health in this area, as in most others in India, has been eradication of malaria. This has meant elimination of the greatest killer and debilitator of man. Moreover, since other diseases like cholera and dysentery, which are prevalent in most other parts of India, have always been less important in the Punjab, eradication of malaria has meant elimination of epidemic disease as a major problem in village life. Campaigns for eradication of small-pox and trachoma are now being carried out as part of country-wide campaigns, and it is expected that these two diseases will also be eliminated in a few years time.

The author had occasion to discuss the availability of medical facilities and attitudes towards treatment of disease with the village leaders and with the lady doctor in charge of the hospital at the Block headquarters town. The hospital, which has 24 beds, has one doctor, besides nurses and other auxiliary staff. Similar hospitals are located at distances of 5 to 15 miles along all the roads going out from the town. In addition, there are sub-centres located in the larger villages, which provide maternity aid and guidance in child-care. Three such sub-centres are located in this Block, and this village is included in the area of one of these.

The doctor explained that as part of the work of the sub-centres, house-to-house surveys of all pregnant women were conducted from time to time, that the women were persuaded to come to the sub-centres for ante-natal consultation and were given advice and necessary medicines. Cases in which any complication was likely at the time of delivery were detected at this stage, and deliveries of such women were attended to either by the nurse-midwife in their homes, or if necessary, at the hospital. At the time of this survey, about a dozen women from this village were visiting the sub-centre for ante-natal or family planning consultation. All the three *dais* of the village had received the training prescribed by the Health Department and were associated with the programme of the sub-centre. The maternity and child guidance service now available to this village is comparable to that available to any protected section of the population of the middle or lower income group, *e.g.* participants in the Employees State Insurance Scheme, and is very much better than that available to any ordinary urban group.

Attitude towards Treatment of Disease

Treatment of disease, especially serious disease or injury by modern medicine has become accepted. All cases of serious sickness or of injury are taken normally to the hospital at the Block headquarters and more serious ones are taken to the hospital at the district headquarters town. But, for treatment of common diseases, there is considerable resort to private practitioners, a *vaidya* in the village and two *vaidyas* and two medical practitioners in the Block headquarters town. The reason for the popularity of the private practitioners is either because the hospital cannot provide all the medical facilities that a villager may need or desire *e.g.* supply of medicines—or because he feels that he will get better medical attention with a private practitioner. But since even the *vaidyas* have begun to use sulpha-drugs and antibiotic, use of modern medicines is extensive, and the knowledge that a penicillin injection is an effective cure for many a disease has become part of the culture of the village.

Family Planning

A beginning has been made with this programme also. Facilities for consultation and free contraceptives are provided to the women at the sub-centres, and to both men and women at the hospital. The hospital provides facilities for vasectomy also and six of these were reported to have been done during the two years preceding this survey. The doctor, the BDO, the VLW, some workers of the Family Planning Programme and the village leaders with whom the author had occasion to discuss the subject, summed up the present practice and attitudes towards family planning as follows :

- The number of people using family planning practices is still quite small. The *Mahajans* and the *Mistris* use these practices more than people of the other castes.

- But knowledge of family planning practices is spreading rapidly, and the number of people who have begun to be aware of the need for these practices is growing. The cultivators in this area have always been acutely conscious of the limitation of land in supporting an increasing population—the tradition of migration among the *jats* is one indicator of this awareness—and the threat to size of holding, and level of income posed by a large number of births is being increasingly realized by them.
- Many, cultivators, especially the young ones, are only watching the experience of those who have begun following family planning practices and especially those who have undergone vasectomies, before adopting these themselves. Use of family planning methods will spread very rapidly in the next few years, as the experience of the small number that is practicing these now becomes widely known.

Sanitation

There has been enormous improvement in sanitation and water supply in the village during the last 15 years. Most of the village streets have been paved and provided with *pucca* side drains with financial assistance from the Community Development Block. Several wells have been made sanitary by provision of well-designed platforms, parapet walls and *pullies*. But the biggest improvement in water supply has come through installation of hand-pumps in a large number of houses. Sanitary water supply now remains a problem only for the Harijans and 'other artisans', who continue to draw water from the wells.

The main sanitation problems of the village now relate to use of latrines and provision of drainage. The drainage problem has been aggravated in recent years, with installation of hand-pumps in the houses and construction of drains because much larger quantities of waste-water now flow into the village pond. No way for draining the pond has been found yet. The *Sarpanch* mentioned that he had sent a proposal to the State Government for draining the pond through a long drainage channel into a *nullah*, and was expecting that a survey of the scheme would be taken up by the State Drainage Department in the near future. However, from the discussions with him and other people in the village it was clear that there was not enough concern about this problem among the village people and progress on it would not be rapid. Similarly, no progress has been made in use of latrines and none can be made unless flush-type latrines, which an average farmer can afford to install in his own house, are introduced. Dry latrines are impractical for the simple reason that nobody would be prepared to clean them. The sweepers of the village already confine themselves to sweeping of only cow-dung and other litter and in the prevailing social climate, it will be impossible to get them to clean latrines.

Levels of Living

Some limited data on character of housing and possession of certain durable consumer goods were collected as part of the household survey. The main object was to get some indication of the advance towards modernization and of improvement in levels of living. The items were selected with this end in view. Another consideration was to select those items which would show significant differences in economic status within the village. Thus possession of a radio set was considered far more significant than possession of several other modern type consumer goods like a torch, a hurricane lantern or even a wristwatch. These have become common in the villages, but the number of radios is still small enough to indicate significant differences in level of living. Similarly, possession of a sewing machine, a kerosene stove or an electric iron indicates not only a certain economic level but even more a definite urban orientation in the household. The items selected for the survey were: type of house—*kutcha, pucca*, or semi-*pucca*; whether having electricity and hand-pump or not; possession of bicycle, sewing machine, radio, kerosene stove and other electric appliances like a fan and electric iron. The data are presented caste-wise in Table 17.11.

Table 17.11 : Levels of Living

	Village	*Jat*	*Ramgarhia*	*Mahajan*	*Harijan*	*Other Artisans*	*Bazigar*
Total number of households	**299**	**105**	**37**	**46**	**87**	**15**	**9**
No. of households living in houses:							
Kutcha	163	41	18	21	62	12	9
Semi-*pucca*	58	18	7	14	12	2	—
Pucca	83	46	12	11	13	1	—
With electricity	108	45	24	31	3	5	—
With hand-pump	168	83	25	35	17	7	1
No. of households possessing							
Bicycles	130	55	33	28	7	6	1
Sewing machine	83	30	23	23	2	5	—
No. of households possessing other appliances	Radio 20; Electric Iron 16, Kerosene stove 10						

It will be seen that about 45 per cent of the households are living in *pucca* or semi-*pucca* houses; about 35 per cent are in houses fitted with electricity; but as many as 55 per cent are in houses having hand-pumps. Over 45 per cent of the households have bicycles and over a quarter have sewing machines. But the number of radios, kerosene stoves and electric irons is rather small.

It may be noted also that living in *pucca* or semi-*pucca* houses with facility of electricity or hand-pump and possession of these durable consumer goods is confined mainly to the three upper groups, the *jats,* the *Ramgarhia Mistris* and the *Mahajans.* The *Mahajans* are visibly lower than the other two groups. This may appear surprising at first; but is readily understood when we consider the fact that a large number of *Mahajans* are either old people or widows living on pensions or remittances from sons and other relatives.

On the other hand the Harijans, the other artisans and the *Bazigars* have these benefits of modernization to a very limited extent. As compared with nearly 40 per cent of Jat families living in electrified houses, only three Harijan families (4% of the total) are living in such houses. Harijans come out very poorly even in possession of the bicycle which has come to be accepted as a necessity over large parts of rural India. This contrast in level of living between the three upper groups and the Harijans reinforces the observations about the failure of the Harijans to rise above the subsistence level and the growing disparity between them and the *Jats* made earlier. It focuses attention on what is perhaps the biggest problem of the village for the future, namely, taking the fruits of higher productivity and income to this large section of the population.

Factors behind Technological Change

The Man

The *Jat* generally, and the Sikh *jat* particularly, is known to be a good cultivator, combining hard work with intelligent use of resources. This fact has been repeatedly stressed by administrators, agricultural officers and others who have had occasion to work with *Jat* cultivators. (See for instance Darling, 1925) In the canal colonies of West Punjab, Sikh *Jats* proved to be particularly adept at intelligent use of irrigation waters, and some of the highest standards of farm husbandry, yields per acre and agricultural incomes to be found anywhere in the country were reached on their farms. The refugee cultivators from the canal colonies are among the most progressive cultivators in this area, and their presence has made a major contribution to Jitpur's agricultural progress, as explained below. Already the standard of farm husbandry in this area was fairly good in pre-Independence years. Cultivation was intensive and crop yields were moderately high. The average yield of sugarcane in 1951-52, just before the opening of the CD block, was 40 to 45 kg (of *gur*) per acre, as compared with 55 kg per acre today. The standard of livestock husbandry was also high, as evidenced by the fairly high yields of milch animals.

Agricultural extension work was well organized in pre-Partition Punjab, its Department of Agriculture being among the best in the country. Several important improved practices such as use of C-591 wheat, and CO-312 sugarcane, growing of *berseem* as green fodder and use of improved implements like iron ploughs, iron Persian wheels, chaff cutters and improved sugarcane presses, had become universally accepted in this area by the time of Independence. The people of Jitpur mentioned in particular the work of a Deputy Director of Agriculture who had in the 1930s taught them the improved method of making *khandsari* sugar, which they are following to this day.

But, rapid advance in techniques and agricultural productivity, with which we are concerned in this study, has occurred only after Independence, and the explanation for it must be sought in the factors operating in this period. A number of factors have been operating simultaneously, and we shall content ourselves with listing the most important among them.

Influence of Refugee Cultivators

After the partition of the Punjab in 1947, large numbers of cultivators from the canal colonies came to East Punjab to their ancestral villages from where they had emigrated 30 or 40 years earlier, or to other villages in which they had been allotted lands. The canal colonists, as stated earlier, had attained high standards of farm husbandry and agricultural incomes in West Punjab and were used to improved methods of farming advocated by the Department of Agriculture. When they came to East Punjab and were given holdings, which were much smaller than those they had left behind, their first endeavour was to re-attain the standard of agricultural income which they had enjoyed earlier. They started building up their new holdings through methods which had given good results in the canal colonies—use of improved seed, use of iron ploughs and other implements, thorough preparation of land and last, but most important, intensive irrigation. From these practices they soon went on to new practices, which were necessary for obtaining higher per acre yields from their smaller holdings. Thus, they were in the forefront of the movement for irrigation by pumping sets, because they realized that irrigation was the key to intensive farming and that the only way to increase water supplies in this area was through the use of mechanical power for lifting water from wells.

Besides generally stimulating the movement towards more progressive, intensive agriculture the refugee cultivators were responsible for popularizing several specific improvements. The rapid spread of American cotton in East Punjab in the early 1950s was due mainly to their influence. They started growing American cotton, which they used to grow in the canal colonies, and the local cultivators followed their example. The large price difference between American and *desi* cotton in the early 1950s aided this movement and growing of American cotton became universal in several districts of the Punjab within a few years.[8] The rapid increase in popularity of the fodder crop, *berseem*, was also because they preferred *berseem* to other fodder crops. Some of the prosperous refugee cultivators, who had owned citrus orchards in the canal colonies, started planting orchards. The Punjab Government encouraged the practice by establishing planned garden colonies, in which besides specialized advice, liberal *taccavi* loans and other facilities were also given to the planters.

Of course, the refugee cultivators were not successful in everything they introduced. Citrus orchards were not successful, because the climate and soils of the Central Punjab districts are different from those of the West Punjab canal colonies. The author saw an instance of failure of citrus plantation in the garden colony, located in this Block, at a distance of about ten miles from Jitpur. The colonists had all planted citrus orchards in the early 1950s; but they had to give up later when they found that the trees did not survive after two or three years, partly because of the presence of a "hard pan" in the sub-soil. The American cotton was also not without its defects. It was more susceptible to diseases like jessids and boll-worm. As a result, after the first wave of spread of American cotton, the *desi* variety staged a comeback. Many agricultural officers now feel that the area is more suitable for *desi* than American cotton.

But the idea of intensive agriculture, use of improved methods and following the advice of extension workers received a definite stimulus from the example of the refugee cultivators. The leadership provided by a refugee cultivator in the village with the co-operative milk producers' society has been described earlier. The garden colony people, though unsuccessful at planting orchards, have nevertheless attained a high standard of cultivation. They are acknowledged to be the best cultivators in the Block and are frequently held up by the extension workers as models for other cultivators. In all our discussions, with the extension staff at the Block and the district level, and even with specialists at the Ludhiana Agricultural University, the role of refugee cultivators in providing a stimulus to the movement towards improved agriculture was emphasized.

Ex-Servicemen and Educated Cultivators

The other groups whose presence has had a significant influence on technological and economic progress in the area are ex-servicemen and educated cultivators. The major contribution of the ex-servicemen has been in spreading the idea of better living—better and cleaner homes, cleaner villages, use of modern medicine, modern-type consumer goods, etc. The Block staff and the village leaders said that ex-servicemen were particularly enthusiastic about building *pucca* or semi-*pucca* houses and installing electricity and hand-pumps in houses. They also took active interest in village sanitation programmes. The spread of the tea-drinking habit after World War II was also attributed to them. Several ex-servicemen were also active in popular institutions like the co-operatives and the *Panchayats* and rose to positions of leadership in them. The extension staff thought that they were good at working the co-operatives because they understood the 'co-operative principle' and were more honest; but they were not particularly successful in the *Panchayats*. Several ex-servicemen, when elected to *Panchayats*, proved unpopular and lost in the subsequent elections. The explanation given for this was that 'they were too strict in the observance of principles'.

But the role of ex-servicemen in the improvement of agriculture was somewhat limited. They undoubtedly influenced technological change, because they were familiar with modern technology and were anxious to adopt labour-saving devices. They were among the first to install electric motors on wells, and to adopt innovations like power or bullock-driven chaff-cutters, sugarcane crushers, in this and the neighbouring villages. But their influence in adoption of other improvements has not been much, because the average cultivator feels that they are not willing to do hard labour and are not particularly good cultivators. This impression is based on the fact that many ex-servicemen were not really interested in agriculture. They drifted to non-agricultural jobs after a period of stay on the farms, and those who did stay back were not happy at doing hard manual labour.

As for educated people, few persons with education above the middle standard stay in agriculture. They are after non-agricultural employment, and leave cultivation as soon as they get suitable jobs. But to the extent that they do stay in agriculture, they are an influence for progress. Some of them like the garden colonists and the chairman of the milk producers' society, are good cultivators. Moreover, like the ex-servicemen, they are anxious to adopt new techniques, especially new implements and other labour-saving devices; and for the same reasons. They have also shown a noteworthy aptitude for taking up new, remunerative types of farm production. The new commercial poultry production is entirely in the hands of educated men. They do not have the prejudice against keeping poultry, which the average cultivator still has. They also have the added advantage of understanding and following the rigorous routine which commercial poultry production requires.

The Environment of Progress

But the most significant influence of the post-Independence years has been the environment of progress. A number of factors, ranging from steady and high prices of agricultural produce and interest shown by government in improvement of agriculture, to the growing interaction between the town and the village, have gone into the making of this environment. Since prices of agricultural produce have remained high, and the government has been making propaganda and giving various incentives and facilities for increasing production, the cultivators feel that the increasing agricultural production is profitable and is likely to remain so for a long time. The various steps taken by the government to increase production have also had their direct effects. It has been explained that in this village, consolidation, digging of new wells and electrification laid the basis of a more progressive agriculture. The work of the extension organization has also been a constant influence for progress. Currently, the propaganda for use of chemical fertilizers, backed by readily available *taccavi* loans, is a major factor in rapid increase in the use of chemical fertilizers.

Increasingly, these influences have operated in a peasantry, which was rising above the subsistence level, was becoming less subject to tradition, and was, therefore, more responsive and better able to benefit from them. The size of holdings in the area is such that with the improved methods of resource use—possible after consolidation and electrification of wells—the average cultivator could raise himself substantially above the subsistence level. As this happened, he acquired not only a desire for a higher standard of living, but also a confidence in his ability to attain it. Eradication of malaria removed a major impediment to economic efficiency—a cause of chronic lassitude and lack of ambition. Spread of education meant penetration of new ideas, decline in influence of tradition and growth of new aspirations, especially among the young who form a steadily more influential section of the population. Even though large numbers of educated young men have gone out after receiving education, the ones who have stayed behind have been on the look for improvements which lighten the burden of work or increase incomes. And as they succeed in their efforts, their influence increases.

Finally, rapid growth of transport and communications has effectively linked the villages with the towns, and made the village people an integral part of contemporary culture and aspirations. Reference was made in the beginning to the ease and rapidity with which the people of Jitpur can travel to the neighbouring town and other places. The material advantages of this which have a direct influence on agricultural improvement are, facility and low expense of taking produce to the market, buying implements, equipment and consumer goods at lower prices and getting repairs and replacement of parts done quickly and cheaply. But the non-material advantages are of equal, if not greater, importance. The average resident of Jitpur today is a full participant in the news, ideas and social currents of contemporary society. Any news or new idea can reach him just as quickly as it reaches a person in the neighbouring town. To an extent he is better informed than the latter, because the channels of informal communication and discussion are much better preserved in the village. Moreover, with his present income and the network of social services available to him, he has a standard of living, which is comparable if not superior in many respects, to that of the resident of the town. All this means that the villager and the town-dweller are part of the same culture and share its values and aspirations. This constant interaction between town and village and the establishment of cultural continuum extending from the large city to the village is a most important influence for economic progress. The distinction between the town and the village—in food, dress, housing conditions, modes of economic activity, patterns of social relation and values—which is still pronounced in many parts of India, has almost disappeared in Punjab.

Simultaneous development of small-scale industry in the towns and technological change in agriculture in the villages is only another aspect of this cultural continuity. The two developments are related in many ways, starting from a common dependence on cheap electricity and mechanical aptitude and skills of the Punjab artisans. Within the village, the relationship between them is expressed in two ways: facility in adoption of new agricultural implements by cultivators because of existence of facilities for repair and manufacture of these in the neighbouring towns; and opportunities for young men of the village for employment in small-scale industry in the towns. An investigation of the relations between the two developments is a fascinating subject for further research.

One result of establishment of this cultural continuum is seen in the mental make-up of the extension workers. The extension agency has here, as in other States, its problems of administrative co-ordination, supplies, credit, etc. But what impresses one here is the lack of distance—social, economic and psychological—between the agricultural extension workers and the cultivators. The Village Level Workers and even the Block and district level Extension Officers speak the language of the cultivators. They have an understanding of their problems and an emotional identification with their interests, which is not found among extension workers in many parts of the country. One reason for this is that most of them come from cultivators' families. But an even more important reason is the fact that levels of living, awareness and income of the average cultivator are comparable to those of the average extension worker. As a result, the extension worker considers the cultivators to be his social and economic equals: he does not think that by joining government service he has become superior to them. Moreover, more extension workers realize that they will have to settle down and work on farms after retiring from service. And since cultivation is profitable, they look forward to it. It may be of interest to mention that many highly paid government officers, especially of the Department of Agriculture, have settled down after retirement, on 15-20 acre farms, and are quite happy with the income and living conditions, which these farms provide. This aspiration to return to agriculture, even more than the farm background, is responsible for ready and sympathetic appreciation of the problems of the cultivators. When both the cultivator and the extension worker feel that they have not merely a common past but also a common future, mental reservations disappear and a community of interest is established, which is rarely established otherwise.

The Role of Emigration

It has been explained earlier that the area has a tradition of emigration. The effect of the recent economic and social changes has been to accelerate the rate at which aspirations for non-agricultural employment and emigration grow. It is true that two reasons for emigration of educated young men from the village in the past—low productivity in agriculture and unattractiveness of village life—no longer operate. A 10-acre holding now offers a similar or higher income than clerical or skilled jobs in town. Secondly, life in the village after coming of electricity, hand pumps, roads and bus transport is not unattractive. But these changes cannot check growth of off-farm employment and emigration, because continued advances in agriculture and levels of living are themselves dependent upon a continuing exodus of workers from the village.

Let us analyze this separately for each of the principal castes. Among the *Jat* cultivating owners, continued agricultural progress and prosperity are dependent upon the size of holding not falling much below the present level. This means that a certain proportion of young men must continuously go out. The *Mahajans* already have a limited economic role in the village. They depend mainly upon income originating from outside and their position cannot change significantly unless some manufacturing industry or urban-oriented commercial activity, in which a large number can get employment, is established in the village. As for the *Mistris*, technological change has undoubtedly opened opportunities for work within and near the village. But as explained above, even they have found employment outside the village more attractive. Increasing number of *Mistri* young men is either going out of the village or are working outside while living in the village. Emigration and work outside the village have been the least among the Harijans and 'other artisans', who are the poorest and most backward people in the village.

The much repeated argument that emigration of its educated and most intelligent people robs the village of its best talent and slows down economic and social progress has no relevance in this situation. As stated earlier the major role of emigration has been to provide opportunities for gainful employment to people who had only a limited role in the economic system of the village and to bring into the village money, new ideas, new techniques and higher aspirations. This contribution of emigration has been far more significant than any loss caused to the village by migration of its educated young men.

Gains of Progress and the Weaker Sections

It has been explained above that the gains of recent economic progress have not been shared equally by all sections of the village community and that the Harijans and other artisans in particular have not benefited, adequately from such progress. These groups have made some economic gains undoubtedly, but they are much smaller than those made by the *Jat* cultivators and the *Mistris*. The difference in levels of living of different castes and groups in the village is much larger today than it was a generation ago, simply because conveniences like electricity and hand-pumps in the homes or durable consumer goods like bicycles and sewing machines which the *Jats* and the *Mistris* have in considerable numbers and which the Harijans do not have, were not available earlier. Moreover, from the (limited) data on earnings of Harijans given earlier, it would appear that increase in agricultural productivity has not been accompanied by a proportionate increase in earnings of agricultural labourers. The result is that the difference between owners of land and their labourers has increased.

But the Harijans cannot obtain a significantly higher income within the economic framework of the village. (Revitalization of their traditional crafts offers no solution to their economic problem, because the economic changes of recent years have accelerated the decline of these crafts.) They can achieve it only through greater participation in the economy of the area, the State and the country. In other words they must do what the *Mahajans* and the *Mistris* (and to a lesser extent the *Jats*) have done before them. They must take up white-collar and skilled-labour jobs in increasing numbers. The process has begun already—recent increase in the number of Harijan young men going into the armed forces is an indicator—and will gather momentum as education spreads among the Harijans. Already, the more advanced and prosperous families among Harijans are those in which skilled work or white-collar service, or other non-agricultural pursuits, is an important source of contribution. As the number of such families increases, the economic and social levels of the group will rise.

Conclusion

This Chapter based on a study of technological change in agriculture and in certain other aspects of change, *e.g.* in levels of living, education, health and attitudes of people, have been analyzed with a view to seeing the relation between them and change in agriculture. Perhaps the most significant conclusion emerging from the study is that change in agricultural techniques is part of a larger change process, which affects many aspects of the life of the villagers, and also the entire region. Change in agriculture is but one aspect of the process of economic growth in Central Punjab. Further, it is necessary to mention that what we have described here is the *beginning* of a process of technological change. It should gather momentum in future and produce larger and more important changes—intensive use of chemical fertilizers and pesticides, use of small tractors, increasing emphasis on specialized farming (poultry keeping, dairying, horticulture), and change in attitudes towards the role of agriculture. These changes can be seen already among the more progressive farmers like the dairy farmer and the garden colonists.

This study throws up many questions relating to the analysis of change, *e.g.* the role of innovators, channels of communication within the village, reasons for acceptance or rejection of specific practices, and the contribution of Sikh religion, better nutrition or health to the enterprise and vigour of the villagers. These and other questions are being investigated by a number of investigators working in different parts of India which will give us a better understanding of the process described in this study.

NOTES

1. The author studied Jitpur 'The New Village' in Punjab first in 1963 to assess the impact of use of modern implements for cultivation on productivity and on several other areas of life in the village. The findings of the study were published in a series of articles in The *Economic Weekly* (now named as *Economic and Political Weekly*) during 1963-64 and are reported in the Chapter. The village was resurveyed by the author 12 years after in 1975 when the effects of Green Revolution were also available. Findings of the later survey were presented in a conference and are published and included in Chapter 18.
2. The author had studied three villages in 1961 in one of the most backward areas in then one of the backward States i.e. Rajasthan. Analysis of data of the study on several socio-economic aspects of the Rajasthan villages have been included in Chapters 14, 15 and16 in this volume.
3. I know of villages in another State where cultivators who grow sugarcane and make *gur* do not own the cane presses, but hire these from smiths in towns, who look after the repairs, also because the local smiths cannot repair these presses.
4. The correct word appears to be Ravidasias, *i.e.* followers of Ravidas, the celebrated *Chamaar* Saint; but the word Ramdasias is more commonly used.
5. See the occupational change among *Berwa Chamaars* in Sawai Madhopur district of Eastern Rajasthan described in Chapter 15.
6. Headman of a group of villages. The post was abolished after Independence.
7. No young man from Jitpur had gone for such work to the UK till the time of this study. But two young men explained to me that they were thinking

of going and had sent the necessary applications for employment vouchers, passports, etc.

8. The Programme Evaluation Organization of the Planning Commission made a study of the spread of American cotton in certain Community Development Blocks of PEPSU in 1954. It was found in this study that 70 to 90 per cent of the cultivators were growing American cotton and that the example of the refugee cultivators who had brought American cotton with them was a major factor in its spread ("Cotton Extension in PEPSU" 1955. PEO Planning Commission).

REFERENCE

Darling M.L.: *Punjab Peasant in Prosperity and Debt,* Oxford University Press, 1925.

ANNEXURE

Annexure Table 17.1 : Selected Economic Data for Households—Caste-wise

		Jats	*Ramgarhia Mistris*	*Mahajans*	*Harijans*	*Other Artisans*	*Bazigars*	*Total*
Number of households		105	37	46	87	15	9	299
Population	Male	472	110	154	281	57	25	1099
	Female	308	95	135	236	32	23	829
	Total	780	205	289	517	92	48	1926
Population above 15 years	Male	271	74	94	134	37	12	622
	Female	170	56	77	108	19	9	439
	Total	441	130	171	242	56	21	1061
Number of literate persons above 15 years	Male	68	37	71	30	8	1	215
	Female	8	17	13	—	—	—	38
	Total	76	54	84	30	8	1	253
Number of children going to school	Male	91	30	32	56	8	8	225
	Female	49	29	40	19	4	2	143
	Total	140	59	72	75	12	10	368
Land ownership and cultivation								
Number of land-owning households		96	3	4	1	—	—	104
Area owned (acres)		1033	11.5	28.5	6	—	—	1079
Number of cultivating households		76	2	4	—	—	—	82
Area cultivated (acres)		1065	9.5	28.5	—	—	—	1103
Economic Activity								
Number of workers								
(i) including migrants		245	70	83	120	29	13	560
(ii) excluding migrants, *i.e.* in village		213	56	53	110	26	13	

(Contd.)

Annexure Table 17.1 : (*Contd.*)

	Jats	*Ramgarhia Mistris*	*Mahajans*	*Harijans*	*Other Artisans*	*Bazigars*	*Total*
Number of workers in village in:							
Cultivation	194	—	9	—	—	—	203
Agricultural labour	121	—	1		4	1	127
Non-agricultural labour	4	4	4	91	5	12	120
Skilled work	1	43	7	5	8	—	64
Service	1	1	13	8	2	—	25
Others (including shopkeeping, contract work, traditional village crafts, etc.)	5	7	14	5	5	4	40
Emigrants in:							
Military service	24	—	10	7	1	—	42
Skilled work (including drivers of motor vehicles)	11	9	2	—	—	—	22
White collar services and professions	6	4	18	2	2	—	32
Others	—	1	—	2	—	—	3
Total							675*
No. of households living in houses							
Total	105	37	46	87	15	9	299
Kutcha	41	18	21	62	12	9	163
Semi-*pucca*	18	7	14	12	2	—	53
Pucca	46	12	11	13	1	—	83
With electricity	45	24	31	3	5	—	108
With hand-pumps	83	25	35	17	7	1	168
No. of households owning							
Bicycles	55	33	28	7	6	1	130
Sewing machines	30	23	23	2	5	—	83

* The disrespect in the number of workers (560) and the number of jobs (678) is due to several persons having more than one occupation and this listed twice.

ANNEXURE 17.I

Women in the New Village*

Kamla Nath

The rapid technological change in agriculture and economic progress sweeping through some of the villages in Central Punjab are also affecting the women of the area. In this chapter an attempt has been made to describe the pattern of work, practices relating to home-making, treatment of diseases, maternity and child care and attitudes towards education of girls among women of *Jat* cultivator households of a small village about three miles from Jitpur.

The agricultural economy and techniques in this village are very similar to those described for Jitpur. It received electricity at about the same time: the bulk of the cropped area is irrigated, and majority of the irrigation wells are fitted with electric motors. The cropping pattern and use of improved practices (chemical fertilizers, improved seeds, and improved implements) are also similar to Jitpur. I selected this village in preference to Jitpur because it is a small village of *Jat* cultivators, and it was much easier for me to know the women. Besides the extremely co-operative attitude of women of the family of the *Sarpanch* (father) and President of the dairy cooperative (son) enabled me to know the women of the village. The educated young wife of the President is much respected in the village for her family background—she comes from a well-known *Jat* family of the district—education and competence in managing the home. She introduced me to the village women, helped explain the object of my work, and was always available for any assistance that I might need. I found discussions with her and the older women of the family an interesting supplement to the data collected through the sample survey. The *dai* of the village, a *Chamaar* woman, assisted me as a companion and interpreter, and also gave useful information on local customs and practices. I am grateful to these women for their assistance.

The village had a total of 104 households and population of 626 (1961). There are 76 households of *Jats*, but only 36 of them are cultivators. In the remaining households, the small holding is given out for cultivation on *batai* (crop sharing) and work outside the village, army pensions or

* Published in *Economic Weekly.*

remittances from sons or nephews working outside are the principal sources of income. This study was confined to the *Jat* cultivators. A sample survey of 18 households (50% of the total) was undertaken, with a view primarily to meeting and knowing a sufficiently large number of women. Emigration and dependence upon outside income is rather more in this village than in Jitpur. The *Jats* of the village have been prominent in the military service. Several even received awards for valour in World War I and II. A *pucca* well situated at the entrance to the village was built by the District Board in 1937 in recognition of the services rendered by men of the village during the First World War.

The 18 households have 123 persons; an average of 6.8 persons per household. The comparatively large size of households is due to the strength of the institution of joint family. As many as 10 households consist of joint families—7 are two-unit families, while the remaining 3 are three-unit families. The number of males is much larger than of females (68 males and 55 females). The excess of males creates a serious problem of finding wives for men. The problem is discussed at the end.

Pattern of Work

The women's pattern of work is described first, because of its influence on home-making, child care, personal hygiene and even attitude towards education of girls. Most women of the sample households reported that they did not do any work in the fields. One of them to emphasize her point said, "We do not go out to even pick *sag* (green leaves of mustard, turnips etc. used as a vegetable). Only two women said that they went to the fields to pick cotton or to supervise the work of hired labourers, during peak period of agricultural work.[1]

Women in the villages of this area probably never worked in the fields in the way in which women of some other cultivating groups in North India do. But the trend towards women not doing any work in the fields is more recent. The change has occurred only during the last 15-20 years and is related to agricultural prosperity, increase in education and urban influences. The older women in several households said that earlier they used to go to the fields to pick cotton, bring fuel and vegetables for the home and fodder for the livestock. One woman regretting the change said, "The young women do not do hard work now, they do not work in the fields and they do not have to grind corn on the *chakki* (hand mill) or to fetch water from the wells, as we had to do. That is why they cannot deliver their babies easily". Domestic work for the women has also become much lighter. Since hand pumps have been installed in most homes the women do not need to bring water from the village wells. Grinding corn on the *chakki* is no longer necessary, because there is a flour mill in the village. This work, which was generally entrusted to the young daughter-in-law, was often the cause of quarrels in the joint family. Its elimination has been welcomed particularly by the younger women.

The main work of the women now, besides looking after the home, is care of the livestock. This takes a lot of their time, because the animals are kept within the houses at night and also for part of the day. Indeed they go out to the fields mainly for exercise. The women feed and look after the animals, and milk the buffaloes and cows. But they will not clean the cattle-shed; cleaning the cattle-shed and carrying refuse to the compost pit are the jobs of the sweeper women. The women do not mind looking after the animals—indeed they are proud of it, because presence of such animals in the house has always been considered a sign of prosperity in Punjab villages. Even the educated wife of the President of the dairy cooperative society spent lot of time attending to her milch animals and disposing of the milk.

Poultry farming is now becoming popular in this area. In this village, one young man is keeping about 400 birds in a part of his house. His mother and wife do all the work—feeding the birds, collecting the eggs, cleaning the bird house periodically. Two other men have also started keeping a few birds each. One of them is thinking of setting up a big modern poultry farm. But the attitude of women towards this work is not favourable. In some of my group interviews, women jeered at the mother of the young poultry farmer and showed pity for the young wife. "Chicken are dirty", they said, "and looking after them is the job of the sweeper women. Besides, what is the use of keeping poultry, when we can get the same income from one buffalo as from a hundred chickens"! These attitudes may change, if poultry farming continues to be as profitable as it has been during the last few years, and the movement towards establishing poultry farms continues among educated farmers.

Elimination of farm work and lighter domestic chores have given these women a lot of free time, which they are now devoting to cooking, better care of home, the children and themselves and to practicing of traditional crafts such as *durry* making, and learning new ones such as knitting and sewing.

These women devote much more time to cooking than the women who work in the fields. Two full meals (sometimes three) are cooked daily[2] and the food is substantial and adequate.[3] They are also becoming increasingly conscious of personal hygiene and their own appearance. They bathe much more frequently than they did in the past. A daily bath is now the rule in the summer; but in the winter they bathe only once in two or three days. Presence of hand pumps in the houses encourages frequent bathing. A number of women use cheap face cream or talcum powder. The wife of the President of the dairy cooperative was using cream, face powder and lipstick of well-known brands. All the younger women said that they used toilet soap and applied oil to the hair. But some of the older women continue the old practice of applying *ghee* to the hair. None of the women, young or old had ever used mud for washing their hair, which the *Meena* women of Sawai Madhopur use. The children too were clean and well clothed.

Most women possess quite a few changes of clothes. Every time the family goes to the town, new clothes and sometimes new shoes are bought for one or the other member. Silk or rayon clothes are bought for festive occasions, woollens are bought for winter. All men, women and children were wearing some woollen garment at the time of this study which was conducted during December. Some men possess western style woollen suits and the women have woollen *salwar-kamiz* suits. These are worn on special occasions—visiting the town to see a 'high officer', or visiting a prosperous relative. A large proportion of the cash income of the families is spent on clothing. It is interesting to note that with somewhat higher incomes, the trend among the *Meenas* of Sawai Madhopur is to spend more on silver ornaments; but in this group the emphasis is *now* on clothing. That they have gone through the stage of spending more on ornaments was clear from the remarks of the 90-year old mother of the Sarpanch. She said, "I have seen three *zamanas* (periods) in my life. First there was the 'silver age' when all of us wore silver ornaments. Then there was the 'gold age'; now it is the 'cloth age'. "The women do have gold and silver ornaments but they were not wearing any ornaments at all. This is a significant trend, for it shows that in course of time possession of ornaments may not retain the same value it enjoys today with villagers in most parts of India.

Washing clothes is almost a daily routine. Frequent washing of clothes is necessary because of the preference for lighter shades of colours in clothes, in contrast to the dark colours worn in Rajasthan. Ordinary washing soap, surf and even Lux flakes are used.

Houses and Household Goods

Most of the houses (16 out of 18 among the sample households) are *pucca*. All houses have hand pumps, nearly two-third are fitted with electricity.

Electricity is used mainly for lighting; only 5 households possess radios and 3 have electric fans. However, 13 households possess bicycles, 11 own sewing machines and 9 have kerosene stoves or electric heaters. In the house of the President of the dairy co-operative, the drawing room was furnished with a cane sofa set (without cushions), chairs, a dressing table, a bedstead and curtains. There was some modern furnitures in his father's house also. But the family is clearly an exception. The other households cannot set apart a room in their small crowded homes as a drawing room. The only modern furniture in their homes was a few chairs. However, old style bedsteads (called *palangs*) of good workmanship were seen in a number of homes.

There is a definite trend towards modernizing the home and buying new durable consumer goods. Several women showed me their radios, sewing machines and other possessions with obvious pride. In most cases the articles had been brought by the daughter-in-law married to the educated son employed in the town in her dowry.

But most of the houses are congested and are not very clean. This is due partly to the large size of families and partly to the practice of keeping animals within the homes. Moreover, installation of hand pumps has made the houses damp—a portion of the courtyard always remains wet. It has also made the lanes outside the houses wet and dirty, and given the village pond a permanent existence. Most of the women did not show any concern about the unsanitary conditions of the street or the congestion and damp within the houses. This lack of concern may be due partly to the feeling that nothing can be done about these things. Tightly clustered houses, narrow dirty lanes, lack of drainage and presence of stagnant water at various places are common features of villages (and most towns) in North India, and are accepted. But some of the younger men and women are thinking of getting away from it all, by building their new houses outside in the fields.

The need for additional space felt by these families has been met in the recent past by construction of one or more rooms on the first floor. These rooms are well lighted and are of relatively of modern design. They are generally used either by the young educated daughter-in-law (if she is staying with the family) or are reserved for guests, such as the son-in-law.[4] But addition of rooms on the first floor has cut off sunlight from the ground floor rooms and has made the principal living quarter darker and more dingy.

Women in the two households having *kutcha* houses said that they had not made their houses *pucca* because they were thinking of building new houses outside the village. But the movement towards living outside the village has not yet started. So far, only the *Sarpanch*, a refugee from the West Punjab canal colonies, has built a house on the outskirts of the village. His house with its enormous courtyard *(aahata)*, cattle-sheds, and feeding stalls, well separated from the living rooms, is patterned after houses in the canal colonies. It presented a pleasant contrast to the other houses. But no other family has followed his example so far.

Health

Modern facilities for treatment of diseases, maternity and child-care are within easy reach of the village and are being used by the people. There is good hospital at the Block headquarters' town Samrala. Besides, there are three sub-centres, each under the charge of a trained nurse-midwife, which provide assistance for maternity and family planning. The village is in the area of the sub-centre located in the next village, a mile away. The village *dai* is undergoing training at the sub-centre. She assists the nurse mid-wife in conducting delivery cases and will be authorized to handle these cases on her own, after she has completed the one-year training course. According to an order of the Punjab Health Department, no untrained *dai* can handle delivery cases on her own. I did not have the opportunity to investigate how strictly this order was actually being followed.

All the women reported that for all ailments, major or minor they consulted a doctor; the qualified private medical practitioner at Samrala. He lives in the next village and can make the rounds of the village on his way to and from the town. They said that they went to the Government Hospital only when this doctor was not available. Cases of serious sickness or serious injury were taken to one of the hospitals at Ludhiana. The city has a number of good hospitals including one attached to Medical College. In half of the sample households, the women reported that they kept medicines such as Anacin, Tincture Iodine, *Amritdhara*, and brandy at home, and used them for minor ailments. Women in the other households also knew about these medicines, but they were not keeping them. Resort to the doctor is so common that one woman said, "We go to the doctor, even when a thorn pricks us".

All pregnant women are expected to be registered with the sub-centre and visit it regularly for getting ante-natal advice. The nurse mid-wife is also expected to conduct house to house surveys periodically, in order to make sure that all pregnant women are contacted. But she is confronted with an interesting problem arising from the practice (in this area as in many others in India) of women going to their parent's homes for childbirth. She said that a number of women for whom she had been maintaining ante-natal records went away for their deliveries to their parents' homes while she had to conduct deliveries of many women for whom she had no records !

The sub-centres also provide advice and assistance on family planning. Of the 32 women in the sample households, three, all below aged 35 were using family planning devices. Two more showed interest, but were not using any device. One woman, who complained about having a large number of children, was hesitant about using any family planning devices. Most women knew about family planning practices and were not unwilling to talk about them; some expressed a desire for birth control pill. The lady doctor at Samrala hospital mentioned that some men of the village had vasectomies done. But no such case was mentioned among the sample households.

Education

All the girls of primary school aged 6-11 years are going to the village school. Half a dozen of the older girls go to higher secondary school at Samrala. I used to meet these girls going to school or returning from the school, on their bicycles, on my way to or from the village. They all rode gent's bicycles: the families perhaps could not afford to buy separate ladies' bicycles. This phenomenon—young girls going out on bicycles—would have been unthinkable a generation earlier, when a girl was not allowed to go out of the village unescorted. Girls from some of the more prosperous and progressive families are receiving education in colleges (or other training institutions) in towns. They stay in hostels. Two daughters of the President of the dairy co-operative are studying outside the village—one is in a college in Ludhiana while the other is in a higher secondary school at Samrala. The daughter in another household is receiving the Physical Training Instructor's training at Patiala. In another household, the daughter is receiving basic teacher's training. Among girls (not of the sample households) one is studying for the Bachelor of Teaching (B.T.) diploma. A sister of this girl had recently flown to Canada to get married to a man (of the caste) settled in Canada. The village women were referring to this as an example of the 'forwardness' of the family. There was no hint of disapproval or of embarrassment that such a thing should have happened in their village.

Education of girls has become a thing of value with the group. All families are sending their girls to school, and the more progressive ones are sending them to institutions of training, which will equip them for careers. Some young women from the village have already taken up jobs. The Deputy Inspector of Schools at Samrala is the daughter-in-law in one of the sample households. Both the teachers in the village school are women from the village. The preference for 'career training' to getting a university degree is significant. Some of the women said that they would like to see their daughters equipped for a career in time of need.

But education of girls is a recent phenomenon. This is brought out very well by data on the number of educated females of different age groups presented in Table 17.2. It will be seen that all the 14 women above the age of 35 are illiterate; among those below 35 more than half are educated, but all the girls of school-going age are attending school. It may be noted that all the daughters-in-law living outside the village are educated. These women married to educated men—their husbands are all in white-collar or military service—had to be educated to get married to educated men. This shows a pattern of selectivity in emigration, and also provides a clue to the motivation for education of girls. Girls are being educated because educated men, who are in service and who are the prized grooms, want educated wives. The changed work pattern of the women—their being at home all the time and having adequate time for household work and child-care—also helps education of girls. Older girls are not needed to look after younger brothers and sisters or to help the mothers with household tasks.

But this trend towards education of girls, with a view to marrying them to educated young men in service, is creating an interesting situation within the group. On the one hand, the problem of finding suitable grooms for educated girls and giving an adequate dowry—problems characteristic of the urban middle class—are appearing. The recent journey of a girl to Canada shows how far families are prepared to go to meet these problems. At the same time, it is becoming increasingly difficult for illiterate or barely literate, young men who remain in the village and work on the farm to get married. This difficulty caused by the absolute shortage of women referred to earlier has always been there, but it is accentuated by the tendency to educate the girls and to marry them to educated young men in service. The gravity of the problem will be appreciated from the fact that among the 43 males, above the age of 18 in the sample households as many as 15 are unmarried. Reference was made to the problem by the women in three sample households, that of a small farmer with a holding of only 6 acres, four unmarried young sons were living with their aged father and mother. They had no hope of getting married because their holding is so small. In another household, only one of the three sons was married. Their father said, "The *Jats* will not give their daughters to us because our holding is small, and we are not prepared to buy women from outside. He is a lucky father, who can marry all his sons !" The difficulty of finding wives is met to some extent by buying women from outside the State. These women, usually from poor families of low castes, are bought from U.P., West Bengal or the South. There were no such women among the sample households: but there were three in the village. I could meet all three women and listen to their interesting life histories. I met some of them in the neighbouring village, of the sub-centre also. The men of the village are well known in the area for bringing women from outside, and there were about a dozen such women in that village.

Table 17.2 : Number of Educated Women of Different Age Groups in 18 Households

	Total	*Educated*	*Illiterate*
No. of the Women	—	—	—
Above age of 35	14		14
Below the age of 35	22	12	10
Daughters-in-law of the households living outside the village	10	10	—
	Total	Going to school	Not going to School
No. of girls of School Age (6-14 years)	18	18	—

NOTES

1. The *Meena* women of Sawai Madhopur district of Rajasthan among whom I had conducted a similar study earlier (the findings of the Rajasthan study are given in Appendix II to Chapter 16), do all agricultural work except ploughing. In fact, from an analysis of the farm work in this area, I came to the conclusion that they do more work than their men.
2. The *Meena* women of Sawai Madhopur would finish most of their cooking for the day in the morning, before leaving for the fields, and would cook only *chappaties* in the evening.
3. I did not collect any data on food consumption. But use of plenty of milk and *ghee* and vegetables especially green leaf '*saag*' was so evident.
4. The women used the Punjabi word for guest (*Paraohina*) also for son-in-law. Obviously, sons-in-law are the most frequent or the most honoured guests.

18

The New Village—Twelve Years After*

Introduction

Jitpur,[1] the subject of this study, is relatively a large village, which had population of 2,114 according to the Population Census of 1971. It is situated about 175 miles west of India's capital, New Delhi, in the Ludhiana District of the Punjab State. The State bordering Pakistan is the richest in the Indian Union, with an average per capita income during 1970-72 of Rs. 1,053, almost 60 per cent above the national average. The bases of its prosperity are a progressive agriculture—the State has been in the forefront of India's Green Revolution of the late 1960s—and diversified small and medium-scale industries. Ludhiana, the district headquarters, located about 30 miles from Jitpur, is a city with a population of nearly 500,000. It is the principal industrial centre of the State and is also the seat of the Agricultural University, an important centre of agricultural education and research in northern India. Jitpur is located on an all-weather motorable road at a distance of one and a half miles from the market town of Samrala (population 7,500). A second market town, Khanna, with a population of about 25,000 is nine miles from Jitpur at the other end of the road. The principal castes of the village are *Jat,* Harijan[2], *Mistri* and *Mahajan*. The *Jats* are the most numerous followed by the Harijans. The caste-wise distribution of the village households in 1975 was as follows:

Caste	Number of Households
Jat	182
Harijan	101
Mistri	13
Mahajan	25
Others	23
Total	**344**

* This part of the study was published as: '*The New Village — Twelve Years After*' in *Indian Urbanization and Planning—Vehicles of Modernization;* eds. Noble, Allen G. and Dutt Ashok K. Tata McGraw-Hill Publishers 1977.

The *Jats,* besides being the largest caste, are also the most powerful. They own and cultivate nearly all the land, and the village has always been regarded as a *Jat* village. The traditional occupation of the Harijans is stated to have been leather work, but their principal source of livelihood was until recently agricultural labour. Many Harijan heads of households worked as attached labourers to farmers under the crop-sharing *sanjhee* (literally share holder) system. Although bearing all the risks of cultivation and providing bullock power in addition to their own, they had no rights on the land. With growth of opportunities for non-agricultural work in or near the village during the last twenty five years, however, they have taken increasingly to this work, principally as casual, day labourers. A few enterprising young men have become skilled workers, shopkeepers, or white-collar workers. The *Mistries* (lit. artisans), the traditional carpenters, smiths and masons, have with growth of small industries in the region, sought employment in them in increasing numbers. Some, who have become successful entrepreneurs, are the richest people in the village. The *Mahajan* is the composite name for the *Brahmins,* the *Khatris* and the *Aroras,* The *Brahmins* were the traditional priests while the other two were merchant-money lenders. All the three castes have had white-collar service and commerce as their principal occupations for a long time. The 'other castes' group includes castes with traditional occupations of barber, tailor, potter, oil-presser water-carrier-*cum*-cook, etc. All the castes except the Mahajans, who are Hindus, follow the Sikh religion.

The village is well served with social and economic service facilities. It has two primary schools (both co-educational); a maternity, child welfare and family planning centre; a primary cooperative society whose principal functions are provision of agricultural credit and distribution of chemical fertilizers and other agricultural inputs; a bank and a training centre for rural artisans. Frequent minibus service on the road is the principal means of transport. There are ten shops (general stores) and a machine shop, which repairs and fabricates agricultural implements. Furthermore, because of proximity to two market towns, the village has easy access to the various service facilities located in them. Agricultural extension and related rural development services form part of the Community Development Block organization[3]. Jitpur is included in the Samrala CD Block, which has a total of 153 villages and a rural population of approximately 120,000.

Method

The village was first studied in 1963 when a series of five articles describing changes in agricultural technology and various other aspects of economic and social change were published in the *Economic Weekly*. Later in the year, the articles were reprinted as a monograph entitled '*The New Village*' (Nath V., 1965). The present study is based on a two-week re-visit undertaken in December 1975; its primary objective is to describe the changes in the village and the region during the period since the first study; particularly as a result of the Green Revolution. It may be mentioned that the 1963 study had, after describing the rapid economic and social changes experienced by the village and the region during the preceding twelve years, forecast "larger and more rapid changes" in the future.

The focus of the present study and its method are somewhat different from those of the original study. Thus greater attention has been given than in the first study to analyzing the regional aspects of the change and to assessing the prospects for the future. The study within the village concentrates on those aspects, which appeared most significant either for understanding the change process of the preceding 12 years or as indicators of future trends. Accordingly, listing of all households in the village with collection of detailed data on demographic characteristics and economic activities of the members and housing conditions; a survey of holdings of all farmers and a sample survey of production and income of the medium sized farmers, which had been done in the 1963 study, have not been repeated. The principal method of enquiry has been interviews with knowledgeable respondents in the village, with officials of the Community Development Block and local leaders in Samrala, and with district or State level officials in Ludhiana. We hope that what the study may have lost in depth is more than compensated by the gains in terms of broader and more future oriented perspective.

It should be repeated that this is not a study of an average Indian village but of a village in one of the richest and most progressive region of the country. But, while economic and social changes are relatively slow in most regions of India, this regions is by no means unique in the speed or the scope of changes: similar or somewhat less rapid changes have been experienced in the post-Independence period in a number of other regions or micro regions of the country. The principal value of this and other studies of progressive rural communities is that (a) they demonstrate the possibility of rapid economic and social changes within the matrix of peasant agriculture and the social structure of rural India which is dominated by the institution of caste; (b) describe the nature of the changes, outlining the areas of rapid and slow advance; and finally (c) draw attention to the factors which induce or retard the change process.

The Village and the Region in 1963

The principal points made in the study were the following :

(i) The village was, like the central Punjab region[4] of which it formed a part, in the midst of the process of rapid economic and social change. The process began with the land reform of consolidation of land holdings[5] which was undertaken at the initiative of the State Government in the early 1950s. It was aided by the well developed physical and economic infrastructures of the region, but its vigour, speed and broad range were due primarily to the people of the region. They had shown a remarkable readiness and capacity to use the various infrastructure facilities effectively; to adopt the changes in agricultural production techniques, health practices, consumption, living patterns etc., recommended by the various extension and service agencies quickly, and finally, to innovate and adapt the recommended practices, as also commercially viable tools and equipments, more closely to their particular needs and financial resources.

The principal component of the infrastructure were approach roads linking most of the villages of the region with trunk highways; bus, minibus and truck services providing motorized transport to almost all villages; the extensive rural electrification network; primary schools in almost all villages, secondary schools in the larger villages and the market towns and colleges in the latter; medical, maternity and family planning services provided both by the centre and run by the government as well as by private practitioners; agricultural and animal husbandry extension services supported by services for distribution of inputs, needed for modernization of agriculture (improved seeds, chemical fertilizers, improved implements etc.) and for provision of agricultural credit at low rates of interest and finally, markets regulated by committees dominated by the farmers themselves.

The people had demonstrated their readiness to contribute to the creation and operation of the services, their capacity to use them effectively and their innovative ability in various ways. They had readily contributed land needed for building the approach roads, often destroying their standing crops so that these could be built earlier. The bus service run by the State Government was extremely popular while the minibus and truck service, provided by the local operators, extended the range of motorized transport service to all villages. Similarly, the land reform of consolidation of holdings, which involved pooling of all the village lands and their redistribution and which could proceed only slowly in some parts of the State, had been undertaken speedily in the region with Land Holders' Committees, which had been established in every village, playing an active role in the decision-making process. Furthermore, it had been followed rapidly by the farmers undertaking reclamation of the uncultivated lands allotted to them and expansion of irrigation by sinking new wells and tube-wells, and installing electric pumps on wells.[6] The change-over from lifting water with the aid of bullocks to electric pumps greatly reduced the cost of irrigation.[7] In addition it made possible extension of the areas irrigated by a well; increase in the intensity of cropping, besides extension of areas under highly remunerative crops, such as sugarcane, which, however, require intensive irrigation. Adoption of improved agricultural practices, notably use of improved seed, chemical fertilizers and improved implements, and generally more efficient farm management were also aided by consolidation of holdings, expansion of irrigation and improvement in its efficiency. The total effect was a rapid change process, resulting in significant increase in total agricultural output, through more intensive and efficient use of the resources of land and water, and the labour and capital committed to agriculture. The farmers had also shown a capacity to operate successfully new power driven implements, notably the electric pumps and mechanical grain threshers, which was quite exceptional for Indian farmers, while the small machine shops located in the villages or the market towns could service and repair the machines quickly, efficiently and at low cost. The artisans of the region not only provided these services to the farmers but also displayed considerable innovative ability; the mechanical corn shellers and wheat threshers, which had rapidly become popular, were noteworthy products of this ability. The latest development in the agricultural change process had been growth of poultry keeping, dairying and market gardening in response to the growing urban demand for their products. These were being taken up both by progressive farmers and by other small entrepreneurs; their growth was significant both because of their potential for making major additions to the farmers' incomes and also because it involved giving up strong traditional prejudices against them. The *Jats* did not keep poultry, which was considered dirty; only the Harijans (and before their migration to Pakistan in 1947 the Muslim residents of the region) kept poultry. Market gardening had been the traditional activity of specialized castes like the Sikh *Sainies* and the Muslim *Arains*. As regards dairying, while the farmers kept milch animals, there was a very strong prejudice against selling milk by farmers; it was considered a mark of extreme want or degradation.[8]

(ii) The change in agriculture and animal husbandry which had been the most noticeable and perhaps also the most significant from the economic stand point, had been accompanied by noteworthy advances in literacy, education and use of modern medical and public health services; major changes in the patterns of employment, consumption and levels of living as well as social changes affecting the attitudes and values of the people, inter-group relations and institutions. Attending primary school had become the norm for all children of the relevant age-group (6-11 years) of the upper castes and for most children of the Harijans. Besides large number of boys and girls were attending secondary schools and colleges. Opportunities for non-agricultural employment had expanded rapidly with the growth of construction following increase in agricultural incomes and in economic activity generally. As a result there was accelerated migration from the villages; wage rates had increased, shortages of labour had begun to be experienced, especially in the peak period of agricultural activity during April and May in which several labour intensive operations, notably harvesting of wheat and planting of cotton and sugarcane were in progress and the traditional *sanjhee* system of crop sharing between the farmer and land owner, and their attached Harijan agricultural labourers had begun to decline. Among the changes in consumption and level of living the most noticeable to the outside observer were those resulting from the following :

(a) Improvement in housing and environmental sanitation with construction of new *pucca* (brick and mortar) houses in place of the traditional *kutcha* or mud houses; electrification of the houses and installation of hand-pumps in them for water supply—earlier the women had to go some distance from their homes to fetch water from communal wells—and pavement of village streets with bricks and construction of drains along their sides for efficient flow of waste water;

(b) The rapid increase in the use of durable consumer goods such as bicycles, sewing machines, radio receivers and small kerosene stoves for cooking; and

(c) Cessation of farm work by women of all but the poor Harijan households.

In Jitpur about 50 per cent of the households were living by 1963 in houses that were entirely or partly *pucca*, more than 50 per cent had hand-pumps in their homes while 36 per cent lived in electrified houses. All the streets of the village except a few in Harijan quarters had been paved and provided with drains. Electrification had made the homes brighter while installation of the hand-pumps had eliminated the drudgery of carrying water from the wells for the women. Cessation of farm work by the women and the education of the girls and the young women had been major factors contributing to improvement in home-making, child care and personal hygiene. Freed from farm work, the women had more time for their homes and the children and the educated ones among them acquainted the others with new ideas, practices and consumption goods.

Finally with the spread of education and of the ideas of freedom and equality, especially during the periodic elections to the State and central legislatures and to village *Panchayats*; increasing participation of Harijans in non-agricultural work outside the villages; increasing emigration from the villages and frequent travel of villagers to towns following improvements in transport and communications, there had been a significant decline in untouchability. It had in any case been weak in the region because of the influence of the Sikh religion, which advocated equality of all men before God and prohibited the practice of untouchability.

(iii) Conditions in the region were exceptionally favourable for rapid economic and social change. The region had a strong tradition of peasant proprietorship, and land holdings were on an average larger and the proportion of landless agricultural labourers smaller than in most parts of India.[9] The *Jats*, who constitute the majority of the farmers in the region, were well known for their hard work and love for farming. The *Mistries* were similarly known for their industry, mechanical aptitude and innovative capacity; they were recognized to be the best carpenters, masons and machine workers in India. The Sikh religion, with its doctrines of monotheism and equality of all men, had acted as a major liberating influence. However the Ludhiana district, the micro region of Jitpur, was until the beginning of the above mentioned change process in the early 1950s, a relatively poor area because large part of it either had sandy soil or formed part of the poorly drained floodplain of the river Satluj. But the town of Ludhiana had long been the centre of the hosiery industry, which provided the nucleus for rapid growth of small, light engineering industries after cheap hydro-electric power became available and industrial development began to be encouraged by the State and Central governments through a variety of promotional measures. Secondly, the micro-region had abundant ground-water, exploitation of which became feasible after the cost of lifting water was reduced with electrification of wells, and construction of electric or diesel powered tube-wells made possible lifting of water from much greater depths than had been possible with the aid of bullocks. The consequent rapid expansion of irrigation was the most important factor contributing to increase of agricultural output in the district.

(iv) The willingness and capacity for rapid economic and social change; the mechanical aptitude and the innovative capability owed not a little to the century old tradition of emigration among the people of the region. Emigration had begun with large numbers of people joining the British Indian army during the 50s and 60s of the last century, and had continued: the region had remained a major source of recruitment for the British Indian (and after Independence of the Indian) army. Besides, it had sent out large numbers of white-collar workers, operators of trucks and taxis, and repairmen for machinery and equipment to cities and towns all over India. Furthermore, large numbers had gone down to settle as farmers in the canal colonies of Western Punjab, which were settled in the first-two decades of the century, and in foreign countries notably Malaysia and East Africa. Remittances from the young men working in the towns but maintaining close ties with their 'families' in the villages, and from the emigrants had been an important source of income in the region, while the new ideas and practices introduced by returning migrants had been a major change influence. The ex-soldiers returning after World War II and the refugees, returning from the canal colonies after the creation of Pakistan, had been the leaders in the above mentioned change process. Both groups had useful skills as well as strong motivation for change. Large number of ex-soldiers had worked in the armed forces as electricians, auto mechanics, drivers etc.; all had got used to living in neat quarters, to preventive health practices, such as use of quinine and mosquito nets, and to modern consumer goods such as bicycles and radios. They were not considered to be particularly good farmers by the villagers because of their unwillingness to work hard, but they were recognized as leaders in adoption of environmental sanitation practices, acceptance of education and modern medicine and in running development-oriented institutions such as the cooperative societies, the *Panchayats*, and the market committees. The refugees had been used to following improved agricultural and animal husbandry practices advocated by the extension services in the canal colonies and had also, because of relatively large irrigated land holdings, enjoyed much higher income levels than the farmers of the region.[10] On return to their ancestral villages and faced with the need to work much smaller holdings, they had a strong motivation to intensify land use and increase agricultural output and incomes. In this process, they not only continued practices such as use of improved seeds and implements, growing of fodder crops and stall-feeding of cattle which they had been following in the colonies but also readily took up new ones, such as use of chemical fertilizers and pesticides. They were also the leaders in construction of tube-wells and installation of electric pumps on wells and in taking up remunerative agricultural or animal husbandry enterprises such as growing of vegetables and fruit, dairy farming and poultry keeping which had been shunned by the local farmers because of traditional prejudices. The refugees were generally the most progressive cultivators in the villages in which they had settled while the 'garden colonies', established by the most progressive and affluent among them, had the highest level of husbandry and income to be seen in the region.

(v) At the same time, the process had itself further stimulated migration and added new dimensions to it, notably—(a) spread of migration to the Harijans who had been relatively unaffected by it earlier; (b) much larger intra-regional movement from the villages to the towns because of the above mentioned growth of small-scale industries in the latter; and (c) emigration to Britain for work in factories there.

(vi) The cumulative effect of all these changes was so large that a "new village", which was different from the traditional Indian village in every significant economic and social respect, appeared to be emerging. Hence the title of the study. In the new village', not only were the levels of agricultural technology and income much higher than in the old, but in contrast to the inward orientation, conservative tradition bound attitudes and values and a rigid social structure, dominated by the institution of caste of the latter, it had multiple and expanding relations with the regional and national economies, and attitudes, values and inter-group economic and social relations, that were increasingly responsive to the demands of the changes in technology, employment opportunities, consumption patterns and levels of living.

(vii) But the changes in agriculture and animal husbandry were considered to be only, "the beginning of a process which should gather momentum in future and produce larger and more important changes—intensive use of chemical fertilizers and pesticides, use of small tractors, increasing emphasis on specialized farming (poultry keeping, dairying and horticulture) and changes in attitudes towards the role of agriculture. These changes can be seen already among the more progressive farmers like the dairy farmers and the 'garden colonists'." (Nath V., *op. cit.*, p. 47)

The Green Revolution

The impetus for the "larger and more important changes" came with introduction in 1965-66 of the high-yielding, dwarf varieties of wheat. The region was exceptionally well equipped to benefit from the high yield potential of the new varieties. Wheat was its most important crop; it already had most of the prerequisites for obtaining the high yields and could create the others by further, more rapid progress along lines which were already well established. Thus it had assured adequate and controlled water supplies, provided by well developed irrigation facilities. Use of non-power driven improved implements, such as improved ploughs, harrows and seed drills, was widespread and power-driven implements, such as tractors and grain threshers, were beginning to be used in increasing numbers particularly by farmers with relatively large land holdings (above 20 acres). Similarly, increasing appreciation of the benefits of using chemical fertilizers had been added to the well established tradition of intensive maturing of the wheat crop. Finally, the farmers had become change-oriented after experience with rapid economic and social change for over 15 years during which their productivity, income and level of living had risen rapidly, and the best among them were themselves looking for new improvements in techniques and other ways to increase their income. The high yield potential of the new varieties provided a powerful incentive for further rapid progress while provision of liberal agricultural credit by the State and Central governments at subsidized, low rates of interest (10-12½% per annum)[11] provided the funds needed for adopting the new capital-intensive techniques. Short and medium-term loans, needed for financing current agricultural operations, such as purchase of seeds and chemical fertilizers, payment for labour, or for quick-yielding investments such as purchase of livestock, were given by village-level, primary cooperative societies, while long-term loans, with repayment periods of 7-10 years, needed for investment in land reclamation, development of irrigation facilities and purchase of tractors etc, were given by institutions such as the newly created Land Mortgage Bank. By 1969-70, four years after the introduction of the new varieties, almost 70 per cent of the total area under wheat in Punjab had been sown with them, while the figure for Ludhiana district was 86 per cent. Production of wheat increased very rapidly, as a result both of increase in yields, and diversion of land from other crops to wheat; the diversion was made because with the high yield given by the new varieties, production of wheat became much more remunerative than that of alternative crops. In Ludhiana district; production of wheat increased by 142.8 per cent between 1964-65 and 1971-72; more than half of the increase was contributed by increase in area, which went up by 63.6 per cent, while the remainder was due to increase in yield per acre which went up by 48.4 per cent.

In order to provide a background to the agricultural changes in village Jitpur, described in the next section, and to relate them to the regional change process, data on a number of indicators of agricultural progress are given for Ludhiana district in Table 18.1. Although progress under the Green Revolution was concentrated during the five years, 1966-67 to 1971-72, the figures are given for 1961-62 and 1972-73 in order to facilitate the comparison with Jitpur.

Table 18.1: Selected Indicators of Agricultural Progress in Ludhiana District, 1961-62 to 1972-73

Indicator	1961-62	1972-73	Index value for 1972-73 (with 1961-62=100)
Land use and the Cropping Pattern (Areas in '000 acres)			
Gross cropped area	933.7	1284.4	137.6
Gross irrigated area	521.2	1104.1	211.8
Percentage of gross cropped area Irrigated	55.8	86.0	154.6
Areas under:			
— Wheat	285.3	624.9	219.0
— Corn	98.3	231.2	235.2
— Sugarcane	25.7	17.8	69.2
— Cotton	74.1	59.3	80.0
— Groundnut	71.1	145.2	204.2
— Pulses	126.7	19.3	14.4
— Fodder Crops	232.2	127.0	54.7
Consumption of Chemical Fertilizers			
Total ('000 tonnes)	13.4	251.0	1873.1
Per acre of gross Cropped Area (kg)	14.4	195.5	1360.1
Loans advanced by Cooperative Credit Societies			
Short-term (Million Rupees)	12.5	120.2	963.6
Medium-term (Million Rupees)	3.4	2.5	72.4
Total (Million Rupees)	15.9	122.7	772.4
Total per acre cropped area (Rupees) of gross	17.0	95.5	561.8

Source: *Twelve Years' Assessment of Intensive Agricultural District Programme.* Ludhiana, 1960-61 to 1972-73. IADP. Ludhiana, Punjab, 1975.

It will be seen from Table 18.1 that the gross cropped area in the district increased by more than one-third during the 11-year period. The increase was achieved mainly by increase in the intensity of cropping from 1.25 to 1.61; the physical area under crops went up by only 7 per cent. Expansion of irrigation was even more rapid than the expansion of cropping; the gross irrigated area more than doubled and by 1972-73, 86 per cent of the gross cropped area was irrigated. Changes in the cropping pattern were equally rapid. The areas under wheat, corn and groundnut more than doubled while those under all other crops decreased, the reductions in the areas under the fodder crops and pulses (beans) being the most pronounced. Thus wheat, corn and groundnut were not only the principal beneficiaries of expansion of the cropped area but gained also at the expense of other crops, particularly fodders and pulses.

The changes were related to the introduction of high yielding varieties of wheat and associated programmes, particularly expansion of irrigation, and reflected also changes in the relative profitability of the different crops or crop combinations following the introduction of the new varieties. In order to give some indication of the latter, data on changes in average yields, prices and gross returns for five important crops of the district[12] wheat, corn, sugarcane cotton and groundnut, are given in Table 18.2. The data relate to the period, 1960-61-1962-63 to 1970-73; three-year averages have been used at both ends of the time period in order to minimize the influence of year to year fluctuations in yields or prices, both of which were quite considerable.

Table 18.2 : Ludhiana District, Changes in Yields, Prices and Gross Returns from Selected Crops,1960-61 and 1962-63 to 1970-71and 1972-73.

Crop	*Yield*	*Price per acre*	*Gross Returns*
	(3-year Averages of 1970-71 to 1972-73 divided by 3-year averages of 1960-61 to 1962-63)		
Wheat	0.99	2.04	4.06
Maize	1.29	2.08	2.68
Sugarcane	1.39	2.00	2.78
Cotton (American)	1.29	2.18	2.82
Groundnut	0.97	2.15	2.09

Source: *Twelve Years' Assessment of IADP.*

Prices of all the five crops more than doubled during the period. As regards yields, while that of wheat and that of groundnut decreased slightly, those of the remaining three crops increased by 30-40 per cent. As a result, the gross return from wheat increased four-fold, that from groundnut more than doubled while those from the other three crops increased nearly three-fold. The rapid increase in the area under wheat was due clearly to its becoming the most profitable crop. But the reasons for increases in the areas under corn and groundnut were somewhat different as were those for reductions in the areas under sugarcane, cotton or other crops. The principal reason for the increase in the acreage under corn was that being a shorter duration crop than cotton it fits into the new crop rotation cycle much better. Growing two crops in a year on the same field has become much more feasible, than it had been earlier, because the high-yielding varieties of wheat have a shorter growing season than the older varieties, and the water needs of both crops can be met adequately by the improved irrigation facilities. Accordingly, corn followed by wheat has become the most popular crop rotation. On the other hand, sugarcane, which occupies the land for about ten mouths in the year, makes double cropping impossible. The other disadvantage of sugarcane, and to a lesser extent of cotton, is high requirement of labour: its importance has increased during the period because of increase in the cost of labour and emergence of a shortage of labour at the peak periods of agricultural activity.

The area under groundnut has expanded rapidly despite it giving relatively the lowest increase in gross return because it is the most suitable crop for the areas with sandy soils of low productivity.

The relationship between the changes in relative profitability of different crops and in the areas under them would be seen more clearly if data on costs of production and net returns were available also. But the large changes in the cropping pattern in a time span of little more than a decade give a clear indication of the responsiveness of farmers to changes in the relative profitability of alternative crops, arising from technological and price changes, and their readiness to transfer their resources of land, labour and capital from production of crops giving lower returns to those giving higher returns. This responsiveness confirms the findings of many studies of peasant agriculture which show a remarkable ability on the part of the peasants to make relatively rapid changes in resource allocation in response to changing economic conditions[13].

The Village and the Region in 1975

By the time of the revisit to Jitpur in December 1975, the rapid changes associated with the Green Revolution as described above, had already been completed; the new cropping pattern production practices were well established, and there had been time also for reflection of the effects of the higher incomes in changes in consumption particularly through improvement of housing and possession of durable consumer goods. The changes in land use and the cropping pattern are indicated in Table 18.3 while data on selected other indicators of economic change area given in Table 18.4. In Table 18.3 figures are given for 1951-52 also in order to make possible comparison with the land use and the cropping pattern prevailing in the village before the beginning of the rapid agricultural and economic change process described in Section I.

Changes in Land Use and the Cropping Pattern

Of the total geographical area of 1,239 acres, 1,121 acres or more than 90 per cent was cultivated in 1973-74. The latter figure had remained virtually unchanged since 1951-52 indicating that the limit of expansion of cultivation had been reached by that time (perhaps much earlier). The intensity of cropping also remained almost unchanged during the period, 1951-52 to 1961-62, at 1.45 to 1.47. More than three-fourths of the cropped area was already irrigated by 1951-52, the further expansion of irrigation brought the proportion up to 88 per cent by 1961-62. But the most notable changes were in the cropping pattern.

The acreage under corn nearly doubled, that under the fodder crops grown in the winter (mainly *barseem* clover) increased nearly 80 per cent and cotton which was not grown earlier became an important crop. The increases in the area under corn and cotton were achieved mainly at the expense of the fodder and other crops grown in the summer, while that under the winter fodders resulted from reduction of the area under "other grains and mixtures". This group includes gram or chick-pea and barley, sown either by themselves or in combination with each other or with wheat.

Changes in land use and cropping pattern between 1961-62 and 1973-74 were much greater. The gross cropped area increased by 24 per cent, from 1,639 to 2,034 acres, as a result of increase in the intensity of cropping; The intensity of cropping reached the figure of 1.81 by 1973-74 indicating that 81 per cent of the cropland was double-cropped during that year. Corn and wheat were the principal crops benefiting from the increase in double cropping. The acreage under corn increased from 240 to 604 acres and that under wheat from 436 to 845. But land had to be diverted also from other crops to achieve theses increases in corn and wheat acreage; areas under all the other crops, except the fodders and 'other' crops grown in the summer went down. The area under sugarcane was reduced by almost half and that under 'other grains and mixtures' grown in the cool season from 237 to 37 acres.

Table 18.3 : Changes in Land Use and the Cropping Pattern 1951-52 to 1973-74—Village Jitpur

Sl. No.		1951-52	1961-62	1973-74	% Change During 1951-52 to 1961-62	and 61-62 to 73-74
1.	Total geographical area	1239	1239	1239	—	—
2.	Net area sown	1132	1118	1121	–1.2	+ 0.3
3.	Gross cropped area	1637	1639	2034	0.0	+ 24.1
4.	Intensity of cropping (Line 3/Line 2)	1.45	1.47	1.81	—	—
5.	Gross Irrigated area	1256	1440	2034	+14.5	+ 41.3
6.	Percentage of gross cropped area irrigated	76.7	87.9	100.0		
Crops						
(a) *Kharif (Summer)*						
7.	Corn (Maize)	121	240	604	+98.3	+151.7
8.	Cotton	—	143	92	—	–35.7
9.	Sugarcane	191	178	95	–6.8	–46.6
10.	Fodder crops	295	195	202	–33.9	+3.6
11.	Other	125	28	50	–77.6	+78.6
12.	Total	732	784	1043	+7.1	+26.6
(b) *Rabi (Cool Season)*						
13.	Wheat	474	436	845	–8.0	+93.8
14.	Other grains and mixtures	319	237	37	–24.7	–84.4
15.	Fodder crops	92	164	94	+78.3	–42.3
16.	Other	20	20	15	—	–25.0
17.	Total	905	855	991	-5.5	+15.9
18.	Grand Total (Line 12 + Line 17)	1637	1639	2034	0.0	+24.1

Source: Output 1975/1963= 3885.8 of which half are due to price increase and other to total increase in production.

The other notable change was expansion of irrigation: the gross irrigated area increased by nearly 600 acres, or by more than 40 per cent during this period and by 1973-74 all the cropped area was reported to be irrigated. The number of irrigation sources, which had increased from 36 in 1951-52 to 51 by 1961-62, increased further to 85 by 1973-74 (Table 18.4). Sixteen of the new irrigation sources were tube-wells, which, as mentioned earlier, tap deeper layers of sub-soil water. They also have much larger irrigation capacity; the average capacity of a tube-well is 3-4 times that of an average well. Most of the tube-wells were powered by diesel engines.

Table 18.4 : Selected Other Indicators of Economic Change, between 1963 and 1975—Village Jitpur

S. No.	*Indicator*	*1963*	*1975*
1.	Population	About 1850	2114*
2.	No. of households	299	344
3.	*Irrigation units (No.) :*		
	Wells	45	55
	Tube-wells	—	16
	Additional bores	6	14
	Total	51	85
	No. of units with motive power provided by :		
	Electricity	36	69
	Diesel oil	—	16
	Bullocks	15	—
4.	*Use of chemical fertilizers :*		
	Total (tonnes)	46.1	152.3
	Per acre of gross sown area (kg)	28.1	74.9
5.	Tractors (No.)	—	14
6.	Trucks (No.)	3	16
7.	*Institutional agricultural credit :*		
	Loans advanced by the primary cooperative society :		
	Short-term ('000 rupees)	n.a.	273.6
	Medium-term ('000 rupees)	n.a.	30.0
	Total ('000 repees)	n.a.	303.6
	Short-term loans per acres of gross sown area (rupees)	n.a.	134.5
	Long-term loans advanced by :		
	The Land Mortgage Bank	—	208.6**
	The Central Bank of India	—	50.0
8.	*Daily wage or earning level of male workers :*		
	Casual agricultural labour	Rs. 2 plus food or Rs. 2.50	Rs. 6 plus food or Rs. 8.†
	Loading and unloading bricks on trucks	Up to Rs. 4	Rs. 10-15.
9.	*Housing*		
	Percentage of households living in :		
	Pucca or Semi-*Pucca houses*	47	70
	Houses with electricity	36	81
10.	*Durable consumer goods (Nos.)*		
	Bicycles	130	n.s.
	Sewing machines	83	n.s.
	Radio receivers	20	n.s.
	Cars/jeeps	—	5
	Motor cycles/scooters	—	13
	Refrigerators	—	4

*1971 Census.

** cumulative total for 9 years, 1967-75.

† Rs. 4 plus food for in-migrants from U.P.

n.s.: Too numerous to be used as significant indicators of change.

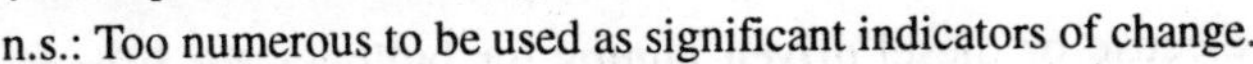

Expansion of irrigation met the water supply requirements of the increased intensity of cropping and also made possible extension of irrigation to about 12 per cent of the cropped area that had remained unirrigated by 1961-62. Improvement of efficiency of irrigation, *i.e*, providing adequate water supply to all the crops, and reduction of the cost of irrigation were secured by further substitution of bullocks by electric or diesel oil operated pumps for lifting the water; substitution had been completed by 1973-74.

Use of Chemical Fertilizers

As may be expected, use of chemical fertilizers, the other essential ingredients of the new agricultural technology, also increased very rapidly during the period. The figures given in Table 18.4 show increase between 1962-63 and 1974-75 from 46.1 tonnes to 152.3 tonnes in the total quantity of fertilizers used, and from 28.1 kg to 74.9 kg per acre of gross cropped area. They do not, give an adequate indication of the trends in fertilizer use during this period because they are partial and are also not comparable. First, they relate only to sales by the village primary cooperative society, which gives short-term (repayable within one year) loans for the purchases. In 1962-63, when supplies were scarce the society was almost the only source of supply of fertilizers; but by 1974-75, additional large quantities were being bought by the farmers from private dealers located in the market towns, against cash payments or under mutually agreed credit arrangements. Second, the figures are for quantities of fertilizers, and not for plant nutrients, so that different fertilizers with different concentrations of nutrients—ammonium sulphate has 16 per cent of nitrogen while urea has 45 per cent—are lumped together in them. In 1962-63, only three of chemical fertilizers—ammonium sulphate, calcium-ammonium nitrate and super phosphate—were being used. But by 1973-74, the number had increased to six; these included both high concentration fertilizers, such as urea, and balanced fertilizers, such as diammonium phosphate and NPK, which contained two or three nutrients. Thus the change in fertilizers use during this period included, besides a major increase in the quantity, increasing application of highly concentrated and/or balanced fertilizers, and increasing willingness of farmers to buy fertilizers on their own.

Mechanization

Substitution of electric or diesel-driven pumps for bullocks for lifting water for irrigation is one important constituent of mechanization of agriculture. The other is represented by increasing use of tractors, combines, grain threshers, corn shellers and other implements driven by mechanical power. In 1963, while two-thirds of the wells in the village were already being worked by electric pumps, the use of the other power-driven implements was limited. There was not a single tractor or grain-thresher although farmers had begun to use their chaff cutters, eight of which were run by electricity, for partial threshing of the wheat, and there were only three corn shellers. By 1975, however, use of other power-driven implements was widespread. There were 14 tractors and as many as 55 grain threshers (Table 18.4) and three large farmers had hired combine-harvesters from the State Cooperative Marketing Federation (MARKFED) for harvesting their wheat crop during April-May 1975. The charges for hiring, reported to be Rs. 150 per acre, were high but the combines were preferred because they saved the farmers the trouble of hiring and supervising the labour needed for the operation. The tractors were all owned by relatively large farmers who cultivated 20 acres or more, but the other farmers could hire them when they were not being used by the owners. Hiring of tractors from owners within the village or others in the neighbouring village of the market town of Samrala was common, the rate being Rs. 12-15 per acre of ploughing.

Increase in Agricultural Output

Precise estimation of the increase in agricultural output during the period is not possible in the absence of data for the village on the yields of crops. However an approximate estimate has been made by using the district data on yields and prices of the principal crops of the village and is shown in Table 18.5. It will be seen that the gross value of agricultural output in 1973-74 was four times that in 1961-62. Somewhat over half of the increase was due to increase in prices—the prices of corn, wheat and sugarcane doubled while those of cotton and gram increased by 118 and 155 per cent respectively—and the remainder represented real increase in output, resulting from expansion of cropped area, substitution of less profitable crops by more profitable ones and increase in crop yields.

It should be emphasized, however, that the increase in net incomes of the farmers would be considerably less than four times, because of the increases in expenditure on inputs, particularly chemical fertilizers, electricity, diesel oil and labour. The increases must be quite large because, as mentioned above, fertilizer use has increased by more than four times.

Furthermore, apart from the quantitative increases in the inputs, their unit costs have increased. Thus wage rates have gone up about three times. An estimate of the net increase in income can be made only if figures on cost of cultivation of all the important crops are available for both the years. However, even after making allowance for all the cost increases, there can be no question that the increase in output represents a substantial gain in real incomes for the farmers.

Table 18.5 : Estimated Value of Output of Principal Crops in 1961-62 and 1973-74—Village Jitpur

(*Value Figures in Rupees*)

Crop	1961-62			1973-74		
	Area (Acres)	Gross* Value (Rs.) Per Acre (y×p)*	Total	Area (Acres)	Gross* Value (Rs.) Per Acre (y×p)*	Total
Corn	240	197.2	47,328	604	506.9	306,161
Wheat	436	264.3	115,235	845	1075.7	908,994
Cotton	143	115.8	16,552	92	208.5	27,466
Sugarcane	178	815.0	145,070	95	2016.1	191,530
Other rabi grains and mixtures	237	161.6†	38,302†	37	460.2†	17,029†
Total	1234		362,578	1673		1,451,180

Note :* Represents product of average yield per acre (*y*) and price (*p*).

† For *gram* or chick pea which is the principal grain among them.

The Role of Institutional Finance

Institutional finance, *i.e.* short, medium and long-term loans, bearing relatively low interest rates and provided by specialized credit institutions or directly by the State Government, has been the principal sources of financing the investment needs of agricultural development. The primary co-operative credit society located in the village has been the principal source of short-term and medium-term loans while long-term loans, repayable in 7-10 years and needed for financing investment in irrigation or farm machinery such as tractors, have been provided since its establishment at Samrala in 1967 mainly by the Land Mortgage Bank. Until the middle 1960s the State Government used to provide medium and long-term loans directly: the loans were the principal source of institutional finance for construction of wells and electrification during the 1950s. But they were discontinued with the growth of lending by the specialized credit institutions. The commercial banking system could emerge as a major source of institutional finance in the future : fostering the banking habit among the rural people and meeting the investment needs of development of agricultural and rural industry were among the most important objectives of nationalization of the 14 largest commercial banks by the Indian Government in 1969. In pursuit of these objectives there has been rapid increase in the number of branches of the banks in the small towns and the large villages since nationalization: there were four such branches in Samrala in 1975 and one, opened in 1970, in the village itself.

The cooperative society had advanced short-term loans totalling Rs. 273,600 during 1974-75 (Table 18.4). Most of them were given in kind, in the form of chemical fertilizers or other inputs distributed by the society. The loans, which bore an interest rate of 12 ½ per cent per annum had been taken by nearly 400 of the 542 members of the society.

The Land Mortgage Bank had advanced a total or Rs. 208,600 to 32 farmers of the village during the nine years of its existence. The loans, ranging from rupees 2,000 to 24,000 each, had been given to finance construction of tube-wells, purchase of tractors, purchase of land or redemption of land from mortgage, etc. Twenty-three loans totalling Rs. 119,500 had been given for development of irrigation, of which 21, totalling Rs. 108,000, had been given for construction of tubewells. The 16 tubewells in operation in the village in 1975 had all been constructed with the aid of these loans, which ranged between Rs. 4,000 to 6,000 each. Five tubewells for which loans had been given during 1974 and 1975 were not operational by the time of this study. The bank had also financed purchase of five tractors to the extent or Rs. 100,600; the individual loans had ranged between Rs. 12,000 and 30,000. The branch of the Central Bank of India, located in the village, had advanced only two loans totalling Rs. 50,000 for purchase of tractors; but at the time of the study it was financing purchase of milch buffaloes by the members of the newly-formed Milk Producers' Cooperative Society. Medium-term loans totalling Rs. 30,000 had been advanced to 15 of the 52 members of the society and the applications of the others were being processed. The loans were being given under a special programme of the Central Government aimed at assisting the small and marginal farmers.

Comparison with Changes in the District

Comparison of the figures of Tables 18.3 and 18.4 with the corresponding figures for the district given in Table 18.1 shows that in case of most of the important indicators of agricultural change—gross cropped area, gross irrigated area, acreage under wheat and consumption of chemical fertilizers—the rates of increase were lower in the village than in the district. In case of gross cropped area and gross irrigated area the lower rates were due to the village having already achieved significantly higher intensity of cropping and proportion of irrigated cropped area than the district by 1961-62, so that the scope for further progress was less. The difference is not large; in case of increase in acreage under wheat, while in case of consumption of chemical fertilizers the village and district figures area not comparable because while the former relate only to the quantities distributed by the cooperative society, the latter include also sales by the private dealers.

Other Aspects of Change

Employment, Wages and the Social Position of the Harijans

Perhaps the most serious criticism of the Green Revolution (or rather of the capital and technology intensive strategy of increasing agricultural output that underlies it is that it has increased disparities in rural incomes and aggravated the problems of labour surplus in agriculture, which was already very serious in many less developed countries, including India, and has thus increased rural social tensions and unrest. It is explained that the large farmers have benefited most from the new technology because they could afford to make the large investment needed for expansion of irrigation and purchase of machinery, chemical fertilizers and other input, and also obtained large increments in output and incomes from the higher productivity of the land; that small farmers have benefited little because of their limited capacity for investment and the small size of their operations, while the landless agricultural labourers are worse off than before because mechanization of agriculture has reduced the demand for labour. It is alleged also that over large regions of India in which the majority of the small farmers are tenants, introduction of the new technology has given the land owners both the incentive and the opportunity to dispossess them by reclaiming the land for 'personal cultivation'.[14] Further since the landless labourers, the tenants and other small farmers belong mainly to the socially depressed scheduled castes and scheduled tribes while the large or medium size farmers belong to the socially privileged and powerful high castes, the increases in economic disparities adds to the tensions generated by the social cleavages[15]

A case study of a single village is not a suitable medium for systematic investigation of such issues for various reasons including the fact that the selected village may not be representative of the region. Thus the size—distribution of cultivated holdings in it may differ significantly from that in the region. The situation relating to the supply or demand for labour may also be different from that in the region because of differences relating to the proportion of landless labourers in the population, the patterns of land use and cropping or the opportunities for off-farm employment. Accordingly, the following observations on changes relating to employment, wages and the social position of the Harijans in village Jitpur during the period 1963-75 are not intended in any way to indicate trends in the district or the State. Their primary objective is to describe how the agricultural changes described above have affected this important section of the village community, which comprises more than one-fourth of its total population. In the process, they draw attention also to some aspects of the change in the labour situation resulting from the Green Revolution which need to be given greater attention in studies of the Revolution.

The principal changes in the labour situation in the village and in the social position of the Harijans since 1963 have been the following :

(i) Virtual disappearance of the slack in the demand for labour during the monsoon months of July and August, which had existed in 1963, despite growth of employment opportunities during the 1950s and the early 1960s and emergence in its place of seasonal labour shortage which is being met by import of in-migrant labour from the neighbouring State of Uttar Pradesh. The change is reported to have taken place towards the end of the 1960s. The labour shortage is pronounced during the peak period of agricultural activity in April and May when harvesting of wheat is in progress along with various operations connected with planting of the summer crops. About 50-75 in-migrant workers come to work in the village for 1-2 months during this period. The monsoon months of July and August instead being a slack period has, with emergence of corn as the second most important crop of the village, become another period of heavy demand for labour which is needed for the weeding of corn. Some farmers face difficulty in obtaining sufficient labour at this time but it is not serious enough to require import of in-migrant labour.

(ii) Progressive replacement of the traditional *sanjhee* system of crop sharing between the farmer-owner and his attached agricultural labourer and of the traditional practice of paying for particular agricultural operations such as harvesting of wheat and picking of cotton in kind, by employing workers on daily wage basis and paying the wages in cash, which had been noted in the 1963 study, has gone even further. The *sanjhee* system, which was still adopted in 1963 study by farmers whose need for agricultural work could not be met by their own family labour has practically disappeared. Employment of agricultural workers on a daily basis is the norm. Secondly, while payments are still made in kind for some operations, notably harvesting of wheat, the dominant mode of payment of wages is in cash. The prevailing rates for the males are Rs. 6 per day plus food (mid-day meal and tea in the late morning and the afternoon) or Rs. 8 without food for local workers, and Rs. 4 plus food for the in-migrants from U.P. The wage differential between the local and the in-migrants workers is justified by the farmers on the ground that the in-migrants do not work as hard or as well as the local workers. They have less stamina than the local workers on account of poor health and small physique and they lack knowledge of local agricultural conditions. They are also considered to be less dependable.

These changes are closely related to the agricultural changes described above, as also to the growth of demand for off-farm labour, notably in construction and transport activities, which is in turn related to a large extent to the agricultural changes. The seasonal slack in demand for labour has disappeared because with more than 80 per cent of the cropland growing two crops in the year, agriculture has become a year-round operation in which there is no slack season, only periods of more or less intensive activity. As regards the total demand for agricultural labour, the increases resulting from expansion of cropped area and the various requirements of obtaining high yields per acre have to be set off against reductions brought about by replacement of bullocks by electric or diesel irrigation pumps and increasing use of tractors, grain threshers, etc. A precise estimate of the net effect on demand can be made only through a detailed study of labour inputs in agriculture.[16] Such a study is needed also for determining the relative contributions of increase in demand for agriculture and growth of off-farm employment in changing the labour situation from one of seasonal labour surplus to that of seasonal shortage.

The agricultural changes of the last 25 years have contributed to the decline of the *sanjhee* system and of the traditional practices of making payments for labour in kind because in a period of rapidly rising yields and prices of crops, the farmers have been increasingly unwilling to share the gains with their labourers particularly since the resource of labour (or of the bullock power, contributed by the *sanjhee)* is not critical to achieving the gains and the labourers cannot contribute the resources of capital and technology that are critical. But as a result of the decline the economic relationship between the farmers and the labourers is no longer governed by tradition, but by the market forces of demand and supply for labour. As a result, the labourers have become a more purely proletarian group with a much less direct stake in the productivity of the land or the profitability of the farm enterprise than they were when they shared the crops with the farmers.

The growth of off-farm employment is a major factor affecting the labour situation in the village. It adds to the demand for labour and keeps wage rates high. The principal sources of such employment are construction works in or near the village; loading and unloading of bricks with trucks which transport them form brick kilns to the constructions sites; hauling produce in the produce market *(mandi)* in Samrala town and various white-collar or unskilled jobs or commercial activity in or near the village. The following admittedly approximate estimates of employment provided by these sources are based on interviews with several knowledgeable respondents in the village; estimates given by different respondents were checked and rechecked in the course of the interviews :

Sources of Employment	*Number of Workers**
Construction work (housing, roads, etc.)	50-60 unskilled workers 15 Masons 2 Carpenters
Loading and Unloading of bricks	40-60
Carrying produce in the market	15-20
White-collar and skilled jobs	20-25
Other* (shop-keeping, repairs of Motors and other skilled work)	15-20
Total	160-200**

Note: * The range of number indicates variations in employment in the course of the year.

** The total number of workers is less than this figure because many workers take up two or more types of work during the year. Furthermore, many workers combine non-agricultural work with agricultural labour.

Since only 637 persons were listed as workers in Jitpur at the time of the Census of Population 1971, it is clear that about one-fourth of the labour force of the village is engaged in non-agricultural work. For most of them it is a year-round activity and the principal source of livelihood.

Agricultural changes have contributed to the growth of off-farm employment because increase in activity levels in most of the source of such employment is related, directly or indirectly to them. The increase in construction activity, which is responsible for the increase in employment in construction works as well as in loading and unloading of bricks with trucks, is the result mainly of increases in agricultural investment or in house construction resulting from increase in income. The principal forms of the activity have been construction of wells, tube-wells, storage facilities and other farm buildings; construction of new houses, shops and community buildings and making additions to or improvements in existing houses. About 100 new *pucca* houses were estimated to have been built during the 12 years since the 1963 study, while the scale of improvements and renovations is indicated by the fact that the proportion of households living in *pucca* or partially *pucca* dwellings had gone up from 47 to 70 per cent and of electrified houses from 36 to 81 (Table 18.4). Construction of new houses and improvements or additions to existing houses has also been the most important indicator of improvement in the level of living and the most important avenue for investment of the higher incomes. That the Harijans and other labouring groups in the village have also benefited from the improvement is indicated by the high proportions of households of these groups that now live in *pucca,* partially *pucca* or electrified houses.

Construction works in the vicinity of the village include besides houses and farm or business related structures in the neighbouring villages, public works such as roads. The second reason for the construction and related haulage of bricks becoming important sources of employment in Jitpur is that its residents own 7 brick kilns and 16 trucks; the more affluent and enterprising *Jat* and *Mistri* families have found these to be a lucrative business enterprises. In 1963, Jitpur residents owned only three brick kilns and three trucks and only 18 Harijans were employment on haulage of bricks.

Wages or earnings in off-farm employment are generally higher than in agricultural work. The workers hauling bricks generally make rupees 10-15 a day, more in periods of brisk activity; the earnings of those hauling produce in the market are similar, while skilled workers such as masons earn Rs. 15 to 20 a day. These relatively high wages or earnings combined with the large volume of off-farm employment keep up the wage level of the agricultural labourers also. Their current wage level of Rs. 6 per day plus food or Rs. 8 without food represents a three-fold increase since 1963, when the prevailing rates were Rs. 2 plus food or Rs. 2.50 without food. The increase has been somewhat higher than the increase in crop prices but less than that in the gross value of agricultural output. It has been explained above that average crop prices in 1970-71 to 1972-73 were twice as high as those during 1960-61 to 1962-63, and that the gross value of agricultural output has gone up by four times during the period, although the increase in net returns to the farmers had been less because of increase in expenditure on inputs. But crop prices have gone up further since 1970-71 to 1972-73 with corresponding increases in the value of agricultural output. Thus the current (December 1975) price of Rs. 110 per quintal of wheat represents a 31.3 per cent increase over the average price of Rs. 83.80 during 1970-71 to 1972-73.

The increase in the total volume of employment, especially disappearance of the period of enforced idleness during the slack season in agricultural activity, and increase in various forms of non-agricultural employment, in several of which wages or earnings are so much higher than in agricultural work, have been major gains for the Harijans (and others such as barbers, oil-pressers, etc.) who depend mainly on labour. It has contributed more to improvement in the economic condition of these groups than the rise in the wages of agricultural labourers.

Another development which has contributed to improvement in both the economic and social position of these groups has been increase in their employment in white-collar or skilled jobs. Ten Harijans of the village are employed as white-collar workers and five are working as masons; in 1963 there was only one Harijan white-collar worker and no Harijan mason or other skilled worker. The upward occupational mobility of the Harijans, as also its principal cause—grant of scholarships by Government for education of Harijan children and reservation of posts for them in the government service—are accepted by the *Jats* and other high castes and are also considered justified and necessary by the more enlightened members of these castes. The acceptance has gone to the extent that a Harijan youth of the village was working as the successful secretary of the primary co-operative society. The job carries a good salary and is, besides, a position of some power because of the role of the society in disbursement of low interest short-term loans and in distribution of chemical fertilizers.

Improvement in the Levels of Living

The following brief remarks are limited to a few, more obvious changes which were observed during this study: an adequate discussion would have to be based on a detailed survey of the level of living. Reference has already been made to improvements in housing resulting from construction of new houses and improvements in existing ones. This constitutes, in our view, the most important change in the level of living. Most of the new houses, built outside the circular road round the village, which was demarcated at the time of the consolidation of holdings and was built soon after, are spacious and well built. Some of them, belonging to the more affluent households, are built in the architectural styles, which are popular in the Punjab towns. Another notable change relates to possession of durable consumer goods. In 1963, possession of goods such as bicycles, sewing machines and radios was considered by the villagers to be significant indicators of modernization of consumption and of improvement in the level of living. But not so in 1975 ! The goods had become common, because their price was low in relation to the income level of the villagers. The price of a bicycle represented 40-60 days' wages of an agricultural labourer and that of a radio the wages for only 15-20 days. The new goods regarded as significant indicators of rise in level of living were automobiles, motor cycles, scooters and refrigerators. But their number was small and would remain so for a long time (Table 18.4) because of the high cost of buying and keeping them. With the possible exception of refrigerators, we regard these goods more as indicators of economic status, which distinguish the affluent from the rest of the community than as indicators of improvement in level of living. Their appearance in the village is an indicator primarily of increase in disparities in income and the level of living.

An interesting change, which indicated the villagers' readiness to adopt urban middle class norms, was the opening in 1969 of an English medium, 'model' primary school. It had been opened by a woman teacher belonging to the village who had returned home after teaching for some years at an English medium high school, located at Dehra Dun in Western Uttar Pradesh. In contrast to the Government primary school in which instruction was free, the new school charged a high fee of Rs. 20 per month per child. But it was popular and as many as 110 children including 10 Harijan children were attending it because the level of instruction in it was considered to be higher than that in the Government School.[17] The Government primary school had 250 children. Thus with a total of 360 children in the two schools, almost every child, boy or girl, of the age-group, 6-11 years, appeared to be attending school. The change since 1963 related primarily to increase in school-going by the children of the Harijans, because at that time a proportion of their children were not attending school. The Headmaster of the Government school mentioned that the primary school would be raised to the middle level (Grade VI to VIII) from the 1976-77 school year; the villagers had built at their own expense a handsome new three-room wing to the school building to provide accommodation for the new classes.

The Prospect

The process of rapid change in agricultural technology (and associated increase in agricultural output) which has been the main theme of this study had been completed by 1971-72 and the next three years was a period of stagnation or retrogression. This is indicated by data on several indicators of agricultural change for both Ludhiana district and the village. Thus output of cereals in the district declined from its peak of 1,009,000 tonnes in 1971-72 to 969,000 tonnes in 1972-73 and 964,000 tonnes in 1974-75. Consumption of chemical fertilizers had peaked at 251,000 tonnes in 1972-73 and was only 160,000 in 1974-75. The yield of wheat had declined from 33.1 quintals per acre in 1971-72 to 29.7 quintals by 1974-75. In case of the village, data on gross cropped area, gross irrigated area, and distribution of chemical fertilizers and short-term credit by the primary cooperative society showed similar stagnation or small decline after 1971-72 or 1972-73. This development was attributed to a combination of unfavourable factors; low rainfall in 1972-73 and again in 1974-75; shortages of chemical fertilizers and diesel oil and sharp increases in their prices after the quintupling of the prices of crude oil by the OPEC countries in 1973-74; and finally, shortage of electricity because of fall in generation as a result of the low rainfall (most of the electricity in the State is supplied by a hydroelectric plant). In 1975-76, a favourable monsoon had resulted in a bumper summer crop and the cool season crop was also expected to be very good. But the farmers had found themselves caught in a squeeze between rising prices of inputs and falling prices of crops. The prices of chemical fertilizers and diesel oil had continued to rise and the electricity rates were raised by the State Electricity Board during the summer of 1975. The rates had been earlier held unchanged for several years despite rising generation costs, because of the State governments' policy of encouraging the use of electricity by farmers. On the other hand, the price of corn had, with the end of the scarcity of foodgrains, come down from a peak of about Rs. 130 per quintal in 1974-75 to Rs. 65-70 by December 1975. In the case of wheat, the price at which the Central Government made purchases for meeting the needs of the public distribution system, had remained unchanged at the 1974-75 level of Rs. 110 per quintal, but the premium above it which the farmers got for sales in the free market, had disappeared and the official purchase price had become the support price for the crop.

Do these developments foreshadow a period of stagnation or retrogression for the region or do they constitute only a temporary setback in a vigorous growth process ? A definite answer is not possible at this stage because we are so close in time to the period of growth and the period of stagnation. Instead we list below some of the factors, which are relevant to analysis of this issue and also indicate some developments which have a bearing on the possible directions of future advance.

(i) The rapid progress achieved by the region has been due primarily to two factors—well developed physical and economic infrastructures and the initiative and dynamism of the people. Both have been added to and strengthened very considerably during nearly 25 years of rapid economic growth. The Green Revolution years, in particular, have witnessed significant expansion of irrigation facilities, major additions to the stock of agricultural capital and expansion or strengthening of the institutional structures of agricultural research and extension, supply of inputs, and agricultural credit. The capacity of the people for making rapid progress has been enhanced because of increase in literacy, improvements in health, nutrition and level of living and, most notably, by the experience of rapid progress during the Green Revolution years. The experience has shown them the possibility of rapid economic advance within their own socio-economic matrix besides greatly increasing their technological and income levels.

(ii) The stagnation or retrogression during 1972-73 to 1974-75 had been due either to natural causes or to national level factors, relating to supplies of inputs or prices of inputs or outputs. As for the national level factors, while the exceptionally favourable situation of the Green Revolution years could not continue indefinitely—a period of adjustment was inevitable—it would be unrealistic to assume that in a situation of rapidly rising demand for food and bare self-sufficiency or marginal scarcity in supply, they could long remain unfavourable to growth in the few regions in which rapid growth of food output had been achieved and the potential for further rapid growth demonstrated. According to projections made by the National Commission on Agriculture the demand for foodgrains (cereals and pulses) is expected to increase by 46-64 per cent between 1975 and 2000 (National Commission on Agriculture 1973). The rate of increase may turn out to be higher because the estimates of the Commission on the growth rates of population and per capita income on which the projections are based appear to us to be on the low side. On the other hand despite the Green Revolution in the wheat growing region of North-Western India, the rate of increase of food output during the 1960s (1960-61 to 1971-72) was only marginally higher, at 2.7 per cent per annum, than the rate of 2.5 per cent achieved during the first 12 years of planned development (1952-53 to 1964-65). This was because food output in most of the other regions, which grow rice or other grains continued to be very low. Thus while wheat output increased at an average rate of 8.8 per cent per annum during 1960-61 to 1971-72 the rate for rice was about 2.5 per cent and that for jowar, India's third ranking cereal in acreage and production, was negative (Saran, 1975).

(iii) Further growth of agricultural output in this region may be expected to come from two principal sources: (a) continuing increase in crop output through more careful adoption of recommendations of the extension services, relating particularly to application of chemical fertilizers, and irrigation; progressive improvements in the recommendations as a result of research, and improvements in management by farmers who are increasingly conscious of increasing the efficiency of resource use; and (b) growth of dairying, poultry-keeping, market gardening and other highly remunerative forms of production resulting in progressive transformation of the region's agriculture from a field-crop producing to a mixed, crop-and-livestock enterprise.

(iv) The effect of the price squeeze was reflected in the widespread feeling in the region that agriculture was no longer as 'remunerative' as it had been in the late 1960s and the early 1970s. The feeling was expressed by respondents in Jitpur, by officials and local leaders in Samrala and Ludhiana and by two State level leaders, the Vice Chancellor of the Agricultural University and an ex-Minister of Agriculture. Although some of them were pessimistic about the future, most were not, and thought that steady progress could continue if appropriate changes were made in the pattern of production. The best prospects for growth were seen in development of dairying and poultry keeping. The popular slogan that "The Green Revolution must be followed by a White Revolution" was repeated by several officials and leaders. The State Government was encouraging expansion of dairying, poultry keeping, market gardening, etc. through a variety of promotional measures. It had drawn up a long-term plan for development of dairying, which was built round establishment of a chain of central dairies, and a dense network of milk collection centres to supply them with milk. Four such dairies located in the principal cities of the State and supplying the cities with fluid milk and products such as butter and ghee (butter oil) were already functioning; besides two large, privately owned, milk processing plants which produced powdered milk, baby food, etc. Three additional dairies were under construction and the plan projected establishment of a dairy or processing plant in each of the 12 districts of the State. The plan envisaged also : (a) major increase in the efficiency of milk production by progressive replacement of the existing milch animals with high yielding animals developed by cross-breeding local cows with high yielding European stock of the Holstein, Jersey and Brown Swiss breeds; and (b) development of the Punjab as a major dairy State supplying milk and milk products to cities all over Northern India. The latter objective was based on appreciation of the fact that the level of animal husbandry and the milk yield per animal were already much higher in the State than in the other States of Northern India.

Among the promotional measures being undertaken to increase milk production, the most important was encouraging formation of "milk producers" co-operatives, consisting primarily of marginal farmers of landless agricultural labourers and giving the members liberal medium term loans for purchase of milch animals or other needs. Besides increasing milk output the measure was expected to provide a source of supplementary income to these poorer sections of the agricultural community. It may be recalled that such a co-operative had been established in village Jitpur in 1975 and loans totalling Rs. 30,000 had already been given to 15 of its 52 members, and that a milk collection centre for the central dairy located at the State capital Chandigarh was proposed to be opened in the village early in 1976.

Poultry farming, which had been growing rapidly in the State in the late 1950s and early 1960s but had gone through a period of stagnation and consolidation thereafter was a well organized promotional service, consisting of extension officers posted at the CD Block and multi-village levels; facilities for disease control and treatment of birds, hatching of eggs and supply of chicks to the poultry farmers; provision of credit and supply of inputs particularly balanced feed to them, and marketing of their products. But, as in the case of the dairy development programme, the emphasis in this case also was on encouraging poultry keeping by small farmers of landless labourers in order to provide them with a source of supplementary income. The Samrala Community Development Block was one of the "intensive development areas" in the State and had a number of relatively large poultry units with 1,000 laying birds or more, besides small units with 100-500 birds, Jitpur had five poultry units in 1975 with the number of birds ranging between 300 and 800. All were owned by small farmers and had been started during the previous two years.

It will be noticed from the above description of the dairy and poultry development programme that the primary economic objective of raising income in the agricultural sector of the State's economy and increasing the long-term growth potential of the sector and the welfare objective of raising the income of the poorer section of the agricultural community were mixed in them. While a clear choice between the two objectives may not be necessary immediately, the choice on establishment of priorities between them was essential in order to improve efficiency of performance.

To conclude, the prospect is of: (a) continuation of the process of vigorous agricultural and economic growth in the region and the village to which the Green Revolution has given a 'big push'; but (b) progressive change in the character of the region's agriculture from concentration of production of field crops to mixed crop and livestock economy similar to that of many countries of Western Europe. Most studies of the Green Revolution emphasize technological change in agriculture and the resulting changes in output, income and employment. This case study brings out, however, that even the purely economic changes associated with the Revolution have been broader in scope and more complex in character.

Thus it shows that non-agricultural employment, resulting mainly from the increase in construction activity, has increased to such an extent that it is now the principal source of livelihood for about one-fourth of the labour force of the village. Second, with the virtual disappearance of the *sanjhee* system and further decline in the practice of making payments of agricultural labour in kind, the traditional, institutionalized patterns of inter-group and inter-personal economic relationships have been replaced almost completely by relationships determined by the market forces of demand and supply for labour. Together, these two changes have altered profoundly the relationship between the land of the village and its people. Not only do the labouring groups not share directly in the current crop, but for a substantial proportion of them the land is no longer the source of livelihood. Indeed for the non-agricultural workers working outside the village, the village is not much more than a dormitory. They live in it because of family and community ties and the very considerable advantage of free or cheap housing. But their economic interests are primarily in the wider, micro-regional economy.

The village economy itself is more closely integrated with the larger regional and national economies than ever before and is more dependent upon policies and programmes originating in the changing needs of the latter. These policies and programmes have been the dominant agents in the change process of the past 25 years. The people of the region and the village have readily accepted the programmes and have through their own initiative and innovative ability added to their beneficial effects. But that does not alter the change-agent role of the policies and programmers. And as the reference to economic stagnation during 1972-73 to 1974-75 indicates, even temporary changes in national level factors, such as supplies of inputs or prices of inputs and outputs have a profound effect on the village economy. We believe that the 'self-sufficiency' of the Indian village was always over stated. But with the economic changes, such as those reviewed here, the village is now as much a part of the wider regional and national economies as any urban community.

NOTES

1. The name is fictitious.
2. Harijan: literally children of God. The term was first used by Mahatma Gandhi, the great leader of India's Independence, for the socially depressed, untouchable Hindu castes, such as leather workers and sweepers, in his campaign for abolition of untouchability and improvement of the social

and economic status of these castes. After the Independence of India, the castes are designated as "scheduled castes", but the term 'Harijans' continues to be used in many regions including this one.

3. The community development block organization was developed as part of the community development programme, the broad ranging rural development programme which the Government of India started in 1952. The rural areas of India are covered by nearly 5,500 Blocks with population varying between 50,000 and 150,000. Every Block has a team of specialists in agricultural extension and related rural development services.
4. The pre-1966 State of Punjab was divided into three parts in that year. The central region in which Sikhs are in a majority, was constituted into the new State of Punjab; the eastern region was constituted into the new State of Haryana, while the small Himalayan portion was merged with the existing State of Himachal Pradesh.
5. Consolidation of holdings is the reform through which the small, scattered plots of land owned by the land-owning families of a village are pooled and each family is then allotted in their place one to three much larger plots. It makes possible more efficient and more intensive cultivation.
6. Wells tap shallow layers of groundwater, located in this region at depths of 15 to 50 feet while tube-wells tap the layers at depths of 50 to 150 feet. The motive power for lifting the water in wells had been provided traditionally by bullocks which have, however, been replaced increasingly by electric to diesel powered pumps: tube-wells are generally powered by the latter.
7. The comparative cost figures for irrigating a field preparatory to sowing of wheat in it were estimated in 1963 as follows :

	Rs. per acre
(i) Using electric pump set	3.87
(ii) Using a pair of bullocks	25.00

   V. Nath *op cit.*, p. 15
8. A popular Punjabi proverb equates selling milk by a farmer with selling his son.
9. According to the Census of Population, agricultural labourers constituted 17.3 per cent of the agricultural labour force and 9.7 per cent of all workers in Punjab in 1961; the corresponding figures of India were 23.7 per cent and 16.7 per cent respectively (Registrar General and Census Commissioner, *India: Census of India.* Series 1. India Paper 1 of 1971. Supplement: *Provisional Population Totals* (New Delhi: 1971) pp. 62-63.
10. The canal colonies of Punjab had among the highest level of agriculture and animal husbandry and of rural incomes in pre-Independent India. The extension service had made a major contribution to this achievement. They were efficient and the farmers, new to a region with an unfamiliar, harsh environment, were more receptive to their advice than farmers in most regions of India.
11. Rate of interest for loans taken from village money lenders vary between 25 and 100 per cent per annum.

12. Pulses or beans of several kinds have an important place in cropping system in most regions of India. They are the principal source of proteinless diet of the Indian farmers. Secondly being legumes, they increase the fertility of the soil.
13. An interesting historical analysis of price responsiveness of Sierra Leone peasants whose principal commercial crops are palm kernels, cocoa and coffee and of substitution between the first-two are contained in: Saylor, R.G., *The Economic System of Sierra Leone*. (Durham, N.C.: Duke University Press, 1967), pp. 58-73.
14. & 15. See for instance:

Ladejinsky, Wolf. "Ironies of India's Green Revolution". *Foreign Affairs,* Vol. 48, No 4 (July 1970), p. 764.

________ *"Green Revolution in Bihar, the Kosi Area; A Field Trip"* refers specifically to ejection of tenants as a result of the Green Revolution in a field trip report on Bihar, *Economic and Political Weekly,* Bombay, Vol. IV, No. 39 (September 27, 1969) pp. A- 147-162

Frankel, F., "Agricultural Modernization and Social Change." *Mainstream* (November 29, 1969)

16. One such study, which contains a detailed analysis of the supply and demand for labour in agriculture of Punjab-Haryana, in 1968-69 and projections up to 1983-94 is Billings, Martin H., and Arjun Singh, "Mechanization and Rural Employment," *Economic and Political Weekly,* Bombay, Vol. V., No. 26 (June 27, 1970), pp. A –61-69. The study indicated that the marginal shortage of labour in the peak demand months for September and October already experienced during 1968-69 would become progressively worse unless the conventional technology was replaced by increasing use of machinery particularly pump-sets, tractors and threshers.
17. Sending children to English Medium 'model' or public schools (following the British practice the term 'public' is used for expensive private schools) has become very popular among the urban middle and upper income groups in the Punjab. The older and best known among the 'public' schools were originally established in the pre-Independence period for the children of British officers or the Indian Princes and many parents make considerable financial sacrifice to send their children to them in order to give them a better start in life.

REFERENCES

Billings, Martin H., and Arjun Singh, "Mechanization and Rural Employment" *Economic and Political Weekly,* Bombay, Vol. V., No. 26 (June 27, 1970), pp. A –61-69

Frankel, F., "Agricultural Modernization and Social Change." *Mainstream* (November 29, 1969)

Frankel, F., "Green Revolution in Bihar, the Kosi Area; A Field Trip" refers specifically to ejection of tenants as a result of the Green Revolution in a field trip report on Bihar *Economic and Political Weekly,* Bombay, Vol. IV, No. 39 (September 27, 1969) pp. A- 147-162

Ladejinsky, Wolf. "Ironies of India's Green Revolution". *Foreign Affairs,* Vol. 48, No 4 (July 1970) p. 764.

Nath, V., "The New Village", *The Economic and Political Weekly,* Bombay 1965, p. 58

National Commission on Agriculture: *Projections of Demand for Selected Agricultural Commodities in India, A.D. 1975-2000.* (Mimeo.) New Delhi, 1973.

Saran Ram, "Growth in Indian Agriculture—An Analysis", Presidential Address to the *Second Annual Conference of the North India Economic Association* (Mimeo.), New Delhi, 1975, pp. 3-6.

Index